CRUSADE TEXTS IN TRANSLATI[...]

About the volume:

The Seventh Crusade, led by King Louis IX of Franc[...] for the recovery of the Holy Land actually to re[...] invasion of Egypt (1249–50), followed by h[...] [...]o retrieve the disaster, had a profound impact [...] [...]ouis's operations in the Nile delta indirectly precipit[...] [...]at, which ended the rule of the Ayyubids, Saladin's dynasty, [...] the transfer of power there to a military elite that would prove to [...] formidable enemy to the Franks of Syria and Palestine.

This volume comprises translations of the principal documents and of extracts from narrative sources – both Muslim and Christian – relating to the crusade, and includes many texts, notably the account of Ibn Wasil, not previously available in English. The themes covered include: the preparations and search for allies; the campaign in the Nile delta; the impact on recruitment of the simultaneous crusade against the emperor Frederick II; the Mamluk coup and its immediate consequences in the Near East; Western reactions to the failure in Egypt; and the popular 'crusade' of the Pastoureaux in France (1251), which aimed originally to help the absent king, but which degenerated into violence against the clergy and the Jews and had to be suppressed by force.

About the series:

The crusading movement, which originated in the 11th century and lasted beyond the 16th, bequeathed to its future historians a legacy of sources which are unrivalled in their range and variety. These sources document in fascinating detail the motivations and viewpoints, military efforts and spiritual lives of the participants in the crusades. They also narrate the internal histories of the states and societies which crusaders established or supported in the many regions where they fought, as well as those of their opponents. Some of these sources have been translated in the past but the vast majority have been available only in their original language. The goal of this series is to provide a wide ranging corpus of texts, most of them translated for the first time, which will illuminate the history of the crusades and the crusader-states from every angle, including that of their principal adversaries, the Muslim powers of the Middle East.

About the translator:

Peter Jackson is Professor of Medieval History at Keele University, UK.

THE SEVENTH CRUSADE, 1244–1254

Crusade Texts in Translation

Titles in the series include

Colin Imber
The Crusade of Varna, 1443–45

Carol Sweetenham
Robert the Monk's History of the First Crusade
Historia Iherosolimitana

Bernard S. Bachrach and David S. Bachrach
The *Gesta Tancredi* of Ralph of Caen
A History of the Normans on the First Crusade

D.S. Richards
The Chronicle of Ibn al-Athir for The Crusading
Period from *al-Kamil fi'l-Ta'rikh*. Part 1
The Years 491–541/1097–1146: The Coming of
the Franks and the Muslim Response

D.S. Richards
The Chronicle of Ibn al-Athir for the Crusading
Period from *al-Kamil fi'l-Ta'rikh*. Part 2
The Years 541–589/1146–1193: The Age of Nur al-Din and Saladin

Paul Crawford
The 'Templar of Tyre'
Part III of the 'Deeds of the Cypriots'

Damian Smith and Helena Buffery
The Book of Deeds of James I of Aragon
A Translation of the Medieval Catalan *Llibre dels Fets*

The Seventh Crusade, 1244–1254
Sources and Documents

PETER JACKSON
Keele University, UK

ASHGATE

Published by

Ashgate Publishing Limited
Wey Court East
Union Road
Farnham
Surrey GU9 7PT
England

Ashgate Publishing Company
Suite 420
101 Cherry Street
Burlington, VT 05401-4405
USA

http://www.ashgate.com

British Library Cataloguing in Publication Data
The Seventh Crusade, 1244–1254: Sources and Documents. –
(Crusade Texts in Translation)
1. Crusades – Seventh, 1248–1250 – Sources. I. Jackson, Peter, 1948 Jan. 27– .
962'.02

Library of Congress Cataloging-in-Publication Data
The Seventh Crusade, 1244–1254: Sources and Documents / translated by Peter Jackson.
p. cm. – (Crusade Texts in Translation; 16)
Includes bibliographical references and index.
1. Crusades – Seventh, 1248–1250 – Sources. I. Jackson, Peter, 1948 Jan. 27–
D167.S48 2007
962'.02–dc22 2007001998

ISBN 978-0-7546-5722-4 (hbk, reprint 2009)
ISBN 978-0-7546-6923-4 (pbk)

Printed and bound in Great Britain by
MPG Books Group, UK

Contents

List of Maps

Preface

This volume has its remote origins in a shorter collection of documents and sources which I began translating in the early 1980s for a Special Subject at Keele University, entitled most recently 'Crusaders, Muslims and Mongols: St. Louis and the East'. I owe a great deal to successive generations of finalists who have kept alive my enthusiasm and have stimulated me with their ideas and questions. I should further acknowledge at this point the help of my medievalist colleagues in the History Department in closing ranks during 2004–2005, and thereby enabling me to spend the best part of a sabbatical year turning the collection into something fit (I trust) for publication. Thanks are due also to my colleague Andrew Lawrence, of the Keele University Digital Imaging/Illustration Service, for drafting the maps.

I have accumulated many debts to institutions outside my own university: the Cambridge University Library, the British Library, the libraries of the Warburg Institute and of the Institute of Historical Research in London, the Sydney Jones Library in the University of Liverpool and the John Rylands University Library in Manchester. I am grateful to the Bibliothèque Nationale, Paris, for supplying me long ago with a microfilm of the unpublished sections of Ibn Wāṣil's *Mufarrij al-kurūb* (ms. arabe 1703) and with a printout of the relevant folios of Ibn ʿAbd al-Raḥīm's revised version of that work (ms. arabe 1702). It is likewise many years since the Forschungs- und Landesbibliothek Gotha kindly sent me a microfilm of Qaraṭāy's *Kitāb al-Majmūʿ al-nawādir* (now ms. Orient. A 1655), and I am no less indebted to the staff there for furnishing me more recently with a printout of the first volume of al-Jazarī's *Ḥawādith al-zamān* (ms. Orient. A 1559).

Professor Malcolm Barber has earned my gratitude by reading through the entire text and offering suggestions and emendations. I alone am responsible for any errors that remain.

Peter Jackson
Keele, September 2006

Abbreviations

AFH	*Archivum Franciscanum Historicum*
Annales Monastici	*Annales Monastici*, ed. Henry Richards Luard (5 vols, London: Longman, 1864–69)
AOL	*Archives de l'Orient Latin*
BEC	*Bibliothèque de l'Ecole des Chartes*
BEO	*Bulletin d'Etudes Orientales de l'Institut Français de Damas*
Berger	*Les registres d'Innocent IV*, ed. Elie Berger
Berger, *Saint Louis*	Elie Berger, *Saint Louis et Innocent IV* (= Berger, II, pp. i–ccxciii)
BIHR	*Bulletin of the Institute of Historical Research*
CTT	Crusade Texts in Translation
DRHC	Documents relatifs à l'histoire des croisades
*EI*²	Charles Pellat et al. (ed.), *The Encyclopaedia of Islam*, new edn (12 vols, Leiden: Brill, 1954–2004)
Foedera	*Foedera, Conventiones, Literae et Cuiuscumque Generis Acta Publica inter Reges Angliae et Alios Quosvis Imperatores, Reges, Pontifices, Principes vel Communitates ab Ineunte Saeculo Duodecimo, viz. ab Anno 1101 ad Nostra usque Tempora Habita aut Tractata*, ed. T. Rymer
Huillard-Bréholles	*Historia Diplomatica Friderici Secundi*, ed. J. L. A. Huillard-Bréholles
JMH	*Journal of Medieval History*
Layettes	*Layettes du Trésor des Chartes*, ed. Alexandre Teulet, H. de la Borde et al.
MGHS	*Monumenta Germaniae Historica. Scriptores*, ed. G. H. Pertz et al. (32 vols, Hanover: Weidmann, 1826–1913)
MHR	*Mediterranean Historical Review*
MM	*The Mariner's Mirror*
RHC HOcc.	*Recueil des Historiens des Croisades. Historiens Occidentaux* (5vols,Paris Imprimerie Royale/Impériale/Nationale, 1844–95)
RHGF	*Recueil des Historiens des Gaules et de la France*, ed. G. Bouquet (24 vols, Paris: Imprimerie Royale/Impériale/Nationale, 1840–1904)
Rodenberg	*Monumenta Germaniae Historica. Epistolae Saeculi XIII e Regestis Pontificum Romanorum Selectae*, ed. Carl Rodenberg (Berlin: Weidmann, 1883–94)

'Rothelin'	'Continuation de Guillaume de Tyr, de 1229 à 1261, dite du manuscrit de Rothelin'

Proper Names and Dates

I have retained Anglicized forms for the names of familiar places: for instance, Cairo rather than al-Qāhira. The names of the majority of Westerners mentioned in the texts appear in their French form (for example, Guillaume de Sonnac), but I have adopted an Anglicized form for a few (thus William of Holland, William of Rubruck).

Dates in the Islamic calendar sometimes present a problem. I have normally given the equivalent according to the Common Era in square brackets. But where a weekday is specified which fails to match that equivalent, I have inserted '=' in square brackets immediately beforehand.

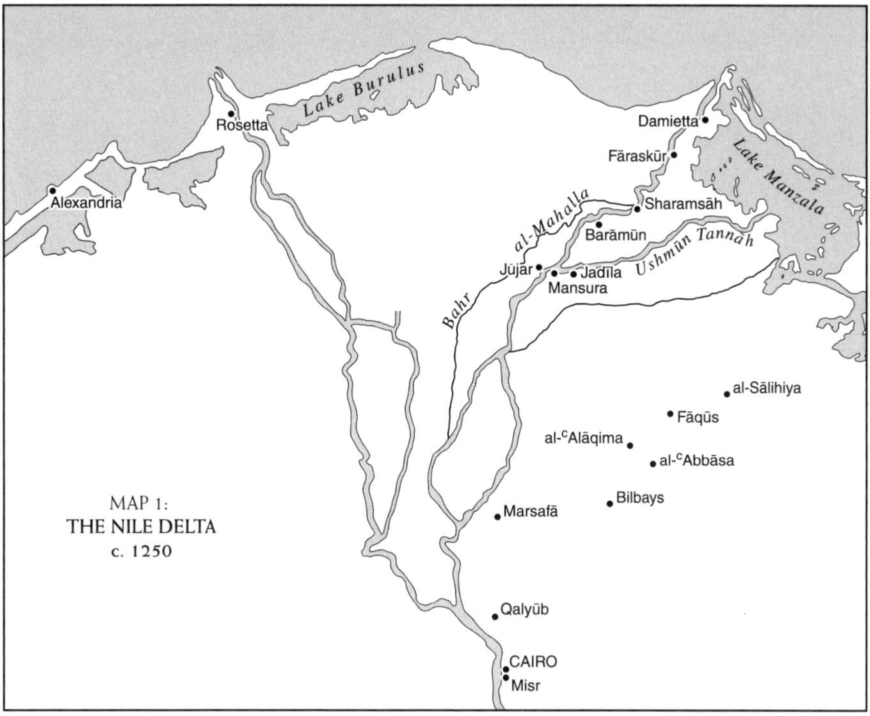

Lake Burulus
Rosetta
Alexandria
Damietta
Fāraskūr
Lake Manzala
al-Mahalla
Bahr
Sharamsāh
Barāmūn
Ushmūn Tannāh
Jūjār
Jadīla
Mansura
al-Sālihiya
Fāqūs
al-cAlāqima
al-cAbbāsa
Bilbays
Marsafā
Qalyūb
CAIRO
Misr
MAP 1:
THE NILE DELTA
c. 1250

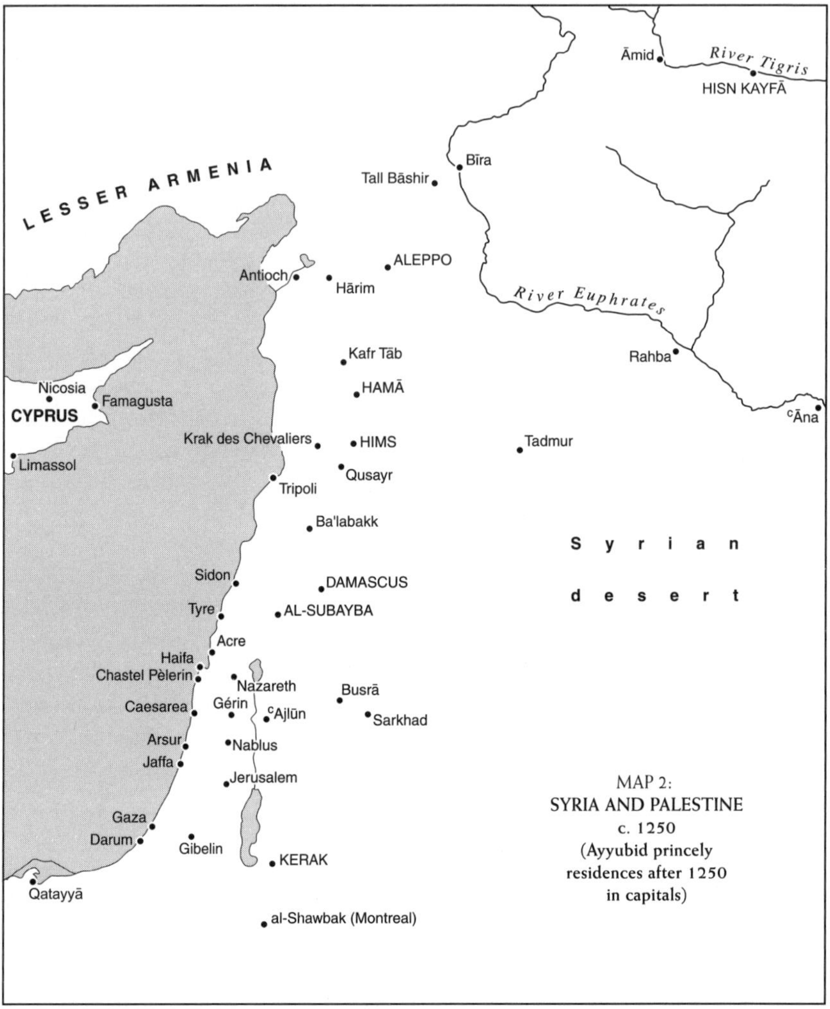

MAP 2:
SYRIA AND PALESTINE
c. 1250
(Ayyubid princely residences after 1250 in capitals)

Introduction

The literary sources in Latin and Old French for the first crusade (1248–54) of King Louis IX of France – the 'Seventh' in the somewhat unsatisfactory notation that has become entrenched in historiography – were conveniently listed over a century ago by Reinhold Röhricht.[1] The principal Western narrative sources are all now available in English translation. The best-known, the *Vie de Saint Louis* of Jean, lord of Joinville, who accompanied the crusade and entered Louis's service in 1248, has been accessible in various versions for several decades.[2] A translation of the account given by someone who was probably also a participant, in the so-called 'Rothelin Chronicle', which continues William of Tyre's great history from 1229 down to 1261, was published in this series in 1999.[3] And the somewhat problematic account of the late thirteenth-century author known as the 'Minstrel of Reims' exists in two translations.[4] We should also include in this group the late thirteenth-century annalistic account preserved in the 'Estoire de Eracles', which was written at Acre.[5] It is a great pity that the *Gestes des Chiprois*, generally believed to be the work of an anonymous Templar knight in the early fourteenth century, contains a lacuna at precisely the period covered by the Seventh Crusade, since the information it yielded would surely have been invaluable; though it must be admitted that the fifteenth-century source known (after a sixteenth-century owner of the manuscript) as the 'Chronicle of Amadi', which is otherwise heavily dependent on the *Gestes* for this period, yields relatively sparse material on the crusade.[6]

---

1 R. Röhricht, 'Der Kreuzzug Louis IX. gegen Damiette (in Regestenform)', in his *Kleine Studien zur Geschichte der Kreuzzüge*, Wissenschaftliche Beilage zum Programm des Humboldt-Gymnasiums zu Berlin, Ostern 1890 (Berlin, 1890), pp. 11–25 (no. IIIa).

2 References will be given here to the second edition by Natalis de Wailly (Paris, 1874), and the translations by René Hague, *The Life of Saint Louis by John of Joinville* (London and New York, 1955), and by M. R. B. Shaw, *Joinville and Villehardouin. Chronicles of the Crusades* (Harmondsworth, 1963).

3 'Rothelin', pp. 566–71, 589–630; trans. Janet Shirley, *Crusader Syria in the Thirteenth Century* (Aldershot, 1999), pp. 66–9, 85–113.

4 Robert Levine, *A Thirteenth-century Minstrel's Chronicle* (New York and Lampeter, 1990), where the Minstrel's account of the crusade is at pp. 88–94, 100. Edward Noble Stone, *Three Old French Chronicles of the Crusades* (Seattle, WA, 1939), pp. 334–9, 346. For the original text, see *Récits d'un ménestrel de Reims au treizième siècle*, ed. Natalis de Wailly (Paris, 1876), §§ 367–97, 430, pp. 189–204, 220–21.

5 For the relevant section, see 'L'Estoire de Eracles empereur', in *RHC HOcc.*, vol. 2, pp. 436–42 (trans. in Shirley, *Crusader Syria*, pp. 137–40).

6 *Chronique d'Amadi*, ed. René de Mas Latrie (Paris, 1891), pp. 198–203: the majority of this material is also available in the 'Annales de Terre Sainte', ed. R. Röhricht, *AOL*, 2 (1884), documents: 442–6 (version 'B'). The *Gestes* is translated by Paul Crawford, *The 'Templar of Tyre': Part III of the 'Deeds of the Cypriots'* (Aldershot, 2003).

In this collection I have given priority to contemporary or near-contemporary letters and documents. The earliest surviving document to cover events in the crusader army once it reached the East is a report from the papal legate, Eudes de Châteauroux, cardinal-bishop of Tusculum, to Pope Innocent IV, written in Cyprus on 31 March 1249, not long prior to the attack on Egypt [**doc. 56**]. Here Eudes refers to a previous report which he had sent to the Pope but which is now lost. Two letters from King Louis himself have come down to us, one of which is addressed to his subjects in August 1250, following his release from captivity and his arrival in Palestine, and throws light on his plans at this critical juncture [**doc. 70**]. We know that this letter was also sent to the Pope and to Louis's fellow-monarchs.[7] In October 1251 the Pope learned from Louis that Henry III had written to him to commiserate on the disaster in Egypt and to offer aid;[8] but neither Henry's letter nor Louis's reply has come down to us. The French King's messengers were again at the Curia in January 1254;[9] but the letter carried on this occasion has likewise not survived.

The many surviving letters from participants vary in value, depending, perhaps, on the closeness of the writer to the decision-making process at councils of war. Letters from the royal chamberlains, Jean Sarrasin (incorporated in the 'Rothelin' account)[10] and Jean de Beaumont [**doc. 58**], announcing the capture of Damietta in 1249, for instance, or the two letters from Patriarch Robert of Jerusalem, dating from the years 1250–51 [**docs 68, 115**], are highly informative. By contrast, that of Gui, a household knight of the Viscount of Melun [**doc. 59**], is likely to be less reliable: the information it supplies, that the crusade was heading for Alexandria but was blown onto the coast at Damietta by chance, doubtless represents the confused perspectives – or the aspirations – of the rank and file. It is clear that other participants wrote back to the West about the progress of the crusade, such as the Teutonic Master, Eberhard, who is cited in the annals of Erfurt [**doc. 80**].

Papal correspondence is a major source of information on the Seventh Crusade, and I have included here a selection of letters from the register of Innocent IV and from other sources. They deal above all with matters of fundraising, recruitment and the payment of subsidies, though one or two throw light on the Pope's response to the news of Louis's failure in Egypt in 1250. Not the least important categories comprise papal letters that aimed to raise reinforcements for King Louis's depleted force in Palestine between 1250 and 1254 [**docs 98–105, 107 and 109–12**] and those dealing with other crusades contemporary with Louis's expedition [**docs 35–55**], in particular that against the Emperor Frederick II and his supporters in Germany and Italy. It should be noted that the loss of the seventh year of Innocent's register (June 1249–June 1250) doubtless means that we lack a good many letters from precisely the period when the crusade was in Egypt, though two, from February–March 1250, have survived in the archives of the province of Rouen [**docs 18 and 19**]. In those cases (the majority) where the prolixity of curial scribes threatens to mask the

7 'Annales monasterii de Burton', in *Annales Monastici*, vol. 1, p. 293.

8 Ibid., p. 294 [**doc. 103**].

9 Berger, no. 7167. Berger, *Saint Louis*, p. cclxxii.

10 See 'Rothelin', pp. 568–71, 589–93 (trans. Shirley, pp. 68–9, 85–8).

information that might be gleaned from a particular letter, I have abridged or simply calendared it rather than translating the entire text, in order to save space.

From the fact that the English Franciscan Adam Marsh mentions having acquired a copy of Louis's letter of August 1250, together with a (no longer extant) letter from the Legate Eudes,[11] it is clear that some of these documents circulated widely. One English author who gained access to a great many of them is the English Benedictine Matthew Paris (d. *c.* 1259), whose *Chronica Majora* turns repeatedly to the crusade and events in the East. In the *additamenta*, or supplementary collection of documents, which he compiled to accompany the chronicle, Matthew transmits a letter from Louis's brother, Count Robert of Artois, to his mother, Queen Blanche [**doc. 57**], and a number of letters from lesser participants. The *Chronica Majora* is a problematic work, given the author's tendency to doctor his material for various purposes: to show the Emperor Frederick II in a favourable light, for example, and to denigrate the Pope and the Military Orders. It is possible, on occasions, to detect phrases or passages that have been inserted in an original.[12] Two letters written by non-participants, Benedict of Alignano, Bishop of Marseilles [**doc. 66**], and the Templar Nicholas de la Hyde [**doc. 65**], are of considerable interest inasmuch as they reflect the way in which rumours of totally spurious triumphs reached Western Europe and buoyed up enthusiasm. Regrettably, the two English translations of the *Chronica Majora* are both incomplete: the modern one by Professor Richard Vaughan covers only the years 1247–51,[13] and even the more comprehensive nineteenth-century translation by Giles[14] lacks some of the documents from the *additamenta*. All the relevant documents assembled by Matthew are therefore included here.

A number of chronicles composed in France during the last decades of the thirteenth century and the early fourteenth survey the events of the Seventh Crusade. The great historical encyclopaedia *Speculum Historiale* (*c.* 1253) of the Dominican Vincent de Beauvais furnishes us with the earliest narrative account.[15] Although Vincent did not accompany the King to the East, his proximity to the Capetian dynasty gave him access to letters and reports, which he summarized. He incorporated in the *Speculum Historiale* the contents of Eudes's report of 1249 and of the King's letter of August 1250, in each case largely verbatim, and apparently also used Robert of Artois's above-mentioned letter to Queen Blanche and her own letter to Henry III of England [**doc. 62**], or perhaps a letter from Louis to his mother on which it was

11 'Adae de Marisco epistolae', nos 17, 22, 23, 181, in *Monumenta Franciscana*, ed. J. S. Brewer, vol. 1 (London, 1858), pp. 103, 108, 109, 327: on two occasions the letters are said to be *de christiani exercitus excidio in Aegypto et statu terrae*, a description strongly evocative of Louis's letter of August 1250.

12 Richard Vaughan, *Matthew Paris* (Cambridge, 1958), pp. 131–5. See also Helen Nicholson, 'Steamy Syrian scandals. Matthew Paris on the Templars and Hospitallers', *Medieval History*, 2/2 (1992): 68–85.

13 Richard Vaughan, *Chronicles of Matthew Paris: Monastic Life in the Thirteenth Century* (Gloucester and New York, 1984).

14 J. A. Giles, *Matthew Paris's English History from the Year 1235 to 1273* (London, 1853).

15 Vincent de Beauvais, *Speculum Historiale*, ed. Johann Mentelin (Straßburg, 1473), xxxii, 89–102.

based.[16] He appears to have had access to other documents which no longer survive, and the data derived from these are therefore included here [**doc. 72**].

Unfortunately, Vincent's work goes down no further than the return of Louis's brothers to France in August 1250. It served as the basis for all subsequent accounts produced in or around the French court, notably the *Gesta sanctae memoriae Ludovici* of Guillaume de Nangis (*c.* 1300) and the survey of Louis IX's reign found in the *Grandes Chroniques de France* which is in turn borrowed from Guillaume.[17] But for the period after August 1250 these later accounts had to rely on the Latin text composed by Primat. This, designed as a continuation of Vincent's work,[18] has reached us only in the French version of Jean du Vignay, and covers Louis's stay in Palestine in far less depth. Significantly, for this later period authors like Guillaume de Nangis are much less informative; they were otherwise almost entirely dependent on Geoffrey de Beaulieu, Louis's confessor and the author of the earliest of the 'lives' of Louis written with a view to his canonization.

Most of the surviving evidence from the canonization process relates merely to miracles witnessed at the King's tomb.[19] The only documentation that provides any information about the Seventh Crusade is a fragment of the submission made by King Louis's brother, Charles of Anjou [**doc. 71**], which speaks of the disaster in Egypt and its immediate aftermath. This eyewitness testimony is important, not least because it pre-dates Joinville's account by over two decades. I have omitted from this collection the various lives of Louis the Saint, since what they add to our knowledge of the events of the Seventh Crusade is meagre: the information given by Geoffrey de Beaulieu (*c.* 1272), for instance, that the Sultan had the captive King carefully tended and cured by his own doctors and that Louis made the pilgrimage to Nazareth (probably in 1251).[20]

Authors writing within the Islamic world do not significantly enhance our knowledge of the course of the crusade. What they provide instead, of course, is a good deal of information on contemporary events within Egypt in the last months of Sultan al-Ṣāliḥ Ayyūb (d. 1249), during the brief reign of his son and successor, al-Muʿaẓẓam Tūrān Shāh (1249–50) and in the wake of the latter's murder by members of his father's household slave (mamluk) guard. The writers whom historians

16 Eudes: ibid., xxxii, 89–94, 96. Louis's letter of 1250: xxxii, 102. Robert's letter: xxxii, 89 (mentioning Charles of Anjou's quartan ague while in Cyprus), 97–8. Blanche's letter to Henry III; xxxii, 97. For Vincent of Beauvais's use of letters from Damietta, see Jacques Monfrin, 'Joinville et la prise de Damiette (1249)', *Académie des Inscriptions et Belles-Lettres: Comptes rendus des séances* (1976), pp. 268–85 (here p. 271).

17 *Les Grandes Chroniques de France*, ed. Jules Viard, vol. 7 (Paris, 1932).

18 'Chronique de Primat, traduite par Jean du Vignay', in *RHGF*, vol. 23, pp. 63, 105–6.

19 H.-F. Delaborde, 'Fragments de l'enquête faite à Saint-Denis en 1282 en vue de la canonisation de saint Louis', *Mémoires de la Société de l'histoire de Paris et de l'île-de-France*, 23 (1896): 1–71.

20 Geoffrey de Beaulieu, 'Vita Ludovici Noni', in *RHGF*, XX, pp. 14 (Nazareth), 16 (the Sultan's physicians). On this work, see Natalis de Wailly, 'Examen critique de la Vie de Saint Louis par Geoffroy de Beaulieu', *Mémoires de l'Académie Royale des Inscriptions et Belles-Lettres*, 15 (1845): 403–37.

usually cite for this period, namely Ibn al-Furāt (d. 1405) and al-Maqrīzī (d. 1442), wrote compilations, based in large measure on earlier works which they had usually abridged.[21] I have included in this collection, therefore, two contemporary sources which they used, and which are of particular value. The first is a history of the Ayyubids, the *Mufarrij al-kurūb fī akhbār banī Ayyūb* ('The Dissipator of Cares in the Account of the Ayyubid Dynasty'), by Jamāl al-Dīn Muḥammad ibn Sālim, known as Ibn Wāṣil (d. 1298) [**doc. 73**].[22] The other principal Muslim source is a general chronicle, the *Mir'āt al-zamān fī ta'rīkh al-a'yān* ('The Mirror of the Age in the History of Notable Men') of Shams al-Dīn Abū'l-Muẓaffar Yūsuf ibn Qizūghlī (d. 1256), known as the Sibṭ ('maternal grandson') of Ibn al-Jawzī (an earlier historian) [**doc. 74(a), (d), (f) and (i)**]. In my notes to the extracts from the works of Ibn Wāṣil and the Sibṭ Ibn al-Jawzī, I have frequently referred to two other contemporary works: the *Dhayl 'alā'l-Rawḍatayn* ('Supplement to the Two Gardens', a continuation of his earlier history), by the Damascene Muslim Abū Shāma (d. 1268), and the *Kitāb al-majmū' al-mubārak* ('The Fortunate Compilation') of the Coptic Christian al-Makīn Jirjīs Ibn al-ʿAmīd (d. *c.* 1272). An excerpt from the somewhat suspect work of the later mamluk author Qaraṭāy al-ʿIzzī al-Khazāndārī, *Ta'rīkh majmū' al-nawādir* (*c.* 1330), describing how Emperor Frederick II warned Sultan Ayyūb of Louis's impending attack [**doc. 32**], is included here together with a passage of Ibn Wāṣil which at least corroborates it in outline [**doc. 33**].

Ibn Wāṣil was in Cairo for most of the period of the crusader operations in Egypt, but spent some days in the Sultan's headquarters at Mansura and was generally well informed about what transpired in the delta. The Sibṭ Ibn al-Jawzī, by contrast, wrote in Damascus, at some remove from the events of the crusade. But he drew a good deal of his material from the highly placed Saʿd al-Dīn Ibn Ḥamawiya al-Juwaynī (d. 1276), who had been in Egypt at the time and whose memoirs, in their original form, are long lost; and this gives the Sibṭ's *Mir'āt* a special value. The text that has come down to us is regrettably corrupt in places, but can be corrected from the work of later historians who made extensive use of it, such as al-Jazarī (d. 1338). I have also included with extracts from the Sibṭ's work other passages from Saʿd al-Dīn preserved by the later author, Shams al-Dīn Muḥammad ibn Aḥmad al-Dhahabī (d. 1348) [**doc. 74(c), (e), (g), (h) and (j)**], and an additional excerpt which al-Dhahabī borrows from the *al-Jāmi' al-mukhtaṣar* ('The Abridged Compilation') of

---

21 Extracts from Ibn al-Furāt's *Ta'rīkh al-duwal wa'l-mulūk* are edited and translated by U. and M. C. Lyons (with introduction and commentary by J. S. C. Riley-Smith) as *Ayyubids, Mamlukes and Crusaders* (Cambridge, 1971). That portion of al-Maqrīzī's *al-Sulūk li-ma'rifat duwal al-mulūk* covering the Ayyubid era is translated by R. J. C. Broadhurst, *A History of the Ayyubid Sultans of Egypt* (Boston, MA, 1980).

22 Francesco Gabrieli, *Arab Historians of the Crusades*, trans. E. J. Costello (London, 1969), pp. 276–80, 284–300, includes extracts on the Seventh Crusade purportedly taken from Ibn Wāṣil's work. Unfortunately, these are based on the Bibliothèque Nationale, Paris, ms. arabe 1702, which is a reworking of Ibn Wāṣil's history by his continuator Ibn ʿAbd al-Raḥīm. I have instead used ms. arabe 1703, which is apparently a copy of Ibn Wāṣil's original work, while citing Ibn ʿAbd al-Raḥīm in the footnotes. The printed edition of Ibn Wāṣil's history stops at 645 H. [1247–48].

the Baghdad chronicler Ibn al-Sāʿī (d. 1276) [**doc. 74(b)**].[23] Further extracts from Ibn Wāṣil [**doc. 118**] and the Sibṭ [**doc. 119**] and passages from Ibn al-ʿAmīd [**doc. 120**] are incorporated in the section on King Louis's four-year stay in Palestine. They tell us nothing of the Franks' activities, but they throw valuable light, again, on developments within the Islamic Near East.

I have included here a number of sources that illustrate the impact of the disaster in Egypt on the Christian world, particularly back in Western Europe, and seek to apportion blame [**docs 75–83**]. Such material is inevitably fragmentary. It includes papal letters; two sermons by the Legate Eudes de Châteauroux, probably delivered in the Holy Land in 1251; a troubadour's song, and the versified chronicle *De triumphis ecclesiae* of Jean de Garlande (*c.* 1252).[24] Some of the sentiments expressed, of course, may simply be designed to vindicate already firmly held views about the crusade or crusade strategy. One notable reaction to the bad news from the East was the popular movement of 1251 known as the 'Crusade of the Shepherds' (or 'Pastoureaux'), which began with the aim of going to Louis's assistance, but degenerated into violence against clerics, friars and Jews and had to be suppressed by force. The principal sources for the outbreak form a discrete section in this volume [**docs 84–97**].

23 For excerpts derived from Saʿd al-Dīn, see Claude Cahen, 'Une source pour l'histoire ayyūbide: Les mémoires de Saʿd al-Dīn Ibn Ḥamawiya Djuwaynī', in his *Les peuples musulmans dans l'histoire médiévale* (Damascus, 1977), pp. 457–82. For Ibn al-Sāʿī's work, of which only the years 596–606 H./1198–1209 survive, see Cahen, *La Syrie du Nord à l'époque des croisades et la principauté franque d'Antioche* (Paris, 1940), p. 72.

24 On him, see Louis J. Paetow, 'The crusading ardor of John of Garland', in Paetow (ed.), *The Crusades and Other Historical Essays Presented to Dana C. Munro by His Former Students* (New York, 1928, reprinted 1968), pp. 207–22 (here pp. 220–21). Jean's verses, of course, are not the most reliable account of the Seventh Crusade itself.

List of Sources and Documents

I KING LOUIS TAKES THE CROSS

1. Baudouin d'Avesnes, 'Chronicon Hanoniense', *MGHS*, vol. 25, p. 453
2. Troubadour's song [1245?]: Joseph Bédier and Pierre Aubry (ed.), *Les chansons de croisade* (Paris, 1909), pp. 240–43
3. Troubadour's song [1245?]: Bédier and Aubry (ed.), *Les chansons de croisade*, pp. 251–3

II PREPARATIONS FOR THE CRUSADE

(a) Preaching and finance

4. Pope Innocent IV to Henry III, King of England, 23 January 1245: *Foedera*, vol. 1/1, pp. 148–9
5. Pope Innocent IV to [Eudes,] Bishop of Tusculum, papal legate, 6 November 1246: J. B. Hauréau, 'Quelques lettres d'Innocent IV extraites des manuscrits de la Bibliothèque Nationale (N° 1194–1203 du fonds Moreau)', in *Notices et extraits des manuscrits de la Bibliothèque Nationale*, vol. 24/2 (Paris, 1876), p. 209; summary in Berger, no. 2228
6. Pope Innocent IV to [Eudes,] Bishop of Tusculum, papal legate, 6 November 1246: Hauréau, 'Quelques lettres d'Innocent IV', pp. 209–10; summary in Berger, no. 2229
7. Pope Innocent IV to the Bishop of Worcester, 8 February 1247: Berger, no. 2962
8. Pope Innocent IV to [Eudes,] Bishop of Tusculum, papal legate, 29 October 1247: Hauréau, 'Quelques lettres d'Innocent IV', pp. 213–14; summary in Berger, no. 3383
9. Pope Innocent IV to P[eter], Cardinal-deacon of San Giorgio in Velabro, papal legate, 29 October 1247: Berger, no. 3384
10. Pope Innocent IV to [Eudes,], Bishop of Tusculum and papal legate, 9 July 1247; Berger, no. 3065
11. Pope Innocent IV to [Eudes,] Bishop of Tusculum, papal legate, 16 March 1248: Berger, no. 3719
12. Pope Innocent IV to the Bishop of Troyes, 27 June 1248: Berger, no. 4038
13. Pope Innocent IV to William Longespee, 6 June 1247: Berger, no. 2758
14. Pope Innocent IV to William Longespee, 19 March 1248: Berger, no. 3723
15. Pope Innocent IV to the Bishops of Lincoln and Worcester, 7 June 1247: Berger, no. 2843

16. Pope Innocent IV to the Archbishop of Narbonne, 15 March 1248: Berger, no. 3727
17. Pope Innocent IV to the barons, knights and other nobles and all crusaders and the faithful of Christ in the territories overseas, 23 February 1248: Berger, no. 3661
18. Pope Innocent IV to the Archbishops of Reims, Bourges, Sens, Rouen and Narbonne and to the Dominican Prior and Franciscan Minister of the province of France, 28 February 1250: *Regestrum Visitationum Archiepiscopi Rothomagensis. Journal des visites pastorales d'Eude Rigaud, archevêque de Rouen. MCCXLVIII–MCCLXIX*, ed. T. Bonnin (Rouen, 1852), appendix, pp. 737–40
19. Pope Innocent IV to the Archbishops of Reims, Bourges, Sens, Rouen and Narbonne and to the Dominican Prior and Franciscan Minister of the province of France, 4 March 1250: *Regestrum Visitationum Archiepiscopi Rothomagensis*, ed. Bonnin, appendix, pp. 740–41

(b) Recruitment of former rebels and heretics

20. Pope Innocent IV to the Archbishop of Auch, 4 December 1247: Berger, no. 3508
21. Hugues le Brun, Count of Angoulême, announces that he will travel overseas with Alphonse, Count of Poitou, to relieve the Holy Land, 24 June 1249: *Layettes*, vol. 5, pp. 177–8 (no. 529)

(c) The search for allies

22. Pope Innocent IV to Haakon IV, King of Norway, 6 November 1246: *Diplomatarium Norvegicum*, ed. C. C. A. Lange and Carl R. Unger, vol. 1 (Christiania, 1849), p. 27 (no. 33); summary in Berger, no. 2218
23. Pope Innocent IV to Haakon IV, King of Norway, 19 November 1247: *Diplomatarium Norvegicum*, ed. Lange and Unger, vol. 1, p. 31 (no. 40); summary in Berger, no. 3439
24. Pope Innocent IV to Henry III, King of England, 30 August 1247: Berger, no. 4054
25. Georgios Akropolita, *Khronike syngraphe*, ed. Immanuel Bekker, *Georgii Acropolitae Annales* (Bonn, 1836), p. 94 (chapter 48)

III THE ATTITUDE OF THE EMPEROR FREDERICK II

(a) Correspondence of the Emperor

26. Frederick II to his officials in Sicily, November 1246: Huillard-Bréholles, vol. 6/1, pp. 465–6
27. Frederick II to all who see the letter, November 1246: Huillard-Bréholles, vol. 6/1, pp. 466–7

28. Louis IX to Frederick II [February or March 1247]: Huillard-Bréholles, vol. 6/1, pp. 501–2
29. Frederick II to the Count of Caserta, [May or June] 1248: Huillard-Bréholles, vol. 6/2, pp. 626–7
30. Frederick II to Louis IX [July 1249]: Huillard-Bréholles, vol. 6/2, pp. 745–6
31. Frederick II to Louis IX [July 1249]: Huillard-Bréholles, vol. 6/2, pp. 748–50

(b) Other evidence

32. Qaraṭāy al-ʿIzzī al-Khazāndārī, *Ta'rīkh majmū' al-nawādir* (*c.* 1330), Forschungs- und Landesbibliothek Gotha, ms. Orient. A 1655, fols 39–40
33. Ibn Wāṣil (d. 1298), *Mufarrij al-kurūb fī akhbār banī Ayyūb* (1263), ed. Jamāl al-Dīn al-Shayyāl, Hasanein Rabie and Saʿīd al-Fatḥ ʿĀshūr (Cairo, 1953–77), vol. 3, pp. 247–8
34. *Annales Ianuenses*, ed. Luigi Tommaso Belgrano and Cesare Imperiale de Sant'Angelo, *Annali Genovesi di Caffaro e de' suoi continuatori dal MXCIX al MCCXCIII* (Genova and Rome, 1890–1929), vol. 3, pp. 178–9

IV RIVAL CRUSADES

35. Pope Innocent IV to archbishops, bishops and prelates of other churches who see the letter, 13 September 1245: *Preußisches Urkundenbuch*, ed. Rudolf Philippi, Max Hein et al. (Königsberg and Marburg, 1882–1986), vol. 1/1, p. 125 (no. 169)
36. Pope Innocent IV to Béla IV, King of Hungary, 4 February 1247: *Vetera Monumenta Historica Hungariam Sacram Illustrantia*, ed. Augustin Theiner (Rome, 1859–60), vol. 1, pp. 203–4 (no. 379); summary in Berger, no. 2957
37. Pope Innocent IV to the Preceptor and brothers of the Hospital of Jersusalem in Hungary, 24 June 1248: *Vetera Monumenta Historica*, ed. Theiner, vol. 1, p. 206 (no. 388); summary in Berger, no. 4000
38. Pope Innocent IV to [Eudes,] Bishop of Tusculum, papal legate, 5 July 1246: Berger, no. 2935; also in Rodenberg, vol. 2, pp. 161–2 (no 214)
39. Pope Innocent IV to the bishops in Frisia, [28 July–9 August] 1246: Berger, no. 2054; also in Rodenberg, vol. 2, pp. 172–3 (no. 234)
40. Pope Innocent IV to O[ttaviano], Cardinal-deacon of Santa Maria in Via Lata, papal legate, 8 March 1247: Berger, no. 3002; also in Rodenberg, vol. 2, p. 219 (no. 292)
41. Pope Innocent IV to P[eter], Cardinal-deacon of San Giorgio in Velabro, papal legate, 18 March 1247: summary in Berger, no. 2964
42. Pope Innocent IV to Louis IX, 17 June 1247: Rodenberg, vol. 2, pp. 287–8 (no. 394); summary in Berger, no. 3040

43. Pope Innocent IV to [Eudes,] Bishop of Tusculum, papal legate, 5 July 1247: Berger, no. 3054; also in Rodenberg, vol. 2, pp. 296–7 (no. 408)
44. Pope Innocent IV to P[eter], Cardinal-deacon of San Giorgio in Velabro, papal legate, 19 November 1247: Rodenberg, vol. 2, p. 329 (no. 459); summary in Berger, no. 4065
45. Pope Innocent IV to Hydus, Provincial Prior of the Dominican Order in Germany, 22 June 1248: Rodenberg, vol. 2, p. 409 (no. 579); summary in Berger, no. 3967
46. Pope Innocent IV to [Albrecht Suerbeer,] Archbishop of Prussia, papal legate, 17 November 1247: Rodenberg, vol. 2, p. 326 (no. 453); summary in Berger, no. 4070
47. Pope Innocent IV to P[eter], Cardinal-deacon of San Giorgio in Velabro, papal legate, 20 November 1247: Berger, no. 3433; also in Rodenberg, vol. 2, p. 335 (no. 470)
48. Pope Innocent IV to preachers in Frisia, 19 November 1247: Berger, no. 4068
49. Pope Innocent IV to P[eter], Cardinal-deacon of San Giorgio in Velabro, papal legate, 20 November 1247: Berger, no. 4060; also in Rodenberg, vol. 2, p. 332 (no. 465)
50. Pope Innocent IV to P[eter], Cardinal-deacon of San Giorgio in Velabro, papal legate, 8 April 1248: Rodenberg, vol. 2, pp. 373–4 (no. 534); summary in Berger, no. 3779
51. Pope Innocent IV to the Dominican Priors of Louvain and Antwerp, in the dioceses of Cambrai and Liège, 19 September 1248: Rodenberg, vol. 2, p. 418 (no. 589); summary in Berger, no. 4166
52. Pope Innocent IV to the Dominican Willem Van Eyk, diocese of Liège, 11 May 1249: Berger, no. 4525; also in Rodenberg, vol. 2, p. 531 (no. 718)
53. Pope Innocent IV to the Dominican W[illem] Van Eyk, diocese of Liège, 14 May 1249: Rodenberg, vol. 2, p. 533 (no. 721); summary in Berger, no. 4510
54. Pope Innocent IV to Henry III, King of England, 11 April 1250: *Foedera*, vol. 1/1, p. 159
55. 'Menkonis Chronicon', *MGHS*, vol. 23, pp. 540, 542

V THE FIRST PHASE OF THE CRUSADE: VICTORY AND DISASTER IN EGYPT

56. Eudes de Châteauroux, Cardinal-bishop of Tusculum and papal legate, to Innocent IV, 31 March 1249: *Spicilegium sive Collectio Veterum Aliquot Scriptorum Qui in Galliae Bibliothecis Delituerant*, ed. Luc d'Achéry, new edn by Étienne Baluze and L. F. J. de la Barre (Paris, 1723), vol. 3, pp. 624–8

57. Robert, Count of Artois, to Queen Blanche, 23 June 1249: Matthew Paris, *Chronica Majora*, ed. Henry Richards Luard (London, 1872–83), vol. 6: *Additamenta*, pp. 152–4; text reproduced in *Lettres françaises du XIII*[e] *siècle*, ed. Alfred L. Foulet, Les classiques français du moyen âge (Paris, 1924), pp. 16–18
58. Jean de Beaumont, royal chamberlain, to Geoffrey de la Chapelle, Damietta 25 June 1249: Comte [P.] Riant, 'Six lettres relatives aux croisades', *AOL*, 1 (1881): 383–92; text reproduced in *Lettres françaises du XIII*[e] *siècle*, ed. Foulet, pp. 18–20
59. Gui, a household knight of the Viscount of Melun [late in 1249], to Master B. de Chartres: Matthew Paris, *Chronica Majora*, vol. 6: *Additamenta*, pp. 155–62
60. Guillaume de Sonnac, Master of the Order of the Temple, to Robert de Sandford, Preceptor of the Temple in England [1249]: Matthew Paris, *Chronica Majora*, vol. 6: *Additamenta*, p. 162
61. Gui de Burcey (passed on by Master Jean, a monk of Pontigny): Matthew Paris, *Chronica Majora*, vol. 6: *Additamenta*, p. 163
62. Queen Blanche to Henry III, King of England [1249]: Matthew Paris, *Chronica Majora*, vol. 6: *Additamenta*, pp. 165–7
63. Philippe, his chaplain, to Alphonse, Count of Poitou and Toulouse, 20 April 1250: T. Saint-Bris, 'Lettre adressée en Égypte à Alphonse, comte de Poitiers, frère de saint Louis', *BEC*, 1e série, 1 (1839–40): 389–403
64. Foundation charter of the cathedral church of Damietta, November 1249: ed. in Jean Richard, 'La fondation d'une église latine en Orient par saint Louis: Damiette', *BEC*, 120 (1962): 39–54; reprinted in Richard, *Orient et Occident au Moyen Age: contacts et relations (XIIe–XVe s.)* (London, 1976)
65. Nicholas de la Hyde to the Abbot of St Albans [1250]: Matthew Paris, *Chronica Majora*, vol. 6: *Additamenta*, p. 167
66. B[enedict of Alignano], Bishop of Marseilles, to Pope Innocent IV, 20 May [1250]: *Spicilegium*, ed. D'Achéry, vol. 3, p. 628
67. A Templar [1250; probably in fact a Hospitaller]: Matthew Paris, *Chronica Majora*, vol. 6: *Additamenta*, pp. 191–7
68. Robert, Patriarch of Jerusalem, to the Cardinals, 15 May 1250: 'Annales monasterii de Burton', in *Annales Monastici*, vol. 1, pp. 285–9
69. Troubadour's song: Bédier and Aubry (ed.), *Les chansons de croisade* pp. 263–5
70. Louis IX to his subjects in France, [before 10] August 1250: *Historiae Francorum Scriptores ab Ipsius Gentis Origine*, ed. André Du Chesne, vol. 5 (Paris, 1649), pp. 428–32
71. Fragments of the deposition made by Charles of Anjou [1282], King of Sicily: Comte Paul Riant, 'Déposition de Charles d'Anjou pour la canonisation de saint Louis', in C. Jourdain (ed.), *Notices et documents publiées par la Société de l'histoire de France à l'occasion du cinquantième anniversaire de sa fondation* (Paris, 1884), pp. 170–76
72. Vincent de Beauvais, *Speculum Historiale*, ed. Johann Mentelin (Straßburg, 1473), xxxii, 89, 95 and 97–8

VI EVENTS IN THE MUSLIM CAMP, AND THE MAMLUK *COUP D'ÉTAT*

73. Ibn Wāṣil, *Mufarrij al-kurūb*, Bibliothèque Nationale, Paris, ms. arabe 1703, fols 60v–66r, 74v–92r *passim*

74. Sibṭ Ibn al-Jawzī (Shams al-Dīn Abū'l-Muẓaffar Yūsuf ibn Qizūghlī) (d. 1256), *Mir'āt al-zamān fī ta'rīkh al-a'yān*, vol. 8/2 (Hyderabad, A.P., 1372 H./1952), pp. 772–83; Shams al-Dīn Muḥammad ibn Aḥmad al-Dhahabī (d. 1348), *Ta'rīkh al-Islām*, ed. ʿUmar ʿAbd al-Salām Tadmurī, [vol. 5:] *641–650 H.* (Beirut, 1419 H./1998), pp. 45, 50–51, 53, 55–6, 358, 373–4, 387–8 (for extracts from Ibn al-Sāʿī and from the memoirs of Saʿd al-Dīn Ibn Ḥamawiya al-Juwaynī)

VII THE REACTION TO FAILURE: CRITICISM AND RATIONAL EXPLANATION

75. Pope Innocent IV to Queen Blanche, [August 1250]: Hans Martin Schaller, 'Eine kuriale Briefsammlung des 13. Jahrhunderts mit unbekannten Briefen Friedrichs II.', *Deutsches Archiv für Erforschung des Mittelalters*, 18 (1962): 171–213; reprinted in Schaller, *Stauferzeit. Ausgewählte Aufsätze* (Hanover, 1993), pp. 283–328 (no. 15)

76. Pope Innocent IV to Eudes Rigaud, Archbishop of Rouen, [second half of August] 1250: *Historiae Francorum Scriptores*, ed. Du Chesne, vol. 5, pp. 415–17

77. Eudes de Châteauroux, *Sermo in anniversario Roberti comitis Attrabatensis et aliorum nobilium qui interfecti fuerunt a Sarracenis apud Mansuram in Egipto* ('Sermon on the anniversary of Robert, Count of Artois, and of other nobles who were killed by the Saracens at Mansura in Egypt') [1251?], in Penny J. Cole, *The Preaching of the Crusades to the Holy Land, 1095–1270* (Cambridge, MA, 1991), appendix D, pp. 235–9

78. Eudes de Châteauroux, *Sermo de eodem anniversario* ('Sermon on the same anniversary') [1251?], in Cole, *Preaching of the Crusades*, appendix D, pp. 240–43

79. Frederick II to [Ferdinand III], King of Castile, [May or June 1250], in Huillard-Bréholles, vol. 6/2, pp. 769–71

80. 'Annales Erphordenses', *MGHS*, vol. 16, pp. 37–8

81. Jean de Garlande [*c.* 1252], *De triumphis ecclesiae libri octo*, ed. Thomas Wright (London, 1856), pp. 135–9 *passim*

82. Austorc d'Aurillac, *Sirventés*, ed. A. Jeanroy, 'Le troubadour Austorc d'Aurillac et son sirventés sur la septième Croisade', in *Mélanges Chabaneau. Festschrift Camille Chabaneau zur Vollendung seines 75. Lebensjahres 4 märz 1906 dargebracht von seinen Schülern, Freunden und Verehrern*, Romanische Forschungen, vol. 23 (Erlangen, 1907), pp. 81–7

83. Salimbene de Adam, *Cronica* [*c.* 1285], ed. Giuseppe Scalia (Turnhout, 1998–99), vol. 2, pp. 672–3

VIII THE 'CRUSADE' OF THE *PASTOUREAUX* (1251)

84. Guillaume de Nangis, 'Gesta sanctae memoriae Ludovici regis Franciae', *RHGF*, vol. 20, p. 382
85. 'Chronique de Primat, traduite par Jean du Vignay' [before 1289], *RHGF*, vol. 23, pp. 8–10
86. Giovanni de Columna, 'E Mari Historiarum', *RHGF*, vol. 23, pp. 123–4
87. 'Extraits des Chroniques de Saint-Denis', *RHGF*, vol. 21, pp. 115–16
88. 'E Chronico Sancti Laudi Rotomagensis', *RHGF*, vol. 23, pp. 395–6
89. 'Chronique anonyme des rois de France finissant en 1286', *RHGF*, vol. 21, p. 83
90. *Actus pontificum Cenomannis in urbe degentium* [1255–72], ed. G. Busson and A. Ledru (Le Mans, 1901 = *Archives Historiques du Maine*, vol. 2), pp. 500–501
91. 'Richeri Gesta Senoniensis ecclesiae', *MGHS*, vol. 25, pp. 310–11
92. 'Balduini Ninovensis chronicon', *MGHS*, vol. 25, p. 544
93. 'Chronica universalis Mettensis', *MGHS*, vol. 24, p. 522 (from ms. 'A')
94. 'Annales monasterii de Burton', in *Annales Monastici*, vol. 1, pp. 290–93
95. Salimbene de Adam, *Cronica*, vol. 2, pp. 672, 673
96. Thomas de Cantimpré, *Bonum Universale de Apibus*, liber II, iv, 15, ed. Georgius Colvenerius (Douai, 1627), vol. 1, pp. 140–41
97. Roger Bacon, *Opus Maius* [1267], ed. John Henry Bridges (Oxford and London, 1897–1900), vol. 1, pp. 401–2

IX EFFORTS TO SEND ASSISTANCE TO KING LOUIS FROM THE WEST

98. Pope Innocent IV to the Bishops of St Andrews and Aberdeen, 17 October 1250: Berger, no. 4868
99. Pope Innocent IV to the Bishops of Paris, Évreux and Senlis, 29 November 1250: Berger, no. 4926
100. Pope Innocent IV to the Dominican Prior and the Franciscan Minister of the province of Germany, 29 November 1250: Berger, no. 4927; also in Rodenberg, vol. 3, pp. 15–16 (no. 20)
101. Pope Innocent IV to the Bishop of Angoulême, 1 February 1251: Berger, no. 5028
102. Pope Innocent IV to the archbishops and bishops in the English kingdom, 16 February 1251: Berger, no. 5106
103. Pope Innocent IV to Henry III, King of England, 18 October 1251: 'Annales monasterii de Burton', in *Annales Monastici*, vol. 1, pp. 293–5

104. Pope Innocent IV to Henry III, King of England, 1252: 'Annales monasterii de Burton', in *Annales Monastici*, vol. 1, pp. 298–9
105. Pope Innocent IV to the archbishops and bishops of England, Ireland and Gascony, 3 September 1252: Berger, no. 5979
106. Henry III, King of England, to Louis IX, 8 June 1252: *Foedera*, vol. 1/1, p. 167
107. Pope Innocent IV to the Prior of the Dominican Order in Paris, 2 April 1253: Berger, no. 6469
108. Philippe, chaplain to Alphonse, Count of Toulouse, to Louis IX, [before 28 November] 1252: *Layettes*, vol. 3, pp. 170–71 (no. 4030)
109. Pope Innocent IV to [Philippe,] treasurer of the Church of Saint-Hilaire at Poitiers, 19 March 1253: Berger, no. 6440
110. Pope Innocent IV to [Philippe,] treasurer of the Church of Saint-Hilaire at Poitiers, 21 March 1253: *Layettes*, vol. 3, p. 176 (no. 4043)
111. Pope Innocent IV to [Philippe,] treasurer of the Church of Saint-Hilaire at Poitiers, 29 March 1253: *Layettes*, vol. 3, pp. 177–8 (no. 4047)
112. Pope Innocent IV to Alphonse, Count of Poitou and Toulouse, 17 October 1253: *Layettes*, vol. 3, pp. 196–7 (no. 4081)

X THE SECOND PHASE: KING LOUIS'S FOUR-YEAR STAY IN PALESTINE

113. Guillaume de Châteauneuf, Master of the Hospital, to the Dominican Walter de St Martin [1251]: Matthew Paris, *Chronica Majora*, vol. 6: *Additamenta*, pp. 204–5
114. Guillaume de Châteauneuf, Master of the Hospital, to the Dominican Walter de St Martin [1251]: Matthew Paris, *Chronica Majora*, vol. 6: *Additamenta*, pp. 203–4
115. Robert, Patriarch of Jerusalem, to Queen Blanche, [summer] 1251: 'Annales monasterii de Burton', in *Annales Monastici*, vol. 1, p. 296
116. Louis IX to Alphonse, Count of Poitou and Toulouse, Caesarea, 11 August 1251: *Layettes*, vol. 3, pp. 139–40 (no. 3956)
117. Joseph de Cancy to Walter de St Martin, 6 May 1252: Matthew Paris, *Chronica Majora*, vol. 6: *Additamenta*, pp. 205–7
118. Ibn Wāṣil, *Mufarrij al-kurūb*, Bibliothèque Nationale, Paris, ms. arabe 1703, fols 92v–98v, 102r–106r, 107v, 108v, 111r
119. Sibṭ Ibn al-Jawzī, *Mir'āt al-zamān*, vol. 8/2, pp. 779–81, 785, 789
120. Ibn al-ʿAmīd (al-Makīn ibn Jirjīs), *Kitāb al-Majmūʿ al-mubārak*, ed. Claude Cahen, 'La "Chronique des Ayyoubides" d'al-Makīn b. al-ʿAmīd', *BEO*, 15 (1955–57): 161–4 *passim*
121. Guillaume de Saulx and Hugues de Bordeaux to Louis IX, Chastel-Pèlerin, 31 October 1251: Pierre-Vincent Claverie, 'Un nouvel éclairage sur le financement de la première croisade de saint Louis', *Mélanges de l'École Française de Rome, Moyen Age*, 113 (2001): 621–35, annexes, no. 2

122. The magnates of the kingdom of Jerusalem to Henry III, King of England, [late] September 1254: 'Annales monasterii de Burton', in *Annales Monastici*, vol. 1, pp. 368–9

I

King Louis Takes the Cross

Louis IX took the Cross in December 1244,[1] on, or perhaps before, his recovery from a severe illness. At this juncture he cannot have received the terrible news of the battle of La Forbie (17 October), in which the forces of the kingdom of Jerusalem and of their confederates among the Syrian Ayyubid princes were decimated by the army of the Egyptian Sultan, al-Ṣāliḥ Najm al-Dīn Ayyūb, and his Khwarazmian allies. The fact that even Pope Innocent IV, writing in January 1245, does not refer to this disaster [**doc. 4** below] strongly suggests that it was not yet known in the West. Like the Pope, King Louis had, in all probability, heard the first reports of the Khwarazmians' sack of Jerusalem on 11 August 1244, which had been swiftly followed by the massacre of most of its fleeing Christian population. Most of the Holy City had been restored to Christian rule through the treaty between the Emperor Frederick II and Ayyūb's father al-Kāmil in 1229, and it had been entirely in Christian hands since 1243. Its loss, and its desecration by the infidel, would have dealt a heavy blow to a man imbued with Louis's profound piety and who was, moreover, gravely ill. As a result – rather like his great-grandfather Louis VII, prior to the Second Crusade almost a century earlier – he made his crusading vow quite independently of the papal summons. The Legate Eudes, arriving in Paris in August 1245 with a letter from Pope Innocent IV which urged the King to move to the relief of the Holy Land, found Louis already *crucesignatus*.

The decision to take the Cross may have been an expression of gratitude for having surmounted a life-threatening malady, and triggered by disastrous news from the East; but it is likely that the King was gradually prepared for it by a combination of circumstances over a lengthy period, and these have been ably analysed by William C. Jordan and by Jean Richard.[2] The three near-contemporary sources below do not add anything of significance to the story of how Louis took the Cross for the first time. But the two *chansons* [**docs 2 and 3**] vividly convey the joy and optimism that greeted the King's vow. It is evident from the tone and content that they were both

1 The date given by Matthew Paris, *Chronica Majora*, vol. 4, p. 397: *in Adventu Domini* (trans. Giles, vol. 2, p. 37).

2 William C. Jordan, *Louis IX and the Challenge of the Crusade: A Study in Rulership* (Princeton, NJ, 1979), chapter 1. Jean Richard, *Saint Louis: Crusader King of France*, ed. and abridged by Simon Lloyd and trans. Jean Birrell (Cambridge, 1992), pp. 87–98; original edn, *Saint Louis roi d'une France féodale, soutien de la Terre Sainte* (Paris, 1983), pp. 159–80. There are also interesting discussions of Louis's spirituality in Étienne Delaruelle, 'L'idée de croisade chez saint Louis', *Bulletin de Littérature Ecclésiastique*, 61 (1960): 241–57, reprinted in his *L'idée de croisade au Moyen Age* (Torino, 1980), pp. 189–207; in Edmond-René Labande, 'Saint Louis pèlerin', *Revue d'Histoire de l'Église de France*, 57 (1971): 5–18, and in Jacques Le Goff, *Saint Louis* (Paris, 1996), *passim*.

written before Louis sailed for the East; the first, in Bédier's view, may well date from the end of 1244 or the beginning of 1245. Both the first anonymous troubadour and Baudouin d'Avesnes [**doc. 1**] broadly confirm the picture drawn by Joinville many decades later. Interestingly, the account given in the first *chanson* possibly also confirms Joinville's statement that Blanche was appalled at her son's decision to take the crusading vow [see note 8 below].[3] This seems more plausible than the story retailed by Matthew Paris, in which she vowed on the King's behalf that he would take the Cross should he recover,[4] especially since Matthew later has Blanche, among others, seeking to dissuade her son from fulfilling his vow on the grounds that he had been in no fit state when he made it. At this point, allegedly, Louis discarded the vow, only to retake it again at once, announcing that now he was in perfect health and the objection could no longer stand.[5] Although it is quite conceivable that Blanche subsequently repented of an earlier enthusiasm once Louis had recovered and his preparations were under way, it seems more likely that, as the French sources claim, she was opposed to his plans from the outset.

DOCUMENTS 1–3

1. Baudouin d'Avesnes, 'Chronicon Hanoniense', MGHS, *vol. 25, p. 453*

In that same year, King Louis contracted a serious illness at Pontoise, and was brought so low that he was believed to be dead. The physicians left, and prayers were said for an hour, to the point where all the doors were open and everyone in the [royal] residence went wherever he pleased. The prelates were summoned to commend his soul. But at that juncture they saw him stir and heard him groan. So the physicians were recalled, and with great effort they opened his mouth to the extent that he swallowed a little cordial. Thereafter they worked hard, so that by the will of Our Lord the King began to recover. And when he was recovered, he took the Cross to go overseas.

2. Troubadour's song [1245?]: Joseph Bédier and Pierre Aubry (ed.), Les chansons de croisade *(Paris, 1909), pp. 240-43*[6]

[p. 240] The whole world must be delighted and be given up to rejoicing. [p. 241] The King of France has taken the Cross to go on that journey which he does not

---

3 On all this, see Jean de Joinville, *Vie de saint Louis*, ed. Natalis de Wailly (Pari,: 1874), §§ 106–7, pp. 60, 62 (trans. Hague, p. 51; trans. Shaw, p. 191).

4 Matthew Paris, *Chronica Majora*, vol. 4, p. 397 (trans. Giles, vol. 2, pp. 37–8).

5 Ibid., vol. 5, pp. 3–4 (trans. Giles, vol. 2, pp. 253–4; trans. Vaughan, pp. 131–2).

6 First edited by Wilhelm Meyer, 'Wie Ludwig IX d. H. das Kreuz nahm (Altfranzösisches Lied in Cambridge)', *Nachrichten der königlichen Gesellschaft der Wissenschaften zu Göttingen* (1907), pp. 246–57. Bédier gives a modern French rendering at pp. 244–5, based on the more reliable text established by Hermann Suchier, 'Ein Kreuzlied von 1245', *Zeitschrift für Romanische Philologie*, 32 (1908): 73–6. There is another translation of all but the final stanza in Richard, *Saint Louis roi*, pp. 172–4.

undertake who is held back by all his sins. He is saved who drowns at sea. I have taken too long to go where God was crucified. The man does not exist who ought not to go thither.

Do you not know the experience that led the King to take the Cross? He is faithful and complete, and truly a *prud'homme*. As far as his realm extends, he is loved and esteemed. The life the King leads is holy, clean and pure, free from sin and filth. You must know that he cares nothing for wickedness.

He succumbed to a prolonged sickness; and that was why he took the Cross. For it was a good hour and a half [p. 242] that they believed him lifeless. Some said that he had died. The elegant Lady Blanche, who is his mother and his friend, cried out in anguish, 'My son, how painful is this separation!'

Everyone was truly of the opinion that the King was dead. A sheet was cast over him, and they wept bitterly around him. All his people entered; there never was such mourning. The Count of Artois, truly, said softly to the King, 'Fair, sweet brother, speak to me if Jesus will allow you.'

At that the King gave a sigh, and said, 'Fair brother, sweet friend, where is the Bishop of Paris?[7] Quickly now! He will give me the Cross. For my spirit has long been overseas; and my body will go there, if it is God's will, and will wrest [p. 243] the land from the Saracens. Blessed is he who aids me in that.'

Everyone was happy and rejoiced when they heard the King, and held their peace, except his elegant mother, who gently embraced him: 'Fair son, hearken to me. I shall give you forty pack-loads of *deniers*: I make you a free gift of it, to pay for mercenaries.'[8]

At this news everyone must be quite overjoyed; for in my view it is fine and welcome. He who strews his brains, or his blood or his innards, on the soil of the land where God was born of His handmaiden, will have a lofty seat before God in Paradise.

3. Troubadour's song [1245?]: Bédier and Aubry (ed.), Les chansons de croisade, *pp. 251–3*

At God's command, I shall begin a *serventois*, calling for good cheer and rejoicing, that He may teach us the right path to reach Him without any obstacle. Let us all go forth, and without delay, together with Him who summons and entreats us, ready to join Him at the point of assembly. As our reward He grants us Paradise eternally for our salvation.

...[9]

7 Guillaume d'Auvergne (1228–49).

8 This is a trifle obscure, but it appears that Blanche may be hostile to her son's intention and is offering him funds with which he might send mercenaries instead of leaving France with his own barons and knights.

9 There is a lacuna here.

Jerusalem, how great is your suffering! It is on you that disaster has fallen. Christendom has too long abandoned you. The Sepulchre and the Temple, once so greatly cherished, are lost. It was surely right that you received service and honour, for in you did God hang on the Cross. And now the pagans have destroyed and ruined you. But they shall have their reward!

[p. 252] ...[10] when the King of Paris was despaired of, and it was thought his soul had left him. And when he returned to life, he asked for the Cross, and it was given him by him[11] who had witnessed such splendid miracles.

France, you must indeed have great glory; you should be honoured everywhere. God is asking you for aid and succour, to free His land from the pagan. That is why He has revived the King. He has taken the Cross in order to amend his life and will go overseas, if God wills it. All the barons will bear him company. The Count of Artois will guide his host.

Go, *serventois*, give your message to the wealthy King who governs France. Let him not forget the land of Syria; he cannot long remain here. [p. 253] Paris gives him counsel in all loyalty, to lead his host swiftly to Romania. He will be able to conquer it with ease, and baptize the Sultan of Turkey.[12] Thereby will he liberate the whole world.

...[13] Reconcile the Emperor with the Pope;[14] and then he will cross the sea with a great fleet. The pagans will be unable to withstand him. He will conquer Turkey and Persia, and will go on to be crowned in Babylon.

10 Another lacuna.

11 Clearly an allusion to the Bishop of Paris.

12 The Seljük Sultan of Anatolia (Rūm), at this time ʿIzz al-Dīn Kaykāʾūs II.

13 Another lacuna.

14 Matthew Paris, *Chronica Majora*, vol. 4, pp. 484, 523–4 (trans. Giles, vol. 2, pp. 112–13, 145–6), has Louis endeavouring unsuccessfully to reconcile Pope and Emperor during a meeting with Innocent IV at Cluny in 1246. Guillaume de Nangis, 'Gesta sanctae memoriae Ludovici regis Franciae', in *RHGF*, vol. 20, pp. 352, 354, speaks of a visit to the Pope in Lyons in 1245. Innocent himself refers to a peacemaking mission from the King, headed by the Bishop of Soissons and the warden of Bayeux (Berger, no. 2948, 5 November 1246).

II

Preparations for the Crusade

The Popes traditionally launched a crusade to the East with *excitatoria*, letters appealing to secular princes and lords to go to the aid of the Holy Land in the wake of some particularly grave disaster. Although Innocent IV's letter to King Louis has not survived, we have the (presumably) almost identical missive to Henry III [**doc. 4**], as also the Pope's letter of 6 February 1245, ordering the Minister-General, provincial ministers and guardians of the Franciscan Order to preach the Cross in aid of the Holy Land.[1] The privileges attaching to those who took the Cross had largely been laid down during the Fourth Lateran Council in 1215 and were reiterated at the Council of Lyons in June 1245.[2] In England the Pope authorized the nomination of commissioners whose duty was to see that the status of *crucesignati* suffered no infringement [**doc. 7**]. Innocent would add further privileges as the crusade progressed (see, for instance, page 196 and **doc. 109** below).

Although participants were expected to meet at least some of the costs of crusading from their own resources, since the pontificate of Innocent III it had been customary to raise additional funds for the crusade by taxing the revenues of the Church as a whole. Innocent IV granted Louis one-twentieth of ecclesiastical revenues throughout Christendom; though the French Church, doubtless under pressure from the King's officers, volunteered to provide one-tenth [**doc. 8**]. Sums raised from legacies and bequests specifically made for the crusade, served to swell the total available; so too did those generated by the redemption of vows, first deployed by Pope Gregory IX from 1234 onwards as a major source of crusade funding.[3] Such monies were made over on collection to great magnates who had taken the Cross. Thus the Pope ordered funds raised within specific regions to be placed at the disposal of the King's brothers, Robert of Artois and Charles of Anjou. Within French territories they were granted only the proceeds of vow redemption and legacies,[4] whereas Robert was allocated the twentieth from the kingdom of Navarre, the cities and dioceses of Metz, Toul and Verdun, and those parts of the diocese of Artois that lay outside the French kingdom [**doc. 10**], and Charles was to have access to the twentieth from his county of Provence, which was technically part of the Empire [**doc. 11**]. In both

1 Ferdinand M. Delorme, 'Bulle d'Innocent IV pour la Croisade (6 février 1245)', *AFH*, 6 (1913): 386–9. Except for the insertion of the passage ordering the preaching of the Cross, the text is identical to that of the letter to Henry III.

2 See *Decrees of the Ecumenical Councils*, vol. 1: *Nicaea I to Lateran V*, ed. Norman P. Tanner SJ (London and Georgetown, DC, 1990), p. 299.

3 See Michael Lower, *The Barons' Crusade: A Call to Arms and its Consequences* (Philadelphia, PA, 2005), pp. 14–17, 31–2.

4 For Charles's counties of Anjou and Maine, see Berger, no. 3769.

cases, the Pope took care to guarantee the rights of local magnates who might yet take the Cross [**docs 11 and 12**].

Similar arrangements were in place in England, although here the subsidies tended to be distributed among crusaders at large rather than concentrated in the hands of prominent magnates [**doc. 15**]; when granting funds to William Longespee, the Pope specified an upper limit to the sum allocated [**docs 13 and 14**]. King Henry III's assumption of the Cross in March 1250, and the consequent papal grant of English ecclesiastical revenues, complicated matters, since he could now be deemed to enjoy precedence over other recipients; consequently, in October the Pope had to instruct the Bishops of Chichester and Exeter to make good the sums promised to various *crucesignati* prior to the King's taking the Cross but which were still outstanding.[5] Some of the monies from vow redemptions were additionally made available to impecunious crusaders [**doc. 16**].

Louis took care to ensure that supplies were awaiting his army when it reached Cyprus. His agents reached the island over a year before the crusaders' own arrival,[6] and Joinville describes the sight that greeted them as they approached: barrels of wine stacked up on the hillside, resembling wooden barns, together with great quantities of wheat and barley, on which grass had sprouted so that they looked like hillocks.[7] The French King's naval preparations, however, were less well-laid than his measures for the supply of his army on Cyprus. The contracts for ships that have come down to us are the earliest to stipulate dimensions.[8] The number of passengers that could be conveyed in these vessels is not stated; but we know that Louis returned to France in 1254 in a Marseillais ship, which carried over 800 souls.[9] It has been pointed out that he did not charter enough of the flat-bottomed horse transports that would have enabled him to land cavalry directly on the beach at Damietta [below, **pp. 63–4**]. More seriously, he failed to gather a sufficient number of oared war-galleys for his operations in Egypt. The overwhelming majority of the vessels that accompanied the French King to Damietta were apparently large sailing-ships. This oversight would severely impair the effectiveness of the crusade in the Nile delta.[10]

Measures were taken to draw in former heretics from Languedoc by commuting any penance imposed upon them to service in the crusading army [**doc. 20**]. It is by

5 Berger, no. 4881.

6 'L'estoire de Eracles empereur', in *RHC HOcc.*, vol. 2, p. 436 (trans. in J. Shirley, *Crusader Syria in the Thirteenth Century*, CTT, vol. 5, Aldershot, 1999, p. 137).

7 Joinville, §§ 130–31, pp. 72, 74 (trans. Hague, pp. 56–7; trans. Shaw, p. 197).

8 For contracts with Genoa, see *Documents historiques inédits tirés des collections manuscrites de la Bibliothèque Royale et des archives ou des bibliothèques des départements*, ed. M. Champollion-Figeac (Paris, 1841–43), vol. 2, Latin text, pp. 54–61 (no. 29); Old French version, pp. 61–7 (no. 30); Louis IX to all who see the letter, October 1246, in L. T. Belgrano, 'Une charte de nolis de s. Louis', *AOL*, 2 (1884), documents: 231–6. For Marseilles, see Jal, 'Pacta naulorum', in *Documents historiques inédits*, ed. Champollion-Figeac, vol. 1, pp. 605–9; also in *Layettes*, vol. 2, pp. 632–3 (no. 3537).

9 Joinville, § 653, p. 358 (trans. Hague, p. 192; trans. Shaw, p. 327); for the numbers on board, ibid., § 15, pp. 8, 10 (trans. Hague, pp. 25–6; trans. Shaw, p. 165).

10 John H. Pryor, 'The crusade of Emperor Frederick II, 1220–29: the implications of the maritime evidence', *The American Neptune* 52/2 (Spring 1992): 113–32 (here 116–23).

no means clear that this elicited an enthusiastic response;[11] but some erstwhile *faidits* are known to have availed themselves of the opportunity, notably Olivier de Termes, who left for the East at an uncertain date but who subsequently went on to have a distinguished crusading career.[12]

For a time Louis was given reason to anticipate the presence of at least one royal colleague on his expedition. King Haakon IV of Norway had already taken the Cross for the Holy Land in 1237.[13] Subsequently, he may have commuted his vow in order to fight against the Mongols, for in 1243 Innocent IV allowed the Norwegian duke Knut to commute a vow for the Near East for this purpose should the Mongols again invade Hungary within twelve months.[14] Haakon had certainly taken the Cross for the East once more by the autumn of 1246 [**docs 22–3**]. During the years 1246–47 he and Louis negotiated over Norwegian participation in the expedition; if Matthew Paris, our principal source for these contacts, is to be believed, Louis offered Haakon command of the combined fleet.[15] But nothing came of the negotiations. Haakon, who was illegitimate, appears to have taken the Cross with a view to buttressing his tenuous claim to the throne. It is surely no accident that shortly after his coronation by a papal legate in July 1247 his desire to sail to the East noticeably abated. To the best of our knowledge, no Norwegians participated in the Seventh Crusade, although in November 1250 the Pope would speak of some as having taken the Cross [**doc. 100** below].[16] Contrary to the impression sometimes given in the secondary literature, however, Haakon did not, it seems, abandon the idea of crusading in Palestine altogether, for in December 1252 Innocent again felicitated him on having taken the Cross for the Holy Land (for the third time) and took him, his wife, his household and his kingdom under the protection of St Peter.[17] This vow similarly remained unfulfilled.

For all the frustration and disappointment that Louis might have experienced as a result of Haakon's tergiversations, the narrative sources reveal that the Seventh Crusade did attract knights from outside France. One, the Count of Saarbrücken, was an imperial vassal, although his participation may be explicable on the grounds that

---

11 Christoph T. Maier, *Preaching the Crusades: Mendicant Friars and the Cross in the Thirteenth Century* (Cambridge, 1994), p. 70.

12 See Caroline Smith, *Crusading in the Age of Joinville* (Aldershot, 2006), pp. 158–70; W. C. Jordan, *Louis IX and the Challenge of the Crusade: A Study in Rulership* (Princeton, NJ, 1979), pp. 17–19, 69–70.

13 The chequered history of Haakon's crusading vows is surveyed in Paul Riant, *Expéditions et pèlerinages des Scandinaves en Terre Sainte au temps des croisades* (Paris, 1865), pp. 345–9; see also Maureen Purcell, *Papal Crusading Policy 1244–1291: The Chief Instruments of Papal Crusading Policy and Crusade to the Holy Land from the Final Loss of Jerusalem to the Fall of Acre* (Leiden, 1975), pp. 110–11, 165.

14 See *Diplomatarium Norvegicum*, ed. C. C. A. Lange and Carl R. Unger, vol. 1 (Christiania, 1849), pp. 21–2 (no. 27), and *Codex Diplomaticus Hungariae Ecclesiasticus ac Civilis*, ed. György Fejér (Buda, 1829-44), vol. 4/1, p. 303; summary in Berger, no. 46.

15 Matthew Paris, *Chronica Majora*, vol. 4, pp. 651–2 (trans. Giles, vol. 2, p. 248; trans. Vaughan, pp. 125–6).

16 For a noble previously believed to be Norwegian but now known to have come from the Pas-de-Calais, see p. 195, note 6.

17 *Diplomatarium Norvegicum*, ed. Lange and Unger, vol. 1, pp. 35–6 (nos 47–8).

he was of French stock and was a cousin of Joinville, with whom he joined in hiring a ship and travelled to the East.[18] No other source corroborates Matthew Paris's claim that Venetian crusaders joined Louis on Cyprus in the winter of 1248-9.[19] A number of English knights took the Cross, and Henry III appointed his half-brother, Gui de Lusignan, as their commander [**doc. 24**]. We know that Gui did travel east, since his return around Christmas 1250 prompted the malicious suggestion from Matthew Paris that he might have made a rapid escape following the surrender of Damietta.[20] But in the event the leader of the English crusaders who joined the French King in Egypt, probably in the summer of 1249,[21] was William Longespee, titular Earl of Salisbury. If Matthew is to be trusted, Longespee, leading a contingent of 200 knights, so distinguished himself as to arouse the jealousy of his French colleagues; he would be killed in the disaster at Mansura in February 1250.[22] The pope wrote in 1248 to a Scottish knight who had taken the Cross,[23] and Patrick, Earl of Dunbar, died at Marseilles in that year while preparing to embark on crusade; whether his contingent, or any other Scottish nobles, joined Louis is unknown.[24]

Stronger support was forthcoming from the Frankish settlements in the East. According to one French participant, the total number of knights from Syria and Cyprus, including those supplied by the Temple and the Hospital, stood at 700 [see **doc. 58**], which may have amounted to a quarter of the total number of knights on the crusade prior to the arrival of Alphonse of Poitou. It was perhaps natural that the Palestinian and Cypriot nobility should be well represented on the crusade by the time it weighed anchor at Damietta. Joinville singles out for mention the Count of Jaffa, Jean d'Ibelin (the celebrated jurist), whose ornate galley clearly made a profound impression on him;[25] and more than once describes the Count's Ibelin relatives, Gui and Baudouin (of whom the latter was Constable of Cyprus), as 'commanding the barons of Outremer', from which it should perhaps be inferred

18 Joinville, §§ 109, 113, 119, pp. 62, 64, 68 (trans. Hague, pp. 51, 52, 54; trans. Shaw, pp. 191, 192, 194).

19 Matthew Paris, *Chronica Majora*, vol. 5, p. 70 (trans. Giles, vol. 2, p. 306; trans. Vaughan, p. 180).

20 Ibid., vol. 5, p. 204 (trans. Giles, vol. 2, p. 417). Berger, *Saint Louis*, pp. clviii–clix.

21 By mentioning his name in connection with Alphonse of Poitou, who left France only in the summer, Jean de Garlande (*c.* 1252), *De triumphis ecclesiae libri octo*, ed. Thomas Wright (London, 1856), p. 134, appears to confirm Matthew Paris's date for his arrival in Egypt.

22 See Simon Lloyd, 'William Longespee II: the making of an English crusading hero', *Nottingham Medieval Studies*, 35 (1991): 41–69, and 36 (1992): 79–125. For the figure of 200 knights, see *Chronica Majora*, vol. 5, p. 76 (trans. Giles, vol. 2, p. 311; trans. Vaughan, p. 185).

23 Berger, no. 3794.

24 Matthew Paris, *Chronica Majora*, vol. 5, p. 41 (trans. Giles, vol. 2, p. 283; trans. Vaughan, p. 158). 'Estoire de Eracles', p. 436 (trans. in Shirley, *Crusader Syria*, p. 137). See Alan Macquarrie, *Scotland and the Crusades 1095–1560* (Edinburgh, 1985), pp. 47–9.

25 Joinville, §§ 158–9, pp. 86, 88 (trans. Hague, p. 63; trans. Shaw, pp. 203-4). On Jean, see Peter W. Edbury, *John of Ibelin and the Kingdom of Jerusalem* (Woodbridge, 1997).

that they commanded on behalf of King Henry of Cyprus.[26] We know also from a later reference that Philippe de Montfort, lord of Tyre, fought with the crusade in Egypt [**doc. 68** below].[27]

We might not, however, have expected the Prince of the Morea (Achaea) in Frankish Greece, Guillaume II de Villehardouin, to have joined the crusading fleet after it left Cyprus in May 1249 [see **doc. 59**].[28] Marino Sanudo, writing early in the following century, heard that he was accompanied by 400 horsemen;[29] though en route he left a contingent of more than 100 knights to assist his Genoese allies in their attack on Rhodes [**doc. 25**]. Given the fact that the Empress Marie of Constantinople visited Louis on Cyprus in 1248–49 with a view to securing military assistance from the crusading army against the Greeks,[30] and given, too, the commonly held notion that the creation of new Frankish settlements in Greece ('Romania') by the Fourth Crusade sapped recruitment for the crusade to Syria, it is interesting that Joinville, in a speech made at the council of war in Acre in the summer of 1250, still saw the Morea as a possible source of mercenary knights on which Louis might draw to replenish his decimated force.[31]

The Seventh Crusade was thus an overwhelmingly French affair, reinforced by knights and other soldiers from Latin Syria and Palestine and to a lesser extent from Latin Greece.

DOCUMENTS 4–25

(a) Preaching and finance

4. Pope Innocent IV to Henry III, King of England, 23 January 1245: Foedera, *vol. 1/1, pp. 148–9*

The Holy Land, bespattered with Christ's blood, in the wake of the grave disasters of frequent devastation and following her continuous laments for the frequent slaughter of her people, now experiences the lash at enemy hands even more harshly; now mourns [p. 149] more bitterly and expresses the sharpness of inward pain with cries of still deeper lamentation; and we, stung by her bitter tears, and spurred on by her powerful cries, are with her worn down by the hammer-blows of a persecution that is hers and ours, and with her mourn equally her and our own wretched fate.

---

26 Joinville, §§ 268, 339, 344, pp. 148, 184, 188 (trans. Hague, pp. 91, 109, 110; trans. Shaw, pp. 232, 247–8, 250).

27 See also ibid., §§ 310–12, p. 170 (trans. Hague, p. 102; trans. Shaw, pp. 241–2).

28 Ibid., § 148, p. 82 (trans. Hague, p. 61; trans. Shaw, p. 201). Two knights-bachelor from the Morea were in Joinville's longboat during the landing at Damietta: ibid., § 154, p. 86 (trans. Hague, p. 62; trans. Shaw, p. 203).

29 Marino Sanudo Torsello, *Istoria del Regno di Romania*, in *Chroniques gréco-romanes*, ed. Charles Hopf (Berlin, 1873), p. 102.

30 Joinville, §§ 137-9, pp. 76, 78 (trans. Hague, p. 58; trans. Shaw, pp. 198–9).

31 Ibid., § 427, p. 232 (trans. Hague, p. 131; trans. Shaw, p. 270).

How grievous it is for all the faithful that a place sanctified by Christ's presence should be desecrated by being home to those who blaspheme Him! How much to be bewailed that the land in which the human race was freed from the yoke of age-old captivity should be reduced to shameful slavery! What a reproachful disgrace, and a disgraceful reproach, to Christians that in the place where the Son of God, by means of temporal death on the Cross, snatched them from the agony of eternal death, there He is crucified by the pain of blasphemies and the horror of godlessness! What an incalculable injury that our predecessors, whose keen and assiduous concern did not forsake that land, seem now to have watched over her defence as if to no purpose! That the Christian people, whose sweat, poured forth with the aim of aiding her, bedewed that land on so many occasions and whose blood, spilled so often, turned her red, are seen on this account to have sustained efforts that are useless and to have incurred expenses that brought no profit!

For behold, the faithless race of the Khwarazmians, bursting out from the limits of their territory and through the strength of great numbers devastating all the lands in their path, recently occupied the Holy City of Jerusalem following the rigours of a close siege. And as its Christian inhabitants sought refuge in flight, they drenched them with the poison of their savagery so dreadfully as to annihilate them all alike with the sword and spatter the fields with their blood. And what pierces the depths of our heart with still more bitter grief, and ought to sting every one of the faithful by the enormity of the outrage, is that their fury extended to the holy and venerable Sepulchre of the Saviour. Laying sacrilegious hands on it, they are said, alas, to have violated it, so that the frenzy of their minds, burning to heap abuse on Christ, might not even leave undefiled the places where He was bodily present, but after demolishing [these places] might extinguish all feelings of devotion for them in the minds of the faithful. And persisting in their savagery as far as the Temple of the Lord, they began to destroy it the more unrestrainedly, the more passionately they burn to undermine the principles of the Christian religion and to shatter the edifice of the orthodox faith. This race is said to have committed in those regions other acts of horrific cruelty which are shocking to hear; but since we are not fully informed about these we are omitting to pass them on. If only they might be far removed from the truth, so that it proved unnecessary to recount them!

Ah, who of the faithful is not cast down at the terrible oppression of that land? Ah, what Christian is not also moved by so many appalling injuries to Christ? Is the wickedness of that people to go unpunished, and are they to be allowed freely to run amok with the sword? Is not the mind of every Christian kindled against them by the zeal of devotion, the heart strengthened by the shield of steadfastness and the right hand armed with the sword of vengeance? For indeed it is advisable that the might of this people meets with powerful and swift resistance, so that they are not free to go on to destroy other regions.

We therefore keenly urge, request and exhort Your Royal Serenity, and beseech you through the blood of Christ, prudently to reflect that the more you are known to have received from the Lord the more you are obliged to serve Him and the more wholeheartedly and steadfastly you are bound to defend His faith, and to rise up passionately to assist that land against the faithlessness of the aforementioned race; and so to bring it prompt and effective relief, in a moment of such great need, that through the arrival of your aid and that of others it can be snatched from the polluted grasp of pagans and, with God's favour, completely restored to Christian worship.

For we, trusting in the mercy of Almighty God and the authority of His Apostles, the Blessed Peter and Paul, by virtue of the power of binding and loosing which God has conferred on us (albeit undeserving), grant to all who undertake this task in person and at their own expense, full pardon of their sins that they have truly repented in their hearts and confessed with their lips and we promise them, as the reward of the just, a greater share of eternal salvation. On those who do not go there in person but despatch suitable men at their own expense according to their capacity and rank, and on those, likewise, who go in person though at the expense of another, we bestow full pardon of their sins. It is also our desire and grant that all those should share in this remission – in proportion to their aid and the depth of their devotion – who make suitable provision for the relief of that land from their own resources or offer timely advice or help for this purpose.[32] We further desire that crusaders enjoy that privileged status and that immunity which are incorporated in the General Council. We shall devote to the assistance of that land the greatest care that we can, by way of effort, resources and attention.

Dated Lyons, the 10th Kalends of February, in the second year of our pontificate.

5. Pope Innocent IV to [Eudes,] Bishop of Tusculum,[33] *papal legate, 6 November 1246: J. B. Hauréau, 'Quelques lettres d'Innocent IV extraites des manuscrits de la Bibliothèque Nationale (N° 1194–1203 du fonds Moreau)', in* Notices et extraits des manuscrits de la Bibliothèque Nationale*, vol. 24/2 (Paris, 1876), p. 209; summary in Berger, no. 2228*

Since many vows have been made to set out in aid of the Holy Land, we order Your Fraternity that you straitly command all who have taken the sign of the Cross, whether long ago or recently, to bear the sign of the Cross in public and to set about their preparations in such fashion that they may set out overseas in the forthcoming general passage together with our dearest son in Christ, the illustrious King of France, with the exception of those whom the King shall leave behind for any business of his own; constraining them to do so, if necessary, by ecclesiastical censure, without [right of] appeal.

Dated Lyons, the 8th Ides of November, in the fourth year of our pontificate.

32 Cf. the relevant decree of the Council of Lyons: *Decrees of the Ecumenical Councils*, ed. Tanner, p. 301.

33 Eudes de Châteauroux (d. 1273), Cardinal-Bishop since May 1244. A report from him to the Pope, dated 1249, has survived [**doc. 56** below], and two of his sermons are included later [**docs 77 and 78**].

6. Pope Innocent IV to [Eudes,] Bishop of Tusculum, papal legate, 6 November 1246: Hauréau, 'Quelques lettres d'Innocent IV', pp. 209–10; summary in Berger, no. 2229

Since we are greatly exercised by the business of the Holy Land, we order Your Fraternity [p. 210] to have the Cross preached in England, Germany, Scotland, Denmark and Brabant by men of discretion whom you know to be suitable for this task, and in whose mouth 'the word of the Lord is not bound',[34] conferring on those whom you choose for the purpose, by our authority, the power to grant limited indulgences to the faithful who assemble to hear their preaching,[35] as they see fit. Those who resist, etc.

Dated Lyons, the 8th Ides of November, in the fourth year of our pontificate.

7. Pope Innocent IV to the Bishop of Worcester,[36] *8 February 1247: Berger, no. 2962*

[Authorizes him to appoint special commissioners to protect the privileges of those who have taken the Cross]

8. Pope Innocent IV to [Eudes,] Bishop of Tusculum, papal legate, 29 October 1247: Hauréau, 'Quelques lettres d'Innocent IV', pp. 213–14; summary in Berger, no. 3383

In giving careful consideration to the pious intentions of our dearest son in Christ, the illustrious King of France, regarding the business of the Holy Land, we willingly seek to cultivate that forethought through which, with God's favour, the King's purpose may arrive at the hoped-for conclusion. Hence it is that, looking kindly on his requests, which merit our favour, we order you to have the tenth of all ecclesiastical revenues in the Kingdom of France which accrue to churches and ecclesiastical personnel from whatever source, collected thoroughly for three years (as has been conceded to him) and assigned to him in its entirety, in those regions in which [the tenth] has been granted to the King, before anything is collected for the Church of Rome or the Empire of Constantinople or under any other head whatsoever. You should also see that the twentieth, which has been, and is to be, collected in that part of the diocese of Cambrai lying outside the kingdom, is delivered to the King, or make appropriate compensation to him where it has been collected already and assigned to someone else, notwithstanding any indulgence granted to any persons whatsoever by the Apostolic See, but with the exception of those whom we have

34 Cf. II Timothy, ii, 9.

35 A partial indulgence for those attending crusade sermons first became customary during Innocent IV's pontificate: Purcell, *Papal Crusading Policy*, pp. 62–3. In his letter of February 1250 to the French prelates [**doc. 18** below], the Pope specifies indulgences ranging from 10 to 60 days.

36 Walter de Cantilupe (1236–1266).

specifically exempted from the tenth. Those who resist, [p. 214] by our authority etc.

Dated Lyons, the 4th Kalends of November, in the fifth year of our pontificate.

9. Pope Innocent IV to P[eter], Cardinal-deacon of San Giorgio in Velabro,[37] *papal legate, 29 October 1247: Berger, no. 3384*

It is the fervent desire of our dearest son in Christ, the illustrious King of France, that the business of the Holy Land may, with God's favour, be brought to a successful conclusion. We, therefore, delighting to agree to the requests, which merit our favour, that he has addressed to us for the promotion of that business,[38] by the authority of this letter order you not to allow vows made in the dioceses of Liège, Metz, Verdun, Cambrai and Toul in aid of the aforesaid land to be commuted or the preaching of the Cross in its support in the said dioceses to be hindered by any person. Those who resist etc.

Dated Lyons, the 4th Kalends of November, in the fifth year of our pontificate.

10. Pope Innocent IV to [Eudes], Bishop of Tusculum and papal legate, 9 July 1247; Berger, no. 3065

[Orders him to assign to Robert, Count of Artois, when he sets out, the proceeds of vow redemptions and offerings for the Holy Land, together with the twentieth of ecclesiastical revenues from the kingdom of Navarre, the bishoprics of Metz, Toul and Verdun, and those parts of the diocese of Artois that lie outside the French kingdom]

11. Pope Innocent IV to [Eudes,] Bishop of Tusculum, papal legate, 16 March 1248: Berger, no. 3719

[Orders him to assign to Charles of Anjou one-twentieth of ecclesiastical revenues, together with vow redemptions, legacies and other donations made for the Holy Land crusade, in the county of Provence, excepting the lands of those who take the Cross for the East][39]

37 Pietro Capocci (d. 1259). He had been Cardinal-deacon since May 1244.

38 This is usually taken as evidence that Louis had protested about the effect which the preaching of the anti-Hohenstaufen crusade in the French-Imperial borderlands might have on recruitment for his own expedition: see, for example, Gary Dickson, 'The advent of the *Pastores* (1251)', *Revue Belge de Philologie et d'Histoire*, 66 (1988): 249–67 (here 260), reprinted in his *Religious Enthusiasm in the Medieval West: Revivals, Crusades, Saints* (Aldershot, 2000).

39 See also Berger, no. 3755 (to Philippe, canon of Orléans, 28 March 1248).

12. Pope Innocent IV to the Bishop of Troyes,[40] *27 June 1248: Berger, no. 4038*

[Orders him to collect the proceeds of vow redemptions and donations towards the crusade from Champagne and Brie, the lands of the Viscount of Limoges and those of the Count of Eu, and to assign them to Robert, Count of Artois, unless the Count of Champagne and Brie (that is, the King of Navarre), or the Viscount of Limoges, or the Count of Eu themselves take the Cross][41]

13. Pope Innocent IV to William Longespee, 6 June 1247: Berger, no. 2758

[Grants him up to £1000 sterling from the proceeds of vow redemption in the diocese of Lincoln]

14. Pope Innocent IV to William Longespee, 19 March 1248: Berger, no. 3723

[Grants him up to 2000 marks sterling from the proceeds of vow redemption in England]

15. Pope Innocent IV to the Bishops of Lincoln[42] *and Worcester, 7 June 1247: Berger, no. 2843*

[Orders them to collect sums bequeathed and promised in support of the Holy Land, and from vow redemptions, in the English kingdom and to distribute the proceeds among crusaders in that realm]

16. Pope Innocent IV to the Archbishop of Narbonne,[43] *15 March 1248: Berger, no. 3727*

[Authorizes him to receive the proceeds of vow redemption within his province and to disburse it, on the Pope's advice, to crusaders who are poor or otherwise suitable]

---

40 Nicolas (1233–1269).

41 See also Berger, no. 3754 (to the Bishop of Troyes, 27 March 1248); also ibid., no. 4039, where the Pope makes the same stipulation regarding the lands of the Countess of Nevers. On 4 July 1248 Innocent ordered Nicolas, Minister of the Order of the Holy Trinity, to make over to Count Robert the proceeds of any redemptions dating from after the departure of the legate Eudes on crusade (ibid., no. 4120).

42 Robert Grosseteste (1235–1253).

43 Guillaume de Broue (1245–1257).

17. Pope Innocent IV to the barons, knights and other nobles and all crusaders and the faithful of Christ in the territories overseas, 23 February 1248: Berger, no. 3661

[Informs them that he is sending Eudes with King Louis, as legate with the crusade and in the Christian territories overseas, recommends him to them and urges them to follow his advice and instructions][44]

18. Pope Innocent IV to the Archbishops of Reims, Bourges, Sens, Rouen and Narbonne[45] *and to the Dominican Prior and Franciscan Minister of the province of France, 28 February 1250:* Regestrum Visitationum Archiepiscopi Rothomagensis. Journal des visites pastorales d'Eude Rigaud, archevêque de Rouen. MCCXLVIII–MCCLXIX, *ed. T. Bonnin (Rouen, 1852), appendix, pp. 737–40*

In no small degree has Mother Church until now bemoaned her suffering, namely the wretched state of that most Holy Land, which was at one time promised to the Holy Fathers and which, when the Heavens unbent, the Son of God, having become Man and dwelling there, chose as His own inheritance, to display there the mysteries of human redemption, and consecrated with His precious blood. She grieves still, full of bitterness and weakened by mourning, since the sword kills outside and there is a similar death at home; for on that side her chief enemies who worship alien gods have laid profane hands on the object of her desire, polluting the Lord's sanctuary, which Divine prohibition forbids them even to enter, while from this side Christians rise up against Christ's bride, in the viper-like manner of sons tearing apart the mother at whose breasts they had been weaned.[46] She sheds floods of tears, groaning and weeping repeatedly and between sobs and sighs scarcely draws breath. She cries out to those close at hand, runs to the renowned, and represents to those at home the urgent plea of the Saviour of the Faith, Who unceasingly calls upon each and every one of the faithful to become His knights, and the most pressing needs of the Holy Land. For if it is not (God forbid) delivered from the hands of the pagans by the energy and power of our dearest son in Christ, the illustrious King of France, there can scarcely be any hope of its subsequent recovery.

---

44 For a very similar letter to Eudes himself and to the same addressees, dated 21 July 1248, see Berger, no. 4662; trans. in *The Crusades: Idea and Reality, 1095–1274*, ed. Louise and Jonathan Riley-Smith (London, 1981), pp. 155–6 (no. 38). On 22 June the Pope wrote another letter recommending Eudes to the Patriarch of Jerusalem, the archbishops and bishops, the Masters and brothers of the Orders of the Temple, the Hospital of Jerusalem and the Teutonic Knights, and the prelates of other churches, in the kingdoms of Jerusalem, Armenia and Cyprus (Berger, no. 3965): copies of this were sent to the Kings of France and Armenia, the Prince of Antioch, and the secular magnates of the kingdoms of Jerusalem, Armenia and Cyprus.

45 Reims: Juhel de Saint-Martin (1244–1251). Bourges: Philippe Berruyer (1236–1261). Sens: Gilles Cornut (1244–1254). Rouen: Eudes Rigaud (1247/48–1275). For Narbonne, see note 43.

46 Evidently a reference to the Emperor Frederick II and his supporters.

Consider, therefore, all Catholics, how disgraceful it is that this place, where our salvation first began, should be defiled with filth and for so long violated by the most unclean of peoples. Let each of you reflect how hateful it is to close one's fist to the Giver of all good things and not to aid the Saviour; and then it will become clear that His faithful should be slothful neither in putting an end[47] to these outrages nor in rendering assistance to Him Who gives all things bountifully. Does he not incur the charge of treason who denies assistance to his temporal lord when he is surrounded by enemies, and fails to defend [his lord's] land from foes? And so, since it is worse to commit treason against God than against Man, nobody ought to wait for the blast of the trumpet's summons or for the rousing cry before going to the aid of the Living God and the true Lord, Jesus Christ, but should run at once, not so much in order to escape punishment as to deserve to become joint heir with the Heavenly King. Rise up, then, vigorous warriors of France, divine athletes of the Lord and knights of the Redeemer, and, uniting your power to the full in so holy and praiseworthy a task, like your forebears who proved more eager in times of need, arm yourselves at once with the helmet of the Cross against those who defile the Holy of Holies and [p. 738] introduce into it abominable acts of foulness.

Make haste while you have time and the Lord's hand is against them, lest His anger be turned away from them through the sluggishness of the faithful, since at that point it would not be safe to meet with them or to do battle with such a large host. That you may be swifter in this affair, reflect, we beg, on the noble deeds – unheard-of in our era – of the said King and his brothers, who have abandoned royal resources, the peaks of honour and the heights of rank, or more correctly have converted them to the aid of the King, taking up a cause that was utterly desperate, and are fighting the Lord's fight; and you will clearly see that He Whose cause it is heeds their pious aspirations and aids them miraculously in war, crushing the enemy and smashing them to pieces. Who could ever have believed that Damietta, the head and key of Egypt, a city so heavily fortified and by [man's] device rendered in some fashion impregnable, would be taken by any artifice, when unexpectedly the populace and countless other warriors detailed to garrison it, in whom the Lord struck fear by His power, were put to flight, and He handed it over to the King without a blow [*lancea*] or a fight, with the result that His name is glorified now and for ever. Nobody, indeed, can doubt that this was the doing, not of men but of God. But in order that the aforesaid King should not be seen as the only one to wear the Lord's Cross in those regions, and so that you may be at one with him and his aforesaid brothers, may share in a temporary labour and may not lack an eternal prize: rise up to assist him, manfully and mightily taking up arms and shield with the purpose of avenging the insult to Him Who washed away our shame and made Himself a living sacrifice for our sake on the Cross.

And so that you may set about this with the greater eagerness and courage for having thereby gained greater spiritual gifts (which are to be preferred to temporal ones), we, trusting in the mercy of Almighty God, in the authority of His blessed Apostles Peter and Paul and in the power of binding and loosing which God has

47 Reading *profliganda* (as in the similar letter of 2 April 1253: Berger, no. 6469 [**doc. 107**]) for the *prostiganda* of the text.

conferred upon us (undeserving as we are), shall bestow on all who undertake this task personally and at their own expense the full pardon for their sins and promise them a greater share of eternal life as the reward of the just. And to those who do not go there in person, but who send there suitable men at their own expense in accordance with their capacity and status, and likewise to those who go in person, albeit at someone else's expense, and to those who donate in aid of that land a quarter or more of their produce and income to the King, or to collectors appointed for his needs, we grant full pardon of their sins. We also desire and grant that all those who have made available to the King, or to those who collect for his needs, a tenth or some other fraction of their goods, or who give timely advice or assistance in this regard, and those who on our authority have preached the Cross for this enterprise, should share in this remission in proportion to the amount of assistance and the depth of their devotion …[48]

[p. 739] … Wherefore we order Your Discretion by Apostolic letter that you, [our] brother archbishops, throughout your cities, dioceses and provinces, and you, [our] sons, the Prior and the Minister, throughout the same cities, dioceses and provinces and the entire realm of France, proclaim the crusade, and cause it to be proclaimed by others whom you know to be suitable for the task, compelling them to do so, if necessary, by ecclesiastical censure with no [right of] appeal. And in order that Christ's faithful may hurry to hear the word of the Lord with greater willingness and passion, you are to bestow on all who truly repent and have been confessed, and who attend official preaching in any city, town or village whatsoever, and in any assembly or context whatsoever, by yourself or those to whom you have delegated it, an indulgence of 10, 20, 30, 40 or 60 days, as you and those to whom you have seen fit to entrust the duty of preaching deem advisable …[49]

[p. 740] … Dated Lyons, the 3rd Kalends of March, in the seventh year of our pontificate.

19. Pope Innocent IV to the Archbishops of Reims, Bourges, Sens, Rouen and Narbonne and to the Dominican Prior and Franciscan Minister of the province of France, 4 March 1250: Regestrum Visitationum Archiepiscopi Rothomagensis, *ed. Bonnin, appendix, pp. 740–41*

[Instructs them not to permit preaching for any crusade but that to the Holy Land, until the March passage in the following year, in order that the resources of the French kingdom are not diverted to any other cause, however pious]

---

48 The following section details the crusader's material privileges, including a moratorium on interest payments, the right of crusading clerics to enjoy the income from their benefices, the protection of the Holy See for *crucesignati*, their families and possessions.

49 The remainder of the document is concerned with authority to grant absolutions and dispensations and to collect funds deposited for the crusade, and with other logistical matters.

(b) Recruitment of former rebels and heretics

20. Pope Innocent IV to the Archbishop of Auch,[50] *4 December 1247: Berger, no. 3508*

Since, as we are informed, some from the lands subject to the lordship of our beloved son, the noble [Raymond], Count of Toulouse, in performance of the penalty enjoined upon them for heresy, are for the moment imprisoned, while others are likewise for a time required to wear a cross as a sign of penance, we delegate to Your Fraternity by the terms of this letter that if such people wish to assume the sign of the Cross and set out in person for the relief of the Holy Land, you may commute their penances of the kind specified to one in aid [of the Holy Land].[51]

Dated Lyons, the 2nd Nones of December, in the fifth year of our pontificate.

21. Hugues le Brun, Count of Angoulême, announces that he will travel overseas with Alphonse, Count of Poitou, to relieve the Holy Land, 24 June 1249: Layettes, *vol. 5, pp. 177–8 (no. 529)*

Hugues le Brun, Count of Angoulême,[52] to all who see this letter, greetings. Know that, when consultation took place between ourselves and our most beloved lord Alphonse, Count of Poitou, regarding our journeying overseas with him in the coming passage, an agreement on this matter was finally reached between ourselves and him on the following terms: We promised on oath, with our hand on the holy Gospels, that we shall cross overseas with him in that passage together with eleven knights; and once we are overseas, we shall be bound to serve him, or a person he appoints in his stead, for one year with the aforesaid number of knights. If we shall happen to die (God forbid), we shall substitute another in our place who shall serve the Count of Poitou, or a person he appoints or assigns in his stead, with the said number of knights, as specified above. When the said terms have been faithfully observed and fulfilled by us, as we have promised and are bound, the said Count is bound to give to us and the heirs of our body, born and [yet] to be born of lawful matrimony, 600 *livres* of Poitou a year, in his own coffers, in two instalments, namely one half at Christmas and the other half at the following feast of the Blessed John [p. 178] the Baptist following, to be paid at Niort, Poitiers or La Rochelle, wherever it best pleases him. In return for these payments, we are bound to do liege homage to him or to his heirs or successors. The Count of Poitou is further bound to pay us wages,

---

50 Hispan de Massas (1245–1261).

51 On 30 April 1248 Innocent ordered the Bishop of Agen to fulfil the instructions previously issued to the Archbishop, who had been unable to implement them (Berger, no. 3866). For other instances involving former heretics, see the Pope's letter of 2 March 1248 to the Bishop of Albi (ibid., no. 3677); also Smith, *Crusading in the Age of Joinville*, pp. 121, 157–8.

52 This is not Hugues X de Lusignan (d. 1249: see below, p. 89), but his son and heir, Hugues XI, who died in Egypt in April 1250. Joinville, § 109, p. 62 (trans. Hague, p. 51; trans. Shaw, p. 191), refers to their embarkation, though his phrasing suggests that they embarked around the same time as the King and most of the other leaders (that is, August 1248).

namely: 40 *sous* for our [service in] person, and compensation for our mounts on the basis that is paid to a noble of this status by our dearest lord, the King of France, and his brothers overseas; to pay wages to the rest of our knights and compensation for their mounts on the same basis as others pay other knights overseas; and our passage for ourselves and our knights on a reasonable basis. We and our knights must also eat daily, if we choose to do so, in his quarters. He further promised to lend us 4000 *livres tournois*, to be repaid by us to him or his representative or his heirs or successors in four instalments, namely in four successive years from the feast of the Blessed John the Baptist celebrated in the year of the Lord 1249, on condition, however, that he receives, in payment in the aforesaid four years, the 600 *livres* of yearly income that he has given us; and in respect of the balance of the loan we are bound to repay to the Count, or to his representative, in each of the said four years 400 *livres*. And for the repayment of the money in the aforesaid instalments, namely in respect of the abovementioned balance, we are liable to the Count of Poitou and his heirs or successors for all our land, wherever it lies; willingly conceding that if we default on the payment of the money, as specified, he and his heirs or successors may keep the said 600 *livres* and may seize our land and hold it, without [incurring the charge of] misappropriation and without detriment to anyone, until he receives full satisfaction for the said sum. If, in fulfilment of the said terms, we default in paying the money, we shall have no respite from him, but shall be bound immediately to make payment to him and his heirs or successors. Should we happen to die while travelling to the port or while halting there, or not to sail through some fault of the lord Count of Poitou, the legitimate expenses that we have incurred, on our own and our knights' behalf, in travelling to the port will be deducted from the loan he has made us, and our heirs shall be bound to repay the balance of the loan to the Count and his heirs or successors at the aforesaid dates, as is specified above. If it transpires that we do not sail, or if we sail and it transpires that we return in person before the term is reached without completing our year's service, or if it transpires that we have already died at sea or overseas and our knights do not serve in our name for the whole term of one year, the Count is not bound to us in any of the aforesaid respects. But if we happened to die at sea, having set out to travel overseas in good faith, or even to die naturally overseas, provided that our knights complete the aforesaid service, the Count of Poitou would be bound to pay our heirs the 600 *livres*' income at the said dates. If we die, having set out to travel overseas by the said date in good faith, the Count shall receive our heirs, whatever age they shall have reached, into the same state of homage that we were in towards him prior to the aforesaid agreement, according to the usages and customs of [our] homeland, and also in respect of the said 600 *livres*, once the said terms are fulfilled as is specified above, saving his rights and those of anybody else. When all these conditions have been fully observed and fulfilled by ourselves, the Count shall have his letters patent, drawn up in respect of the aforesaid income and deposited at the Temple in Paris, delivered to us or to our heirs. In witness whereof we have had this document sealed with our seal.

Done at Paris, on the feast of St. John the Baptist, in the year of the Lord 1249.

(c) The search for allies

22. Pope Innocent IV to Haakon IV, King of Norway, 6 November 1246: Diplomatarium Norvegicum, *ed. C. C. A. Lange and Carl R. Unger, vol. 1 (Christiania, 1849), p. 27 (no. 33); summary in Berger, no. 2218*

[Having learned that the King has taken the Cross for the Holy Land, the Pope takes him, his wife and his sons under his protection and that of St Peter]

23. Pope Innocent IV to Haakon IV, King of Norway, 19 November 1247: Diplomatarium Norvegicum, *ed. Lange and Unger, vol. 1, p. 31 (no. 40); summary in Berger, no. 3439*

[At Haakon's request, the Pope grants him the twentieth of all ecclesiastical revenues in his kingdom, except the bishopric of Hamar[53]]

24. Pope Innocent IV to Henry III, King of England, 30 August 1247: Berger, no. 4054

Having frequently experienced the purity of devotion and faith that you have towards the Roman Church your mother, we intend to consent to [those of] your wishes and requests with which we can, with God and without scandal, comply, and we hope to demonstrate good will. We were recently asked on your behalf that, since you, in your desire to give the Holy Land appropriate assistance, intend to set the general passage of crusaders from your realm one year after the passage of the French crusaders and [to put] our beloved son, your brother the noble Gui de Lusignan – the son of the noble [Hugues] Count of La Marche, the vassal of our dearest son in Christ [Louis], the illustrious King of France – in command of these crusaders from England, we might take care, in the kindness of the Holy See, to grant that Gui, notwithstanding the sworn obligation he is under to sail in the aforementioned passage of the French, might be enabled to postpone the fulfilment of his vow until the passage of the English. Nevertheless, however much love we bear your person deep within, it was not fitting to agree to your request without the consent of the aforesaid King, to whom the nobleman in question made this oath. But in our desire to attend to your will and pleasure with fatherly affection, we have seen fit, by letter, to ask the King more keenly and to recommend that, carefully bearing in mind that your design can bring him a fairly considerable advantage, he generously gives his consent to this request and sends back to us his approval in writing.[54] We are also writing to our dearest daughter in Christ, B[lanche], the illustrious Queen of the French, the King's mother, asking her more pressingly and urging her to advise and persuade the King

53 Bishop Paul, who had himself taken the Cross, was granted the twentieth within his own diocese: *Diplomatarium Norvegicum*, ed. Lange and Unger, vol. 1, pp. 31–2 (no. 41): summary in Berger, no. 3440.

54 For the Pope's letter to King Louis, dated 8 August 1247, see Berger, no. 4056.

to [agree to] it,[55] and will make still more assiduous requests to them on this matter should it prove necessary and should you wish it.

You asked in addition that we should grant you, as a special favour, the legacies for the Holy Land and the redemptions of the vows of crusaders from your realm, so that you might fulfil your desire more splendidly and more honourably regarding the aforementioned assistance. On this head we are giving Your Serenity such reply as we saw fit to give, some time ago, at the instigation of your envoys and those of the prelates of the whole English church, our venerable brothers, Bishops [Robert] of Lincoln and [Walter] of Worcester – that when collecting legacies and redemptions of this kind they should use their discretion in making provision from them to needy crusaders and inhabitants of your realm at the time of the general passage; and we shall be unable to revoke this by giving contrary instructions, in view of the scandal. Since, however, we wish to defer to you, as a most dear son of the Church, we are ordering the aforesaid bishops by letter that they pay appropriate attention to the purpose and the zeal of the royal sublimity and, as regards the aforesaid redemptions and legacies, should attempt to contrive something that Your Excellency can justifiably accept, though in such fashion that the inhabitants of the realm of England are not cheated of the expectations raised by our first letter.[56]

Dated Lyons, the 3rd Kalends of September, in the fifth year of our pontificate.

25. Georgios Akropolita, Khronike syngraphe*, ed. Immanuel Bekker,* Georgii Acropolitae Annales *(Bonn, 1836), p. 94 (chapter 48)*

As Prince Villehardouin of Achaea and the Peloponnese was setting out for Syria, bringing reinforcements to the Franks who were on their way to Syria, and had cavalry forces in his triremes, he put in at the island of Rhodes and made an agreement with the Genoese there. He left with them more than a hundred fine knights of high birth; this would force the Byzantines[57] to abandon the siege of the city …

55 For this letter, of 8 August 1247, see Berger, no. 4057.

56 For this letter, of 30 August 1247, see Berger, no. 4055.

57 *Rhomaioi.*

III

The Attitude of the Emperor Frederick II

From the Empire, Louis received little or no military assistance. As far as Germany is concerned, one important reason for this was the fact that the kingdom was in the throes of civil war between the supporters of the Emperor Frederick II and those of Pope Innocent IV and the anti-kings whom he supported. The Pope had solemnly excommunicated and deposed Frederick at the Council of Lyons in 1245, and a crusade had been launched against him (see the following section). Nevertheless, Frederick was still at large in his kingdom of Sicily, and his assistance with Louis's expedition would have been invaluable. Sicily traditionally occupied an important place in the provisioning of crusading armies which travelled by sea,[1] and in 1239 the Emperor had invited the 'Crusade of the Barons' to use its ports en route for the East, although the majority of the leaders neglected to take advantage of this offer.[2]

The Emperor's own attitude towards the Seventh Crusade is opaque.[3] As early as 1246, he ordered his representatives in the Regno to furnish Louis's forces with provisions, horses, arms and other necessities [**docs 26 and 27**], an action for which the French King wrote to thank him – despite the fact that he was an excommunicate – in the following year [**doc. 28**]. Subsequently Frederick ordered the Count of Caserta to make arrangements for Louis's honourable reception [**doc. 29**]; and in 1249, on hearing rumours of the dispersal of the crusading fleet in a storm, he wrote to Louis to express his dismay and sympathy [**doc. 30**]. Later that year he notified the King that he had made a present of victuals and 50 warhorses to Alphonse [**doc. 31**]. This may be the occasion mentioned by Matthew Paris, who speaks of Frederick both encouraging the despatch of provisions to the crusaders on Cyprus and sending abundant supplies himself.[4] The statement in a hostile Frisian source, that as a result of Frederick's intervention Louis was able to muster only half the necessary

---

1 See Norman Housley, *The Italian Crusades: The Papal-Angevin Alliance and the Crusades against Christian Lay Powers, 1254–1343* (Oxford, 1982), pp. 66–8. For earlier Sicilian participation, see Helene Wieruszowski, 'The Norman kingdom of Sicily and the crusades', in R. L. Wolff and H. W. Hazard (eds), *The Later Crusades, 1189–1311*, A History of the Crusades (general ed. K. M. Setton), vol. 2, 2nd edn (Madison, WI, 1969), pp. 3–42, reprinted in Wieruszowski, *Politics and Culture in Medieval Spain and Italy*, Storia e Letteratura. Raccolta di studi e testi, vol. 121 (Rome, 1971), pp. 3-49, and James M. Powell, 'Crusading by royal command: monarchy and crusade in the kingdom of Sicily', in *Potere, società e popolo tra età normanna ed età sveva, 1189–1210. Atti delle quinte giornate normanno-sveve, Bari-Conversano, 26–28 ottobre 1981* (Bari, 1983), pp. 131–46.

2 Lower, *The Barons' Crusade*, p. 162.

3 For the fullest treatment, see Berger, *Saint Louis*, pp. ccxxiii–ccxxvi, ccxlvii–ccxlix.

4 Matthew Paris, *Chronica Majora*, vol. 5, p. 70 (trans. Giles, vol. 2, pp. 306-7; trans. Vaughan, p. 180).

fleet [**doc. 55** below], can doubtless be discounted. The most we can say is that misapprehensions may have arisen because Frederick was at odds with the Genoese, who were supplying Louis with many of his galleys and transports. He seems to have feared that Genoa would seize the opportunity to attack Sicily, and the operations he threatened against the city in 1248 were certainly portrayed there as an attempt to obstruct the French King's expedition [**doc. 34**].

Frederick was not only king of Germany and Sicily, but also claimed to be king of Jerusalem, a position he had inherited through his second wife, though since her death in 1228 he had technically been merely regent for his young son Conrad. In 1242, however, an opposition party within the kingdom of Jerusalem had declared that because Conrad had come of age, Frederick was no longer regent and they had appointed as regent Conrad's closest relative (and heiress), Alice, dowager Queen of Cyprus, expelling the Emperor's officials from Palestine.[5] Frederick's other preoccupation, therefore, was undoubtedly the future of his – or Conrad's – rule in Palestine. He had evidently raised the prospect that his enemies in the East might profit from the crusade in a letter (now lost) to the French King, who was at pains to reassure him [**docs 27 and 28**]. Louis would do nothing prejudicial to Frederick's or his son's interests (or for that matter, those of any other Christian); and he would do his best to prevent any of the provisions or arms he purchased from finding their way into the hands of the Emperor's enemies. Frederick wrote to Louis again on at least two occasions following the disaster in Egypt and the King's arrival at Acre, when his aim was to secure the installation of his own lieutenants and serjeants in Acre and other Palestinian towns.[6] One of these embassies is possibly described by Joinville, who dates its arrival soon after the departure of Louis's brothers for the West, perhaps in the early autumn of 1250. The envoys, who had first travelled to Egypt, assured the French King that their mission had been to treat with the Sultan (of whose murder Frederick had been unaware) for the release of Louis and his staff; but it was widely rumoured that the Emperor had intended to delay their release.[7] This seems improbable, and in all likelihood the interpretation placed on Frederick's action represents nothing more than scurrilous anti-Hohenstaufen gossip.

In all this, it is difficult to know what to make of the allegation in two Arabic sources that the Emperor tried to persuade Louis to abandon his expedition and then wrote to the Egyptian Sultan al-Ṣāliḥ Ayyūb to warn him of the impending attack. The more detailed account, which includes an apocryphal meeting between Frederick and Louis, is found in the relatively late work of Qaraṭāy [**doc. 32**], a source of dubious reliability.[8] Yet the authenticity of an imperial embassy sent to warn Ayyūb receives support from a much more trustworthy author, Ibn Wāṣil [**doc. 33**]. Ibn Wāṣil cites

5 Peter Jackson, 'The end of Hohenstaufen rule in Syria', *BIHR*, 59 (1986): 20–36. David Jacoby, 'The kingdom of Jerusalem and the collapse of Hohenstaufen power in the Levant', *Dumbarton Oaks Papers*, 40 (1986): 83–101.

6 'Rothelin', p. 624 (trans. Shirley, *Crusader Syria*, p. 109).

7 Joinville, § 443, p. 242 (trans. Hague, p. 136; trans. Shaw, p. 274).

8 See Robert Irwin, 'The image of the Byzantine and the Frank in Arab popular literature of the late Middle Ages', in Benjamin Arbel, Bernard Hamilton and David Jacoby (ed.), *Latins and Greeks in the Eastern Mediterranean after 1204* (London, 1989 = *MHR*, 4/1), pp. 226–42 (here p. 237; on Qaraṭāy more generally, pp. 236–40).

as his informant a Western knight who had acted as the Emperor's envoy in 1248 and whom he himself met, presumably, when he accompanied an embassy from Cairo in 1261 to the court of Frederick's son Manfred in Sicily.[9] This does not, of course, tell us what was the Emperor's true purpose in contacting the Sultan. The sparse information supplied by these Arabic sources hardly indicates that al-Ṣāliḥ Ayyūb was told anything he might not have learned from his own spies. Frederick had been corresponding with the Egyptian court since his return from his own crusade in 1229.[10] His concern now may simply to have been the preservation of good relations with Cairo, without necessarily undermining the crusade. In general, we are justified, perhaps, in seeing the crusade as a potential embarrassment to Frederick, who may have tried, without any great hope, to dissociate himself from it while deriving some benefit from it for his kingdom of Sicily.

DOCUMENTS 26–34

(a) Correspondence of the Emperor

26. Frederick II to his officials in Sicily, November 1246: Huillard-Bréholles, vol. 6/1, pp. 465–6[11]

Frederick, by God's grace ever august Emperor of the Romans, King of Jerusalem and Sicily, to his justiciars, master chamberlains, master procurators, master *fundicarii*[12] and all his vassals in the kingdom of Sicily: favour and good wishes. Since our beloved friend L[ouis], illustrious King of the French, whom we embrace with totally sincere love, has – to the honour of Him Who grants kings salvation – assumed the sign of the wondrous Cross in aid of the Holy Land and has made the praiseworthy decision to sail overseas on the forthcoming feast of Saint John in the Sixth Indiction [24 June 1247], we, in our desire that the (we trust) successful voyage of him and his men be sustained by the productivity of our kingdom, give Your Fidelity the following orders, inasmuch as we might seem to be acting thereby virtually in our own interests and those of our dearest son Conrad, King-elect of the

9 For the 1261 embassy, see Ibn Wāṣil, *Mufarrij al-kurūb*, partial edn by Jamāl al-Dīn al-Shayyāl et al. (Cairo, 1953–77), vol. 3, p. 248. Ibn Wāṣil's testimony is briefly discussed in Edgar Blochet, 'Les relations diplomatiques des Hohenstaufen avec les sultans d'Égypte', *Revue Historique*, 80 (1902): 51–64 (here 62–3); and see further Reuven Amitai-Preiss, 'Mamluk perceptions of the Mongol-Frankish rapprochement', *MHR*, 7 (1992): 50–65 (here 53).

10 Nevill Barbour, 'The Emperor Frederick II, King of Jerusalem and Sicily, and his relations with the Muslims', in J. M. Barral (ed.), *Orientalia Hispanica sive Studia F.M. Pareja Octogenario Dicata* (Leiden, 1974), vol. 1, pp. 77–95 (here pp. 89–90). For a new interpretation of Frederick's stance *vis-à-vis* the Muslim powers, see James M. Powell, 'Frederick II and the Muslims: the making of an historiographical tradition', in Larry J. Simon (ed.), *Iberia and the Mediterranean World of the Middle Ages: Studies in Honor of Robert I. Burns, S.J.* (Leiden, 1995–96), vol. 1, pp. 261–9.

11 Also edited in *Layettes*, vol. 2, pp. 641–2 (no. 3562).

12 Probably officials in charge of the markets (*fondachi*).

Romans and heir of the kingdom of Jerusalem. You are to permit horses, weapons, provisions and any [other] necessities, both for the said King and for those of his household and retinue, to be purchased throughout our realm without restriction at the common price for which they may generally be sold in the realm at the time of purchase and, from the Kalends of March next in the Sixth Indiction [1 March 1247] onwards for the whole duration of the said King's stay overseas in Christ's service, to be freely purchased and exported from the realm and to be conveyed there by land or by water for this same business, without any let or hindrance whatsoever.
[p. 466] Dated Lucera, in the month of November in the year 1246 of the Incarnation of the Lord, in the Fifth Indiction.

27. Frederick II to all who see the letter, November 1246: Huillard-Bréholles, vol. 6/1, pp. 466–7[13]

Frederick, by God's grace ever august Emperor of the Romans and King of Sicily and Jerusalem. We wish it hereby to be known to all that we have granted licence and safe-conduct to all merchants, whether from our Empire and kingdom or from the kingdom of France and any other regions whatever, who wish to sail to the Holy Land with our beloved friend Louis, the illustrious King of the French, so that throughout our Empire and kingdom they may be able to buy wheat and any [other] necessities on behalf of either the aforementioned King or the barons, knights, nobles and other crusaders who are about to set out with the King in aid of the Holy Land, commencing from the forthcoming Kalends of March in the Sixth Indiction and lasting for the entire duration of the King's stay overseas in Christ's service; and to export it and convey it to the crusaders for their troops, without any obstacle, once we, if we are in the kingdom, or, in our absence, whoever is acting there as our deputy, are fully aware through a letter of the said King that he is in port and about to cross to the aforesaid regions in Christ's service; appropriate guarantees having been obtained from the aforesaid merchants, and undertakings given either to us or to the abovementioned person who acts as our deputy, by special royal letters, that they will not dare to convey goods they have purchased from our kingdom and Empire to anyone other [p. 467] than crusaders and for their troops, and especially that they will not turn them over to the use and advantage of the people of Acre or of anyone else whatsoever who is under the ban of, or disloyal to, or at enmity with, ourselves and the Empire. Wherefore we order, by the authority of this letter, that no man may make so bold as to dare to obstruct or harass these merchants with the foodstuffs and other goods which they carry with them to the said [crusaders].

Dated Lucera, in the month of November in the year 1246 of the Lord's Incarnation, in the Fifth Indiction.

13 Also edited in *Layettes*, II, p. 642 (no. 3563).

28. Louis IX to Frederick II [February or March 1247]: Huillard-Bréholles, vol. 6/1, pp. 501–2

To his most excellent and dearest friend Frederick, by God's grace illustrious and ever august Emperor of the Romans, King of Jerusalem and Sicily, Louis, by the same grace King of the French: greetings and sentiments of sincere affection. We have received with fitting gladness and joy your ambassador, the knight Hugh de Albamara, bearer of this letter, along with the letter which Your Benevolence despatched to us by his hand. We have learned both through the reliable reports of our own envoys and through your letter patent which Hugh presented to us, as well as by his own statements to us, that you have been so gracious as to give a friendly hearing to the requests we made to Your Serenity through the said envoys, and particularly for the export of provisions and other things necessary from the territories of the Empire and your realms for our passage in aid of the Holy Land. And so we give you thanks, and in friendship agree to the request of this your ambassador, that if by chance (which God forbid!) we and our dearest brother Robert, Count of Artois, are prevented by some mishap from crossing to the aid of the Holy Land, as is our fixed purpose with the sure and unchanging aid of God, the letter addressed to us with your aforesaid concession will be null and void. But as to what your said ambassador added, namely that whatever lands are acquired through the *crucesignati* who are about to cross to the Holy Land by the next passage should become the rightful property of the kingdom of Jerusalem, we hereby inform Your Highness that, since we have entered upon the said business only for the honour of the Divine Majesty and the exaltation of the Christian faith, we intend to do nothing in pursuit of that business, with God's favour, that could prejudice any Christian or infringe his rights – let alone you or our beloved friend, your son C[onrad], illustrious King-elect of the Romans and heir to the kingdom of Jerusalem. As to your ambassador's request also that [p. 502] neither should provisions be taken from your territories to your enemies to be employed in their interests, nor should your enemies or rebels against you be allowed to attempt anything to the disadvantage of you or your people, by enjoying free access and egress in the guise of traders on the pretext of seeking provisions in your lands under cover of the generous grant made to us: we wish Your Serenity to know that this will not happen through our desire, and that we shall also willingly take care that it does not occur through our vassals and subjects. But since it is neither appropriate nor possible for us adequately to give a more certain undertaking regarding these matters, which are contingent on the actions of others, Your Serenity could, if it seems advisable, require a sworn guarantee in this regard from those traders who will have access to your territories for the export of provisions according to the terms of your grant. As to what your ambassador added regarding the renewal of the treaty we made some while ago, moreover, we have given him a private response which he can reliably convey to Your Serenity by word of mouth.

Dated etc.

29. Frederick II to the Count of Caserta, [May or June] 1248: Huillard-Bréholles, vol. 6/2, pp. 626–7

[Appoints him as his special Vicar in the Sicilian kingdom, ordering him to betake himself there immediately with the purpose of suitably receiving King Louis, who wishes to pass through Sicily or to winter there]

30. Frederick II to Louis IX [July 1249]: Huillard-Bréholles, vol. 6/2, pp. 745–6

Frederick etc. to L[ouis], illustrious King of the French etc. The common affection in which a shared faith envelops us with all Christians, and the sincere affection in which we hold your person in particular, give rise to an especial anxiety of the heart, amid the many different and heavy kinds of care that unceasingly crowd our thoughts. We aspire to hear at once accurate but welcome news of you, and to learn in full the outcome of your pilgrimage to aid the Holy Land, as one who, from devotion to the enterprise, has ever (as the Supreme Judge is witness) longed that it should thrive and, from personal affection, that it ever be as successful as you desire. Regarding the onset of the enterprise, tested in such a mighty tempest of time and circumstance, the matter indeed full of rising fear, the love for you and your forefathers which we are agreeably mindful we have held undiminished, frequently renders us apprehensive and has many times made us fear that through hostile fortune the outcome might be at variance with the general desire. For amid these anxieties and cares, with which fear for the future weighed down our feelings, there came the chatter of fickle rumour spread abroad in various versions and belching forth reports (we trust) devoid of truth: it claimed that the royal fleet, assembled some time ago by the holy purpose of the faithful not without great outlay of effort and funds, had been scattered by clashing winds in a heaving tempest at sea, over which there is no authority but the power of God.[14] This has [p. 746] afforded us reason for all the greater dismay, in that we cherish your person with a more sincere love than all the kings and princes of the world and that, since the plans of many of Christ's faithful and our own are thereby held in abeyance, we grieve wholeheartedly, too, at the ruin of the Holy Land, which was awaiting such imminent relief from French power. Yet though perplexed by these diverse reports, we have been unwilling to put simple trust in garrulous rumour until the true facts which may calm these storms of fear are clearer to us. Wherefore we have seen fit to despatch specially to your presence …,[15] the bearer of this letter, that he may come back to report to us well-

14 Louis's fleet encountered a storm on its way from Cyprus to Damietta in May 1249, and his ships were scattered, some as far as the coast of Palestine: see Joinville, § 147, p. 82 (trans. Hague, pp. 60–61; trans. Shaw, p. 201), and the letters of Jean Sarrasin (in 'Rothelin', p. 571; trans. Shirley, p. 69) and Jean de Beaumont [**doc. 58**]. See also Joinville, § 182, p. 100 (trans. Hague, p. 69; trans. Shaw, p. 210), for a storm off Damietta in October 1249, which sank 140 vessels, just prior to Alphonse's arrival; according to 'Estoire de Eracles', p. 437 (trans. in Shirley, *Crusader Syria*, p. 137), and 'Annales de Terre Sainte', p. 442 (version 'A'), 32 ships were sunk at Damietta; 'Estoire de Eracles' adds 'and 10 other vessels'. This tempest is also mentioned in 'Rothelin', p. 596 (trans. Shirley, p. 90).

15 The name is omitted.

informed of your (we trust, successful) operations. We should wish, nevertheless, if the turbulence in Italy subsided, to be near you geographically so that, whatever the state of affairs, the right hand of Our Magnificence might despatch aid to you not merely in writing but in other ways. But what the extent of our business and the current situation will permit, we offer to you no less willingly than we [should] put it at the disposal of ourselves or of the dearest to us among our sons. And so we earnestly ask Your Benevolence that you refresh Our Serenity's inner agitation with news of your condition and location and the fate of your fleet.

31. Frederick II to Louis IX [July 1249]: Huillard-Bréholles, vol. 6/2, pp. 748–50

Frederick etc. to the King of the French etc. Hitherto, to speak literally, we have ever been firm in our constant purpose as to how we might honour you and your people with clear signs of proof of the sincere affection in which we hold you. We have persisted all the more strongly – nay, indeed, have been encouraged the more stoutly – in the fulfilment of this purpose, in that we have seen you both willingly and manfully take up the business of the Cross in the service of the Holy Land (for the speedy aid of which we are activated by a special concern above the rest of the princes [p. 749] of the earth). Our Puissance would wish to arise in person and in force along with you at this moment (as the Supreme Judge is witness), so that we might be able to rejoice because supported by the association of such great princes in so welcome a league, where our own interests are especially at stake – if the long-conceived or, rather, outdated malice of our Pope did not obstruct and resist our desires both in this and in other respects, as is already public knowledge. We should wish, nevertheless, as long as we are unable to extend our personal assistance to you and your people, to make splendid provision by way of other aid and the wealth of our realm, were we not prevented by the dearth of supplies that has obtained in our realm for the past two years and has curtailed our ability to fulfil our wishes, which we offer ready and prepared in this matter. Although, therefore, for the reasons we have given, Our Serenity's goodwill has proved unable to make the friendly provision to you and your people that it wished, we are, however, no less moved by love of you and won over by so wholesome an opportunity; and we have preferred that we ourselves and our faithful royal subjects should be in want by foregoing provisions than that you, your vassals and the other nobles of your kingdom who have passed through our realm should, in the fulfilment of so useful and holy a purpose, lack things of which our generosity might supply your need and theirs. For recently, to demonstrate a sign of the pure love that we have always felt – and still hold undiminished – towards you and yours, we have courteously had 1000 *saumas* of provisions and 50 warhorses[16] freely made over to Jean de Treux [?],[17] the envoy of your dearest brother A[lphonse], Count of Poitou, to be presented

16 Old French *destrier*.

17 Possibly identical with a Syrian Frankish knight of this name found making a grant at Acre to the Hospitallers in April 1245.

to the said Count on Our Highness's behalf for his voyage;[18] and Our Majesty has even so granted him licence that he may purchase freely in [p. 750] our realm things necessary for the Count's use which he may deem appropriate for his purposes and those of his household.

(b) Other evidence

32. Qaraṭāy al-'Izzī al-Khazāndārī, Ta'rīkh majmū' al-nawādir *(c. 1330), Forschungs- und Landesbibliothek Gotha, ms. Orient. A 1655, fols 39–40*[19]

When the Emperor, the leader of the Franks, had left the Holy Land and bade farewell to al-Malik al-Kāmil at Ascalon, the two sovereigns had embraced and promised mutual friendship, assistance and fraternity. Now the only route by which the Frenchman could reach Egypt lay across the Emperor's territory. The latter first went to him and offered him help in terms of horsemen, money and livestock. But subsequently the two sovereigns had an interview,[20] in which the Emperor said to the Frenchman: 'Where do you intend going?' 'To Egypt and to Jerusalem', [was the reply]. To which the Emperor responded, among other things: 'That will do you no good. Do not go to Egypt, but reconsider, along with your barons … I was there in the year [626/1229], in the reign of al-Kāmil. I took from the Muslims Jerusalem and all the villages between it and Acre, and stipulated with al-Kāmil that these localities should belong to the Franks, and that there should no longer be a Muslim force at Jerusalem.[21] If I limited myself to that much, it is because I had realized the impossibility of fighting the princes, the amirs and all the troops in the country, and my powerlessness before them. And so how do you hope to take Damietta, Jerusalem and Egypt?' But on hearing this the Frenchman was scandalized and told the Emperor: 'Say no more. Nothing, by God and by the truth of my Faith – nothing shall prevent me from attacking Damietta, Jerusalem and Egypt, and nothing shall deflect me from it except my death and that of my people.'

So then, irritated by his obstinacy, the Emperor wrote to King al-Ṣāliḥ[22] a letter in which he said, among other things: 'In such-and-such a year the King of the French has arrived in my country accompanied by a vast host.' And further on: 'My lord Najm al-Dīn,[23] take good care. You must know that your attackers' intention is to take Jerusalem, and for that purpose to conquer Egypt first.' And again: 'The King of the French is convinced he will conquer Egypt in a few hours'; and 'this prince is the most powerful of the princes of the West – animated by a jealous faith, the

18 Alphonse embarked at Aigues Mortes on 25 August 1249, and arrived at Damietta on 24 October.

19 There is a French translation of this passage in Claude Cahen, 'Saint Louis et l'Islam', *Journal Asiatique*, 257 (1970): 9–10, reprinted in his *Turcobyzantina et Oriens Christianus* (London, 1974).

20 To the best of our knowledge, Louis and Frederick never met in person.

21 A somewhat oversimplified reference to the Treaty of Jaffa (February 1229).

22 That is, al-Kāmil's son, Sultan al-Ṣāliḥ Ayyūb (1240–1249).

23 This was Ayyūb's *laqab* or honorific ('Pillar of the Faith').

importance of his actions as a Christian and his attachment to his religion set him against everyone else.' And he ended: 'My nephew, in vain have I opposed his plans and sought to put him on his guard against the danger he runs in attacking you. To shake him I have insisted on the numbers and strength of the Muslims and on the impossibility of taking Jerusalem if one has not first reduced Egypt, which is [in any case] unfeasible. The Frenchman has not fallen in with my views. The number of those who follow him is constantly on the increase: they total more than 60,000, and in the course of this year they will land in Cyprus.'

33. Ibn Wāṣil, Mufarrij al-kurūb fī akhbār banī Ayyūb *(1263), ed. Jamāl al-Dīn Shayyāl, Hasanein Rabie and Sa'īd al-Fatḥ 'Āshūr (Cairo, 1953–77), vol. 3, pp. 247–8*

When the King of France,[24] one of the greatest Frankish kings, attacked Egypt in the year 647 [1249–50], the Emperor sent word to him in order to restrain him from doing so, to fill him with fear and to warn him what would come of it; but he did not accept [his advice]. Sir ***,[25] who was master of ceremonies[26] to the Emperor's son Manfred, told me: 'The Emperor sent me in secret to al-Malik al-Ṣāliḥ Najm al-Dīn to inform him of the King of France's determination to invade Egypt, to put him on his guard and to advise him to make preparations against it. al-Malik al-Ṣāliḥ made ready, and I returned to the Emperor. I had gone out to Egypt, and come back, in the guise of a merchant, and not one person learned that I had met with al-Malik al-Ṣāliḥ to alert him to the danger from the Franks or that the Emperor had made common cause with the Muslims against them.'

[p. 248] When al-Malik al-Ṣāliḥ died and there befell the King of France what transpired – the destruction and annihilation of his army, his being taken prisoner by al-Malik al-Ṣāliḥ's son, al-Malik al-Muʿaẓẓam Tūrān Shāh, then his release from captivity following al-Malik al-Muʿaẓẓam's murder, and his return to his own country – the Emperor sent to remind him of his [own] sound advice and the consequences of his obstinacy and recalcitrance, and to upbraid him for it.

34. Annales Ianuenses, *ed. Luigi Tommaso Belgrano and Cesare Imperiale de Sant'Angelo,* Annali Genovesi di Caffaro e de' suoi continuatori dal MXCIX al MCCXCIII *(Genova and Rome, 1890–1929), vol. 3, pp. 178–9*

[p. 178] That year [1248], while the Podestà was intent on the despatch of the ships which were being made in San Pier d'Arena for the passage of the lord Louis, illustrious King of France, the lord Frederick, the said Emperor, who was besieging the city of Parma, was very apprehensive concerning this passage, particularly on

---

24 *raydāfrans*.

25 The name, which is given as the three consonants *NRD* in the Arabic script, is indecipherable. Gabrieli, *Arab Historians of the Crusades*, p. 276, n. 3, hazarded a guess at 'Berto'; but perhaps 'Bernard' is more probable.

26 *mihmāndār*. At the courts of Muslim rulers, this official was responsible for seeing to the reception of foreign ambassadors and visitors.

account of the great fleet of Genoese ships and galleys and the warriors who were to travel in them, for fear lest they might land on the island of Sicily and completely reduce it. He sent word to his subjects and supporters everywhere to make ready their forces against the Genoese by land and sea; and he promised to come in person. Thus 25 armed galleys arrived at Savona from the Regno. Oberto Pallavicini, with the Pisans and many others from Tuscany, Lunigiana and Graffignana, fitted out an army against the commune of Genoa. The Genoese Mascarati, who were in exile, planned to raise an army among the Lombards against the commune of Genoa; and Jacopo, marquis of Carretto, who claimed to be the vicar of the lord Frederick from above Asti, likewise prepared his forces to the best of his ability. [p. 179]

At this the lord Podestà, having summoned a general council in Genoa, stood up and gave a wonderful address to everyone in order to hearten their resolve, so that everybody might be intent on protecting their liberty and their homeland, since all this was being done in order to hinder the lord King's passage. For the wise Genoese, with one accord, were shouting lion-heartedly throughout the city that everybody should be ready to arm and that the ships and galleys that were being made should be greatly increased for the lord King's passage. By the decision of the council two ambassadors were sent to Piacenza, namely the lords Amigo Streiaporco and Giovanni di Turca, to hire 400 knights to serve the commune of Genoa as mercenaries. Within the city of Genoa 300 horses were impounded, and [a further] 100 horses in the Oltregiogo; and to every castle and locality of the Riviera, both east and west and to the Oltregiogo, there were despatched a fine guard of serjeants, crossbowmen and provisions. Straight away 32 galleys were armed, that is to say four in each *compagna*. And word was sent from the commune of Genoa to the lord King of France regarding what the lord Frederick was doing in order to hinder his passage, but that he should in no way be apprehensive, since he would have the ships and galleys, fitted out in all respects, for his passage just as the commune of Genoa had promised …

IV

Rival Crusades

King Louis's projected expedition to the East was not the only crusade under way or envisaged in Europe at this time. At the Council of Lyons it had been decreed that financial aid should be mustered for the beleaguered Latin Empire of Constantinople ('Romania'),[1] and Innocent ordered the Franciscans in Provence to preach the crusade in aid of the Latin Empire in September 1245.[2] King Jaime I of Aragon may have contemplated leading an expedition to its relief in that year; but the plan appears to have been jettisoned.[3] Nor is there any evidence that crusaders left Western Europe for Romania in substantial numbers, and it seems fair to conclude that, apart from the knights whom the Prince of Achaea left on Rhodes to fight the Greeks (see above, page 25, and **doc. 25**), this theatre did not serve as a distraction from Louis's own expedition. In December 1247 the Pope expressed concern about the burden borne by French churches and monasteries in meeting the stipulations of the Lyons decree concerning funds for Romania.[4] It has been suggested, in fact, that propaganda on behalf of the Latin Empire was kept 'on a low flame' because the threat to it had receded in the early 1240s.[5]

Innocent was insistent that the crusade in the Baltic region should not suffer through preaching there on King Louis's behalf [**doc. 35**]. The threat in Eastern Europe came not only from local pagans, but from the Mongols, who had devastated Hungary and Poland as recently as 1241–42. This is the explanation usually given for the poor response from Eastern Europe to the papal summons on behalf of the Holy Land a few years later. It is true that Hungary was subject to fresh alarms concerning Mongol activity in 1246–47.[6] In February 1247 the Pope promised King Béla IV that once intelligence arrived of a fresh Mongol invasion, he would immediately send *crucesignati* to his assistance, even expressly including those who had vowed

1 *Decrees of the Ecumenical Councils*, ed. Tanner, pp. 295–6.

2 Ferdinand M. Delorme, 'Bulle d'Innocent IV en faveur de l'empire latin de Constantinople (29 sept. 1245)', *AFH*, 8 (1915): 307–10.

3 Joseph O'Callaghan, *Reconquest and Crusade in Medieval Spain* (Philadelphia, PA, 2003), p. 107; and compare José Manuel Rodríguez García, 'Henry III (1216–1272), Alfonso X of Castile (1252–1284) and the crusading plans of the thirteenth century (1245–1272)', in Björn K. U. Weiler (ed., with Ifor Rowlands), *England and Europe in the Reign of Henry III (1216–1272)* (Aldershot, 2002), pp. 99–120 (here p. 102).

4 Berger, no. 3468.

5 Maier, *Preaching the Crusades*, pp. 78–9.

6 *Vetera Monumenta Historica Hungariam Sacram Illustrantia*, ed. Augustin Theiner (Rome, 1859-60), vol. 1, pp. 203–4 (no. 380, 4 February 1247); summary in Berger, no. 2958. Matthew Paris, *Chronica Majora*, vol. 4, p. 546 (trans. Giles, vol. 2, p. 165). Boniface, Archbishop of Canterbury, to Peter of Savoy, ibid., vol. 6, p. 133.

to crusade in the Holy Land [**doc. 36**], and in June 1248 he granted those who went to Hungary to fight against the Mongols the indulgence associated with the Holy Land crusade [**doc. 37**]. Such solicitude on the part of the Curia did not prevent the Hungarian monarch from protesting vigorously in November 1247 that Innocent allowed Louis to leave for the East when the Mongols threatened the very heart of Europe.[7] It is also true that the Pope's agents were then active even in Poland, where they were seeking to recruit crusaders both against the Emperor Frederick II and in defence of Constantinople.[8] But to point to the distraction of Eastern European rulers is to ask how far these regions were traditionally a source of men and money for the Near Eastern theatre. Hungary was in fact the only Eastern European kingdom to have any serious historic connection with the Holy Land crusade, and that relatively recently, since Béla's father, King András II, had briefly participated in the Fifth Crusade in 1217–18.[9]

We can be more certain that the struggle between Frederick II and Pope Innocent IV impaired recruitment for the Seventh Crusade. In 1246 Frederick's enemies in Germany elected an anti-king, Heinrich Raspe, Landgrave of Thuringia; and on his death in 1247 they chose Count William of Holland, who injected fresh vigour into the crusade against Frederick's supporters and in the course of a longer reign was able to inflict greater damage on the Hohenstaufen cause. The struggle in Germany undoubtedly had implications for King Louis's expedition. In the first place, the spiritual reward available to those who enlisted in the struggle with Frederick was identical with that offered to those who fought in the East [**doc. 40**]. The two crusades were clearly competing for the same group of nobles and knights, not just in the imperial territories, but even to a lesser extent within France itself, particularly following the election of an anti-king with a power-base in the north-west, close to the French border. And secondly, the Pope himself exhibited a marked ambivalence towards the French King's expedition. It is easy to gain the impression that he was more interested in the struggle with the Hohenstaufen than in the Seventh Crusade, regarding it as an unwelcome distraction; but the reality was more complex. He was anxious that Louis's absence would render the papal Curia at Lyons more vulnerable to attack by the Emperor, and for this reason urged the French King not to depart

---

7 *Vetera Monumenta Historica*, ed. Theiner, vol. 1, pp. 231–2 (no. 440). This letter, traditionally allocated to 1254, has now been persuasively re-dated to 1247 by Toru Senga, 'IV Béla külpolitikája és IV Ince pápához intézett "tátár" levele', *Századok*, 121 (1987): 583–612 (French summary at 611–12).

8 Frederick: Rodenberg, vol. 2, p. 235 (no. 309, 18 March 1247); also in *Vetera Monumenta Poloniae et Lithuaniae Gentiumque Finitimarum Historiam Illustrantia*, ed. Augustin Theiner (Rome, 1860–64), vol. 1, pp. 44–5 (no. 90); David Abulafia, *Frederick II: A Medieval Emperor* (London, 1988), p. 385. Constantinople: *Kodeks diplomatyczny wielkopolski*, ed. Societas literaria Poznaniensis (Poznań, 1877-8), vol. 1, pp. 207–9 (nos 246–7).

9 See generally James Ross Sweeney, 'Hungary in the crusades, 1169–1218', *International History Review*, 3 (1981): 467–81; and for András II, James M. Powell, *Anatomy of a Crusade 1213–1221* (Philadelphia, PA, 1986), pp. 127, 132–4.

until given papal leave to do so [**doc. 42**];[10] he would manifest the same concern about the prospective departure of Henry III of England for the East in 1250 [**doc. 54**].

Although for much of 1247 Innocent seems to have been opposed to the commutation of vows for the Holy Land in order to furnish recruits for the crusade against Frederick [**docs 9, 43 and 44**], and to have been concerned not to permit preaching within France for any crusade other than that for the East, even before the news reached him of Louis's defeat and capture [**doc. 19** above], other evidence suggests that papal policy was in a state of flux. In November 1247 a group of nobles whose vows were commuted from the Holy Land to the anti-Hohenstaufen crusade actually included five from the French kingdom [**docs 48 and 49**]. This is perhaps hardly worth mentioning, nevertheless, alongside the diversion of resources from the French-Imperial borderlands, namely the Low Countries. In July 1246 Innocent had instructed the Legate Eudes to discontinue the preaching campaign in Germany on the French King's behalf, on the grounds that the response had been poor and that the crusade was being preached there against the former Emperor; his insistence, nevertheless, that this order should be kept secret suggests that he knew it would be resented, not least by Louis [**doc. 38**]. In November of that year, he ordered the crusade to the Holy Land to be preached in Germany, Brabant and Denmark, among other regions of the Latin world [see **doc. 6** above]; but in March 1247 crusade preaching against Frederick was extended to Denmark and Poland [**doc. 41**].

One of the first casualties was the adhesion of William's maternal uncle, Duke Heinrich II of Brabant, who had taken the Cross for the Holy Land but who in 1247 was involved in the struggle against Frederick [**doc. 47**].[11] The consequences are most obvious in Frisia. This region, as Innocent himself would observe in 1250 [**doc. 100** below], was traditionally a source of doughty combatants for the campaigns in the East. Certainly the Frisians had distinguished themselves on the Fifth Crusade in 1218–19;[12] and there is evidence of support in the region for Louis's expedition. In the summer of 1246 the Pope had strongly encouraged Frisians who had taken

10 As noticed by Salimbene de Adam, *Cronica*, ed. Giuseppe Scalia (Turnhout, 1998–99), vol. 1, pp. 318–19. This request must be the reason that the Erfurt chronicler describes Louis as leaving on crusade against the Pope's advice: 'Chronica minor auctore minorita Erfordiensi', in *MGHS*, vol. 24, p. 200.

11 See also Berger, no. 3430; Berger, *Saint Louis*, p. clxvi. In the spring or early summer of 1246 he had expressed a desire to take the Cross for the Holy Land: Rodenberg, vol. 2, pp. 169–70 (nos 229–30; summaries in Berger, nos 2016, 2032). But already in January 1247 the pope described him as 'applying himself to the service of the Church [*servitio Ecclesiae insistens*]', which suggests, rather, that the Duke was supporting the crusade against Frederick: Registrum Vaticanum, Innocent IV, annus 4, fol. 356v (no. 355; summary in Berger, no. 2351). He would be with King William at the siege of Aachen (1248): Dickson, 'The advent of the *Pastores*', p. 261.

12 Which they had joined in the spring of 1218: Powell, *Anatomy of a Crusade*, pp. 137 ff. For Frisian enthusiasm on that crusade, see J. J. Van Moolenbroek, 'Signs in the heavens in Groningen and Friesland in 1214: Oliver of Cologne and crusading propaganda', *JMH*, 13 (1987): 251–72; more generally, Johannes A. Mol, 'Frisian fighters and the crusade', *Crusades*, 1 (2002): 89–110.

the Cross for the Holy Land to set out [**doc. 39**]. As late as June 1248 he was still insisting on the fulfilment of crusading vows to the East from Frisia [**doc. 45**]. But in the previous November, at King William's request, he had also begun to countenance the commutation of such vows to participation in the war in Germany [**doc. 46**], though subsequently requiring his legate to set a limit on the number of commutations to be permitted [**doc. 50**]. Logistical difficulties in getting Frisian crusaders to travel east also surfaced, so that after the date for their embarkation had been set back a further twelve months in May 1247, many Frisians were drawn into the siege of Aachen on King William's behalf and would-be Frisian participants in the Seventh Crusade were allowed to commute their vows to the war against the deposed Emperor [**doc. 55**].

Later, Innocent took another significant step, by ordering William to be allocated funds from the redemption of vows that were earmarked for Louis's expedition, and that hitherto had been kept strictly separate from the monies designed to support the crusade in Germany – a shift that papal letters enable us to date precisely to 11–14 May 1249 [**docs 52 and 53**].[13] It was only after the news arrived of the disastrous outcome of Louis's Egyptian campaign that the Pope again began to encourage the recruitment of crusaders from the imperial territories for the war in the East [**doc. 100** below]. In other words, Innocent's stance varied with the fortunes of the respective crusades in Germany and in the Near East. *Prima facie* this conclusion might have seemed only too likely, and we might have reached it without documentary evidence. But it seems worth emphasizing nevertheless.

DOCUMENTS 35–55

35. Pope Innocent IV to archbishops, bishops, archpriests, provosts and prelates of other churches who see the letter, 13 September 1245: Preußisches Urkundenbuch, *ed. Rudolf Philippi, Max Hein et al. (Königsberg and Marburg, 1882–1986), vol. 1/1, p. 125 (no. 169)*

Although we have given orders for the Cross to be preached in aid of the Holy Land in every quarter, it is our intention, even so, that the Cross should be preached for the business of Livonia and Prussia within their own regions notwithstanding, as is evident in our other letters. Wherefore we instruct Your Discretion by apostolic letter that since both are necessary you see to both attentively and effectively by word and by action.

Dated Lyons, the Ides of September, in the third year of our pontificate.

13 Maier, *Preaching the Crusades*, p. 152.

36. Pope Innocent IV to Béla IV, King of Hungary, 4 February 1247: Vetera Monumenta Historica Hungariam Sacram Illustrantia, *ed. Augustin Theiner (Rome, 1859–60), vol. 1, pp. 203–4 (no. 379); summary in Berger, no. 2957*

Since it is our policy to show ourselves favourable and well disposed towards you in your affairs, and especially in the business of the Tartars, which is not [just] your own but a general one that affects each and every Christian, we are intent on doing our utmost to help you and provide you with powerful aid and defence in this regard. Wherefore we keenly request and urge Your Royal Highness to prepare manfully to resist them, to have careful enquiries made concerning their arrival in your territories, and not to delay in notifying us as soon as you have reliable information, in the sure knowledge that we shall immediately cause all those who have taken the Cross in aid of the Holy Land and [p. 204] of the Empire of Romania, and others wheresoever they may be, to move swiftly to your assistance.

Dated Lyons, the 2nd Nones of February, in the fourth year of our pontificate.

37. Pope Innocent IV to the Preceptor and brothers of the Hospital of Jerusalem in Hungary, 24 June 1248: Vetera Monumenta Historica, *ed. Theiner, vol. 1, p. 206 (no. 388); summary in Berger, no. 4000*

[Urges them to see to the defence of Hungary against the Mongols and grants to their families, and to all those who take the Cross and go to Hungary to fight the Mongols, the same indulgence as is conferred on those who sail to the aid of the Holy Land]

38. Pope Innocent IV to [Eudes,] Bishop of Tusculum, papal legate, 5 July 1246: Berger, no. 2935; also in Rodenberg, vol. 2, pp. 161–2 (no 214)

It is our wish, and our authorization by means of this letter, that you do not delay in ordering those to whom you have entrusted the preaching of the Cross throughout Germany in aid of the Holy Land, to see to the suspension of preaching of this kind during the present time, particularly since it is currently reported to be having little effect in those parts and since we have ordered that the Cross be preached in the same region against Frederick, the former Emperor. But we desire you to keep this secret, to be revealed to absolutely nobody.

Dated [Lyons, the 3rd Nones of July, in the fourth year of our pontificate].

39. Pope Innocent IV to the bishops in Frisia, [28 July–9 August] 1246: Berger, no. 2054; also in Rodenberg, vol. 2, pp. 172–3 (no. 234)

In order that those who take the vow may, in accordance with the choicest of the prophets,[14] render their vows to the Lord, we order Your Fraternity, on the authority of this letter, to take steps diligently to advise and persuade those in your dioceses in Frisia [already] signed with the Cross, and those yet to be signed, who are about

14 Reading, with Rodenberg, *prophetarum eximium* for the *prophetam eximium* of the text. Compare Psalms xxii, 25, lxvi, 13, cxvi, 14 and 18.

to set out to aid the Holy Land – and to compel them, if it proves necessary, by excommunicating their persons and pronouncing an interdict on their lands – to put an end to all vacillation, with the sole exception of those who have encountered the sort of obstacle on account of which their vow ought, by the providence of the Apostolic See, to be commuted or postponed; and to make themselves ready in such a way that they may commence their journey within a year of the coming March and, with the Lord's permission, make the passage overseas with our dearest son in Christ, the illustrious King of France, since in those circumstances their crossing the sea may be more advantageous and more successful.

Dated Lyons, the 5th Nones of August, in the fourth year of our pontificate.[15]

40. Pope Innocent IV to O[ttaviano], Cardinal-deacon of Santa Maria in Via Lata,[16] papal legate, 8 March 1247: Berger, no. 3002; also in Rodenberg, vol. 2, p. 219 (no. 292)

Since we shall be sending you to Lombardy after entrusting you with the office of full legate, we grant Your Discretion, by the authority of this letter, the power to confer on knights, and others who accompany you in order to serve the Church, or who themselves are present on campaign or elsewhere against Frederick, former Roman Emperor, that full pardon for their sins which was granted in the General Council to those who aid the Holy Land.

Dated Lyons, the 8th Ides of March, in the fourth year of our pontificate.

41. Pope Innocent IV to P[eter], Cardinal-deacon of San Giorgio in Velabro, papal legate, 18 March 1247: summary in Berger, no. 2964

[Orders him to instigate crusade preaching against Frederick in Germany, Denmark and Poland]

42. Pope Innocent IV to Louis IX, 17 June 1247: Rodenberg, vol. 2, pp. 287–8 (no. 394);[17] summary in Berger, no. 3040

[p. 288] Let the heavens rejoice and the earth be glad that God has once again shown His face in such a way to His Church, which was founded in the precious blood of His only-begotten Son, that what was thought, in the vortex of rising storms, to be about to undergo, as it were, extreme danger is [now] seen suddenly to be attended by the outcome of secure freedom together with the fullness of honour: as you, our dearest son, glorious above all the earth's princes in the sight of God and of men, who trace your origin to a royal lineage that has always been wont to yield for the Church a harvest of honour and of grace, without a moment's hesitation and with an ardour conceived by the Holy Spirit, together with our dearest daughter in Christ,

---

15 Berger detects an error in the date given and points out that the year must be Innocent's third.

16 Ottaviano degli Ubaldini (d. 1273).

17 Also printed in Huillard-Bréholles, vol. 6/2, pp. 544–6.

the illustrious Queen of the French, your mother, and our beloved sons, your noble brothers the Counts, have decided with one voice, putting aside all delay, to move with a victorious army to the defence of ourselves, whom in reverence for God you recognize as a father, and of the Church itself. Filled with incredible joy at the divine glory of this action, we and our brethren glorify with humble hearts the clemency of the Eternal King, Who has filled you, His own king, with so pious and praiseworthy a desire that it is deservedly wondrous in the minds of ourselves and others and ought to be brought to the everlasting knowledge of every nation. Nor is it surprising, since in response to the groans of the Church and the constant perils with which it is beset – only to consider the harassment continuously inflicted on the Church's sons by the disturber of the world[18] – you alone, outshining all the other kings of the earth and while others are virtually silent, have chosen not merely to lay out your wealth in aid of Mother Church but to serve in person. May God reserve for you the inexpressible quantity of this kind of merit for the bestowal of that reward with which the blessed ranks of everlasting princes are known to be crowned. May God's kindness also bring some of the power of that merit to your forebears of renowned memory, so that their fortunate souls may rejoice to be set amid the light above; granting to us meanwhile that we, who gladly feast our hearts on rejoicing at the abundance of divine kindness and of yours [here] below, are able to recompense you and yours with what is a fitting honour and a due reward.

Behold, my son of blessing and grace, you have heard our gladness and have observed the Church's rejoicing. However desirable and necessary it is for her, having once drunk bitter draughts, that the light of solace should approach her and that especial food for gladness should be forthcoming, we beg Your Serenity, through God's mercy, and enjoin on you for the remission of your sins, that, in accordance with the design which, with pious intention, you conceived for her honour, you instantly add to it and in the Lord multiply the joy in your heart over it. For when the enemy becomes aware of the abundance of grace with which the kindness from on high is known to have bathed the Church through you, he may perhaps forsake the darkness of a perverse mentality and turn his heart to reverence for the divine majesty; or if he has any inner light remaining he may of necessity see that the Son of God, the Church's founder and governor, does not allow the dignity granted to the Church from Heaven to be nullified by his manifold wickedness. But although a glorious host may, at your order, be deployed most readily for its defence, it is nevertheless our wish that you do not make ready for the journey, and do not send any troops, until you learn the will of the Apostolic See in this matter through our envoy or special letter.

Dated Lyons, the 15th Kalends of July, in the fourth year of our pontificate.

43. Pope Innocent IV to [Eudes,] Bishop of Tusculum, papal legate, 5 July 1247: Berger, no. 3054; also in Rodenberg, vol. 2, pp. 296–7 (no. 408)

Since at the present time the Holy Land stands in need of military reinforcements, and our dearest son in Christ, the illustrious King of France, has assumed the sign of the

18 Evidently an allusion to the Emperor Frederick II.

life-giving Cross, not by the agency of men but rather through divine intervention, and is making mighty and manful preparations to aid that country, and since we wish to be favourably at hand and of use to him in an enterprise of this nature, we order you to prevent and cause to be prevented, on our behalf, anyone in the cities and dioceses of Cambrai, Liège, Toul, Utrecht, Metz and Verdun from daring, on the authority of our letters, to absolve anyone in those regions from a vow to crusade to Jerusalem or to commute such a vow to another. You should, after issuing a warning, compel those who presume to the contrary to desist altogether from their presumption by ecclesiastical censure, without right of appeal, and pronounce it nevertheless null and void should any challenge be made through however pious a presumption, notwithstanding any letter obtained, or even to be obtained, from the Apostolic See, in general or in particular terms, which might serve to obstruct this, although express mention of them is not made here.

Dated Lyons, the 3rd Nones of July, in the fifth year of our pontificate.

44. Pope Innocent IV to P[eter], Cardinal-deacon of San Giorgio in Velabro, papal legate, 19 November 1247: Rodenberg, vol. 2, p. 329 (no. 459); summary in Berger, no. 4065

Since many in the Empire have assumed or received the sign of the Cross as the fulfilment of various pious works, and because we regard it as a most pious task at this moment to aid our dearest son in Christ, the illustrious King of the Romans,[19] against the faithlessness of Frederick, who aspires to destroy the faith, we grant you, by the authority of this letter, full power to commute the vows of those same crusaders to the assistance of the aforesaid King, with the exception of those who have taken the Cross in aid of the Holy Land.

Dated [Lyons, the 13th Kalends of December, in the fifth year of our pontificate].

45. Pope Innocent IV to Hydus, Provincial Prior of the Dominican Order in Germany, 22 June 1248: Rodenberg, vol. 2, p. 409 (no. 579); summary in Berger, no. 3967

In order that those who take the vow may, in accordance with the choicest of the prophets, render their vows to the Lord, we order Your Discretion, by the authority of this letter and in the power of obedience, that you keenly urge and persuade, in person or through any of the Friars of your Order whom you know to be suitable for this purpose, all who have taken the Cross from Frisia, Holland and Zealand, and compel them, if necessary, by ecclesiastical censure without [right of] appeal, to make themselves ready to set out in aid of the Holy Land in the month of March next. Notwithstanding the privilege granted to the aforesaid Order by the Apostolic See that the Friars of the Order should not be bound to take cognizance of, or involve themselves in, cases and matters referred to them by that See, against their will; or [notwithstanding] an indulgence issued to anybody by that See that they may not be

19 William, Count of Holland, elected German King in 1247, following the death of Heinrich Raspe: he would be crowned at Aachen in 1248.

subjected to interdict, suspension or excommunication by apostolic letter and without special instructions from that See which make full mention of that indulgence; or any other [indulgence], of which particular mention ought to be made in our letter; or the constitution *De duabus dietis* issued in the General Council.

Dated Lyons, the 10th Kalends of July, in the fifth year of our pontificate.

46. Pope Innocent IV to [Albrecht Suerbeer,] Archbishop of Prussia,[20] *papal legate, 17 November 1247: Rodenberg, vol. 2, p. 326 (no. 453); summary in Berger, no. 4070*

An urgent request has reached us from our dearest son in Christ, the illustrious King of the Romans, that since many Frisians from the county of Holland, which belongs to him by hereditary right, have received the sign of the Cross in aid of the Holy Land, we should see to it that the Cross is commuted from this [purpose] to the King's support and, with our customary kindness, that the same pardon is bestowed upon them for their sins as if they had personally gone overseas. Wherefore we instruct you to arrange and implement what we have said to you by word of mouth, on the advice of our beloved son, P[eter], Cardinal-deacon of San Giorgio in Velabro, legate of the Apostolic See, and of the aforesaid King, or of either one of them.

Dated Lyons, the 15th Kalends of December, in the fifth year of our pontificate.

47. Pope Innocent IV to P[eter], Cardinal-deacon of San Giorgio in Velabro, papal legate, 20 November 1247: Berger, no. 3433; also in Rodenberg, vol. 2, p. 335 (no. 470)

In order that those who fight on the Church's behalf against its persecutors may gain a reward that does not perish, it is our wish, and our command to Your Devotion by the authority of this letter, that by apostolic authority you bestow on our beloved son, the noble Duke of Brabant and Lorraine,[21] as he manfully and powerfully[22] assists us and the Roman Church, in his own person and those of his men, against F[rederick], former Roman Emperor, and his sons, and their helpers and well-wishers, and also on anyone else who aids the said Duke in this matter, full pardon of the sins that they have truly repented and have confessed.

Dated Lyons, the 12th Kalends of December, in the fifth year of our pontificate.

48. Pope Innocent IV to preachers in Frisia, 19 November 1247: Berger, no. 4068[23]

A humble request has reached us from our dearest son in Christ, the illustrious King of the Romans, that since certain noblemen from the kingdom of France as well as

20 Albrecht Suerbeer (d. 1272). Currently unable to enter into possession of his see, he was employed on other commissions (see below, **doc. 55**; also note 28). He would be made Archbishop of Riga in 1252.

21 Heinrich II (d. 1248).

22 Reading *potenter* for the *patenter* of the text.

23 This letter is also partially printed in Rodenberg, vol. 2, pp. 330–31 (no. 462).

from Germany who have taken the Cross are eager to go to the aid of the said King against his enemies, we should, with fatherly forethought, see to it that the crusading vow in the case of these crusaders is commuted to [one in] support of the King. Wherefore we order you to proceed in this, and in other matters pertaining to the business of the Cross, on the advice of our beloved son, Peter, Cardinal-deacon of San Giorgio in Velabro, legate of the Apostolic See.

Dated Lyons, the 13th Kalends of December, in the fifth year of our pontificate.

49. Pope Innocent IV to P[eter], Cardinal-deacon of San Giorgio in Velabro, papal legate, 20 November 1247: Berger, no. 4060; also in Rodenberg, vol. 2, p. 332 (no. 465)

A humble request has reached us from our dearest son in Christ, the illustrious King of the Romans, that since certain noblemen from the kingdom of France as well as from Germany who have taken the Cross are eager to go to the aid of the said King against his enemies, we should, with fatherly forethought, see to it that the crusading vow in the case of these crusaders is commuted to [one in] support of the King. Because the King, whose cause is that of the Faith and the Church, has need of military reinforcements, we order you to commute the crusading vows of these crusaders, of whom five are from the kingdom of France and fifteen from the Empire, to [one for] the King's assistance. Those who resist, etc.

Dated Lyons, the 12th Kalends of December, in the fifth year of our pontificate.

50. Pope Innocent IV to P[eter], Cardinal-deacon of San Giorgio in Velabro, papal legate, 8 April 1248: Rodenberg, vol. 2, pp. 373–4 (no. 534); summary in Berger, no. 3779

[p. 374] Our dearest son in Christ, W[illiam], the illustrious King of the Romans, has requested us, in a special letter, that since it is necessary for the business of the Church to make impressive headway in Germany we should commute the vows of Frisians who have taken the Cross in aid of the Holy Land to one for the promotion of that business. Trusting in your discretion, we delegate to you, by the authority of this letter, the release of *crucesignati* of this kind from their crusading vows, up to the number that you judge expedient when all circumstances are taken into account, in order that they may assist the aforesaid King manfully and conscientiously in the advancement of that business until the deadline that you see fit to prescribe for them, having bestowed on them for this purpose the pardon for their sins which is granted to those who go to Jerusalem.

Dated Lyons, the 6th Ides of April, in the fifth year of our pontificate.

51. Pope Innocent IV to the Dominican Priors of Louvain and Antwerp, in the dioceses of Cambrai and Liège, 19 September 1248: Rodenberg, vol. 2, p. 418 (no. 589); summary in Berger, no. 4166

As we are gaining in the Lord full confidence regarding your discretion, we instruct you to collect, personally or through others whom you deem suitable for the task, the redemptions and offerings (whatsoever the cause for which they arrive) of the vows of crusaders, whether against Frederick, the former Emperor, and Conrad, his son, and their supporters, or in aid of the Holy Land, who have been held back by a proper obstacle and so have been unable to fulfil their vows in person, as well as the bequests made for these categories of assistance in the province of Cologne and in those parts of the dioceses of Cambrai and Tournai which are recognized as lying in the Empire, and the twentieth of ecclesiastical revenues throughout Germany, and cause to be made over to yourselves what has already been collected by others, and further to keep [it all], awaiting our pleasure. Those who resist etc. You are faithfully to report to us the total amount by letter. Notwithstanding that an indulgence has been granted by the Apostolic See to your Order or to a person of another [Order] to whom you may have seen fit to delegate this task, to the effect that the Friars or the relevant person of that Order are not bound to take cognizance of, or intervene in, cases or affairs that have been entrusted to them by the Apostolic See; and [notwithstanding] any other [privilege] that any persons may not be subjected to interdict, suspension or excommunication by apostolic letter that does not make full mention of an indulgence of this kind.

Dated Lyons, the 13th Kalends of October, in the sixth year of our pontificate.

52. Pope Innocent IV to the Dominican Willem Van Eyk, diocese of Liège, 11 May 1249: Berger, no. 4525; also in Rodenberg, vol. 2, p. 531 (no. 718)

We order Your Discretion, by this letter, that on our authority you collect, either in person or through others who are suitable, the redemptions of the vows of crusaders in the kingdom of Germany, whether against F[rederick], the former Emperor, or even in aid of the Holy Land, and in addition sums bequeathed or left, or other offerings, for whatever reasons they were made over to the said land or to the business of the Church at large, notwithstanding any grants, indulgences or letters whatsoever regarding these redemptions and the other things aforementioned, made by the Apostolic See, or to be made in the future, to any persons whatsoever, even if mention ought to be made of them in this letter. You should see that the proceeds of the redemption of crusading vows against the said F[rederick] or sums made over from any other sources for that purpose, are granted and assigned to our dearest son in Christ, W[illiam], illustrious King of the Romans, just as we are said to have granted them in our earlier letters. As for the proceeds of the vows of crusaders to the Holy Land, or even of legacies from any other sources whatever that are due to that land, you are to have them kept in a safe place under trustworthy guard, awaiting our pleasure. Those who resist, etc.[24]

Dated Lyons, the 5th Ides of May, in the sixth year of our pontificate.

24 For a letter (dated 14 May 1249) ordering Friar William and his fellow Dominican, Johann von Diest, to keep the proceeds of vow redemptions and other offerings for the Holy Land crusade until they learned the Pope's pleasure, see Berger, no. 4508. This is difficult to reconcile with **doc. 53** below.

53. Pope Innocent IV to the Dominican W[illem] Van Eyk,[25] *diocese of Liège, 14 May 1249: Rodenberg, vol. 2, p. 533 (no. 721); summary in Berger, no. 4510*

We instruct Your Discretion, by the authority of this letter, to see that the redemptions of crusading vows in aid of the Holy Land, which we ordered through you to be kept until our pleasure, are assigned in their entirety, once you have collected them, to our dearest son in Christ, the illustrious King of the Romans.

Dated [the 2nd Ides of May, in the sixth year of our pontificate].

54. Pope Innocent IV to Henry III, King of England, 11 April 1250: Foedera, *vol. 1/1, p. 159*

We rejoice in the Lord and commend with suitable praise your pious intention, in that, as we learned recently from your letter and envoys, you are kindled with zeal for the faith and devotion and are making splendid and mighty preparations, as befits Your Highness, to bring aid to the Holy Land.

You have requested previously, and again on this occasion, that in order to conclude this business, since it entails heavy expenditure, you should be granted by us a tenth of the ecclesiastical revenues of your kingdom and of the other territories subject to your jurisdiction. We wrote back to you some time ago that although it is our policy to comply with your wishes in all matters, so far as we are able with God, nevertheless following his assumption of the Cross we did not grant our dearest son in Christ, the illustrious King of France, a tenth of this kind in his realm, which he had requested in similar circumstances, until the prelates of that kingdom had granted it; and for this reason we would make efforts to see that the prelates of your realm would prove accommodating in this regard, and were prepared, once you had taken the Cross, to persuade them to [accept] your need and to ask them to consider the urgency of the affair and the pious nature of your intention and to comply with your wishes both generously and willingly. Those prelates have requested us by letter that, as is gratifying and acceptable to us, we should see to it that you receive abundant funds for such an important business from the ecclesiastical revenues of the kingdom of England.

But in order that we do not seem guilty of neglect, by ignoring the ruinous consequences for Christendom, it is a vital part of our function, as one set (albeit undeserving) over the Lord's flock, that we bring to your attention the critical and perilous situation that threatens the entire Christian people. For you know, dearest son, that since Mother Church is upheld by these two realms, where through God's grace the Christian confession is thriving, were their kings thus to abandon her in exile on the pretext of any pious duty whatever, the effect would be nothing other than to expose her to pillage and plunder by her enemies and to pay no regard to the Catholic faith, which is being undermined on this side of the sea. For this reason, since the King [of France] has crossed overseas together with all his brothers, it would be inhuman, and far removed from filial kindness if, when she has no one else left, you were to abandon her to be tossed to and fro on stormy seas. As, therefore,

25 The text reads 'de Cybea' in error for 'de Eyka'.

the burden for which two of you were responsible is left – by divine dispensation, perhaps – to be carried on your shoulders alone, we ask you to reflect carefully that, since it is more [important] to aid the head than any limb, however noble, you recognize forthwith what is to the advantage of Christendom and [what] of the honour and safety of yourself and your kingdom.

But since – whatever you conclude in these matters – expenditure is necessary to see these things to fulfilment and Holy Mother Church ought to nurture the praiseworthy intention of [Your] Royal Magnificence with careful advice and with help where she can, we have seen fit to grant Your Highness a tenth of all the ecclesiastical revenues of your kingdom, and also of the other territories subject to your jurisdiction, for up to three years in aid of the aforesaid land. And we are ordering our venerable brothers, the Archbishop of Canterbury and the Bishop of Hereford,[26] by letter to have that tenth made available to you without any difficulty and in its entirety, once it is collected and you wish to set out overseas; constraining by ecclesiastical censure, without [right of] appeal, those who resist. The collection of this tenth is to be postponed, however, until the [date of your] passage is determined on oath; and the time at which its levy will commence, and the persons to whom it will be entrusted, will be arranged as seems to be in your interests and those of the business.

Dated Lyons, the 3rd Ides of April, in the seventh year of our pontificate.

55. 'Menkonis Chronicon', MGHS, *vol. 23, pp. 540, 542*[27]

[p. 540] In the year 1247 one of the Order of Minor Friars arrived together with a man from Rome of the same order. Claiming that his name was Renold, he showed a letter of the lord Pope addressed to a certain Renold, and demanded urgently the money in the chests, the deposits [made] for the crusade and the sums bequeathed by dead persons for the crusade, as if for the purpose of the lord Pope's expenditure. But the lord Sicco, who was dean of Farmsum, and the nobles of the region took a vigorous stand on behalf of the Frisians' liberty and openly opposed him, saying that this money was being kept in order to be used for poor pilgrims who were about to leave Frisia, since a general crusade was under way. And thus [the two Franciscans] withdrew in confusion with empty purses. It was later learned by the friars that Renold was an impostor. That letter had been addressed to a certain Renold, but death had overtaken him; and this man had obtained the letter by some means or other and adopted a false name, with the aim of using it to gather the money and of either abandoning the order or perhaps, rather, securing the favour of the Curia by presenting the money. For this he was seized by his fellow-friars, as was appropriate, and thrown into prison …

In that same year Friar Wilbrand travelled to the court of the lord Pope, and because he carried with him a great sum of money which he had obtained through

26 Canterbury: Boniface of Savoy (1241–1270). Hereford: Peter d'Aigueblanche (1240–1268). The Pope in fact wrote letters to this effect to the Archbishops of Canterbury and York and the Bishops of Hereford, Ely and Durham on 30 April 1250: *Foedera*, vol. 1/1, p. 161.

27 This testimony is discussed in Maier, *Preaching the Crusades*, pp. 66–7.

the redemption of crusading [vows] and made in the Curia on the Frisians' behalf many great promises of help by way of goods and men, he found considerable favour there. While he was at the Curia, the King of France, who had already begun preparations for a crusade to the Holy Land, which was wretchedly befouled by the pagans, requested the lord Pope to send preachers to Frisia who might encourage the Frisians to accompany him. And so this business was entrusted to Friar Wilbrand. Overall, however, it was entrusted to the lord Albrecht, Archbishop of Livonia, Estonia and Prussia, so that as he passed through Frisia he might reinforce Friar Wilbrand by his preaching and protect him.[28] They reached Groningen after the Exaltation of the Holy Cross [14 September], furnished with many letters giving them authority to dispense [vows], as well as privileges concerning the Frisians' liberties.[29] An assembly of abbots, other Frisian prelates, jurors and lay nobles, and in particular crusaders, was held, and they showed their letters of authority, setting May of the following year as the time of the sea-crossing and ordering all the crusaders to make ready for that date. But everybody protested that in view of the shortness of the time, a lack of money and the uncertainty of [finding] ships they could in no way get ready so early; and so it was postponed until May of the year following. Yet then in turn the journey overseas was put off on account of the siege of the city of Aachen,[30] for which many Frisians had departed, and the vows were commuted on the lord Pope's authority …

[p. 542] In that same year [1248] King Louis of France set out for the Holy Land. He had given orders for 100 ships to be made ready for him at Marseilles; but because of obstruction by Frederick he got only half of these, each of them with the capacity to carry 1000 men. And thus with 50,000 men he sailed to Cyprus, where he spent the winter, ordering his brother Robert, Count of Artois,[31] to follow him in the spring with the remaining fifty ships. And in this way they sailed together to the Holy Land.

28 During the years 1246–48 Albrecht was engaged in negotiations on the Pope's behalf with Rus's princes regarding ecclesiastical union: see Joseph T. Fuhrmann, 'Metropolitan Cyril II (1242–1281) and the politics of accommodation', *Jahrbuch für Geschichte Osteuropas*, 24 (1976): 161–72 (here 163 and 165, n. 18).

29 For an undated papal letter granting 40 days' remission of penance to those who attended Willibrand's crusade sermons, see Paolo Sambin, *Problemi politici attraverso lettere inedite di Innocenzo IV*, Memorie del Istituto Veneto di Scienze, Lettere ed Arti, Classe di Scienze Morali e Lettere, 31/3 (Venezia, 1955), p. 70 (no. 53).

30 Below (p. 541), the author describes the siege as lasting throughout the summer of 1248 and into the autumn.

31 An error, of course, for Alphonse, Count of Poitou.

V

The First Phase of the Crusade: Victory and Disaster in Egypt

NUMBERS

Although we have no reliable total for the force that invaded Egypt in June 1249, we do at least have figures for the knights. Louis's chamberlain, Jean de Beaumont, sets at more than 1900 the number of knights from France who accompanied the King and gives 700 for the knights who joined him from Cyprus and Syria, including those supplied by the Temple and the Hospital [**doc. 58**]. The total – 2600 – tallies with that of '2500 or more' furnished by Jean Sarrasin for the number of knights who embarked for Egypt at Limassol in May 1249, though slightly lower than the figure of 2800 specified by Joinville at two points in his narrative. Sarrasin is also the only source to supply a figure (of 5000) for the crossbowmen.[1] It is usual to multiply the number of knights by a factor of four or five in order to arrive at a total for the entire force. Strayer estimated the total size of the army, at the peak of the crusade in the spring of 1249, as 25,000 men, but went on to suggest that even this figure appears too high in view of what is known of Louis's overall expenditure and the costs of maintaining knights, serjeants and crossbowmen, and that the true figure is likely to have been nearer to 15,000.[2] These estimates exclude the unknown number of knights brought by Alphonse, who joined his brother at Damietta in October. It is worth noting that the contemporary Muslim author Saʿd al-Dīn would set the total number of Franks taken prisoner in April 1250 at over 20,000 and the slain at 7000 [**doc. 74(h)** below], figures that have a more realistic ring than the higher totals found in some Muslim sources.

The number of ships in the crusader fleet is equally difficult to establish. Both Jean de Beaumont [**doc. 58**] and Gui de Burcey [**doc. 61**] specify 120 larger vessels, and the former mentions also 800 others. The higher figures of 1500 vessels given by Gui, a knight in the service of the Viscount of Melun [**doc. 59**], like the 1800 furnished by Joinville,[3] must have included even the very smallest boats such as longboats and the smaller craft carried on board. Our sources, testifying as they do that on arrival in the delta the crusader knights were obliged to leave their ships,

1 'Rothelin', p. 571 (trans. Shirley, p. 69). Joinville, §§ 147, 423, pp. 82, 230 (trans. Hague, pp. 60, 131; trans. Shaw, pp. 201, 269).

2 J. R. Strayer, 'The crusades of Louis IX', in Wolff and Hazard, *The Later Crusades*, pp. 493–4.

3 Joinville, § 146, p. 82 (trans. Hague, p. 60; trans. Shaw, p. 201).

enter smaller vessels and galleys and then wade ashore [**docs 57-59**],[4] amply bear out Professor Pryor's suggestion that Louis had either failed to bring enough of the requisite landing-craft in the form of shallow-draught horse-transports or, more probably, had lost them in the storm off Cyprus. Had the crusaders possessed these vessels, which had an opening in the stern, the oarsmen could have manoeuvred them in reverse towards the shore and the knights would have been able to mount a charge against the enemy directly from the galleys.[5] More important still was the lack of sufficient war-galleys for amphibious operations further up the Nile.

THE HALT ON CYPRUS

Most of the King's ten-month stay on Cyprus until May 1249 is covered by a report from the legate Eudes de Châteauroux to the Pope [**doc. 56**]. Various preoccupations surface in this report. One is Louis's concern that the army should not disintegrate during this period of inactivity, a possibility thrown starkly into relief by the behaviour of the Viscount of Châteaudun, who had quarrelled with his ship's crew and attempted to sail to Acre; the dispute was still not resolved when the Legate wrote. In responding to an appeal from the hard-pressed Prince of Antioch and sending only crossbowmen, Louis similarly demonstrated his awareness of the risk that undisciplined Western knights would interpret fulfilment of their vows as military assistance to Christians against the Muslim menace in any locality, rather than participation in an organized and focused campaign under his own leadership. He seems also to have turned down a personal appeal for reinforcements from the Empress of Constantinople, who visited him on Cyprus (see above, page 25).

The King was determined from the outset, moreover, that under his leadership the Christian establishment should act as one in the diplomatic context and that there should be no separate negotiations with the Muslims. The Master of the Temple notified him of the arrival of envoys from Ayyūb, the Sultan of Egypt; but when he heard rumours that the Egyptian embassy had come at the Master's own instigation Louis was angry, on account of the impression of weakness to which this *démarche* might have given rise. Joinville reports a similar incident some years later, in Palestine, when the Templar Master had entered into discussions, this time with al-Nāṣir Yūsuf of Aleppo, over mutual territorial interests, and the King obliged him to undergo a humiliating climbdown in public; the order's Marshal, who had conducted these negotiations, was banished from Palestine.[6]

Another theme to emerge from Eudes's letter is the relatively heavy toll taken of the crusaders by the prolonged stay on Cyprus, even before a blow had been struck against the Muslim enemy. He lists several prominent figures who had died, and towards the end of his report he says that 260 barons and knights had perished

4 See also Jean Sarrasin, in 'Rothelin', p. 590 (trans. Shirley, p. 86).

5 John H. Pryor, 'Transportation of horses by sea during the era of the crusades: eighth century to 1285 A.D. Part II: 1228–1285', *MM*, 68/2 (May 1982): 102–25 (here 103–4). Pryor, 'The crusade of Emperor Frederick II', pp. 116–19.

6 Joinville, §§ 511–14, pp. 280, 282 (trans. Hague, pp. 154–5; trans. Shaw, pp. 293–4).

(doubtless in many cases from malaria), a figure that at this stage is likely to have represented as much as 10 per cent of the total number of knights accompanying King Louis. It was for this reason, no doubt, that the halt on Cyprus was subsequently criticized. Joinville appears a trifle anxious to dissociate the King from the decision. Louis had allegedly wanted to sail straight to Egypt but had been dissuaded by the advice of his barons;[7] though the pretext given – to wait until the entire army had assembled – is eminently reasonable. The author of a crusade treatise around the turn of the century, who is flatly hostile to using Cyprus as a base, cites in support the regret expressed by Louis and his staff in view of the consequences for the Seventh Crusade.[8]

The King was also called upon, not for the first time, to act as peacemaker in a long-standing dispute that had arisen in the Christian East. He sent envoys with a view to securing a truce between Prince Bohemond V of Antioch and King Het'um of Armenia. We are not told what, if anything, they achieved: it was not until October 1254 that the prince's son and successor, Bohemond VI, married Het'um's daughter Sibylla,[9] which might suggest that Louis's efforts were unavailing at this early juncture. No other source corroborates Matthew Paris's assertion that the King reconciled the Templars and the Hospitallers in Cyprus and other regions of Christendom, and this may be simply another instance of the way the St. Albans chronicler denigrates the Military Orders.[10]

RELATIONS WITH THE MONGOLS

A significant proportion of Eudes's report is taken up with diplomatic dealings with the Mongols. The initiative here did not, as sometimes suggested in the secondary literature, come from Louis.[11] In fact, it was the Mongols who sought out the French King. The general Eljigidei, who had recently arrived in western Persia, despatched an embassy to him, which joined the crusade in Cyprus in December 1248. Eudes preserved a translation of the letter that the envoys carried; and Louis also had a French version drawn up and forwarded to his mother.[12] The letter contrasted sharply with the ultimatums that hitherto had characterized Mongol diplomacy towards the West, on which the French King was well informed. If Matthew Paris is to be trusted,

---

7 Ibid., § 132, p. 74 (trans. Hague, p. 57; trans. Shaw, p. 197).

8 *Via ad Terram Sanctam*, ed. Charles Kohler, in 'Deux projets de croisade en Terre-Sainte composés à la fin du XIIIe siècle et au début du XIVe', *Revue de l'Orient Latin*, 10 (1903–1904): 406–57 (here 428). The *Memoria Terre Sancte* (ibid., p. 450), to which in places this text bears a marked similarity (though in Old French as opposed to Latin), advances the same arguments against Cyprus, but omits the King's regret.

9 'Estoire de Eracles', p. 442 (trans. in Shirley, *Crusader Syria*, p. 140). 'Annales de Terre Sainte', p. 446 (version 'B').

10 Matthew Paris, *Chronica Majora*, vol. 5, p. 71 (trans. Giles, vol. 2, p. 307; trans. Vaughan, p. 181). On this, see Nicholson, 'Steamy Syrian scandals'.

11 See, for example, Louis Hambis, 'Saint Louis et les Mongols', *Journal Asiatique*, 258 (1970): 25–33 (here 28–9).

12 Reproduced by Matthew Paris, *Chronica Majora*, vol. 6: *Additamenta*, pp. 163–5.

Louis himself had received such an ultimatum in France in 1247;[13] and in 1248, not long before he embarked on crusade, Innocent had sent to his court the papal envoy Carpini, who had recently returned from the Mongol dominions.[14]

Eljigidei expressed cordial good wishes towards Louis and for his victory. He claimed to have arrived with an edict exempting Christians from servitude, tribute, labour services and other impositions and granting them freedom of worship (though in reality the immunities applied only to Christian priests and monks, rather than to the Christian population at large, and the same privileges were extended to the 'religious classes' in other faiths, including Islam and Buddhism).[15] He assured Louis, lastly, that under Mongol rule there was no discrimination between different Christian sects, and asked the French king to apply the same principle. There was no mention whatever of Frankish submission to the Mongols, although Eljigidei was in effect asking Louis to implement one of Chinggis Khan's edicts (*yasas*). And it should further be noted that he twice addressed Louis as 'son', implying that the King was of lower rank; Chinggis Khan had similarly addressed the Muslim Khwārazmshāh in the diplomatic exchanges that preceded the Mongol invasion of Western Asia.[16]

It was, however, the oral statements of the two emissaries – both Christians from the Mosul region – which appeared to offer the strongest grounds for optimism. They claimed not merely that Eljigidei was a Christian but that the qaghan Güyüg himself, whose mother was a Christian and the daughter of Prester John, had been baptized. Moreover, in order to avenge the injuries done to Jesus Christ by the Khwarazmians and other Muslims – a reference to the sack of Jerusalem in 1244 – Eljigidei planned to attack Baghdad in the summer of 1249, and the envoys urged King Louis to invade Egypt in the spring so that the Sultan would be unable to send help to the Caliph. It is instructive to compare these statements, which the Legate took care to pass on to Pope Innocent, with other versions that reached Western Europe. Jean Sarrasin reported that the Mongols wanted King Louis to invade Egypt to prevent the Sultan and the Caliph assisting each other.[17] For Matthew Paris, the 'Tartar King' had sent Louis an encouraging message, urging him to attack the Muslims and offering swift and effective aid.[18] Many years later, Joinville would likewise ascribe the embassy to the 'Great King of the Tartars' and would describe the Mongols as offering to help the crusaders recover the Holy Land and the kingdom of Jerusalem from the Muslims.[19] Although some elements in the crusading army were deeply sceptical that anything good might come from the 'faithless' and 'inhuman' Mongols [**doc. 59**], the news of Eljigidei's overture evidently created a sensation in Western

13 Ibid., vol. 4, pp. 607–8 (trans. Giles, vol. 2, p. 214; trans. Vaughan, p. 94).

14 Salimbene de Adam, *Cronica*, vol. 1, p. 321.

15 Peter Jackson, *The Mongols and the West, 1221–1410* (Harlow, 2005), pp. 100, 174.

16 David Morgan, *The Mongols* (Oxford, 1986), p. 68.

17 Jean Sarrasin, in 'Rothelin', p. 570, reading *ne pourroient il aidier li unz l'autre* for *se pourroient* ..., as adopted by the editor (trans. Shirley, p. 69).

18 Matthew Paris, *Chronica Majora*, vol. 5, p. 87 (trans. Giles, vol. 2, p. 319; trans. Vaughan, p. 193).

19 Joinville, §§ 133, 471, pp. 74, 258 (trans. Hague, pp. 57, 144; trans. Shaw, pp. 197, 282):

Europe.[20] In the fourteenth century, when the idea of collaboration with the Mongols against the Mamluk regime was well-established, two crusade propagandists would see Eljigidei's embassy as presaging these amicable relations and would derive encouragement from it, since at this early date the Mongol attitude to the Christian West had been more uncompromising.[21]

It is possible that Louis and his advisers would not have attached as much credence to Eljigidei's letter and his envoys' assurances had they not appeared to be confirmed by the tone of a letter from the Armenian Constable, Smbat, received a few weeks earlier, around the time of King Louis's arrival in Cyprus,[22] and similarly incorporated in Eudes's report. Smbat had been sent by his brother, King Het'um I, on an embassy to convey to the Mongols the submission of the Christian kingdom of Lesser Armenia. His letter, addressed to his brother-in-law, the King of Cyprus, among others, testified to the destructive and demoralizing impact of the Mongol conquests on the Islamic world and to the existence of large numbers of eastern Christians throughout the Mongol empire. This incidental corroboration may have persuaded Louis and the legate to send back to the Mongols an embassy of their own, headed by the Dominican Friar André de Longjumeau and carrying a portable chapel and other gifts.[23]

Any expectations raised by Eljigidei, however, were disappointed when André de Longjumeau's party rejoined the King in 1251,[24] bringing with them an ultimatum in the more familiar style of Mongol diplomacy, which instructed Louis to send gold and silver annually as tribute. André's report has not survived, and we are dependent for the Mongol response on Joinville, who again speaks of the 'Great King of the Tartars' when in fact the letter came from Güyüg's widow, the regent Oghul Qaimish. But there is nothing implausible in his claim that Louis's overture had been interpreted as an act of submission and has been deployed as a means of intimidating other rulers who were not yet subject to the Mongols. Nor have we any reason to doubt Joinville's assertion that the French king greatly regretted having sent envoys to them.[25] It was precisely to avoid giving a similarly submissive impression that the

20 The Mongol general's letter was inserted both in Vincent de Beauvais's *Speculum Historiale* and in 'Annales Sancti Rudberti Salisburgenses', in *MGHS*, vol. 9, p. 790. For the arrival of the news of the conversion of the 'Tartar King' in the West, cf. also Matthew Paris, *Chronica Majora*, vol. 5, p. 80 (trans. Giles, vol. 2, p. 314; trans. Vaughan, p. 188).

21 Guillaume Adam, *De modo Sarracenos extirpandi* (*c*. 1318), in *Recueil des Historiens des Croisades. Documents arméniens*, vol. 2 (Paris, 1906), p. 535. Raymond Étienne ('Pseudo-Brocardus'), *Directorium ad passagium faciendum* (*c*. 1332), ibid., p. 504.

22 As Vincent de Beauvais, *Speculum Historiale*, ed. Johann Mentelin (Straßburg, 1473), xxxii, 91, makes a point of mentioning.

23 The evidence (such as it is) relating to this embassy and its composition is discussed by Paul Pelliot, 'Les Mongols et la papauté: chapitre 2 (suite)', *Revue de l'Orient Chrétien*, 28 (1931–32): 3–84 (here 37–54, 67–77 = pp. 175–92, 205–15 of the separatum).

24 While the king was fortifying Caesarea: Joinville, § 470, p. 258 (trans. Hague, pp. 143–4; trans. Shaw, p. 282). The author of 'Rothelin', p. 624 (trans. Shirley, p. 109), heard that they had been detained in Aleppo on their return through northern Syria.

25 Joinville, §§ 490–92, pp. 268, 270 (trans. Hague, pp. 148–9; trans. Shaw, pp. 287–8).

Franciscan William of Rubruck, setting out to take the Gospel to the Mongol world in 1253 and carrying a letter from King Louis that requested safe-conduct on his behalf, would be at pains to stress that he was not the king's ambassador.[26]

What was the purpose of the embassy? The importance that Eljigidei attached to it is perhaps highlighted by the date of his letter, which corresponded to May 1248 – some months before Louis even left France. We know that his commission from the late qaghan Güyüg was to administer the territories of 'Rūm [Anatolia], Georgia, Aleppo, Mosul, and Takāvor [Lesser Armenia], in order that no one else might interfere with them'.[27] It seems that the qaghan was primarily concerned about the influence of his cousin Batu in these regions. From his base in the Pontic and Caspian steppes, Batu had extended his authority over the general Baichu, who was in overall command of the Mongol forces in Persia,[28] and one of Eljigidei's first actions had been to arrest Batu's representatives in the Transcaucasus.[29] But Güyüg had died in April 1248, even before Eljigidei's embassy reached the French King, and it is highly probable that the Mongols in the Near East were by now anxious about the advent of the crusade. In his report Carpini had drawn attention to the Mongols' diplomatic subterfuge: they would deal leniently with powers which adjoined states that they had not yet subjugated and of which they were somewhat afraid, in order to ensure that these more distant powers did not enter the fray against them.[30] And King Louis's army, hovering on the fringes of the Islamic Near East, would certainly have appeared worth cultivating. A few years later, William of Rubruck, visiting the Mongols of the Pontic steppe, would find that Louis enjoyed greater prestige there (this despite his failure in Egypt) than did the Emperor.[31] Simon de Saint-Quentin,

---

26 William of Rubruck, *Itinerarium*, i, 6, ix, 1, xix, 5, and xxviii, 2, in *Sinica Franciscana*, ed. Anastasius Van den Wyngaert, vol. 1 (Quaracchi-Firenze, 1929), pp. 168, 188, 213, 244; trans. Peter Jackson and David Morgan, *The Mission of Friar William of Rubruck: His Journey to the Court of the Great Khan Möngke 1253–1255*, Hakluyt Society, 2nd series, 173 (London, 1990), pp. 66–7, 97, 131–2, 172. See also the editors' introduction, ibid., pp. 43–4; Jean Richard, 'Sur les pas de Plancarpin et de Rubrouck: la lettre de saint Louis à Sartaq', *Journal des Savants* (1977), pp. 49–61, reprinted in his *Croisés, missionnaires et voyageurs. Les perspectives orientales du monde latin médiéval* (London, 1983).

27 Juwaynī, *Ta'rīkh-i jahān-gushā*, ed. Mīrzā Muḥammad Qazwīnī, Gibb Memorial Series, new series 16 (Leiden and London, 1912–37), vol. 1, p. 212; trans. J. A. Boyle, *The History of the World-Conqueror* (Manchester, 1958, reprinted in one volume 1997), vol. 1, p. 257.

28 Ibn al-ʿAmīd, *Kitāb al-majmū' al-mubārak*, ed. Claude Cahen, 'La "Chronique des Ayyoubides" d'al-Makīn b. al-ʿAmīd', *BEO*, 15 (1955–57): 108–84 (here 130); trans. Anne-Marie Eddé and Françoise Micheau, *Al-Makīn ibn al-'Amīd. Chronique des Ayyoubides (602–658/1205–6–1259–60)* (Paris, 1994), p. 25. See generally Peter Jackson, 'Bāyjū', *Encyclopaedia Iranica.*

29 See Peter Jackson, 'Eljigidei (2)', *Encyclopaedia Iranica.*

30 Giovanni di Pian di Carpini (Plano Carpini), *Ystoria Mongalorum quos nos Tartaros appellamus*, vii, 8, ed. Enrico Menestò et al., *Storia dei Mongoli* (Spoleto, 1989), pp. 288–9, and trans. in *The Mongol Mission: Narratives and Letters of the Franciscan Missionaries in Mongolia and China in the Thirteenth and Fourteenth Centuries*, ed. Christopher Dawson (New York, 1955), p. 41.

31 William of Rubruck, xv, 3, p. 201 (trans. Jackson and Morgan, p. 115).

who had accompanied Innocent IV's envoy Ascelin on an embassy to the Mongol general Baichu in 1247–48, tells us that their hosts repeatedly questioned them about the date when the crusading army would arrive in Syria. In Simon's view, their aim was merely to dupe the Westerners by simulating friendliness towards Christians and thus to deflect the crusading army away from territories, like Aleppo and Anatolia, which lay within their immediate sphere of operations.[32] Certainly Mongol concern about Frankish intervention here would have been borne out later, when a body of French serjeants crossed to Cilicia in anticipation of a struggle between King Het'um and the Seljüks[33] and Louis himself despatched 600 crossbowmen to aid the Prince of Antioch against the Türkmen.[34]

THE LONG-TERM AIMS OF THE CRUSADE: THE EGYPTIAN STRATEGY

In keeping with the conception of the crusade that we may call the 'Egyptian strategy', and which was by now well established,[35] Louis appears to have had in mind the permanent occupation of at least the Nile delta and possibly of the whole of Egypt. For this we have more, fortunately, than the questionable testimony of a letter found in Matthew Paris's *additamenta*, claiming that the King had brought to Egypt even the wherewithal to cultivate the soil [**doc. 61**]. Greater weight certainly attaches to the assertion of the Master of the Temple that Louis planned the conquest of the entire country [**doc. 60**]. And a still more substantial piece of evidence is the charter drawn up on the French King's own behalf in November 1249, which determined the endowment of the cathedral church of Damietta [**doc. 64**]. This was the church to which Joinville refers as 'the Church of Our Lady'.[36] In itself the charter is an unusual and highly valuable document since, as its most recent editor points out, no earlier charter relating to the foundation of any other Latin see in the East has come down to us.[37] The very fact that a Christian cathedral had been established and endowed strongly suggests that a short-term occupation of Damietta was not in view; and the King confirms this by speaking more than once of 'perpetuity'. The Muslims, too, appear to have been convinced that the crusaders aimed at the conquest of Egypt and, for what it is worth, the 'Rothelin' chronicle imputes this belief to them.[38]

---

32 Simon de Saint-Quentin, ed. Richard, pp. 97–8 (= Vincent de Beauvais, xxxii, 41: the view expressed is conceivably an interpolation by Vincent).

33 Joinville, § 143, pp. 78, 80 (trans. Hague, p. 59; trans. Shaw, p. 200).

34 Eudes de Châteauroux to Innocent IV [**doc. 56**], p. 76 below; hence Vincent de Beauvais, xxxii, 96.

35 See Joshua Prawer, 'Crusader security and the Red Sea', in his *Crusader Institutions* (Oxford, 1980), pp. 471–83 (here pp. 482–3).

36 Joinville, § 181, p. 98 (trans. Hague, pp. 68–9; trans. Shaw, p. 209).

37 Jean Richard, 'La fondation d'une église latine en Orient par saint Louis: Damiette', *BEC*, 120 (1962): 39–54 (here 39), reprinted in his *Orient et Occident*.

38 Ibn Wāṣil [**doc. 73**], p. 141 below. 'Rothelin', p. 597 (trans. Shirley, p. 91); and cf. also p. 599 (trans. p. 92) for the probable consequences of the crusaders crossing the Ushmūn Ṭannāḥ.

The language of the foundation charter, notably its use of the phrase 'when this land is liberated', indicates that the crusaders attached no little importance to the fact that Egypt had once been under Christian rule and still contained a Christian population. This same perspective emerges from other contemporary documents. Gui of Melun alludes to the fact that Christians had long ago openly worshipped in Damietta,[39] and the Templar Master writes of restoring the country to Christian worship [**doc. 60**]. The crusaders evidently saw Egypt as a land at one time in Christian hands; it was incumbent upon them to wrest it from the Muslims who had conquered it five centuries previously. During the Fifth Crusade, Jacques de Vitry, Bishop of Acre, in what is possibly the fullest exposition of the thinking behind the 'Egyptian strategy', had articulated a similar rationale for the invasion of Egypt, alluding also to the fact that the infant Jesus had been taken to Egypt when his life was threatened by Herod.[40]

It is noteworthy, moreover, that Louis envisages a future time in which the country will be under the rule of someone else 'in our stead' and that the document is witnessed, significantly, not by barons of the Frankish East but only by three great officers of the French Crown. What is implicit here, clearly, is that Louis regarded Damietta as his by the law of conquest. Just as in 1190, in advance of the Third Crusade, Philippe Augustus had agreed with Richard Coeur-de-Lion to divide equally any conquests they might make without reference to the King of Jerusalem,[41] so Philippe's grandson would exercise full rights over any territories acquired in the course of his own expedition. It may be telling, in this context, that the charter is completely silent about the capture of Damietta in 1219, during the Fifth Crusade, when it had been assigned to Jean de Brienne as King of Jerusalem. Although the 'Rothelin' chronicle suggests that the cathedral church was established by King and Legate jointly,[42] and the charter itself refers to 'the customs of the East', Damietta was to be treated as a Capetian possession and any claim of the absent Conrad, as King of Jerusalem, was to be ignored (although Louis seems in other contexts to have been very scrupulous regarding Conrad's rights). There would, in consequence, be no question of using the city as a bargaining-counter in order to secure the return of Jerusalem and other lost territories of the kingdom of Jerusalem. This was in sharp contrast with developments in 1219, when the campaign had been vitiated by dissension between King Jean and the Legate Pelagius over war aims – whether to proceed with the capture of Cairo or to make a treaty with the Sultan whereby Damietta would be exchanged for territories in Palestine.[43] In 1249, of course, Louis

39 Matthew Paris, *Chronica Majora*, vol. 6: *Additamenta*, p. 160 [**doc. 59**].

40 Jacques de Vitry to Pope Honorius III, 21 Sept. 1218: *Epistolae*, no. 4, ed. R. B. C. Huygens, *Lettres de Jacques de Vitry (1160/70–1240) évêque de Saint-Jean-d'Acre* (Leiden, 1960), p. 102.

41 R. C. Smail, 'The international status of the Latin Kingdom of Jerusalem, 1150-1192', in P. M. Holt (ed.), *The Eastern Mediterranean Lands in the Period of the Crusades* (Warminster, 1977), pp. 23–43 (here p. 31).

42 'Rothelin', p. 594 (trans. Shirley, p. 89).

43 See Powell, *Anatomy of a Crusade*, pp. 160–61, 164–5; a different interpretation (more hostile to Pelagius) in T. C. Van Cleve, 'The Fifth Crusade', in Wolff and Hazard, *The Later Crusades*, pp. 409–10.

benefited from the fact that he was in unchallenged command of the crusading forces and that he enjoyed a good working relationship with the Legate Eudes.

And yet it is far from certain that a permanent occupation of Egypt was in Louis's mind from the very outset of the campaign. In this connection the date of the foundation charter may be significant. It was drawn up in November – after the arrival of Alphonse and after the council of war, described by Joinville, in which the rival merits of Alexandria and Cairo were debated.[44] It is difficult to explain the lapse of five months between the capture of Damietta and the establishment of the cathedral church except on the grounds that during the summer Louis and his advisers were still open to the possibility of a diplomatic bargain. That Alexandria seemed a natural goal to some crusaders might well be inferred from the implausible claim that the crusading fleet was blown to Damietta after setting a course for Alexandria [**doc. 59**].[45] Both Gui of Melun and the Templar Master [**doc. 60**] make it clear that the rival merits of Alexandria and Cairo were discussed over the summer. We should note, incidentally, that the choice between the two objectives was not necessarily one between the use of major cities as a bargaining-counter and the permanent occupation of all or part of Egypt.[46] Whichever longer-term strategy had been in view, the seizure of Alexandria – Egypt's most important port, which William of Tyre more than sixty years previously had called 'a general market for two worlds'[47] – would itself have been seen as a vital stage in the reduction of the country.

All the contemporary documents translated here that describe the rapid fall of Damietta agree in seeing it as an unmistakable sign of God's favour. To have been spared the trials of protracted siege operations, of the kind that their precursors on the Fifth Crusade had been obliged to sustain for eighteen months, demonstrated, in the eyes of Louis and his troops, that Christ stood alongside His army as it embarked on the struggle with the Muslims.[48] We do not find in these sources any recognition that Damietta had in fact fallen *too* swiftly: that in view of the imminence of the Nile floods (July–October) the crusading army was now condemned to spend several enervating months in Damietta before it could move onto the next phase of the campaign. This long wait would only sap its morale. And – worst of all – the overwhelming joy and gratitude evinced by the crusaders following their unlooked-for triumph in June 1249 would make the grief and despair that accompanied the abject collapse in March–April 1250 all the more poignant.

---

44 Joinville, § 183, p. 100 (trans. Hague, p. 69; trans. Shaw, p. 210).

45 See note 118 below.

46 As Strayer, 'The crusades of Louis IX', p. 497, seems to suggest.

47 William of Tyre, *Historia*, xix, 27, ed. R. B. C. Huygens, *Guillaume de Tyr. Chronique*, Corpus Christianorum Continuatio Mediaevalis, vols 63–63A (Turnhout, 1986), vol. 2, p. 903, *forum publicum utrique orbi*; cf. the translation by Emily Atwater Babcock and A. C. Krey, *A History of Deeds Done Beyond the Sea, by William Archbishop of Tyre* (New York, 1943; repr. New York, 1976), vol. 2, p. 336.

48 Cf. also Joinville, § 165, p. 90 (trans. Hague, p. 64; trans. Shaw, p. 206).

THE INVASION OF EGYPT

The story of the Egyptian campaign is well known.[49] In November the King and his forces, reinforced now by Alphonse of Poitou, set out upstream with the intention of advancing on Cairo. For several weeks they were held up on the banks of one of the Nile tributaries, the Baḥr al-Ṣaghīr or Ushmūn Ṭannāḥ (the 'Tanais', as the French called it),[50] and unable to cross in the face of powerful Muslim opposition; their catapults were under constant attack from Greek Fire, and their efforts to build a causeway were unavailing. Then, on 7 February 1250, someone variously described as a Muslim deserter or as a Bedouin revealed the existence of a ford. At dawn on the following day the vanguard, commanded by Robert of Artois, led the way across the river and took the Muslim camp by surprise; the Egyptian commander Fakhr al-Dīn, among others, was cut down, and many of the Muslims in the camp were massacred. Fortified by another unexpectedly swift triumph and seeking to capitalize on it before the enemy could regroup, Robert disregarded his brother's orders and rashly charged into the town of Mansura, where he and his men, lacking the support of infantry and crossbowmen, were at a disadvantage amid the buildings and the narrow streets and were annihilated. The situation was only partly retrieved when the King and the main army, having crossed the river, occupied the site of the Muslim encampment and repulsed the enemy. Both sides then dug in once more. But following the arrival of the new Sultan, Tūrān Shāh, the Muslims launched ships on the Maḥalla canal, which were thus able to enter the main branch of the Nile and to intercept Frankish vessels bringing provisions from Damietta. Their supply-lines cut, the crusaders were further assailed, during the ensuing weeks, by a number of diseases, principally scurvy and dysentery. Louis himself succumbed, and it was decided to retreat to the safety of Damietta on 5 April. Pursued by the Muslim forces, the crusaders were surrounded on land near Fāraskūr, while most of their ships were seized by the crews of Egyptian galleys. The King and his staff were taken prisoner; only a handful of the more prominent leaders, including the Legate Eudes and the Patriarch of Jerusalem, got through to Damietta.

Joinville has been accused of turning Robert of Artois into the scapegoat for the failure of the crusade, which was a foregone conclusion in any case.[51] Louis himself, of course, is not made to decry his brother's conduct in Joinville's version of events: one cannot fail to be struck by the contrast with the King's reaction (as described by Joinville) to the indiscipline of Gautier d'Autrèche, who had broken ranks at Damietta and sallied forth alone against a Muslim squadron, only to be cut down.[52] Neither Louis's letter to his subjects in France a few months later [**doc. 70**] nor the Patriarch of Jerusalem's letter to the Cardinals [**doc. 68**] criticizes Count Robert; for the King, the turning-point in the campaign is Tūrān Shāh's arrival at Mansura,

49 See Strayer, 'The crusades of Louis IX', pp. 98–104.

50 For Joinville, this is the 'Rexi' (Rosetta) branch of the Nile: § 191, pp. 104, 106 (trans. Hague, p. 71; trans. Shaw, p. 213).

51 Robert Irwin, *The Middle East in the Middle Ages: The Early Mamluk Sultanate 1250–1382* (London and Sydney, 1986), pp. 20–21.

52 Joinville, § 176, p. 96 (trans. Hague, p. 67; trans. Shaw, pp. 208–9).

while the Patriarch identifies it as the onset of disease in the wake of the battle. Yet it should be noted that sources other than Joinville draw attention to the Count's heedlessness and indiscipline.[53] In view of the size of the crusading army, and with no hope of reinforcements, the Franks simply could not risk heavy losses in a single engagement so far from their ultimate goal, Cairo. Still less could they afford to be further weakened by disease.

The Patriarch tells us that approximately two-thirds of the entire crusading army perished between the departure from Damietta in November 1249 and the end of March 1250 [**doc. 68**], that is, as a result of the fighting at Mansura and of the outbreak of disease, but prior to the bloody engagement in which King Louis was finally compelled to surrender. Joinville believed that 300 knights had perished with Robert of Artois and that the Templars had lost 280 horsemen.[54] Matthew Paris has Robert being followed by a third of the army in his advance on Mansura;[55] while a letter which he reproduces alleges that the force which perished there with Robert totalled almost 1000 knights and 7200 other combatants, and that in the final engagement 2300 horsemen and 15,000 others were killed or taken prisoner.[56] Joinville gives the suspiciously round figure of 10,000 for the prisoners.[57] These latter figures are not totally at variance with those in the Muslim sources. Ibn Wāṣil [**doc. 73** below] gives the Franks' losses at Mansura as 1500 horsemen;[58] Saʿd al-Dīn [**doc. 74(e)**] supplies the slightly higher figure of 1600, while Ibn al-ʿAmīd says that Robert of Artois was accompanied by 1400 horsemen.[59] The numbers given by Muslim authors that relate to the final encounter are more diverse and probably less reliable: Saʿd al-Dīn [**doc. 74(h)**] puts the total slain at 7000 and the number of captives at 20,000, while Ibn Wāṣil furnishes a total of 30,000 for those killed.

From the fragmentary deposition of Charles of Anjou [**doc. 71**], which covers the retreat from Damietta, the eventual surrender, the brief captivity of the crusade's leaders and their negotiations with the Muslims, we learn a good deal that is not available elsewhere: the abortive efforts of various nobles to obtain their release and the King's prohibition of such individual negotiations; the pretexts offered for their action by the Sultan's murderers when they came to King Louis's tent; the dispute among the Frankish barons as to who should be left as a hostage until the first instalment of the ransom had been paid and Damietta had been surrendered to the Muslims; and Charles's desire to stay with Louis in Palestine. In some measure, of

53 Matthew Paris, *Chronica Majora*, vol. 5, pp. 147–51, 165 (trans. Giles, vol. 2, pp. 367–70, 382; trans. Vaughan, pp. 239–42, 253); see also **doc. 67** (though this letter is itself taken from the *Chronica Majora*). In 'Rothelin', pp. 604–5 (trans. Shirley, pp. 95–6), the rash speech is attributed to knights in the Count's force but Robert is nevertheless clearly in sympathy with them.

54 Joinville, § 219, p. 120 (trans. Hague, p. 78; trans. Shaw, p. 219).

55 Matthew Paris, *Chronica Majora*, vol. 5, pp. 148, 166 (trans. Giles, vol. 2, pp. 367, 383; trans. Vaughan, pp. 240, 253).

56 Ibid., vol. 5, p. 158 (trans. Giles, vol. 2, p. 376; trans. Vaughan, p. 247).

57 Joinville, § 333, p. 180 (trans. Hague, p. 107; trans. Shaw, p. 246).

58 The same figure is given by Abū Shāma, *al-Dhayl 'alā'l-rawḍatayn*, ed. M. Z. al-Kawtharī as *Tarājim rijāl al-qarnayn al-sādis wa'l-sābi'* (Cairo, 1366 H./1947), p. 183.

59 Ibn al-ʿAmīd, p. 159 (trans. Eddé and Micheau, p. 86).

course, we must treat this evidence with caution: regarding his departure for France in 1250, for instance, it is hardly likely that Charles would have given a version of events that cast him in a poor light.

The King's initial plan, on reaching Acre, was to take ship for France in September [**docs 68, 70**]. It soon became clear, however, that the amirs were failing to release the prisoners, in breach of their oath; and this raised the further possibility that the truce by no means guaranteed the security of the kingdom of Jerusalem. In a series of meetings during June, therefore, Louis consulted the French and, it seems, the Palestinian barons as to the best course of action. Joinville depicts himself as virtually a lone voice in favour of remaining in the East, among a large majority who sought to return to France.[60] At one time it was assumed that there is a discrepancy between Joinville's account of this meeting and the accounts in other sources, namely the King's own letter of August 1250 and the 'Rothelin' chronicle, which speak of a majority view that the King should stay in Palestine.[61] But it has been demonstrated that we can discount 'Rothelin', which derives its information from Louis's letter and in this context is therefore not a first-hand source, and that the King's testimony and the Seneschal's can be reconciled.[62] Joinville was indeed in a minority among the French barons,[63] most of whom would accompany the King's brothers back to the West in the autumn; but Louis's letter, written in his capacity as the crusade's leader, makes no distinction between the French and the Syrian and Palestinian magnates and lumps them together.

DOCUMENTS 56–72

56. Eudes de Châteauroux, Cardinal-bishop of Tusculum and papal legate, to Pope Innocent IV, 31 March 1249, in Spicilegium sive Collectio Veterum Aliquot Scriptorum qui in Galliae Bibliothecis Delituerant, *ed. Luc d'Achéry, new edn by Étienne Baluze and L. F. J. de la Barre (Paris, 1723), vol. 3, pp. 624–8*[64]

To the most holy father and lord, Innocent, by God's grace Supreme Pontiff, Eudes, by God's mercy Bishop of Tusculum, [offers] devoted kisses of his blessed feet, with all manner of obedience, reverence and honour. Among the things that have befallen the Christian army during its stay in Cyprus since I wrote to Your Holiness, I have seen fit to report the following to you.

60 Joinville, §§ 422–30, pp. 230, 232, 234 (trans. Hague, pp. 130-2; trans. Shaw, pp. 269–71).

61 H.-François Delaborde, 'Joinville et le conseil tenu à Acre en 1250', *Romania*, 23 (1894): 148–52.

62 For what follows, see Alfred Foulet, 'Joinville et le conseil tenu à Acre en 1250', *Modern Language Notes*, 49 (1934): 464–8.

63 As Louis's own words indicate: Joinville, § 432, p. 236 (trans. Hague, p. 133; trans. Shaw, p. 271).

64 D'Achéry's text has been checked against the version of the letter found in Bibliothèque Nationale ms. lat. 3768, fols 76v–81r.

On the Friday [23 October 1248] after the feast of St Luke, the Viscount of Châteaudun[65] and several other knights landed in Cyprus. After some days a quarrel arose at the Devil's prompting, [p. 625] between the Viscount and his ship's crew. The Viscount's crossbowmen were responsible for killing two on the Genoese side, of whom one was a man of status and good birth. The Viscount himself, moreover, under what influence I do not know, sought, after a discussion with the Count of Montfort,[66] to sail across to Acre, and many knights with him. But on learning of this the King of France restrained him and the other knights from doing so; for it could have brought about the dispersal of the entire army, and impeded the business of Christendom. Yet since the Viscount wanted at all costs to carry out his intention, the King had his own galleys armed and prevented the ships' captains from trying to take the Viscount or his associates any distance whatsoever. At this the Viscount changed tactics, taking possession of the ship and everything in it, and claiming that according to the contract drawn up between them and the ship's masters both the vessel and all its contents were his by right. It was finally proposed, through the French King's mediation, that the parties should entrust the case to two good men and the King should appoint a third. But the parties would not agree, with the result that the dispute could not be resolved at this juncture.

During this period there went the way of all flesh my lord Guillaume de Merlet the elder, my lord Guillaume de Barre, the Count of Montfort, the Lord of Duech, the Castellan of Burgues, and several other knights.

Around this time the Master of the Temple[67] and the Marshal of the Hospital wrote to the King that the Sultan of Babylonia[68] had arrived in the Gaza region with a large army in order to win over the Sultan[69] of Aleppo and Damascus, and they were afraid that he planned perhaps to besiege Jaffa or Caesarea. The Master subsequently wrote further to the King, saying that he had been visited by one of the Sultan's amirs. However, he did not come on the Sultan's behalf – or so he claimed – and did not carry a letter from him: he had come to ascertain the French King's intentions, since his sovereign would gladly make peace with him. According to some, it was at the Master's own request that the Sultan had sent the amir to him, which greatly displeased the King and all the barons. The King wrote at once to the Master, forbidding him to receive in future any more such envoys, or to dare to talk with them, without his own express authorization. For everyone who was familiar with the Syrian situation was saying that, however hard pressed the Christians were, they never took the initiative in proposing a truce, but did so only when they had received an urgent request for one from the Turks; and by virtue of the Master's having been the first to propose a truce the Christians' position had been weakened,

---

65 Geoffrey VI, who would be killed in Egypt on 6 February 1250.

66 Jean I, son and successor of Amaury, Constable of France (d. 1241).

67 Guillaume de Sonnac (1247–50): see below, note 129.

68 'Babylon' and 'Babylonia' are the most common terms for Egypt (and sometimes for its capital) in medieval Latin sources: see M. M. Alexandrescu-Dersca, 'Babylone d'Égypte', *Revue Historique du Sud-Est Européen*, 20 (1943): 190–201.

69 The text has the plural *soldanos* in error. At this time Damascus was in the hands of Ayyūb's lieutenants, and al-Nāṣir Yūsuf ruled only Aleppo: he did not acquire Damascus until the summer of 1250, after the murder of Ayyūb's son and successor, Tūrān Shāh.

particularly since the Turks could infer from this that the King regarded himself as inferior to them in strength and was in a hurry to make any sort of truce and return home.

Around this time the French King was visited by envoys of the Prince of Antioch[70] and also of the King of Armenia, bringing him gifts from their masters. The Patriarch of Antioch[71] and the Prince also sent envoys to the King and myself, informing us by letter that shortly before the Turcomans had invaded the Antioch region in very considerable numbers and had done great damage to Christendom in terms both of lives and of property. For this reason they begged the King to send them aid as swiftly as possible. The King sent them 600 crossbowmen: he was unwilling to send knights, from fear that the army might break up and that it would prove impossible to reassemble it at the scheduled time.

Around the feast of St Nicholas [6 December 1248] a quarrel broke out in Famagusta between the crews of the royal galleys and the King's serjeants, and some of the serjeants were killed. The King hurried there and had a number from either side arrested, so that he could learn who was responsible for this outrage.

During this period the King and Queen were staying in Nicosia, while the knights were scattered in villages all over the island. The Queen has recovered from the illness she had been suffering.

Around this time the King sent official envoys to the Prince of Antioch and to the King of Armenia, to make peace between them, or at least to arrange a truce.

At this time, too, the Marshal of the Hospital informed the King that the Sultan of Babylonia and the Sultan of Aleppo had angrily parted company without making a truce, and that the Sultan of Aleppo was planning to send envoys to the King to arrange a truce in the near future.

On the Monday [14 December 1248] after the feast of St Lucia, the envoys of the King of the Tartars landed at Castrochernia,[72] which lies six leagues from Nicosia, and entered Nicosia on the Saturday before Christmas [19 December]. They appeared before the King on the following day, and presented him with this letter, written in the Persian language and in Arabic characters, of which the King had a translation made word for word.[73] It read as follows:

> 'In the power of the Most High God, the word of Erchalchai,[74] representative of the Kan, the World-King, to the great king of many territories, the mighty bulwark of the world, the sword of Christianity, the victory of the faith of baptism, the defender of the law of

70 Bohemond V (1233–1253).

71 Opizo dei' Fieschi, a nephew of Pope Innocent IV. He had probably been appointed in 1247, and may have remained patriarch until after the fall of Antioch to the Mamlūks in 1268: Bernard Hamilton, *The Latin Church in the Crusader States, I: The Secular Church* (London, 1980), pp. 231–7.

72 Kyrenia (Cérines).

73 The translator may well have been the Dominican André de Longjumeau, who according to Jean Sarrasin (in 'Rothelin', p. 570; trans. Shirley, p. 68), subsequently acted as interpreter when Louis and the papal legate interviewed the envoys.

74 Eljigidei.

the Evangelist, [our] son[75] the King of France – may God extend his domain, preserve for him his kingship for many years, and fulfil his desires both sacred and profane, now and in the future, through the truth of the Divine Guide of mankind and of all the prophets and apostles, amen. A hundred thousand greetings and blessings. I ask that he accept these blessings, that they may find favour with him. May God grant that I see this magnificent king who has landed, and may the Creator Most High cause us to meet one another in charity and bring it about with ease that we are united as one.

'He should know, after this greeting, that our intention in this letter is nothing other than the advantage of Christendom and, should God grant it, the strengthening of the hand of the king[76] of the Christians. I ask God to bestow victory on the troops of the king of Christendom and make them triumph over his enemies who despise the Cross.

'We are come on behalf of the exalted King – namely, at present Kiokan[77] (may God exalt him; may God increase his magnificence) – in power and with the edict that all Christians be free from slavery, tribute, *corvées*, tolls and the like; that they should enjoy honour and reverence, and that no man should touch their property; that churches that are destroyed are to be rebuilt; that they may beat their tablets,[78] and no one may dare to prevent them praying for our kingdom with a calm and willing heart. We are come here this very hour for the advantage and protection of Christians, so the Supreme God grant it.

'We are sending this by the hand of our faithful envoy, the venerable Sabeldin Mousfat David, and of Markus, so that they may proclaim this good news and pass on by word of mouth what is happening around us. Let [our] son accept and trust what they say.

'In his letter the World-King (may his magnificence increase) decrees as follows: "In the law of God, let there be no distinction between Latin, Greek, Armenian, Nestorian, Jacobite, and all who worship the Cross, for they are all as one among us." And so we ask the magnificent king not to distinguish between them, but that his mercy and kindness [p. 626] extend to all Christians. May his mercy and kindness be abiding. And it will be well, so God Most High grant it.

Dated the end of Muḥarram [646 H. = May 1248].'

Your Holiness should know too that at the time that I and the King first entered Cyprus, the King of Cyprus and the Count of Jaffa presented the King with a letter which ran as follows:[79]

---

75 *Filius* here corresponds to the Persian *pisar* ('son'): for this slightly patronizing form of address, see above, page 66 and note 16.

76 Reading with the ms. here, as also in the next line, *regis* for the *regum* of D'Achéry's edition.

77 Güyüg Khan, who had been elected *qaghan* in 1246. He had in fact died in April 1248, but it appears that, at the time of writing in the following month, Eljigidei had not yet learned of this event.

78 Striking a wooden or iron tablet or board with a hammer was the means traditionally employed in the Eastern Church for summoning the faithful to divine service, since the use of church bells had been prohibited by the Muslim authorities: Jean Dauvillier, in Paul Pelliot, *Recherches sur les Chrétiens d'Asie centrale et d'Extrême-Orient*, ed. Dauvillier (Paris, 1973), pp. 155–6.

79 A critical edition of Smbat's letter, utilizing ms. lat. 3768, is given in Jean Richard, 'La lettre du Connétable Smbat et les rapports entre Chrétiens et Mongols au milieu du XIIIème siècle', in Dickran Kouymjian (ed.), *Études arméniennes in memoriam Haïg Berbérian* (Lisbon,

'To the high and mighty lord H[enry], by God's grace King of Cyprus, to the most noble and mighty lady, my sister E[meline], by the same grace of God Queen of Cyprus, and to the noble lord J[ohn] of Ibelin, my dearest brother, and the noble lady, my dearest sister Maria: greetings from Sembath, Constable of Armenia, and a love that stands ready for your commands.[80] Let me inform you that I am safe and in health and am eager to hear and learn that you are also. Know, my lords, that as I especially subjected myself to a journey for God and for the advantage of Christendom, so Jesus Christ has been my guide as far as a town called Saurequant.[81]

'But what should I say or write to you of the many countries I have seen, given that we have left India behind us to the west,[82] and passed through Baudach and the whole of its territory two months after setting out on our journey? And what should I say of the many cities I saw abandoned, which the Tartars have destroyed and whose wealth and size no man could calculate? For we saw three towns, each one three days' journey in extent. We saw more than a hundred thousand amazingly large heaps of dead men's bones, men slain by the Tartars. And indeed it seems to us that if God had not brought here the Tartars, who have destroyed the heathen in this fashion, there would have been enough of them to fill up and take over all the land on this side of the sea. We crossed one of the rivers of Paradise, which the Scripture calls Gion,[83] greater than we have ever seen, since its bed extends on either side for a good day's journey.

'As for the Tartars, you should know that they are so countless that no one could calculate their number, very accurate and fine archers, terrible in appearance and very diverse of face; we could not describe their practices to you in writing. But should God vouchsafe me life, so that with divine assistance I may see you safe and sound, I shall tell you everything by word of mouth. It is now eight months that we have been on the move day and night, and we are told that at present we are half-way through the journey between our territory and that of the Khan, namely the chief ruler of the Tartars. Concerning our errand, all those we meet, both Tartars and others, tell us that we shall be uncommonly successful. We have learned for a fact that it is now five years since the Khan died who was the father of the current one,[84] and the Tartar barons and knights have so spread themselves throughout [different] countries that in those five years they have scarcely proved able to assemble in one place in order to enthrone the Khan. For some of them were in India, others in the land of Chata,[85] others in the land of Russia, and others in the

---

1986), pp. 683–96 (here pp. 688–92), and reprinted in Richard, *Croisades et États latins d'Orient: Points de vue et documents* (Aldershot, 1992). I have translated from this edition rather than from D'Achéry's text.

80 Emeline, Smbat's sister and the wife of King Henry of Cyprus, is also sometimes called Stephanie. Jean d'Ibelin (d. *c.* 1266), Count of Jaffa, the husband of another sister, Maria, is the celebrated jurist. For these persons, see Count W. H. Rüdt-Collenberg, *The Rupenides, Hethumides and Lusignans: The Structure of the Armeno-Cilician Dynasties* (Paris, [1963]), Table III (H2).

81 Samarqand: Richard suggests that the original read *Samequant*.

82 Reading, as Richard proposes, *ad ponantem* for the *ad pontem* of the text.

83 Smbat is here speaking of the River Oxus, known to the Muslims as the Jayhūn.

84 Güyüg's father Ögödei, who had died in December 1241.

85 'Cathay', that is, northern China; later the term would be extended to cover the entire country.

countries of Chascat[86] and of Tanghat,[87] which is the land from which the Three Kings came to Bethlehem to worship the Lord Jesus at His birth.[88] You should know that Christ's power has been, and still is, great: the peoples of that country are Christians, and the whole of the land of Chata believes in the Three Kings. I myself have been in their churches and have seen paintings of Jesus Christ and of the Three Kings, one offering gold, another incense and the third myrrh. It is through these Three Kings that they believe in Christ and through them that the Khan and all his men have now become Christians. They have their churches in front of their gates, and sound their bells and beat their tablets, with the result that those who go to visit their lord the Khan have first to visit the church and salute the Lord Jesus Christ and only then go and salute their lord the Khan, whether they are Christians or Saracens, and those who disapprove of this [do it] willy-nilly.

'Let me tell you that we have found many Christians scattered throughout the East, and many fine churches, tall and old and well constructed. They had been razed by the Turks, with the result that the Christians of that country appeared before this Khan's grandfather,[89] who gave them a most honourable welcome, conferred enfranchisement upon them, and issued orders prohibiting anyone from saying or doing whatever might justifiably distress them even a little. Consequently, the Saracens, who used to inspire them with fear, now receive back what they did [then] twice over. And since, as our sins required, there was a dearth of preaching, and Christ did not have people to preach His most holy Name on his behalf in those parts, He Himself preaches and has preached on his own behalf by means of His most holy powers, as you will be able to learn the more clearly, in such a way that the peoples of those parts believe in Him. You should know that in my opinion those whose task it is to preach deserve to be severely punished.

'You should know besides that there is in the land of India, which was converted by the Apostle St Thomas, a Christian king, who used to be very apprehensive because he was surrounded by other, Saracen kings who attacked him from all sides, until the point when the Tartars entered that territory and he became their liegeman. He took his own army and Tartar troops, and fell on the Saracens. He obtained as a result so much booty within India that the whole of the East is full of Indian slaves:[90] I have seen more than 50,000 of them, whom this king had captured and ordered to be sold. I could not tell you a twentieth of what we have seen; but from a fraction of it, you can grasp the major part.

---

86 Kāshghar.

87 Probably Tangut, that is, the former empire of Hsi-Hsia in north-western China (*c.* 982–1227).

88 For the development in the East of the story of the Three Wise Men (subsequently metamorphosed into kings) who did reverence to the infant Jesus (Matthew, ii, 1–12), see Ugo Monneret de Villard, *Le leggende orientali sui Magi evangelici*, Studi e Testi, vol. 163 (Vatican City, 1952); more generally, Richard C. Trexler, *The Journey of the Magi: Meanings in History of a Christian Story* (Princeton, NJ, 1997).

89 Chinggis Khan (d. 1227).

90 These sparse details may possibly relate to an episode described by Carpini, *Ystoria Mongalorum*, v, 12, pp. 258–9 (trans. in Dawson, *The Mongol Mission*, pp. 22–3): here Prester John repulsed a Mongol army that had invaded 'Greater India' by sending against them mounted warriors made of copper in which fire had been ignited and fanned by bellows. Large numbers of Indians are known to have been enslaved during the Mongol campaigns of the 1240s and the 1250s: a high proportion of them were exported to Iran. See Peter Jackson, *The Delhi Sultanate: A Political and Military History* (Cambridge, 1999), pp. 236–7, for references.

'You must know that the lord Pope has sent his ambassador to the aforementioned Khan, and told him to say whether he was a Christian or not, why he had despatched his people to trample the world underfoot, and why he was causing poor folk to be killed. To this the Khan replied that God had commanded him and his forebears to send their people to destroy wicked nations. As to the question whether he was a Christian, he replied that God knew, and if the lord Pope wished to know he should come and see and learn [for himself].

'My beloved, the things I have written to you are reliable reports. What I ask from the Lord is that my letter finds you safe and sound. Farewell, etc. Pray God on my behalf, etc.

'Dated 7 February [1248] in the great city of Saurequant.'

Having received Erchelchai's letter, the King that day made enquiries, in my presence and that of his council and certain prelates, how their master had heard of the King's arrival; where the Tartars had come from, and what was the impulse behind their coming; why they were called Tartars; what territory they now dwell in; whether the Great King has a large army; for what reason and in what way he had adopted the Faith, how many years have passed since his baptism, and whether many had been baptized with him. The King also asked about Erchalchai: since what point he had received the sacrament of baptism, and whereabouts he was now. Likewise, why had Bachon given our envoys such a poor reception?[91] He asked similarly about the Sultan of Mosul[92] (which in ancient times was called Nineveh), whether he was a Christian; and again, from what parts the envoys themselves had originated, and for how many years they had been Christians.

[p. 627] Their replies to these questions were as follows. The Sultan of Mosul had forwarded to the Great King Khan a letter which he had received from the Sultan of Babylonia and in which the Sultan of Babylonia referred to the French King's arrival and disembarkation. (He claimed falsely to have seized sixty of the French King's vessels by force of arms and to have brought them to Egypt, seeking by this means to prove that the Sultan of Mosul ought not to rely upon the French King's coming.) Having in this way learned of the French King's arrival, Erchalchai has sent to him envoys with the letter given above. They informed him that the Tartars' plan is to besiege the Caliph of Baldak this coming summer, and asked the King to invade Egypt, to prevent any help reaching the Caliph from the Egyptians. The envoys also stated that it is now forty years since these people who are now called Tartars emerged from their country, which contains no cities, towns or villages, but plentiful pasturelands, for which reason the people of those parts are engaged solely in rearing livestock. It lies forty days' journey from the territory where the Great King Khan now lives and in which he has established his residence.[93] And the country is called

91 A reference to the difficulties encountered by the papal embassy headed by the Dominican Ascelin of Lombardy, who spent several weeks at Baichu's headquarters in the summer of 1247: see Igor de Rachewiltz, *Papal Envoys to the Great Khans* (London, 1971), pp. 115–18.

92 Badr al-Dīn Lu'lu' (d. 1259).

93 For the itinerary followed by Ögödei, and Güyüg after him, in the vicinity of Qaraqorum and the Orqon basin, see J. A. Boyle, 'The seasonal residences of the Great Khan Ögedei', in Georg Hazai and Peter Zieme (eds), *Sprache, Geschichte und Kultur der altaischen*

Trahetar, and hence they are even today called Tartars. The envoys said that they were unaware of the reason for their emigration, but said that the Tartars first of all overcame the son of Prester John, putting him and his troops to the sword. The Tartars had no religion.

They said, moreover, that the Great King of the Tartars has with him almost all the commanders, together with a countless number of cavalry, men and animals. They remain constantly in tents, since no city could accommodate them. Their horses and livestock are always in pasture, because they cannot find barley or straw in sufficient quantities for their mounts. The commanders despatch their men in armies which are sent out to subjugate countries, while they themselves remain with the Great King. The Great King has the authority and the inclination, when someone dies, to install as king one of his sons or nephews. The envoys further declared that the man who currently wields the sceptre, named Kiokan, had a Christian mother, the daughter of the king who is known as Prester John,[94] and it was at her urging, and that of a most holy bishop called Malassias,[95] that he underwent the sacrament of baptism at Epiphany along with eighteen sons of kings and many others, mainly commanders. There are nevertheless many among them who have not yet accepted the sacrament of the Faith. Erchelchai, who sent these envoys, has been a Christian for several years already. He is not of the royal blood, but for all that he is a man of importance and authority: he is at present operating on the eastern borders of Persia. As for Bachon, he is a pagan who has Saracen advisers, which is why he gave your envoys a poor reception. But he no longer enjoys such authority, for nowadays he is under the orders of Elchelchai. Regarding the Sultan of Moyssac or Mosul, they assert that he was the son of a Christian woman, and that he privately favours Christians. He keeps their festivals and does not observe any part of the religion of Mahomet: it is believed that if he had the opportunity, he would willingly become a Christian. The envoys said that they were natives of a city that lies two days' journey from Mosul (formerly called Nineveh), and that they and their forebears were Christians. They further said that the Supreme Pontiff's name was well known these days among the Tartars, and that it was the intention and plan of their master Elchelcai to attack the Caliph of Baldak this coming summer and to avenge the wrong done to the Lord Jesus Christ by the Khwarazmians.[96]

Völker. Protokollband der XII. Tagung der Permanent International Altaistic Conference 1969 in Berlin (Berlin, 1974), pp. 145–51, and reprinted in Boyle, *The Mongol World-Empire 1206–1370* (London, 1977). Güyüg's own appanage, which he had inherited from his father, and where he resided until his election as qaghan, lay further west, in the region of the town of Emil and the River Qobuq.

94 To the best of our knowledge, Güyüg's mother, Töregene, was not a Christian. The allusion to Prester John is curious, given that the burgeoning reputation of this mythical potentate was largely due to his celebrated 'letter', a twelfth-century forgery originating in Western Europe; but it may indicate that rumours about him were also current among Eastern Christians.

95 Otherwise unknown.

96 A reference to the sack of Jerusalem and the massacre of most of its Christian population in August 1244.

On the 8th Kalends of February [25 January 1249] the envoys were given leave by the French King to depart, and they left Nicosia on the 6th Kalends of that month [27 January], accompanied by the Friars Preachers André, Jean and Guillaume, whom the King is sending to the Tartar king with gifts, namely a cross made from the wood of the life-giving Cross, a tent of scarlet, on which are embroidered most accurately scenes of what the Lord Jesus Christ suffered in His Body for our sake; and other items pertaining to the Divine worship and designed to induce the [Tartar] king [to participate in it].[97]

I myself despatched letters to the King Chan, to his aunt,[98] to Elchelcai, and to their prelates, informing them that the Holy Roman Church will rejoice to hear of their conversion to the Catholic faith, and will gladly welcome them as beloved sons, provided, however, that they prove willing to maintain the orthodox creed and confess that she is the mother of all the churches; that he who presides over her is the Vicar of Jesus Christ, and that obedience to this Vicar is rightly due from all who are reckoned to profess Christianity. The prelates are given the same summons in my letters: that they should all recognize this and that there should be no schism among them, but that they should abide in the truth of the faith as proclaimed in the first general councils and approved by the Apostolic See.

At Epiphany [6 January 1249] I catechized 57 Saracen prisoners. Although there was no obligation to set them free, as they were expressly informed,[99] they nevertheless kept asking urgently for the sacrament of the Faith. And after I had baptized thirty of them with my own hand, I went on to meet a procession of Greeks on some river. In the presence of the French King, the King of Cyprus and myself, they acknowledged that there was one God, one Faith and one baptism, and that what they practised they did to commemorate the baptism of the Lord Jesus by John on this day in the waters of the Jordan. They confessed upon dipping the cross in the water, and said nothing except 'The Father [is] Light, the Son [is] Light, the Holy Spirit [is] Light.' They offered up intercessions there and then for Your Holiness; but they would not pray for Vastachius,[100] since you had excommunicated him.

On the Friday [15 January 1249] following the octave of Epiphany, the lord Archambaud de Bourbon went the way of all flesh.

On Quinquagesima Sunday [14 February 1249], when the King's representatives arrived in Acre to fetch the transports, they were unable by any means to induce the Genoese and the Venetians to put a reasonable price on their vessels. In fact, their

97 Joinville, § 471, p. 258 (trans. Hague, p. 144; trans. Shaw, pp. 282–3), mentions the tent of scarlet, containing illustrations of events from the Annunciation down to the coming of the Holy Spirit, and chalices, books and everything necessary for the celebration of Mass; see also § 134, p. 74 (trans. Hague, p. 57; trans. Shaw, p. 198).

98 Ögödei's sister, Altalun, who was subsequently executed on the charge of having poisoned him, though in the Persian sources there is some confusion between her and the Kereyid princess Ibaqa: Jackson, *The Mongols and the West*, p. 72.

99 Pope Gregory IX had ruled in 1237 that Muslim slaves who sought baptism did not thereby lose their servile status: Benjamin Z. Kedar, *Crusade and Mission: European Approaches to the Muslims* (Princeton, NJ, 1984), pp. 147–9.

100 John III Ducas Vatatzes, Emperor of Nicaea (1222–54).

purpose seemed, rather, to be that the enterprise be ruined if they were not given the freight sum they desired.

At this juncture there arose in Acre, at the Devil's prompting, a serious dispute between the Genoese on the one hand and the natives and the Pisans on the other, and one of the Genoese consuls was struck by an arrow and killed.[101]

Around the same time peace was effected between the Sultans [p. 628] of Babylonia and Aleppo through the mediation of the envoys of the Caliph of Baldak,[102] and the Babylonians withdrew from the siege of La Chamelle.[103]

On the Friday [19 March 1249] preceding Passion Sunday, the King and I sent a second time to Acre, [namely] the venerable fathers the Patriarch of Jerusalem and the Bishop of Soissons,[104] the Count of Jaffa, the Constable of France[105]and my lord Geoffrey de Sergines,[106] regarding the matter of the ships and to settle the quarrel that had broken out. But I do not know what they have achieved.

The Count of Vendôme[107] went to the Lord on the Saturday [27 March] before Palm Sunday, and it is said that since the army entered Cyprus 260 knights have died.[108] In all this may God be blessed.

The King has decided to enter Egypt around mid April,[109] God permitting. Holy Father, pray to God on behalf of His army, which is ready and willing to fight and to bear all adversity cheerfully for the honour and reputation of Jesus Christ. Let Your Holiness see to what he thinks will further this holy and godly enterprise. And be assured that from the legacies and redemptions of crusading vows beyond the sea I did not receive 100 *livres tournois*: the money from the redemption of vows beyond the sea did not amount to 300 *livres*.

May God preserve Your Holiness for His Church safe and sound for long to come.

Dated Wednesday before the Lord's Resurrection, in Cyprus.

---

101 This dispute is mentioned also in 'Estoire de Eracles', p. 437 (trans. in Shirley, *Crusader Syria*, p. 137), where it is said to have lasted for 28 days, and in 'Annales de Terre Sainte', p. 442 (version 'A'), with 21 days.

102 See Ibn Wāṣil [**doc. 73**], p. 128 below.

103 *Camelae*, that is, Ḥimṣ.

104 The Patriarch of Jerusalem was Robert de Nantes (d. 1254). Gui de Chastel-Porcien, bishop of Soissons (1245–50), would be killed at Mansura.

105 Humbert de Beaujeu.

106 Geoffrey de Sargines (d. 1269), mentioned frequently by Joinville, had been Louis's vassal since 1236, and would command the force which Louis left in the Holy Land on his departure in 1254, subsequently becoming in turn seneschal and regent (*bailli*) of the kingdom of Jerusalem. Rutebeuf devoted a poem to his exploits: *Onze poèmes de Rutebeuf concernant la croisade*, ed. Julia Bastin and Edmond Faral (Paris, 1946), pp. 22–7. For a brief biography, see Jonathan Riley-Smith, *What Were the Crusades?*, 3rd edn (Basingstoke, 2002), pp. 77–80.

107 Pierre.

108 Vincent de Beauvais, xxxii, 89, and others who followed his account give the figure as 240. The large number of deaths on Cyprus (including specifically Count Jean of Dreux) is mentioned also by Matthew Paris, *Chronica Majora*, vol. 5, pp. 92, 93 (trans. Giles, vol. 2, pp. 323–4; trans. Vaughan, p. 197).

109 In the event, the fleet first put to sea on Ascension Day (13 May).

57. Robert, Count of Artois, to Queen Blanche, 23 June 1249, in Matthew Paris, Chronica Majora, *vol. 6:* Additamenta, *pp. 152–4; this text reproduced in* Lettres françaises du XIIIe siècle, *ed. Alfred L. Foulet, Les classiques français du moyen âge (Paris, 1924), pp. 16–18 (references are to the pagination of the* Chronica Majora*)*

To his most excellent and dearest mother B[lanche], by God's grace illustrious Queen of France, Robert, Count [p. 153] of Artois, her devoted son, greetings and a ready will, in filial love, to do her pleasure.

Since we are aware that you rejoice greatly at the good fortune of ourselves and ours, and at the fine successes which have befallen the Christian people when you gain certain news of them, Your Excellency should know that our dearest brother the King, the Queen, her sister[110] and ourselves are, through God's grace, enjoying full bodily health. It is our fervent desire [to hear] the same of you. But our dearest brother, the Count of Anjou, is still experiencing his quartan ague, though more mildly than usual. Your Benevolence should know that our dearest lord, our brother, the barons and pilgrims, who wintered in Cyprus, embarked on their ships in Limassol harbour late on Ascension Day, in order to move against the enemies of the Christian faith. They left the port and with the Lord's guidance, following many trials and adverse winds at sea, they arrived around midday on the Friday [4 June 1249] after Trinity, and dropped anchor. That same day there was a meeting in the lord King's ship to deliberate what should be done next, since they saw before them Damietta and its harbour, garrisoned by a great number of Turks, both horse and foot, and the mouth of the river, which lay close at hand, [guarded] by a great many armed galleys. At this council it was decreed that the next morning everyone should, to the best of his ability, disembark with the lord King. Your Ladyship should know that just as it had been commanded, on the Saturday morning the Christian army left the large ships and manfully equipped, embarked in the galleys and smaller vessels.. Trusting in God's mercy and in the help of the triumphant Cross, which the lord Legate carried in a vessel alongside the lord King, and deriving joy and strength from God, they drew near to land in the face of the enemy, who were making numerous attacks by firing arrows and [p. 154] other [projectiles]. But when the vessels were unable to reach dry land because the sea was too low, the Christian army, in God's name, left their vessels, leaped into the water and penetrated with their arms to the dry land on foot. And although that mass of Turks defended the shore against the Christians, nevertheless, through the favour of Our Lord Jesus Christ, the Christian people occupied the shore in safety and joy, making a great slaughter of horses and Turks, including some who were said to be of high rank. When the Saracens withdrew into the city, which was very strong both because the river lay in between and because it was surrounded by mighty walls and towers, Our Lord Almighty, 'Who giveth to all men liberally and upbraideth not',[111] on the following day, namely the octave of the Trinity [6 June 1249] around the third hour [9.00 a.m.], without any human effort, made over the city to the Christian people, while the infidel Saracens took flight and

110 Beatrice of Provence (d. 1267), wife of Charles of Anjou and sister of Queen Marguerite.

111 James, i, 5.

abandoned it. This was done by the gift of God alone and by the bounty of the Lord God Almighty. You should know that these Saracens left the city furnished with a great abundance of provisions and meat and engines and other good things, of which the greater part has been kept for the city's maintenance; and from that portion the troops have drawn considerable sustenance.

The lord King stayed there with his army, having his goods unloaded from his ships; and we believed that the army ought not to leave there until the river subsided, which was then due, we were told, to cover the country, for the Christian people suffered much harm in that region on the previous occasion.[112]

The Countess of Anjou gave birth on Cyprus to a son who was extremely handsome and well made,[113] and put him out to nurse there.

Dated in the year of the Lord 1249, the month of June, on the eve of the blessed John the Baptist, in the camp at Damietta.

58. Jean de Beaumont, royal chamberlain, to Geoffrey de la Chapelle, Damietta 25 June 1249, in Comte [P.] Riant, 'Six lettres relatives aux croisades', AOL, *1 (1881): 383–92; this text reproduced in* Lettres françaises du XIIIe siècle, *ed. Foulet, pp. 18–20 (page references are to Riant's edition)*

[p. 389] Jean de Beaumont,[114] chamberlain of France, to his particular friend, Sire Geoffrey de la Chapelle, steward[115] of France, greetings.

You have been sufficiently informed, we believe, of the stay which the lord King and his army made in Cyprus. You should know that the lord King, my lady the Queen, the Counts of Artois and Anjou, the Countess of Anjou, ourselves and our sons Gui and Guillaume, are through God's grace in good health and spirits, and we wish to hear the same of you.

The lord King, his brothers, the barons and the rest put out to sea on Ascension Day [13 May 1249], in order to head for Egypt, with the Lord as their guide, and with God's aid to besiege Damietta. But while it is only three days' voyage from Cyprus to Damietta given favourable weather, we nevertheless remained at sea for twenty-three days,[116] as it pleased the Lord, before reaching our goal, Damietta harbour. So great a fleet left the port of Limassol in Cyprus with the lord King that it is believed such a fleet has not assembled at one time on any previous occasion. The larger ships were estimated at 120 or more; the smaller vessels at 800 or more.

With the Lord as our escort, the greater part of us put in at Damietta harbour on the Friday after Trinity, namely the 2nd Nones of June [4 June 1249], cheerful and in good spirits. And on the following day, a Saturday, at first light, the King, his brothers, the barons and knights and the rest, both serjeants and crossbowmen,

112 During the Fifth Crusade: see Powell, *Anatomy of a Crusade*, pp. 188–90.

113 Charles of Salerno, later King Charles II of Naples (d. 1309).

114 Jean de Beaumont (d. *c.* 1252), is mentioned on occasions by Joinville; he was even deemed sufficiently important to be the recipient of a papal letter in 1247 (Berger, no. 3044).

115 *pannetarius*.

116 Joinville supplies different dates for the events of May–June 1249: his inaccurate chronology is explained in Monfrin, 'Joinville et la prise de Damiette', pp. 274–5.

having heard the hours and divine service, left the large ships and entered the lesser vessels – that is, the galleys and other small craft – which they brought up to the shore in order to land. But when they approached land, they could not bring the vessels right in to the shore; and so the lord King, the barons and knights, and all the rest, without any expression of fear and with glad hearts, waded into the water up to their chests, holding their lances and crossbows, and fell manfully upon the enemies of the Cross like strong athletes of the Lord. The armed Saracens, stationed mounted on the shore, disputed the land with us and defended it with all their strength. They dedicated themselves to resistance, maintaining a dense fire of javelins and arrows against our men. And yet our men, their operations directed by Christ the Lord, manfully pushed on and set foot on the land despite the Saracens. [p. 390] With the Lord's help our men prevailed, and the infidel Saracens were in a short space vanquished and put to flight. Many of them, both great and lesser, were killed, and many more mortally wounded; but of our men, preserved by God, there perished few or none.

And thus the Saracens left the shore in confusion, and the Lord struck such fear into their hearts that on the following day – Sunday – all of them, from the greatest to the youngest, took flight and abandoned the city. They set fire to houses and gates at various points around the city, so that the smoke from the burning city told us of the Saracens' confusion and flight. In this fashion Jesus Christ made over to the Christians an impregnable city, to the honour of His Holy Name and the exaltation of the Catholic faith.

The knights from the kingdom of France at present in the army are reckoned at more than 1900, while those from Syria and Cyprus, from the Temple and the Hospital, and from other regions on this side of the sea are put at 700; and there are many others in the army, whom the knights there present put at 3000.

Dated the year of Our Lord 1249, on the day [25 June] after the blessed John the Baptist.

59. Gui, a household knight of the Viscount of Melun [late in 1249], to Master B. de Chartres, in Matthew Paris, Chronica Majora, *vol. 6:* Additamenta, *pp. 155–62*

Better evidence of the capture of Damietta To his beloved uterine brother and dear friend, Master B. de Chartres, student at Paris, Gui, knight of the household of the Viscount of Melun, greetings and a ready will to do his pleasure.

Since we know that you are concerned about the condition of the Holy Land and of our lord the King of France, as much for the sake of the fortunes of the universal Church as on account of the great number of our kinsfolk and friends serving under the lord King of the French, we have seen fit to inform you more fully of what is rumoured among the common people. When we sailed eastwards from Cyprus, after holding a special council, it was our plan to take Alexandria; but within the next few days we were carried by an unexpected storm a vast distance across the sea, and many of our ships were scattered and cut off from one another.[117] The Sultan of Babylon

117 This storm is referred to briefly by Joinville, § 147, p. 82 (trans. Hague, pp. 60-1; trans. Shaw, p. 201), and in the letter of Jean Sarrasin (in 'Rothelin', p. 571; trans. Shirley, p. 69).

and other Saracen leaders were meanwhile informed by spies of our intention to take Alexandria,[118] and so they gathered an immense number of armed men from among the populations of Cairo, Babylon, and Damietta as well as Alexandria, and waited for our arrival, in order to receive us at swordpoint when we were exhausted. And so, after a night in which we were carried by a violent wind across a wide stretch of sea, in the morning the wind subsided and the calm arose that we longed for, enabling the dispersed fleet successfully to reassemble. We therefore sent up to the top of our ship's mast, namely as the look-out, an experienced climber, who was familiar with all the coasts on this side of the sea and many languages on this side of the sea as well, and who acted as our faithful guide, so that he might tell us if he sighted land and where on earth we were. When he had carefully scanned and thoughtfully regarded all our surroundings, he cried [p. 156] out in astonishment: 'God help us! God help us now, for only He can. Here we are before Damietta!' We were now all in a position to examine the coast. The look-outs on the other ships gave a similar verdict, and they all began to gather together. On learning of this, the lord King, with undaunted spirit, began splendidly to put heart into all of his men and to reassure them, saying as he stood in the midst: 'My friends and vassals, if we remain undivided in love, we shall be unconquered. It is not contrary to God's will that we have been so unexpectedly conveyed here. Let us disembark on these shores, however strongly they are guarded. I am not the King of France; I am not the Holy Church: it is surely you who are the king, and you who are the Holy Church. I am only one individual whose life, when God wills it, will be snuffed out like any other man's. For us, every outcome means deliverance: if we are defeated, we fly forth as martyrs; if we are victorious, the glory of the Lord will be proclaimed and that of all France – indeed of Christendom – will be enhanced. Surely it is madness to believe that the Lord has roused me to no purpose. He Who provides everything has through this designed a mighty business. Let us fight on Christ's behalf, and He shall triumph in us, giving the glory, honour and blessing not to us but to His Own Name.'

In the mean time our ships were already collected and were drawing near the shore, with the result that the citizens of Damietta and those who were on the shore were in a position to contemplate our fleet, namely 1500 ships, not counting those that had been scattered, which numbered 150. And in truth, there was never assembled in our days, we believe, such a great host of noble ships. The people of Damietta were therefore stunned and beyond words amazed and panic-stricken. They sent towards us four very fine galleys with their most nimble corsairs, to reconnoitre and ascertain who on earth we were and what our aim was. [p. 157] When we saw them approach so close that they could distinguish our standards, they faltered and ceased to make such haste as before, as if they had gained the intelligence they were sent for and were about to retire unharmed. But they were meanwhile surrounded by our galleys and swift boats, which cut them off, and they were forced, against their will, to draw close to our ships. Our men, seeing the lord King's steadfastness

118 Gui's letter is not the only evidence that Alexandria was envisaged as the goal at this stage. Curiously, the same claim is also found in Jean de Garlande, *De triumphis ecclesiae*, p. 131: *ad urbem tendit Alexandri, sed negat unda viam*. Matthew Paris refers to the 'diversion' again later: *Chronica Majora*, vol. 5, p. 139 (trans. Giles, vol. 2, p. 360; trans. Vaughan, p. 233).

and unwavering resolve, at his bidding made ready for a naval battle, so as to seize these and any others that might come up; and his orders were to occupy the shore by force and go on land. We therefore hurled at them incendiary darts and stones from the ships' mangonels, which were so fashioned as to fire five or six stones at once from a distance, and phials full of lime, to be discharged at the enemy by bows through small shafts, in the same way as arrows. The corsairs and their vessels were therefore pierced by the darts and crushed by the stones, and blinded by the lime from the smashed containers; with the result that three of their galleys were at once destroyed, though some of the pirates were rescued from drowning. But the fourth escaped, albeit not without damage. We subjected those we had [captured] alive to well-devised tortures, and extracted from them an admission of all the facts, namely that we were expected at Alexandria and that Damietta was emptied of its population. The corsairs who escaped, however, whose galley had been put to flight and some of whom were mortally wounded, reported with tearful howls to the men of Damietta, waiting for them in considerable numbers on the shore, that the sea was full of the fleet that was coming in, since the King of the French was approaching in hostile fashion with an immense body of nobles. In support of this they also claimed that Christ was evidently fighting against the Saracens, since he rained down upon them fire, stones and cloud. 'But while they are weak and exhausted from the buffeting of the sea,' [they said], 'you – as you cherish your lives and homes – must to a man attack and slaughter them, or [p. 158] at least effectively keep them at bay until our men are recalled. We alone barely escaped, to tell you of this and put you on your guard. We recognized the devices of the[ir] great men. See, they are already attacking us in their frenzy, inspired and equipped for a naval or land engagement.' As a result, fear and despondency overtook them.

All our men, once aware of the facts, were buoyed up to the pinnacle of hope, so that in groups they vied with one another in leaping from the ships into the boats, for the sea was rather shallow close in to the shore, so that neither the boats nor the small craft were able to reach dry land. Many, therefore, in accordance with the lord King's strict and most urgent command, hastily leaped into the sea up to their loins. And straight away there began a most bloody battle: our men joined those in front uninterruptedly, and the courage of the Gentiles was shattered. Nobody on our side fell by the sword except one; but two or three died by drowning, having plunged into the sea too hastily in their fervent eagerness to fight and thus perished at their own hands rather than those of others. The Saracens, therefore, of whom many had been killed and a great number mortally wounded or mutilated, withdrew into their city in cowardly flight. Our men would have followed hard on their heels, but were checked by the leaders, who were afraid of treachery. While we were fighting, however, some slaves and prisoners came out, having burst their chains and escaped from confinement, because even their gaolers had left to fight us; and in the city only women, children and the sick [remained]. These slaves and prisoners therefore joyfully hurried to meet us and cheered the King and his troops, saying, 'Blessed is he that cometh in the name of the Lord'.[119]

119 Luke, xiii, 35.

These events constituted an auspicious beginning, namely on Friday, the day of the Lord's Passion.[120] The lord King then landed in safety and in good spirits, as did the [p. 159] remainder of the Christian army, and thus we rested until the following day. But on the next day, a Saturday, we carefully occupied in force the land along the seashore that had yet to be taken, with the guidance and escort of the slaves, who were aware of even the little-used routes. That same night the Saracens, who had learned of the escape of some slaves and prisoners, dashed out the brains of those who remained, and thus made of them glorious martyrs of Christ – and their own damnation. Under cover of the following night and on the Sunday morning, the Saracens, reflecting on the numbers, courage and steadfastness of the approaching [enemy] and the unexpected emptiness of the city, and since they were without commanders, leaders, advisers, strength or weapons, took their women, children and movable possessions, and fled, lightly armed, through small gates on the far side of the city, which some time before they had had the foresight to make ready. And so they suddenly escaped, some by water and some by land, leaving the city replete with everything. On Sunday morning, at the third hour [9 a.m.], two slaves emerged who had by chance avoided the enemy's clutches, and informed us of what had happened. The King, therefore, casting aside all fear of treachery, made his entry into the city before the ninth hour [3 p.m.], not amid bloodshed or the clash of arms, but without any resistance. None of those who entered was even seriously wounded, apart from Hugues le Brun, Count of La Marche,[121] who has lost so much blood from his wounds that we do not think he can escape death. For in view of the disgrace he had incurred he squandered his life by recklessly charging into the thick of the enemy: of his own choice, being distrusted and not unaware of the fact, he was placed in the front rank of the troops. Nor should we fail to mention that when the Saracens planned to take flight, they launched at us powerful Greek fire in large quantities, which was extremely dangerous and deadly for us, since a strong wind blew from the city in our direction. But behold, the wind changed directly and spread fire over the [p. 160] city, which consumed many bodies and much of the fortress. It would have burnt more, but a few slaves who had remained behind came up in quick succession and put it out by means known to them and also by their prayers, which God granted in order that the Lord might not hand over to us a city in ashes.

On that day – truly the Lord's day – then, as we said above, the lord King entered Damietta amid the greatest jubilation, and went into the Saracens' temple there to pray and to attribute all these things, with good cause, to God. Before he took food, the faithful, having shed in their rejoicing tears of gladness and devotion, chanted with the greatest solemnity, and headed by the Legate, the hymn of the Angels, namely the *Te Deum laudamus*. And forthwith, where Christians long ago had been in the habit of celebrating Mass and ringing their bells, he purified the place and sprinkled it with holy water, before having the Mass of the Blessed Virgin celebrated.

---

120 An error: Good Friday had fallen on 2 April, whereas the crusading army landed on 4 June.

121 Hugues X, Count of La Marche and the husband of Isabella (d. 1246), who had previously been the consort of King John of England: he was thus stepfather to Henry III.

Here, three days earlier,[122] the prisoners categorically assured us, the most filthy Mahomet had been glorified with abominable sacrifices, cries from on high, and the blast of trumpets.

We found in the city an immense quantity of foodstuffs, weapons and engines, as well as precious garments, vessels and utensils of gold and silver, and other good things. And in addition to this, we at once had our own provisions, of which we had plenty, and other things which we valued and needed, brought from the ships. By the favour of the divine generosity, therefore, the Christian army was daily increasing, in the manner of a lake which is broadened as it is flooded by torrents. At one point, knights from the territories of my lord Villehardouin;[123] at another, reinforcements from the Temple and the Hospital; not to mention the arrival of pilgrims – each day, through God's grace, our support was on the increase. The Templars and Hospitallers, however, were for a long time unwilling to believe in the glory of such a great triumph; and in truth what happened was completely unbelievable. Since these things happened in miraculous fashion, especially the wind changing and throwing back their hellfire on their own heads (one of Christ's miracles of old, for it thus transpired [p. 161] at Antioch),[124] some were converted to the Lord Jesus Christ, and have until now faithfully adhered to us.

We for our part, though made secure by what has happened, shall proceed warily and carefully in our future operations. For we have alongside us the Eastern faithful, in whose trustworthiness we have full confidence, who know by experience almost all the regions of the East and their hazards and who in proof of their devotion have already undergone the sacrament of baptism.[125] Our nobles, therefore, when this was being written, carefully debated in council whether to attack next Alexandria or Babylon with Cairo.[126] What will come of this, we do not yet know; but while life remains, we shall notify you of what transpires. Hearing this news, the Sultan of Babylon proclaimed a general war against us, so that on the morrow [25 June 1249] of St John the Baptist, on a single day and in a place jointly agreed upon, we should put to the test the fortunes of war between the people of the East and those of the West, in other words between the faithful and themselves; and to whichever side fate allots victory, that side should be glorified while the vanquished humbly yield. To this the lord King replied, 'I do not offer this enemy of Christ my defiance on this or that day; nor do I appoint any date for peace. I defy him tomorrow and all the days

122 *quarta die precedente*.

123 Guillaume II de Villehardouin (d. 1278), Prince of the Morea (Achaea). His arrival is mentioned by Joinville, § 148, p. 82 (trans. Hague, p. 61; trans. Shaw, p. 201), who says, however, that he joined Louis during the sea voyage from Cyprus to Egypt, that is, as early as May 1249. See also **doc. 25** above.

124 I am unable to identify the allusion here.

125 In fact, the Coptic population of Egypt do not appear to have felt any marked partiality for the crusaders: see Françoise Micheau, 'Croisades et croisés vus par les historiens arabes chrétiens d'Égypte', in Raoul Curiel and Rika Gyselen (eds), *Itinéraires d'Orient. Hommages à Claude Cahen* (Bures-sur-Yvette, 1994), pp. 169–85.

126 This debate is mentioned briefly by Joinville, § 183, p. 100 (trans. Hague, p. 69; trans. Shaw, p. 210), though he alleges that it followed the arrival of Alphonse of Poitiers (in October 1249).

of my life, from now for evermore, until he has pity on his own soul and is converted to the Lord, Who desires all men to be saved and unfolds the bosom of His mercy to all those who are converted to Him.'

I am informing you of these events in writing by the hand of our kinsman Guiscard, who has no other object but to begin his promotion to a Master's chair at our expense and to find honourable lodgings for at least two years.

We have heard nothing for certain, or worthy to pass on, concerning the Tartars.[127] Nor do we hope for faith in the faithless, humanity in the inhuman, or charity in curs, unless God, for Whom nothing is impossible, brings about something unheard-of. But [p. 162] God has cleansed the Holy Land of the wicked Chorosmians, and has destroyed and utterly annihilated them from beneath the Heavens.[128] When we hear anything sure or noteworthy about the Tartars or any other matter, we shall inform you, either by word of mouth or by letter, through Roger de Montfage, who in the spring will be visiting the lands of our lord the Viscount in France, with a view to obtaining funds for us.

60. Guillaume de Sonnac, Master of the Order of the Temple,[129] *to Robert de Sandford, Preceptor of the Temple in England [1249], in Matthew Paris,* Chronica Majora*, vol. 6:* Additamenta*, p. 162*

Letter of the Master of the Knights of the Temple regarding the above Brother G[uillaume] de Senay, by God's grace Master of the Poor Knights of the Temple, to his beloved brother in Christ, Robert de Sandford, Preceptor in England, greetings in the Lord.

It is our desire to pass on to you in this letter happy and joyful news. You should know that on the Friday after Trinity last Louis, the illustrious King of the French, by God's grace put into Damietta harbour with his army. On the following Saturday this same Louis with his troops occupied the land along the coast, killing a great number of the heathen but with the loss of only one of our Christians. On the Sunday following, at the third hour [9 a.m.], the royal forces took the city of Damietta, after having utterly put to flight the heathen host. Damietta, then, has been captured, not through our deserts, nor by armed might, but through the workings of God's power and grace. You should know in addition that the lord King plans with God's grace to head towards Alexandria or Babylon, in order to liberate our brothers and several others who are kept in captivity and, with the Lord's aid, to return the entire country to Christian worship.

---

127 André de Longjumeau and his colleagues had left Cyprus for Eljigidei's headquarters in January 1249. According to Jean Sarrasin (in 'Rothelin', p. 624; trans. Shirley, p. 69), Louis had received word of their progress eastwards at mid-Lent.

128 A reference to the Khwarazmians' overthrow at the hands of the armies of Ḥimṣ and Aleppo in May 1246: see R. Stephen Humphreys, *From Saladin to the Mongols: The Ayyubids of Damascus, 1193–1260* (Albany, NY, 1977), pp. 284–7.

129 Joinville, § 270, p. 148 (trans. Hague, p. 92; trans. Shaw, p. 232), says that he lost one eye on Shrove Tuesday [8 February 1250] and the other in the fighting after Louis and the main army had crossed the Ushmūn Ṭannāḥ, as a result of which he died.

61. Gui de Burcey (passed on by Master Jean, a monk of Pontigny), in Matthew Paris, Chronica Majora, *vol. 6:* Additamenta, *p. 163*

With the capture of Damietta, the lord King of France has no anxieties, except that he does not have enough men to garrison and colonize the land he has occupied or has yet to occupy. But the King has brought with him ploughs, mattocks, drays and other farming equipment.[130] When this reached the ears of the Sultan of Babylon, he sent word to the King: 'Why have you had farming equipment brought here in order to cultivate our soil? I shall find you sufficient corn for the duration of your stay here.' This was a piece of irony, as if to say, 'You are a soft and delicate youth and will not be capable of a long stay among Easterners, but will melt away and die'. The lord King retorted, 'I made a vow and an oath to come here, and determined a date in advance, as I was best able. But I took no vow or oath to leave; nor have I set a date for my departure. This is why I have brought with me the tools of cultivation.'

Of all the ships, the lord King's put in first. His fleet included the large ships we call *dromones*,[131] totalling 120, not to mention the galleys and smaller vessels. And leaping nimbly from his ship, he fell forward on his face, praying most devoutly and with tears that God would guide his path and his actions.

62. Queen Blanche to Henry III, King of England [1249], in Matthew Paris, Chronica Majora, *vol. 6:* Additamenta, *pp. 165–7*

To our dearest cousin, the most excellent Henry, by God's grace illustrious King of England, Blanche, by the same grace Queen of France, greetings and sincere love in the Lord.

Since we are aware that you rejoice very greatly over the advantage and honour of the whole of Christendom, [p. 166] we have seen fit to impart to Your Excellency what Our Lord Jesus Christ has deigned to accomplish overseas at this time through our dearest son the King, his brothers, and the Christian army for the exaltation of the Christian faith and of His Own Name, in so far as we have learned of it from a letter of our son the King. Your Lordship should know, then, that when our son the King, his brothers and the army of the Christians accompanying them had agreed in council on the island of Cyprus to cross to Egypt and make for Damietta, they embarked on the Wednesday [19 May 1249] before Pentecost from Cyprus, where they had stayed for the whole of the winter, and on the Friday [4 June] following the Octave of Pentecost they sighted Egypt and shortly afterwards the city of Damietta. Approaching land, they took up position in the harbour close to the city and there dropped anchor. For the Saracens had put the shore in a state of defence with a numerous host of armed foot and horse, who, as the Christians emerged from the vessels and ships, stoutly

---

130 This is also mentioned in Matthew's narrative of the crusade: *Chronica Majora*, vol. 5, p. 107 (trans. Giles, vol. 2, pp. 334–5; trans. Vaughan, p. 209).

131 The Byzantine *dromon* was an oared war-galley: John H. Pryor, *Geography, Technology and War: Studies in the Maritime History of the Mediterranean, 649–1571* (Cambridge, 1988), pp. 58–60. The vessels referred to here were presumably based on the Byzantine model.

hurled projectiles and struck [at them] with swords. But God's grace prevailed, and the knights and serjeants of our son the King manfully occupied the shore, driving off the enemy and killing or mortally wounding many of them, including the more prominent among them. They pitched tent on the shore and invested the aforesaid city, few or none of the Christian army having been wounded. And to this auspicious beginning Almighty God added a more auspicious fulfilment. For that night and on the next day, a Sunday, the Saracens within the city, who were countless in number, were struck with terror by the power of God, and everybody – both the common folk and the grandees – left the city and took to flight, abandoning it after setting it on fire throughout. On learning of this, the Christian army at once entered the city; and once it had been cleansed of the corpses and carcasses to be found there, our dearest son the King, his brothers and all the Christian troops entered in procession with bare feet. The site of the [p. 167] mosque, which some time ago – when the city was previously captured – was the Church of the Blessed Virgin Mary, was reconciled and thanks were given there to God Most High, and the Legate celebrated Mass in honour of the Virgin. Although many of the provisions with which the city was abundantly furnished had been destroyed by fire, nevertheless a good deal remained, which will, we believe, be of great benefit to the Christian army. We wish Your Excellency to know that our son the King, our sons his brothers, the Queen, the wife of our son the King, and her sister the Countess,[132] with the son she bore in Cyprus,[133] are enjoying full bodily health. Please tell your beloved wife, the Queen of England, and give her our greeting.

63. Philippe, his chaplain,[134] *to Alphonse, Count of Poitou and Toulouse, 20 April 1250: T. Saint-Bris, 'Lettre adressée en Égypte à Alphonse, comte de Poitiers, frère de saint Louis',* BEC, *1e série, 1 (1839–40): 389–403*

[p. 394] To his very noble and very dear lord, Alphonse, son of a King of France, Count of Toulouse and Poitiers and Marquess of Provence, Philippe, his devoted chaplain: greetings from one entirely at his service and his wishes.

I received in Paris, on the Monday [21 February 1250] prior to the feast of Saint Mathias the Apostle, your letter, which you sent me via the King's messages closed and open, with joy and with great affection at heart, and from it learned of your arrival at Damietta,[135] of your health, and of the glad welcome given you by the King, your brothers and the barons, and was greatly cheered at heart. But for all that I was very much astonished and distressed by what befell you on Cyprus and by the fact that your passage was so delayed. Yet I believe for sure that Our Lord did it for

132 Beatrice of Provence, the wife of Charles of Anjou: see note 110 above.

133 Charles of Salerno: see note 113 above.

134 We possess another letter from Philippe, to King Louis in 1252 [**doc. 108**], and eight papal letters, from January 1249 and from March 1253 (Berger, nos 4295, 6419–6422, 6440, 6459, 6466), addressed to him as treasurer of the church of Saint-Hilaire at Poitiers, of which three are included in this volume [**docs 109–11**].

135 On 24 October 1249. He had left France on 25 August 1249: Richard, *Saint Louis*, p. 121 (French edn., p. 219); see also below, **doc. 72**.

your good and for the increase of the crown and of merit should you accept these trials, and others that you have endured or shall endure, humbly and with much patience, and dedicate everything you do, whether drinking or eating or all other actions, and do them to the honour of God, according to the Apostle's advice;[136] and I well believe that you have the will to do this and that Our Lord will grant you the strength for it.

And in accordance with the instructions that you have given me in your letter, I am informing you in this present letter of the news and the course of events that have occurred in France since your passage. Know, my lord, that [p. 395] on the very day when you set sail, as soon as I had lost sight of your ships, which caused me great unease and considerable anguish of heart, I left the port and travelled directly to Pontoise, to my lady the Queen, whom I found greatly cheered by the news she had heard, two days before I reached her, of the capture of Damietta. There was a good deal of rejoicing throughout France; and likewise in Paris and its neighbourhood the people engaged in great celebrations, processions, prayers and almsgiving, and humbly and devoutly praised Our Lord for it. When I reached my lady, I told her how long you had spent in the port, the day and hour of your departure, and the heavy expenditure that you had incurred; and I asked her on your behalf that she, as a mother, should take thought for your affairs, since all your trust and dependence was on her. She replied that she would do so most willingly. After this, it was only a short time before she heard news of the death of the Count of Toulouse, who had died, as I recall, on the eve [28 September 1249] of St Michael at Milhaud and had made a very fine end, so they said, and had duly made his will and set matters in order. This you can see from the will itself, which I am sending you, sealed with my own seal …[137]

[p. 400] … In addition, you should know [p. 401] that during Lent the King of England took the Cross, to set out within six years. But many people believe that he did it only in order to delay the journey of the English crusaders.[138] You should know that my lady the Queen sent to the Pope in order to secure their excommunication if they do not sail by the August passage. And this concession was obtained from the Pope…

Know that Earl Richard and his wife arrived in France during this Lent and went to Saint-Calmon, and from there Earl Richard made his way to the Pope, but I do not know for what reason. On his return he visited my lady in Melun, around three weeks from Easter, as did my lord Simon de Montfort, and the truce was discussed and renewed for five years from St. John's day[139] …

---

136 Cf. I Corinthians, x, 31.

137 The remainder of the letter is largely taken up with news from Alphonse's territories in France. Raymond VII of Toulouse was the father of Alphonse's wife Jeanne, and the residue of his county now passed to his daughter and son-in-law by the terms of the Treaty of Paris (1229).

138 Alan Forey, 'The Crusading vows of the English King Henry III', *Durham University Journal*, 65 (1973): 229–47 (here 232), reprinted in his *Military Orders and Crusades* (London, 1994), is sceptical, and attributes this view to Anglo–French rivalry.

139 Matthew Paris, *Chronica Majora*, vol. 5, pp. 97, 110–11 (trans. Giles, vol. 2, pp. 326, 337; trans. Vaughan, pp. 201, 212), mentions Earl Richard's visit to Blanche. Compare

[p. 403] This letter was written at Corbeil on the Wednesday after the third week of Easter.

64. Foundation charter of the cathedral church of Damietta, November 1249, ed. in Jean Richard, 'La fondation d'une église latine en Orient par saint Louis: Damiette', BEC, *120 (1962): 39–54; reprinted in Richard,* Orient et Occident au Moyen Age: contacts et relations (XIIe–XVe s.) *(London, 1976)*

[p. 52] *Charter of the church of Damietta*[140] In the name of the Holy and Indivisible Trinity: Amen. Louis, by God's grace King of the French:

If we were to direct our mind's eye towards the good things we have received at the Lord's hands, and towards our own inadequacy, we surely do not see how we can repay the gifts we have obtained with appropriate acts of gratitude, or in what way we may respond to so great and so magnificent a Giver for all the things He has granted us. For we could not give in return one thing for a thousand. Since, then, we are not adequate to extol such mighty works of God with fitting praise, we rise nevertheless to perform the acts of gratitude that are within our power. Among the blessings of God we have received, we recall in particular how in our own time, when we, albeit undeserving, arrived with the Christian army on the shores of Damietta – namely in the year of the Lord 1249, on the Saturday [5 June] preceding the feast of the Apostle St Barnabas – the aid of the divine clemency was so wondrously and powerfully with us that, when a very great multitude of infidel Saracens had gathered there to strive to oppose the landing of the Christian army, at last the power of God prevailed and the Christians, routing and putting to flight the enemy, successfully entered this country. And – what most clearly demonstrates the divine compassion – on the next day, the Sunday, the King of Virtues, Our Lord Jesus Christ, adding still more success to success, struck such terror into those within the city that with one accord they completely abandoned this most well-fortified city and turned tail, though nobody pursued them; and so we have received it at God's hand, emptied of enemies. And for this we are exceedingly glad and rejoice in the Lord.

To the praise and glory, then, of Our Lord Jesus Christ and of the glorious Virgin His Mother, through the aid of whose intercession so many blessings are believed to have befallen the faithful of Christ, certain ministers have been appointed to conduct the divine service in the principal Church of the Blessed Mary in this city, once it had been utterly purged of the pagans' filth. [p. 53] And we, whose particular desire it is that He Who has given everything and His most glorious Mother may be worthily and admirably served there, do grant the aforesaid church, in perpetual

---

Lloyd, *English Society and the Crusade*, p. 214; for the truce, see also Elie Berger, *Histoire de Blanche de Castille reine de France* (Paris, 1895), p. 382.

140 'Rothelin', p. 594 (trans. Shirley, p. 89), describes how, following the capture of Damietta, Louis and the legate installed an archbishop and canons in the cathedral (formerly the chief mosque) and allocated parts of the conquered city to the archbishop and canons and the various military and other religious orders; the 'barons and princes of the Holy Land' are also said to have been given 'rich and handsome residences'. The Archbishop was Gilles de Saumur (d. 1266), subsequently Archbishop of Tyre: 'Estoire de Eracles', p. 441 (trans. in Shirley, *Crusader Syria*, p. 139); 'Annales de Terre Sainte', p. 445 (version 'B').

alms, two towers together with the neighbouring dwellings, the structure which was known as the Mahomerie, and the courtyard that adjoins these towers, for the use of the Archbishops of the said church; and the compound that extends from the stone stairway ascending to the walls, and which is near the lesser tower of the Archbishop, as far as the street lying between the house which the Patriarch holds and the house of St Lazarus, along with all the dwellings and the courtyards included within it, for the use of the canons, to be held in perpetuity, exempt from all burgage and tax; reserving nothing therein for ourselves or for our successors in the future.

We desire and grant, moreover, that the same Archbishop and chapter shall levy tithes on all leases in the city and diocese of Damietta that would accrue to [its] lord or lords, namely on leases of mills, ovens, baths, fisheries, bird-snares, salt-springs, [money-]changing and minting of coins whether in the diocese or in the city, as well as of the *fonde* and *chaîne* dues,[141] the weighing and measuring of the produce of the soil, animal fodder, and in general all the revenues of the aforesaid city and diocese. (No tithe, however, shall be payable on the fines for offences imposed by those who hold rights of justice.) In addition, for the land's produce which is not leased out, we desire and grant that tithes shall be paid in their entirety to the said church. And of these tithes the Archbishop shall receive two-thirds, and the canons and ministers of the said church one-third. Over and above these tithes, however, we desire and grant that 5000 *besants* of the annual revenues be assigned to the Archbishop and 5000 to the canons and ministers of the said church, both in the rural estates and in property within the said diocese, after this country is liberated from the hands of the infidels.

We desire and grant also that when this land is liberated, the said Archbishop shall be assigned, for himself and his successors, in perpetuity, the fiefs of ten knights, who shall do liege homage to the said Archbishop and shall be bound to perform service for the said fiefs in accordance with the custom of the kingdom of Jerusalem; and that the Archbishop and his successors shall be bound to do service for them both to us, in our support for as long as we are in the country, and [p. 54] to our successors who govern the said country at the time, whenever required by us or by them to do so.

It is also our desire and command that if the above assignments are not made over by us to the same church, either wholly or in part, prior to our departure from the land on this side of the sea, whosoever governs the country in our stead is bound to make them over in their entirety, as detailed above, to the same church. And we further desire and grant that the said Archbishop and canons shall enjoy, both for themselves and their people and goods, free entry and exit for their own purposes to and from the harbour and the city, without any levy or customs dues on the part

141 The *chaîne* dues were those levied at the quayside (the *anchoragium* or port tax; an *ad valorem* tax on the estimated value of goods brought in for resale; a tax on goods exported; and the *terciaria*, an additional harbour tax paid on departure). The *fonde* taxes included both similar dues levied on those entering or leaving by the land gates and charges on transactions conducted in the markets. On these commercial taxes, see J. S. C. Riley-Smith, 'Government in Latin Syria and the commercial privileges of foreign merchants', in Derek Baker (ed.), *Relations between East and West in the Middle Ages* (Edinburgh, 1973), pp. 109–32 (here pp. 112–18).

of the temporal lord. They shall also have, likewise for their own use, weights and measures, and sea-vessels, without any levy or customs dues.

In order that this may have the force of perpetual validity, we have had the present deed confirmed with the authority of our seal and of the royal name as impressed below. Done in the camp near Damietta, in the year of the Incarnation of the Lord 1249, in the month of November, being present in our court those whose names and marks are given below:

> No steward; the sign of Étienne the Butler; the sign of Jean the Chamberlain; the sign of Imbert the Constable.

65. Nicholas de la Hyde to the Abbot of St Albans [1250], in Matthew Paris, Chronica Majora, *vol. 6:* Additamenta, *p. 167*

To my lord, sincerely beloved in Christ, by God's dispensation Abbot of St Albans, his devoted Brother Nicholas de la Hyde, brother of the Temple in England, greetings in the Lord.

It is our desire to announce to Your Lordship happy and joyful news of the Holy Land. You should know that Louis, illustrious King of France, is by God's grace in excellent bodily health, and has landed with his army at the port of Damietta. This same Louis has occupied the coastal region, putting to flight the pagan host. The city of Damietta has been taken into Christian hands and is under their control. Your Excellency should know in addition that the illustrious King of France, in collaboration with the Divine Grace, has taken with his troops the cities of Alexandria and Cairo of Babylon.

66. B[enedict of Alignano], Bishop of Marseilles,[142] *to Pope Innocent IV, 20 May [1250],*[143] *in* Spicilegium, *ed. D'Achéry, vol. 3, p. 628*[144]

To the most holy father and reverend lord, I[nnocent], by divine providence Supreme Pontiff, Brother B.,[145] by God's dispensation Bishop of Marseilles, [sends] reverence and obedience with the greatest devotion, [and] kisses his blessed feet.

---

142 Bishop of Marseilles from 1229 to his resignation in 1267, he died in 1268: see U. Chevalier, 'Alignan, Benoît d'', *Dictionnaire d'Histoire et de Géographie Ecclésiastiques*, vol. 2, coll. 454–5. Benedict accompanied Thibaut of Navarre's crusade in 1239, returning to the West probably in the spring of 1241; and would again visit the Holy Land in 1260, in response to a papal appeal to defend it from the Mongols.

143 Wrongly dated 1249 by the editors.

144 D'Achéry's text reads badly in places, and so I have occasionally corrected this version from that found in Matthew Paris, *Chronica Majora*, vol. 6: *Additamenta*, pp. 168–9 (not in the Giles translation), and from the text in BL ms. Cleopatra, A. VII, fols 103v–104. This latter version had clearly found its way to Tewkesbury: the abbey's cartulary (in which the Bishop's letter is incorporated) and the Tewkesbury annals together make up the bulk of the ms. Matthew, who has just reproduced the letter from Nicholas de la Hyde, also later inserts a rubric: 'Fresh evidence and confirmation of this, albeit fallacious'.

145 D'Achéry's text reads 'H.', but Matthew Paris has the correct initial.

Just as we wish to take care not to assail Your Holiness's ears with falsehoods, so when we hear happy and certain news relating to the honour of God and the Church we pass it on gladly to you. Although we have heard frequent rumours that the fortress of Cairo has been surrendered to the lord King of France, through the divine favour and to the exaltation of Christendom, nevertheless since they were reported by various sources in different terms we postponed writing until we had certain information. But last night the Preceptor of the Hospital of St. John at Marseilles sent us a letter, in which it is stated that eight days [26 January 1250] before the Purification of the Blessed Mary the illustrious King of France reached the fortress of Cairo with his army, and it was handed over to him by certain Saracens who had rebelled against the Sultan, as well as by the Master of the Hospital[146] and other Christians who had been kept there under duress. Two days later the Sultan arrived with 100,000[147] or more mounted Saracens and countless infantry. As God ordained, the lord King drew up four divisions. In the first was the Count of Flanders with the Templars; in the second, the Counts of Brittany[148] and St Pol; in the third, the King himself, the Counts of Poitou and Anjou and Provence, the Duke of Burgundy[149] and many other barons; and in the fourth, Robert Count of Artois, the Master[150] of the Hospitallers and several other barons. Two other squadrons of barons and knights were stationed one on either wing. And when the army of Jesus Christ had been thus drawn up, they met in battle at sunrise. The battle lasted from the third hour [9 a.m.] until nightfall, and the Saracens were massacred in great numbers: the Sultan fled – where, I do not know. On the Christian side it is said that among the knights, crossbowmen and squires up to 1000 died. The lord King, the Queen, who is pregnant, and his three brothers the Counts and their wives are by God's grace in good health, although the Count of Artois has lain a day and a night on the field as if dead, beneath an infinite host of the slain, men and horses alike. The lord King holds Cairo and Babylon; and Alexandria, it is said, has been abandoned. And so, most holy Father, 'bless the God of Heaven', and let us 'confess Him before all men living, that he has shown his mercy upon us',[151] in exalting Christendom in such a fashion under your governance.

Dated Marseilles, the 13th Kalends of June.[152]

---

146 Guillaume de Châteauneuf (1242–58), who had been a prisoner in Egypt since the battle of La Forbie in 1244.

147 Matthew Paris has 200,000.

148 Pierre Mauclerc: he no longer governed Brittany, having surrendered the reins to his son Jean I. He would die at sea during the return voyage in late May or early June 1250: Joinville, § 379, p. 206 (trans. Hague, p. 119; trans. Shaw, p. 258).

149 Hugues IV (d. 1272).

150 Reading *magister* for the *magistri* of the text.

151 Cf. Tobith, xii, 6.

152 The date in Matthew Paris's version. BL ms. Cleopatra, A. VII, fo. 104, has 14 kal. June [19 May]. The date in D'Achéry's text, 5 kal. June [28 May], must be wrong, given that both Matthew Paris, vol. 6, p. 169, and the BL ms. say that the Pope received this letter on the Sunday after Trinity [29 May 1250]. It is puzzling, nevertheless, that by mid-May the Bishop had apparently heard no genuine reports of the defeat of the crusading army in the delta. As well as reproducing it in the *Additamenta* to his *Chronica Majora*, Matthew also refers in the main

67. A Templar[153] *[1250; probably in fact a Hospitaller], in Matthew Paris,* Chronica Majora, *vol. 6:* Additamenta, *pp. 191–7*

The unhappy outcome overseas according to a missive of the Templars In our desire to announce to you the good fortune that has recently befallen the lord King of France with regard to the enemies of the Christian faith, we [hereby] inform Your Benevolence that following the conquest of the territory and city of Damietta the lord King stayed in his camp throughout the summer; and, when the Nile flood had passed, on the advice of wise men who were familiar with the region he struck camp on 22 November[154] with his troops and with a great fleet of ships which were carrying provisions up the river. He advanced towards Babylon and pitched his camp on this side of the river that flows in the direction of Staneis:[155] his purpose, since in view of the depth of the river he could not cross it, was to block the channel of the river, which was a tributary of the great River Nile, and to construct bridges which would enable him to approach the enemy. By having the work maintained without interruption, inasmuch as the Saracen enemy, who were assembled on the opposite bank of the river, had set up several catapults and machines and were endeavouring to impede and terminate the operations, he wasted there the efforts and labours of no mean space of time. The lord King therefore changed his plan. [p. 192] Together with his brothers the Counts of Artois, Poitou and Anjou, and

---

part of the work to the arrival of this joyful 'news', though blaming it on prominent Templars (presumably a reference to the letter of Nicholas de la Hyde) as well as the Bishop of Marseilles, and alleging that it was a ploy to persuade crusaders to go to Louis's assistance: see vol. 5, pp. 87, 118 (trans. Giles, vol. 2, pp. 319–20, 343–4; trans. Vaughan, pp. 193, 217). At vol. 6, p. 169, he also provides an assessment of the two letters:

> From this and other letters it is to be understood that Louis, the most Christian King of the French, whom the Lord, miraculously and not without an excellent and powerful purpose, raised up from death or the threshold of death, is in the year of the Lord 1250 by God's grace master of Damietta, Babylon, Cairo, Alexandria and the shores beyond the sea. Those who have steadily persevered in this glorious conflict and the trials of the expedition are universally considered fortunate; and the prayers poured forth to the Lord on his [Louis's] behalf are deemed to have had a glorious outcome.

153 *Sic* in the rubric. But the perspective – particularly in the latter sections of the document, where we find mention of the Hospitallers' Vice-Master, Jean de Ronay, and their Master, Guillaume de Châteauneuf – is evidently that of a Hospitaller: Lloyd, 'William Longespee II', pp. 66–9. The tone of the opening paragraph, announcing the good news of a crusader victory, is also at variance with the lugubrious news given subsequently; and the last part of the document has much more the bald style of an intelligence report. In addition, the engagement at Mansura is recounted twice. There is consequently a strong possibility that Matthew has dovetailed together two or more letters.

154 This date, confirmed by 'St. Cecilia's day' in 'Rothelin', p. 597 (trans. Shirley, p. 90), appears more reliable than that of 20 November, as given in Louis's own letter [**doc. 70, p. 108**]: see the discussion in Ibn al-Furāt, *Ta'rīkh al-duwal wa'l-mulūk*, partial edn and trans. by U. and M. C. Lyons (with introduction and notes by J. S. C. Riley-Smith), *Ayyubids, Mamlukes and Crusaders* (Cambridge, 1971), vol. 2, n. 3 (to p. 19) at p. 181.

155 The Ushmūn Ṭannāḥ, known to the Franks as the Taneis.

taking with him the Hospitallers, the Templars, and several other barons and knights, he left our men, those of the Hospital of the Germans, the Duke of Burgundy, the Count of Brittany and others to guard the camp, and in the middle of the night of the 8 February he crossed the river at a spot disclosed to him by a Saracen.[156] From there, in accordance with a decision reached beforehand, he advanced straight on the Egyptian camp, which he occupied with a great slaughter of the infidels, who were still lying in bed. As for the lord Count of Artois, together with the Templars and several barons and knights, including William Longespee (being one who excelled in ardour and prowess) – even though the Count was restrained with some courtesy from his intemperately rash course by those whose senses had been sharpened by campaigning experience, and was urgently recalled by an express messenger from the King –, he was nevertheless his own superior,[157] and they charged towards a village called Mansora and there encountered the entire force of the heathen, with whom they struggled all day in a mighty clash of arms. At last, as the enemy gained the upper hand, they were hard pressed and in desperate straits, inasmuch as the Count had made his escape and several – indeed, almost all – of the barons, knights and Templars had pitiably fallen. William Longespee, too, who won for himself in that conflict the title of everlasting blessedness, departed this world with his men to obtain a martyr's reward in Heaven. The King himself, with his men, was meanwhile holding off savage attacks in the camp he had occupied, and [sustained] not a few wounds that day, since the Sultan[158] had gained heart and his men were rendered keener by their success and braver by their victory.

On the following day, Friday, the 11th of the month, rejoicing at their own safety but saddened by the fate of their own people (for they had lost a great number of their more prominent men), they mustered all their strength and, [p. 193] emboldened once more by mutual exhortations, moved in from every side, that is, by land and by water, launching horrific attacks on the Christian army. Advancing with lances, swords and various missiles, and shooting from every direction a virtual hail of arrows from morning until evening, they did not cease to harass the resisting Christians, approaching in their audacity so close as to engage in hand-to-hand combat and attacking the King's own camp. Through the divine aid, however, the enemy forfeited their chief men and their best warriors perished by the sword, so that they lost more than 4000. Indeed, the day on which we heard these reports we made the utmost rejoicing at the King's triumph and success. But at other events which occurred alongside this, we can only grieve. For famine subsequently mounted to an intolerable level, since the sea was not yet navigable and foodstuffs could not be brought to Damietta by sea or to the army by way of the Nile, which was carefully guarded and manfully defended night and day by the enemy's archers. The enemy

---

156 A Bedouin, who had approached the King through the Constable Humbert de Beaujeu, according to Joinville, §§ 215–16, p. 118 (trans. Hague, p. 77; trans. Shaw, p. 218). But 'Rothelin', p. 602 (trans. Shirley, p. 94), describes him as one of a group of Muslim renegades who had joined the crusading army.

157 Thus my conjectural translation of the obscure phrase *major sibi se*.

158 An error: there was of course no Sultan present, until the arrival of Tūrān Shāh later that month.

would lurk in the hills and valleys and keep all the roads and paths under surveillance; and they were all the greater threat to our men because their missiles were poisoned with Greek fire. For these reasons our men endured no slight dearth of victuals in the army, and thus they wasted away with hunger, and horses as well as men were in short supply. Those who earlier had been strong and brave were now enfeebled and languished wretchedly.

At length, then, as our sins required, the chord of our hope has turned to grief, and the joy we felt mixed with sorrow has matured into mourning. The bellies of the faithful who hear this are with reason bound to be convulsed and their eyes to overflow with tears. For the Lord God Himself, like an enemy, has shattered and cast down the crown of the universal church, namely the strength and prosperity of France; He has destroyed the foundations and the glory of the Christian religion and faith. O God, Whose 'ways are past finding out' and Whose many 'judgements are unsearchable',[159] did not [p. 194] Thy faithful come to repulse Thine enemies and to liberate from them the land of Thy birth, Thine own land, and to worship there Thy footprints? But in this affair Thou hast clearly shown mortal men how precarious is the joy of this world. Of a truth the whole of Christendom should duly bewail with bitter groans the terrible fate that befell the King of France and the Christian army as they fought against the infidel that pestilential day, the 6 April. Neither has to this day such an event been witnessed or reported. For as the King advanced to attack the heathen in a town called Mansora, lying approximately three days' journey from Damietta, he was suddenly surrounded there on all sides, like an island in a vast sea, by a countless host of infidels, who sealed off all the approaches by land and water so tightly that our men were now altogether deprived of the relief of provisions. And having often withstood for almost four months the most intense shortage of food, heavy attacks and repeated wounds, they breathed forth their wretched spirits for lack of victuals. Nor was any remedy to hand for men who were deficient in themselves and whose mares were enfeebled, other than to entrust themselves all to the two-edged judgement of war or death. On a day decided upon, therefore, they retreated along the river towards Damietta, weakened and in no state to fight, and as the enemy, who were positioned as guardians of the banks, hurled missiles and Greek fire, they were pierced or set alight, or were slaughtered by the warriors, or drowned. The remainder engaged in close fighting with the enemy for as long as they were able. But what could a few achieve against such a great number of enemies, the hungry and starving against those who were alert and refreshed, those who did not know the terrain against natives? They stood their ground in the conflict, however, though the bloodshed was indescribable, until they were pitiably vanquished – alas! – by the superior numbers of the heathen. Seeing this, several of our men, fearful of death, before which even perfect saints are said to have recoiled, surrendered to the enemy, offering their sword hilts in the hope that at some time [p. 195] they would be ransomed. But almost all fought on until they breathed their last. Preserving true charity towards one another in their lives, these true martyrs were not separated in their dearly-bought deaths, since all, religious and laymen alike, together with the King, suffered the penalty of death or captivity, so that not one of those present at

159 Romans, xi, 33; cf. also Psalm xxxvi, 6.

the battle escaped. Who can tell this story or recall it without tears, when such noble, such elegant, such prominent Franks were massacred, trodden down, or like thieves seized by base men and dragged off to imprisonment, subjected to the judgement and the grinning mockery of God's enemies? Here the *oriflamme*[160] was torn to pieces, the *bauséant*[161] trampled underfoot, a sight nobody remembers having ever beheld. Over there the standards of magnates, since ancient times an object of dread to the infidel, were bespattered with the blood of men and horses and, spurned under the heels of a triumphant enemy who blasphemed against Christ and ridiculed our men, were most vilely destroyed and treated with contempt. How great are the rewards they deserve to expect who for the sake of Christ endured such trials to the point of death! But these are matters to be submitted to the hidden judgement of God rather than that of men.

When the King abandoned the camp, the Legate for his part, along with the Patriarch of Jerusalem, certain prelates and the Duke of Burgundy, who was sick, embarked on galleys and made their way by river as far as Damietta, at great risk and with great effort. Another flotilla of boats, into which the army's foot-soldiers who were unarmed, feeble or sick had been taken in great numbers, was set alight, just as previously, by Greek fire (it might more appropriately be called Hellfire) and sunk together with its equipment, arms, horses and treasure. Let me tell you that this loss was inflicted on us by the Egyptian fleet.

[p. 196] You should know that in the final engagement all the brothers of our convent perished, with the exception of the Vice-Master, Brother Jean de Ronay.[162] Four were taken prisoner, and one in addition was captured with the King. And only three brothers of the Order of the Temple barely escaped, though terribly wounded, as we have been informed at Acre while drafting this letter. Our scouts, whom we sent to Egypt, have not yet returned. In the first encounter, in which the Count of Artois fell, William Longespee died a praiseworthy death and ascended [into Heaven], and none of his companions escaped except Sir Alexander Giffard, who was wounded five times and eventually in the final engagement, we believe, was either taken with the King or killed along with the rest.

Postscript. When the lord King had been captured, he made a truce with the Sultan for ten years, on the following conditions. The King was to give the Sultan 100,000 silver marks, and the prisoners on both sides taken since the battle of Gaza should be exchanged (by this truce our Master and our captive brothers have been released). Damietta was to be handed back with all the equipment, both arms and provisions, found therein when the King took it. The Christians have kept Jaffa, Arsur,[163] Caesarea, Chastel Pèlerin, Haifa, Caymont, Nazareth, Saphed, Beaufort, Tyre, Cavea de Tyron (which the Saracens occupied when the King was at Damietta)

160 The royal French standard.

161 The black and white standard of the Templars.

162 'Bonay' in the text. He had been acting Master since the capture of Guillaume de Châteauneuf at La Forbie in October 1244. Joinville, § 244, p. 134 (trans. Hague, p. 85; trans. Shaw, p. 226), calls him Henri de Ronay in error.

163 *Azothum*.

and Sidon, with their appurtenances which the Christians held at the time of the King's arrival. If prayers are to be offered up for the souls of those who were killed on Christ's behalf, remember the souls of our brethren who fell, and know that as many as 140 picked brethren perished and, it is to be believed for a fact, yielded up their souls to God.

Before the King was captured, and while he was still halted at Mansora and in possession of the camp, the Sultan went so far as to offer him Earl Richard's truce,[164] with Jerusalem, Ascalon and Tiberias fortified. All of this was unhappily prevented on the advice of certain prelates, and in particular of a Dominican [p. 197] Friar. And although we said earlier that the Vice-Master of the Hospital was captured alive, we have since learned that he fell in the final engagement together with the Hospital's standard-bearer.

These tragic reverses, to be mourned for all time, befell the Christians, it is said, through the pride of the lord Pope and his implacable hatred of the Emperor Frederick. In fact, this is what even the Saracens claim. For F[rederick][165] had offered whatever was Christian territory at that time without fighting or bloodshed; and in addition he would put an end to the sedition at Constantinople, namely with the purpose of winning gratitude and peace. But by an evil chance the Pope obstructed the fulfilment of this offer. It is in F[rederick's] bosom, however, that our hope lies that we may breathe awhile; but may the Pope's anger be moderated in some fashion.

We have sent this same letter, though abridged in some respects, to our brothers who reside in France, but we saw fit to forward to you a fuller version. Fresh events that come to light will alter style and content; and if there is any new development, we shall inform you at the earliest opportunity.

68. Robert, Patriarch of Jerusalem, to the Cardinals, 15 May 1250: 'Annales monasterii de Burton', in Annales Monastici, *vol. 1, pp. 285–9*

Letter [describing] how King Louis of France was captured by the pagans, and how the Christian troops were captured or killed To the reverend fathers in Christ and venerable lords, the college of the Cardinals of the Holy Roman Church, Robert, by God's grace (albeit undeserving) Patriarch of Jerusalem, greetings and the due reverence given to fathers. We should more willingly have reported joyful than sorrowful tidings to Your Paternities. But circumstances [p. 286] of unexpected and bitter necessity, into which the Lord Jesus Christ, as our sins required, has brought Christendom in these past days, compel us to report to His Apostolic Holiness and to yourselves tragic news which suffices to move not only the hearts of men to lamentation and mourning but – so dreadful are its contents – the very elements to wailing. It is with great heaviness of heart that we have seen fit to inform Your

164 The truce made in 1241 with Sultan Ayyūb by Richard of Cornwall on behalf of the Emperor.

165 The editor here understands the dative form *Fretherico*; but if that is correct the subject of the sentence is obscure. We might have assumed that it was the Sultan, so that the reference is to the 1229 treaty with Egypt, but this scarcely harmonizes with the offer to end the sedition at Constantinople, which involved Frederick's son-in-law, the Emperor John Vatatzes of Nicaea.

Paternities that the Christian host left Damietta on the 20 November [1249] last, in order to advance against the Egyptian army, which had pitched camp beyond the River Thaneis at a village called Mansora, where the River Thaneis branches off from the main river. When the Christian army approached that point on the Tuesday [21 December] before the Lord's Nativity, they made camp on the opposite bank of the river, facing the Saracens and extending from the main river to the other mentioned above, while the Saracens did their utmost to prevent our troops from crossing over to them. But certain spies were bribed to point out a spot not far from the host; and here, after taking advice from his barons, the lord King of the French crossed over the River Thaneis to the boats [?] on the 8 March[166] with the greater part of his army, meeting no opposition. Before the Saracens realized that he was upon them, he entered their camp and seized their engines which they had set up against ours. But the Saracens gathered together, and a very great struggle took place between them and our men, with no small number killed on both sides. There fell in that engagement the pick of the knights in our army, among them the lord Count of Artois, Earl William Longespee, the lord André de Vitry, the lord of Coucy,[167] the lord Archand de Brienne, the lord Foucard de Merle,[168] almost all the Templars, and a vast number of others, not counting those who were mortally wounded.

From that day forward, by I know not what judgement of God, everything turned out contrary to our desires, as a severe and fatal pestilence afflicted both men and horses. Another type of sickness, too, gained hold of men's mouths, with the gums decaying so that they were unable to chew food. Their feet and legs, moreover, subsequently swelled up and turned black, to the extent that their legs could no longer carry them, and thus within a short time they breathed their last. Why say more? We can claim with assurance that from the time we left Damietta down to the end of March [p. 287] about two-thirds of the army perished, knights, crossbowmen and men-at-arms alike.

At last, when the lord King and the troops, on account of these misfortunes and the dearth of provisions, could remain there no longer, they held a consultation and, around nightfall on the 4 April, set off on the return march to Damietta, both by land and by the river in galleys and armed vessels. The enemy realized that we were retreating, and their galleys fell upon ours, capturing many of them and other boats. Some they burnt, killing for certain, it is claimed, more than three thousand sick men who had been placed in these galleys and boats, not to mention those who were fit; the other galleys and vessels, which were able to escape by rowing, got back to Damietta. On the following day, a Wednesday [6 April], around the first hour [7 a.m.], the lord Legate and I, after riding armed throughout the night, and being so exhausted and broken by excessive and unaccustomed efforts that we were in no way capable of any further exertion by riding, and being alone without any of our

---

166 An error: the correct date was 8 February 1250.

167 Raoul.

168 Joinville, § 218, p. 120 (trans. Hague, p. 78; trans. Shaw, p. 219), describes how this 'very fine knight' was holding Count Robert's bridle and, being completely deaf and unable to hear the Templars' restraining advice, kept urging the company to pursue the fleeing Muslims.

households, boarded a ship which, so it pleased God, we found along the river bank. It was our plan to move along the river until nightfall in the direction of Damietta, where we believed the lord King and the army would come and pitch camp, since we had left behind in the host our knights and all our households along with all our possessions. But as we headed for the place, we heard reports from those who were retreating by water that the lord King and the troops had stayed behind near a village called Sarensa,[169] and that the Saracens had arrived there in vast numbers. Since we could see behind us on the river Christian vessels in flames, and were unable either to go back to the army or to wait there without risk, we moved on ahead and landed at Damietta around sunset that day. We waited until the next day for the lord King and the army to arrive; but nobody returned to Damietta and we were in no position to learn anything for certain concerning the army; and so the next day, a Friday [8 April], on the orders of my lady the Queen and with the approval of the lord Legate and other great men, ten galleys and many other armed vessels were sent with a great number of armed men to the King's aid. These advanced as far as the village of Sarensa, but could get no sure news of the army. Some of the men were put ashore from the galleys to reconnoitre whereabouts the army was to be found, but no intelligence was obtained through them, since they proved unable to sight the army; but they did find, in a field near that village, a great mass of men who had been put to the sword, [p. 288] naked and decapitated, and countless horses that had been killed. They came back from there the next day, Saturday, and gave us this sad news, so that we clearly recognized that our men had fallen in the battle. The next day, a Sunday [10 April], we heard reports that on the Wednesday the Saracens had fought a field engagement with our men, in which – alas! – they had been victorious, with the result that the lord King, his brothers the Counts of Poitou and Anjou, the Count of Brittany, the Count of Flanders, the lord Philippe de Montfort,[170] the lords Baudouin and Gui d'Ibelin, the brothers the Preceptors of both the Temple and the Hospital, and several other barons and knights had been captured in this battle and were being held prisoner at the abovementioned village of Mansora. And, truth to say, of the entire force which was retreating by land, there was not a single Christian who had not been captured or killed.

At length the lord King sent to Damietta official messengers telling my lady the Queen, the lord Legate and the others in the city that he had made a truce for ten years with the Sultan of Babylon, and that it had been confirmed by oath on both sides. In the terms it was expressly stated that the lord King was bound to hand back the city of Damietta to the Sultan and to give as a ransom for himself and the prisoners, as well as for the losses he had inflicted on the Sultan, 800,000 Saracen *bezants*. All the prisoners, whether Christian or Saracen, who had been taken since the time when the lord Frederick came to the Jerusalem region and made a truce with the Sultan of Babylon[171] were to be freed by both sides by a certain date. The lands which the Christians held in the kingdom of Jerusalem when the lord King of France arrived in Cyprus are covered by the truce; but both the cities of Jerusalem and Bethlehem,

169 Sharamsāḥ.

170 Lord of Tyre; he died in 1269/70.

171 A reference to the crusade of the Emperor Frederick II (1229).

and all the other lands that the Saracens had taken and held, they have kept for themselves, nor have they been prepared to return them to the Christians; and the church of Jerusalem, which has been despoiled of its property by these Saracens, has not regained a single village, nor any of its possessions, by this truce.

The lord King saw fit to summon me to go to the place where he was being held prisoner in the Saracen camp, since he had need of my presence. And although I was on good grounds afraid to go, I feared nevertheless that his release might be delayed if I stayed away; and so I exposed myself to danger, and went with an amir who was my escort. I arrived, then, at the place where the King was, on 1 May, and that day long negotiations were held as to the manner of his release [p. 289] and that of the other captives. But on the following morning, while the business was stalled somewhat, the amirs and other Saracens fell upon their lord the Sultan of Babylon, who was present in the camp, and killed him, publicly butchering him with their swords. They took me and all those with me, bound our hands, and inflicted many injuries upon us, confiscating all the property we had brought there with us.[172] Had not God's mercy assuaged their frenzy, they would have put to the sword the lord King, myself and the rest of the Christians alike. How many injuries, threats and frightful ordeals the lord King and the others were subjected to, it would take too long to describe in writing. In sum, after further long and varied negotiations, the Saracens agreed to the truce which the lord King had made with the aforesaid Sultan, and reinstated it under oath. The following day, a Friday [6 May], the lord King's lieutenants and his men handed back the city of Damietta to the Egyptian amirs; and they, once they were in possession of the city, that same day released the lord King and many other nobles whom they held prisoner. When these things had been completed as described, the lord King, together with the Legate, his brothers and many nobles, left Damietta and came to Acre, where he has decided to remain until this next September passage, so as to be present while in the meantime all the terms of the truce are fulfilled.

Dated at Acre, 15 May, in the year of the Lord 1250.

69. Troubadour's song: Bédier and Aubry (ed.), Les chansons de croisade, *pp. 263–5*[173]

---

172 Joinville, §§ 364–5, p. 198 (trans. Hague, pp. 115–16; trans. Shaw, pp. 254–5), says that the 80-year-old Patriarch, who had joined the King in order to secure his release, was seized by the Muslims on the grounds that the safe-conduct granted by the dead Sultan was no longer valid. The proposal by one amir that he be put to death, on the grounds that he had encouraged Louis to resist swearing the oath demanded by his captors, was rejected; but he was bound very tightly to a tent-pole, and urged Louis to swear as required.

173 The poem is also printed in G[aston] P[aris], 'La chanson composée à Acre en juin 1250', *Romania*, 22 (1893): 541–7, and in William Chester Jordan, '"Amen!" cinq fois "Amen!". Les chansons de la croisade égyptienne de saint Louis, une source négligée d'opinion royaliste', in Laurence Moulinier and Patrick Boucheron (eds), *Hommes de pouvoir: individu et politique au temps de saint Louis* (Vincennes, 1998 = *Médiévales*, 34, Spring 1998), pp. 79–90 (here p. 90). Bédier gives a modern French translation at pp. 266–7, and there is a partial rendering into modern French in Richard, *Saint Louis roi*, pp. 240–41.

[p. 263] No man could create or sing
a good song on a bad theme.
And therefore I do not propose to do so,
for I have other things enough on my mind.
[p. 264] And yet I see the land of Outremer
hang so in the balance
That in singing I want to beg the King of France
to put no trust in cowards and flatterers
And to avenge his own and God's shame.

Ah! noble King, when God caused you to take the Cross,
All Egypt trembled at your reputation;
But now you will forfeit it all
if you thus leave Jerusalem a prisoner.
For since God made you His choice
to be executor of His vengeance,
You ought surely to demonstrate your power
to avenge those dead and captured
Who for you and for God were slain or taken.[174]

King, you know that God has few friends,
and never had He greater need of them.
For it is on your account that His people have died and been taken;
nor is there any save you who could aid them.
[p. 265] For those other knights are poor
and are afraid to stay.
And if at this juncture you fail them,
saints and martyrs, apostles and innocents
Will accuse you at the Judgement.

King, you have treasure in silver and gold,[175]
methinks, more than any other king ever had.
So should you give more bountifully
and stay to protect this land.
For you have lost more than you have conquered;
and it would be too great a retreat
To go back home in such misfortune.
But stay, and you will make mighty exploits,
Till France has regained her honour.

---

174 Paris thus restored the line, which is corrupt in the mss.

175 See Joinville, § 427, p. 232 (trans. Hague, p. 131; trans. Shaw, p. 270), where Louis is told that he has spent none of his own wealth but only the funds furnished by the Church. The sentiments expressed in this song are so much in harmony with those voiced by Joinville at the council in Acre that Paris suggested Joinville was the author. It does look as if the song was composed by someone from Champagne, but the views found in it were doubtless widespread among the rank and file; and it is of course possible that Joinville recalled the words of the song when he came to write his account of the council session: cf. Jordan, '"Amen!" cinq fois "Amen!"', p. 84. A different candidate is proposed by Ineke Hardy, '"Nus ne poroit de mauvaise raison" (R1887): a case for Raoul de Soissons', *Medium Aevum*, 70 (2001): 95–111.

King, if at this juncture you return,
France, Champagne and all mankind will say
That you have turned your back on glory
and the booty you have won is less than nought;
That you ought to have taken pity on the captives
who live in agony;
That you ought surely to have sought their release.
Since they are martyrs for you and for Jesus,[176]
It were a great sin to leave them to die.

70. Louis IX to his subjects in France, [before 10][177] *August 1250, in* Historiae Francorum Scriptores ab Ipsius Gentis Origine, *ed. André Du Chesne, vol. 5 (Paris, 1649), pp. 428–32*[178]

Louis, by God's grace King of the French, to his beloved and faithful prelates, barons, knights, citizens and burgesses, and to all others in the kingdom of France whom this letter reaches, greetings. In our desire to pursue the business of the Cross with all our energies, to the honour and glory of the Lord's name, we have thought fit to tell you all [the following]. After the capture of Damietta (which, as we believe you are aware, the Lord Jesus Christ, in His ineffable mercy, had delivered into the Christians' power almost by a miracle surpassing human strength), we held a general council, and left Damietta on the 20th day of November last. Gathering our forces both by land and by water, we advanced against the Saracen army, which had assembled and pitched camp in a place which is popularly called Massoria. In the course of this march we were subjected to Saracen attacks, in which they constantly sustained no small losses: on one day some of them from the Egyptian army, who had met up with our men, were killed. On the march we learned that the Sultan of Egypt had just ended his wretched life. He had sent word, it was commonly said, to his son, who dwelt in the East, to come to Egypt, and had caused an oath of fealty to him to be taken by all the leaders of his army; and the overall command of the troops of his dominions was entrusted to an amir named Fachardin.[179] On our arrival at the locality aforementioned, we discovered that all this was true.

We arrived, then, at this place on the Tuesday [21 December 1249] prior to the Nativity of the Lord; but initially it proved impossible for us to engage the Saracens, on account of a river that flowed between the two armies, which is called the Thaneos and branches off from the main river at that spot. We set up our camp between the two rivers so that it stretched from the main river to the lesser one; and here we had a big clash with the Saracens, in which many of them perished, killed by the swords

---

176 Paris's conjectural restoration of this line.

177 Since we know that this letter was carried back to France by the King's brothers, who sailed on 10 August (note 185 below), this provides a *terminus ante quem* for its date.

178 There is a translation of this letter in Hague's translation of Joinville, *Life of St. Louis*, pp. 247–54; but it errs at times on the free side, and the odd phrase is omitted.

179 Fakhr al-Dīn Ibn al-Shaykh. The oath referred to was in fact imposed upon the amirs by Fakhr al-Dīn and others who were keeping the Sultan's death secret. See **docs 73 and 74(c)** below.

of our men; a very great number of them, moreover, drowned in the strong and deep currents. Indeed, since this river Thaneos was unfordable in view of the depth of the waters and the height of the banks, we began to build over it a causeway, which would enable the Christian army to cross, and we devoted several days to this, with vast effort and at great risk and expense. The Saracens, resisting us with all their efforts, set up against the engines we had built there several machines of their own, and with these they shattered and broke with stones our wooden fortresses that we had placed over the crossing and utterly consumed them with Greek fire.

But when through this we were cheated of almost all hope and expectation of crossing over by the causeway, we received intelligence through a Saracen from the Egyptian army that some way downstream there was a place that was fordable, where the Christian army could cross the river. As a result, after we had taken counsel with the barons and other army leaders on the Monday [7 February 1250] before Ash Wednesday, it was generally agreed that on the next day, the first day of Lent, we should assemble at the aforesaid spot with a view to crossing the river, while deputing part of the army to guard the camp. And so on the following day we drew up our battle-lines and reached the place, where we crossed over the river, though not without grave danger; for [the water] was deeper and the spot more treacherous than we had been led to believe, with the result that our mounts had to swim and the high, muddy banks made emerging from the river hazardous. When we had crossed the river, then, we reached the place where the Saracens' engines stood, close to the causeway. Those of our men who were in the van attacked the Saracens and slaughtered many of them with their swords, sparing them on the grounds of neither age nor sex. Among them they killed there [the Saracens'] general and certain other amirs. At this juncture, however, our forces scattered, and some rushed through the enemy encampment and advanced as far as the town called Massoria, cutting down as many of the enemy as they encountered. But at last the Saracens became aware that they had advanced without due heed, and rallied. Charging upon our men, they surrounded them on all sides and overwhelmed them. And there a great slaughter of our barons and of the knights, both religious and secular, took place, for which we have had [p. 429] good cause to grieve – and grieve still. There too we lost in this world our very dear and illustrious brother of honoured memory, the Count of Artois, a fact we recall with bitter sorrow at heart, even though we should rather rejoice for him than grieve, since we hope and believe for a fact that, crowned as a martyr, he has flown to his heavenly homeland and will there have everlasting joy with the holy martyrs.

On that day, then, as the Saracens charged at us from all directions and rained arrows upon us, we withstood their mighty attacks until around the ninth hour [3 p.m.], though completely lacking the support of crossbowmen. At length, when many of our men had been wounded there, and the majority of our horses had suffered various wounds or been killed, with the Lord's help we rallied our forces and held our position, making camp that day close to the Saracens' engines which we had captured. We stayed there that day with a small force, having first built a wooden bridge to enable those on the other bank to cross to join us. The next day many of our people crossed over the river at our orders, and pitched camp alongside us; and then, having destroyed the Saracens' engines, we made barricades for the bridges of ships so that over them our men might move freely and safely from one army to the other. But the following Friday [11 February 1250], the sons of Perdition mustered their forces on all sides, with the aim of utterly destroying the Christian army, and in the greatest strength and in countless numbers gathered at our barricades, everywhere launching so many troops and such fearful assaults as the Saracens had never been known to do, so many claimed, in the regions on this side of the sea. But with the divine might in the ascendant, and by holding the line throughout our army, we stood firm and repulsed their attacks, so that a very great number of them fell before our men's swords.

When some days had elapsed thereafter, the Sultan's son reached Massora from the East, and the Egyptians beat their drums and rejoiced at his arrival, and received him as their ruler. This gave no small boost to their morale, while on our side from that point onwards, by what judgement of God I do not know, everything turned out contrary to our desires. A plague of different sicknesses broke out, and a general mortality among both men and horses, with the result that there were scarcely any in the army who did not mourn those who had died or were mortally ill. By this means the Christian army was reduced and the greater part perished. Such a shortage of provisions reigned that many died of starvation; for naval vessels from Damietta could not get through to the army, since they were prevented by the Saracen galleys and the pirate vessels which they had [carried] overland and launched on the river. And thus they first seized very many of our vessels on the river, and in time captured two convoys in succession which were bringing provisions and many other good things to the army, massacring a host of sailors and others, to the great loss of the entire army. With a total dearth of foodstuffs and of fodder for the horses, almost everyone in the army began to lose heart and fell into despair and no little fear.

Hard-pressed by these afflictions, as much by the lack of provisions and of fodder for the horses as by the disaster we have previously related, we were compelled by an unavoidable necessity to withdraw from that locality and – had the Lord granted it – to fall back on Damietta. But, since 'the ways of Man are not in himself'[180] but rather in Him Who 'directs all men's steps, and disposes according to what pleases His will',[181] while we were on the return march, namely on the 5th day of April, the Saracens assembled all their forces and attacked the Christian army in countless numbers; and, as it chanced, by the divine permission and as our sins required, we fell into the hands of the enemy. We, our dearest brothers, A[lphonse] Count of Poitou and C[harles] Count of Anjou, and the rest who were retreating with us by land, of whom none whatsoever escaped, were taken and put in chains, not without a very great slaughter of our men and the shedding of no little Christian blood. The majority of those who were retreating on the river were likewise captured or put to the sword, and most of the naval vessels were burned, the flames consuming a tragic host of the sick.

For some days after our capture, the aforementioned Sultan had them demand a truce from us, insisting urgently, with threats and harsh words, that we should have Damietta surrendered to him without delay, with all its contents, and that we should

180 Cf. Jeremiah, x, 23.

181 Cf. Psalm xxxvi (in the Vulgate; otherwise xxxvii), 23.

indemnify him for all the damage [we had done] and all the expense he had incurred from the day that the Christians had occupied [p. 430] Damietta until that moment. At length, after much negotiation, we made a truce for ten years, on the following terms:

1. The Sultan was to release from captivity ourselves and all the Christian prisoners, as well as all others from whatever region they originate, who had been captured since the time that Sultan Keymel, the grandfather of this Sultan, once[182] made a truce with the Emperor, and was to allow them to go freely wherever they wished;
2. The territories that the Christians held in the kingdom of Jerusalem when we arrived, together with all their appurtenances, they were to hold in peace;
3. We for our part were bound to hand over to him Damietta and 800,000 Saracen *bezants* in return for the freedom of the prisoners and the aforementioned damage and expenses, of which we have already paid 400,000; and to free all the Saracens captured in Egypt by the Christians since our arrival, as well as those who had been captured in the kingdom of Jerusalem since the truce once made between the Emperor and the said Sultan; with the addition that all our movable possessions, and everyone else's, remaining in Damietta after our withdrawal should be safe and under the guard and protection of the Sultan, to be conveyed to Christian territory whenever opportunity might offer. All the sick Christians also, and others who were staying in Damietta in order to sell their belongings there, should likewise be safe and were to leave by land or by sea when they wished, without any obstacle or opposition whatever. The Sultan was bound to provide with safe-conduct to Christian territory all those who chose to leave overland.

When the truce on these terms between ourselves and the Sultan had been confirmed by oaths on both sides, and the Sultan was already on the way with his troops towards Damietta with the aim of fulfilling all these stipulations, it transpired by the divine judgement that some Saracen knights, not without the collusion of the majority of the troops, fell on the Sultan in the morning, as he was rising from the table after eating, and severely wounded him; and as he left his tent with the aim of seeking deliverance through flight they hacked him to pieces with their swords before the eyes of almost all the amirs and a crowd of other Saracens. Immediately following this, many Saracens appeared at our tent, armed and inflamed with frenzy, as if they sought – so many feared – to vent their rage on us and other Christians. But the divine mercy allayed their fury, and they pressed us urgently to confirm the truce we had made with the Sultan and to expedite the surrender of the city of Damietta. Although they stormed and threatened, at length, as it pleased the Lord, Who as the Father of mercies and even more a comforter in tribulation heeds the groans of those in bondage, we confirmed with them on oath the truce we had previously made with the Sultan; and we received from each and every one of them oaths, in accordance

182 At this point the text has the corrupt reading *caym*, which I have amended on the basis of the *olim* in the corresponding section of Vincent de Beauvais, xxxii, 101.

with their religion, regarding the observance of the truce. Dates were fixed by which the prisoners were to be freed on both sides and the city of Damietta would be surrendered. We had no little problem in reaching agreement on its surrender with these amirs, as with the Sultan earlier, because there was no hope of holding the city, as we learned for a fact from those who had joined us from Damietta and who were well aware of the true situation. And it was for their sake that, on the advice of the barons of France and a great many others, we decided that it was in Christendom's interest rather that we and the rest of the prisoners be released in accordance with the truce than that the city be lost with the rest of the Christians therein and that we and the others should remain in captivity amid so much danger.

On the day appointed, therefore, the amirs took over the city, and when they had occupied it they released us and our brothers, together with the Counts of Brittany, Flanders and Soissons and many other barons and knights of the kingdoms of France, Jerusalem and Cyprus. At that juncture we were fully confident that, since they had freed us and the others aforementioned, they would be steadfast in keeping their oaths regarding the release and handing-over of the other Christians in accordance with the terms of the truce. And when all this had been done, we departed from Egypt, leaving behind there representatives to take delivery of the prisoners from the Saracens and to keep guard on the goods we had abandoned, since we did not have enough ships to take them away.

Subsequently, however, when we began the process of recovering the prisoners, a matter of anxious concern which plays on our mind a good deal, we sent back other official envoys and ships, to bring back the captives and the other things we had left there, namely our engines, weapons, tents, a certain number of horses, and many other [p. 431] goods. Although these envoys of ours pressed insistently for the prisoners and the other things aforementioned to be handed over to them in accordance with the terms of the truce, the amirs kept them waiting there in Egypt in the expectation of being given everything they were asking for. But at last, when it had been daily anticipated [that they would hand over] all the prisoners whom they were bound to surrender, who number, it is reliably claimed, more than 12,000, both recent and of long standing, they delivered to our envoys no more than a mere 400, of whom some left prison only through a money payment. And of the other things they were not prepared to hand over any whatsoever.

What is still more detestable, indeed, as we discovered from our envoys and from certain trustworthy prisoners who were returning from that country, is that having made and sworn a truce they picked out young men from among the Christian captives and, leading them like sheep to a sacrifice, they did their utmost, by putting swords to their throats, to force them to apostatize from the Catholic faith and to proclaim the religion of the wicked Mahomet. Many of them, in their enfeebled and vulnerable state, turned away from the faith and professed this loathsome religion. But the rest, like strong athletes, rooted in the faith and persisting most steadfastly in their firm resolve, could in no way be overcome by the enemy's threats and blows, but put up a proper resistance and obtained the bloodied crown of martyrdom. Their blood, we are convinced, will cry out to the Lord on behalf of the Christian people, and they will be our advocates in the court of Heaven before the Supreme Judge: in the cause for which we struggle against the enemies of the faith, they will prove of greater value to us in yonder homeland than if they dwelt with us on earth. [The Egyptians] also put to the sword many Christians who were left behind sick in Damietta. We had no assurance that they would hand over the Christian prisoners or restore our belongings, even though we have fully observed the terms of the agreement we have with them and are [still] ready to observe them.

In addition, since following the conclusion of the truce and our own liberation we were firmly convinced that once the prisoners were freed the overseas territories which the Christians held would remain undisturbed for the period specified in the truce, it was our desire and intention to return to the kingdom of France; and we had already begun to arrange for ships and other things which appeared necessary for our passage. But when we saw clearly, through the events related above, that the amirs were openly contravening the truce and had no scruples about making a laughing-stock of ourselves and Christendom contrary to their own oaths, we sought the advice of the barons of France, the prelates, the houses of the Templars, the Hospitallers of St John and of St Mary of the Germans, and the barons of the kingdom of Jerusalem, and consulted them regarding what we ought to do in these circumstances.[183] The majority with one accord declared that if we embarked at this juncture we should be leaving the country on the verge of total loss, and our departure would simply leave it exposed to the Saracens, particularly since at this time it was, alas, in such a weakened and wretched condition. In the wake of our departure the Christian prisoners, too, who were being detained by the infidels could be regarded as dead men, since all hope of their release would have been removed. But if we stayed, some good, it was hoped, might come of our presence, including the liberation of the prisoners, the retention of the fortresses and towns of the kingdom of Jerusalem and, through the Lord, other advantages for the whole of Christendom, especially since a bitter conflict has arisen between the Sultans of Aleppo and Egypt. Already, the former has gathered his forces and taken Damascus and some fortresses that were under Egyptian rule, and is about to advance on Egypt in order, many allege, to avenge the death of the Sultan who was murdered and to do his utmost to conquer the country.[184]

Having given these matters close consideration, although many urged us not to remain overseas, nevertheless in our pity on the miseries and adversities of the Holy Land, to whose aid we had come, and in our sympathy for the incarceration and sufferings of our prisoners, we have chosen to postpone our passage and to stay some time in the kingdom of Syria, rather than to leave the Business of Christ in a state of utter hopelessness and our prisoners in such great peril. We have, however, thought fit to send back to France our dearest brothers, A[lphonse], Count of Poitou, and C[harles], Count of Anjou,[185] to be a comfort to our dearest lady and mother and to the entire kingdom.

---

183 Reading, with Vincent de Beauvais, xxxii, 102, *in eventibus* for the *ineuntibus* of the printed text.

184 For this campaign by Sultan al-Nāṣir Ṣalāḥ al-Dīn Yūsuf of Aleppo, see Humphreys, *From Saladin to the Mongols*, pp. 305–7; also **docs 118–120** below.

185 According to 'Estoire de Eracles', pp. 438-9 (trans. in Shirley, *Crusader Syria*, p. 138), they and Guillaume, Count of Flanders, left for France on St Lawrence's day (10 August

Since, therefore, all who are called by the name Christian ought to be zealous for the aforementioned Business, and you in particular, Franks,[186] being descended by blood from those whom the Lord chose, as His special people, to win the Holy Land, [p. 432] which you ought to deem your own by right of conquest, we invite all of you to render that service [to Him] Who did us service on the Cross and existed to pour forth His own blood for your redemption, so that your hearts may be renewed in Christ Jesus. For in addition to the blasphemies they uttered in the sight of Christian people, that most wicked race has offended the Creator by whipping the Cross, spitting upon it, and finally trampling it vilely underfoot, to the dishonour of the Christian faith. Come, then, knights of Christ, the special property of the Pope of the Living God, make ready and prove yourselves mighty men in avenging these injuries and insults. Make your actions recall those of your forebears, who among the nations were particularly devoted in promoting the faith, and wholeheartedly obeyed their lords in temporal affairs, filling the entire world with renowned deeds. We were before you in obedience to God. Do you now come and follow us for God's sake, so as to gain alongside us, through the Lord's bounty, though you will have come late, the reward which the husbandman in the Gospel gave both to the first who tended his vineyard and to the last.[187] Moreover, those who come or who send adequate reinforcements to aid us, or rather the Holy Land while we are here, will gain, besides the general indulgence vouchsafed to those signed with the Cross, great favour and honour both with God and among men.

But you must make haste. Let those whom the power of the Most High inspires to come out or to send reinforcements, make ready to travel or to send by the coming April or May passage. Let those, on the other hand, who cannot be ready to cross by that passage take care at least to sail to our assistance by the following St. John's Day [24 June 1251] passage. For the nature of the business means that speed is essential and delay dangerous. Do you, prelates and others among Christ's faithful, especially intercede with the Most High with urgent prayers on our behalf and that of the Business of the Holy Land, and have special prayers said in places under your authority, so that, as the divine mercy is assuaged and shows its favour, your prayers and those of other good men will achieve what our own sins prevent.

Dated Acre, the month of August in the year of the Lord 1250.

1250).

186 The text reads *clerici*. But this must be an error for *Franci*, since the allusion is clearly to the First Crusade. For this theme, see Joseph R. Strayer, 'France: the Holy Land, the Chosen People, and the Most Christian King', in Theodore K. Rabb and Jerrold E. Seigel (eds), *Action and Conviction in Early Modern Europe: Essays in memory of E.H. Harbison* (Princeton, NJ, 1969), pp. 3-19, and reprinted in Strayer, *Medieval Statecraft and the Perspectives of History* (Princeton, NJ, 1971), pp. 300–314.

187 Matthew, xx, 1–16.

71. Comte Paul Riant, 'Déposition de Charles d'Anjou pour la canonisation de saint Louis', in C. Jourdain (ed.), Notices et documents publiées par la Société de l'histoire de France à l'occasion du cinquantième anniversaire de sa fondation *(Paris, 1884), pp. 155–76 (here pp. 170–75)*

Fragments of the deposition made by Charles I of Anjou [1282], King of Sicily[188] [p. 170]

(a) … of the 32 columns drawn up in Damietta, there remained for the withdrawal from Mansora, as a result of the engagement and through [spasmodic] killings and those natural deaths that might occur, only six, even including the wounded, the enfeebled and the sick. And those six did not reach the number of warriors, comparing man for man, who were strong and healthy among the original 32. The ailment that had afflicted the Christian army in general was so severe that scarcely anyone avoided it. They suffered in their teeth and gums, and from dysentery, and the sick developed dark patches on their thighs or legs.[189] Two days before we retreated from Ma[n]sorra, the King succumbed to this disease to the point that he was in complete distress. In informal moments he showed [his] brothers extensive dark patches on one of his legs. There was no physician …

(b) Orders were given that the ships should hug the bank as the army moved along it, lest the Saracens' vessels, which lay on the opposite bank of the river, should split up in order to occupy both banks, which would have enabled them to harass our men from two directions, both by land and by water. [The aim was also] that our men should assist each other, by virtue of the ships shielding those who were on land from the direction of the river and, conversely, that those on land might protect the ships from the direction of the shore that they occupied. Because of the need for them [p. 171] to wait for one another, the cavalry were obliged to move more slowly on Damietta than they should have done; and waiting for the weak foot-soldiers, and the sick in the army who could not be accommodated in the ships, further slowed the pace. On the night of the withdrawal from Ma[n]sorra, the King greatly deteriorated. Several times he had to dismount on account of the dysentery from which he suffered along with the other aforementioned ailments. When morning came, which was the Wednesday [6 April 1250] following the octave of Easter …

Then the King dismounted in view of his illness, and stood propped up against his saddle. With him were his close friends, the knights Geoffrey de Sardines,[190]

188 Riant, pp. 162–3, discussing the date, concludes that Charles gave this testimony in Naples in February 1282 to the Cardinal Benedict Caetani (the future Pope Boniface VIII), who had been sent to him by Martin IV.

189 These afflictions are described by Joinville, § 291, p. 160 (trans. Hague, p. 97; trans. Shaw, p. 237): he says that the flesh on the legs grew desiccated and the thighs were covered with black or earth-coloured spots. Hague (note at p. 278) suggests that the symptoms indicate the presence not only of scurvy and dysentery but also of malaria, typhoid and diphtheria.

190 Geoffrey de Sargines: see note 106 above.

Jean Fuinon,[191] Jean de Valéry,[192] P. de Baucay, Robert de Basoches and Gautier de Châtillon,[193] who, seeing his grave condition and the danger if he stayed on land, urged him, singly and in unison, to save himself by going on board ship. And when he refused, so it is said, to abandon his people, his brother, King Charles, who was then Count of Anjou, told him: 'My lord, you do badly in not accepting the sound advice of friends to go on board, since holding back for you on land is dangerously slowing the army's progress, and you could be the cause of our deaths.' He said this, so he himself reported, from a desire to save the King, since he was so afraid that [the King] would die there and then that he would willingly have forfeited his entire inheritance for himself and his heirs, just for the King to be at that juncture in Damietta. But the King, agitated and with a fierce look, twice told him: 'Count of Anjou, Count of Anjou! If you find me a burden, leave me behind, since I will not desert my people.'[194] …

(c) When, therefore, the captured King was being held in a [particular] place, his brother Charles was brought to him, after being kept apart from him for four or five days. Charles now informed him, as he describes in his deposition, that some were negotiating separately for their own release and that of their friends … and were promising the Saracens money in return. At this the King was extremely troubled, and sent for them and certain others; and in the presence of his two brothers and of the knights previously named, he addressed them, saying: 'I hear that some of you are negotiating separately for your release and that of your brethren. This I would on no account permit. I want everybody under my command to know that, if God delivers me from this prison, I shall deprive whoever has acted thus of everything he holds from me or possesses under my rule. I [p. 172] prohibit all under my command from daring to do anything of the kind on pain of death and of everything they hold

191 Joinville, § 392, p. 214, speaks of him as *li bons chevaliers* (trans. Hague, p. 123; trans. Shaw, p. 261). He is presumably to be distinguished from the man of similar name who had been *bailli* of the kingdom of Jerusalem in 1248–49: 'Estoire de Eracles', pp. 436–7 (trans. in Shirley, *Crusader Syria*, p. 137); 'Annales de Terre Sainte', pp. 442, 443 (version 'B').

192 Mentioned by Joinville, who describes him as *le preudome*: §§ 230–32, 339, pp. 126, 184 (trans. Hague, pp. 81–2, 108–9; trans. Shaw, pp. 222-3, 247). It was Jean who, in the division of spoils at Damietta in June 1249, had unavailingly pointed out to Louis that he was disregarding the custom of the kingdom of Jerusalem: §§ 168-9, p. 92 (trans. Hague, pp. 65–6; trans. Shaw, pp. 206–7).

193 Gautier de Châtillon was given command of the rearguard after Louis and the main army had crossed the Ushmūn Ṭannāḥ, and held it during the retreat from Mansura: Joinville, §§ 243, 295, 308, pp. 134, 162, 168 (trans. Hague, pp. 85, 98, 101; trans. Shaw, pp. 225, 238, 241). Curiously, Joinville was under the impression that he had been killed in the fighting: §§ 390–92, pp. 212, 214 (trans. Hague, pp. 122-3; trans. Shaw, p. 261); cf. also § 108, p. 62 (trans. Hague, p. 51; trans. Shaw, p. 190), where he is described as the nephew of Hugues, Count of Saint-Pol.

194 Louis's refusal to abandon his men by boarding a galley is mentioned also by Joinville, §§ 9-10, 306, pp. 6, 168 (trans. Hague, pp. 24, 101; trans. Shaw, pp. 164, 240). 'Rothelin', p. 612 (trans. Shirley, pp. 100–101), claims that the King and his brothers had been urged to take ship for Damietta even before the retreat began.

from me. The reason is that if this came about it would cause the worst trouble and scandal, because the only people to be released by these means would be the wealthy, who could afford the price, while all the poor, who lack the wherewithal to ransom themselves, would remain captives in perpetuity. But let everyone leave it to me to negotiate in general for the release of all the prisoners, since I want nobody to spend any of his own money for his release. I want to be the only person burdened with paying myself the cost of the ransom of each and every one, and I submit to you …'

(d) The King began negotiations for the release of himself and all the others, in return for which he was to pay a specified sum of money, to surrender Damietta and to make a truce for ten years. The King's two brothers went with certain others to receive the Sultan's oath on these matters. When both sides had agreed, the King, his brothers and all the rest were sent off in ships to be taken downstream to Damietta. And when they were approaching close to the city, the Sultan had the King, his brothers and certain others disembarked and placed on land in a tent set up specially for this purpose, while the rest of the prisoners remained on board. At that point, at the third hour [9 a.m.] there arose a great dispute among the Saracens, at which those guarding the King and his brothers appeared extraordinarily bewildered. When asked what was happening, they would not say; but from their behaviour it was clear that it was a mighty commotion and that grave danger threatened. Thereupon the King, turning to the Lord, had the office of the Mass for the Cross recited, and that for the day, for the Holy Spirit, and for Requiem, together with certain other prayers which he knew were beneficial in such circumstances. Then they were visited by those who had recently killed the Sultan, accompanied by a good 200 others, their white clothes bespattered with blood. At that moment the King and the others were firmly convinced that they were to be massacred. But these men began to offer justifications for the Sultan's death, advancing two reasons. One was perhaps fictitious. They claimed to disapprove of the treachery the Sultan intended towards the King and the other Christians, alleging that contrary to his oath he planned to kill the King and all the other Christians, whether or not he gained Damietta; [and so] they had put him to death.[195] [p. 173] The means whereby he had proposed to kill the Christians was this: he planned to tie the King and his brothers and barons to stakes before the walls of Damietta and to use torture to compel them to have Damietta surrendered. Unless they did so, he would have them subjected to exquisite torment; but even if they had complied, he planned subsequently, nevertheless, to put them all to different kinds of death. For even after the aforementioned oath to release the prisoners, he had killed

195 According to Joinville, §§ 353, 357, pp. 192, 194 (trans. Hague, pp. 112–13, 114; trans. Shaw, pp. 252, 253), Fāris al-Dīn Aqṭāy appeared before Louis with his hands dripping blood after cutting out the Sultan's heart, and told him that had Tūrān Shāh lived he would certainly have killed the King; and the following day messengers sent by the amirs told Joinville and other leaders the same thing. It is perhaps for this reason that Joinville, § 401, p. 218 (trans. Hague, p. 125; trans. Shaw, p. 263), later describes Aqṭāy as 'one of the most honourable Saracens I have ever met'.

several of them, and had sent many to Cairo,[196] whom he would not have sent away had he [really] had it in mind to hand them over.[197] But God had turned upon him the death he had devised for the Christians, just as Aman was hanged on the gibbet he had prepared for Mardocheus.[198] The second reason they gave was that the Sultan had deprived of their rank those who had served his father and had aided[199] him in war, and had given them to boys who had not aided him in war. The ambassador of the Caliph of Baghdad, who was with them, was disturbed at the Sultan's murder, and was hostile: he blamed the King for having delayed paying the outstanding part of the ransom, and claimed that this was what had given rise to these disastrous events. This ambassador of the Caliph [also] threatened the Sultan's murderers that the Caliph would rouse up against them the whole of Islam.[200] For this reason, in order not to have a war on their hands, they were in a hurry to get the Christians to shelter in Damietta and [to receive] the sum outstanding.

(e) ... Three times the King refused to add this condition, and on the first two occasions the King's brothers believed that he was to be killed.[201] But on the third occasion, when they were arguing that it was no sin to insert that condition if he intended to observe the aforesaid clauses, whereas it would be a sin if he had no such intention,[202] he replied that he did intend to observe [them] and that he did indeed believe the addition was no sin; but it struck him as appalling that a Christian should employ such phrases, and for that reason he would in no way agree, were it a matter of life or death. On hearing this, everyone believed they would be slaughtered on the spot, and regretted that they had required from the Saracens [a clause stipulating] denial of faith, for their own advantage, in order that the terms might be more surely fulfilled, and it had been turned round against them.

But the Lord, as we have said, calmed [the Saracens'] rage. When the Saracens required payment of the outstanding half of the money and the return of Damietta, in accordance with the terms, the King replied that at the moment [p. 174] he did not have the money: if a deadline was set, he would find and pay it and surrender

196 *Babilonia.*

197 For Joinville, § 358, p. 194 (trans. Hague, p. 114; trans. Shaw, p. 253), too, this was a sign that had the Sultan gained possession of Damietta he would have put the leaders of the crusade to death.

198 Esther, vii, 10.

199 Reading here and in the next line *iuverant* for the *invenerant* of the text.

200 *paganismum.* Riant claims that the presence of a caliphal ambassador is not mentioned elsewhere. But Ibn Wāṣil [**doc. 73**], p. 151 below, says that he was in the camp, and according to the Sibṭ Ibn al-Jawzī [**doc. 74(i)**], p. 161 below, it was he who interceded with the Mamluks in order to secure burial for Tūrān Shāh's corpse.

201 There is a fuller account of this dispute over the phrasing of the oath to be taken by Louis in Joinville, §§ 362-5, pp. 196, 198 (trans. Hague, pp. 115–16; trans. Shaw, pp. 254–5): the King objected to the clause that if he did not keep his word he should be as dishonoured as a Christian who denied God and his law and spat and trampled on the Cross.

202 Joinville, § 365, p. 198 (trans. Hague, p. 116; trans. Shaw, p. 255), attributes this argument to the Patriarch of Jerusalem, who was being manhandled by the Muslims on the suspicion that he had encouraged the King to stand firm [see also **doc. 68** above].

Damietta, but first he wanted the release of himself and the others to be guaranteed, in case it transpired that he lost out on both counts. At this, as their own guarantee and ours, they offered the King a choice: either he alone could remain a prisoner on behalf of all the others, who could go free, or conversely the King might go free and everyone else remain until the money was paid and Damietta surrendered. Thereupon, in the presence of his brothers and the aforementioned knights, the King, without a moment's thought, replied that he chose to remain a prisoner on behalf of everyone [else]. His brothers and knights, however, replied that they could on no account tolerate going free while their lord remained in captivity; the opposite should be done, namely that they would remain on their lord's behalf. There followed a lengthy altercation about this, until the Saracens discovered through the interpreter that they were engaged in a pious dispute about mutual charity, whereby the lord wanted to remain hostage for his subjects and they for their lord; and God touched the tyrants' hearts. Moved by compassion, they proposed that the King choose one of his brothers to remain a hostage for himself and the others until they had handed over Damietta and the money, when he would go free with the rest.[203] But when the King chose to leave behind as hostage the Count of Anjou, [the Saracens] judged that he had more affection for the Count of Poitou, whom he had chosen to keep by his side; and they wanted to hold the latter in their hands so that the King would fulfil his undertakings more promptly to get him back. And so it was done. And when they reached Damietta, the King refused to let the ship leave until he had paid the money, handed over Damietta and had his hostage brother back,[204] and all …

(f) When the [King's] brothers, the two counts, had stayed with the King in Syria until August, the King summoned the Count of Anjou and told him his wishes, namely that both brothers should return to France, while he himself remained. Charles asked [the King] to allow him to remain with him; and he replied that he would be very willing to keep him with him if the Count of Poitou were prepared to go back alone. At that Charles asked that he might himself remain in the country in his place. The King answered that he would not put anyone in his own place as a substitute: he could better recover the prisoners who were still held than [p. 175] anyone else in his stead, since as the most powerful he was more greatly feared than all the rest. This compassion for the captives was his major reason for wanting to stay, so that he could free them just as he [in fact] did: had he returned, they would never have been released. The King, therefore, stayed in Syria and sent his brothers to France;

203 Joinville, § 302, pp. 164, 166 (trans. Hague, pp. 99-100; trans. Shaw, p. 239), describes how the question whether Louis or one of his brothers should be left as a hostage in Muslim hands arose during earlier negotiations with Tūrān Shāh, prior to the final *débâcle*, over an exchange of Damietta for territory in Palestine; the discussions collapsed owing to the Egyptians' insistence that it should be the King.

204 Joinville says at this point only that the Count of Poitou was kept as a hostage, to be released once the first half of the ransom had been paid, and fails to mention the dispute over which brother should be left. He also alleges that, although Louis refused to leave the river for the open sea until the money had been handed over, he set sail without knowing that Alphonse had been freed: §§ 378, 388–9, pp. 206, 212 (trans. Hague, pp. 119, 122; trans. Shaw, pp. 258, 260–61).

and he wrote letters for them to take which, authenticated with his new seal, included everything good and ill that had befallen him and his people and ordered everyone in his realm – great, middling and small – to bring him aid in the Holy Land, which stood in grave danger[205]...

72. Vincent de Beauvais, Speculum Historiale, *ed. Johann Mentelin (Straßburg, 1473), xxxii, 89–98*[206]

(89) How Louis, King of the French, sailed to Cyprus In the year of the Lord 1248, Louis, King of the French, began the journey overseas, inasmuch as on the Friday [12 June] after Pentecost he left Paris, escorted by many from that city as far as Saint-Antoine. He was accompanied by the venerable Bishop of Tusculum, Eudes, the legate of the Apostolic See, and the King's two brothers, Robert, Count of Artois, and Charles, Count of Anjou, their wives, and many barons and bishops of the kingdom of France. The King's brother Alphonse, Count of Poitou, had also taken the Cross for overseas, but he stayed behind with his mother, Queen Blanche, for that year in order to watch over the realm. And so the King and his men took ship on Tuesday, the day [25 August] following St. Bartholomew, and spent the next two days there awaiting a favourable wind. On the Friday following, he left the harbour and, sailing with God's guidance, he at length put into Limassol in Cyprus on the night of Thursday [17 September] preceding the feast of St. Matthew.[207] But the Countess of Artois returned to France from the port of Aigues-Mortes, because she was pregnant, and stayed there until the Count of Poitou sailed.[208] On the advice of his barons and of the barons and landholders of Cyprus, the King made a long halt in Cyprus, because his ships and galleys, with his crossbowmen and [other] men, had not yet arrived, and put off his expedition against the Saracens until Easter on account of the imminence of winter and for other relevant reasons. The King of Cyprus and almost all the nobles and prelates of that realm assumed the sign of the Cross and swore that they would set out with the King of France against the Saracens, wherever he wished to take them, at a prearranged date.

At this time the Sultan of Egypt, who had made preparations to move to the Damascus region through Christian territory, heard rumours of the French King's arrival and abandoned the journey he had planned. There were hostilities between this Sultan and him who was Sultan of Damascus[209] and also the people of Aleppo.

During this period there died among the pilgrims Robert, Bishop of Beauvais, the Count of Montfort, the Count of Vendôme, Guillaume de Mello, Guillaume de Barre, Archambaud, sire de Bourbon, the Count of Dreux, and very many other knights, whose number is estimated at 240; while the Count of Anjou suffered from

205 For this letter, see **doc. 70** above.

206 What follows is reproduced almost verbatim by Guillaume de Nangis, 'Gesta sanctae memoriae Ludovici', pp. 356-82.

207 'Estoire de Eracles', p. 436 (trans. in Shirley, *Crusader Syria*, p. 137), has 28 September, but 'Annales de Terre Sainte', p. 442, has 17 September.

208 Not mentioned in any other source translated here.

209 An error: see above, note 69.

a quartan ague on Cyprus. Since there was a dispute between the Archbishop of Nicosia and the knights of the district, on account of which almost all those knights had been excommunicated, the Legate Eudes mediated a settlement between the parties and had 200 knights absolved. The Archbishop of the Greeks in Cyprus, who had now for a long time been exiled from his church as a schismatic who did not obey his Latin archbishop, returned at this time and both he and the other Greeks who had been excommunicated returned to obedience and were absolved by the Legate, in whose presence they further renounced certain heresies. Many Saracens, too, who were kept in captivity on Cyprus urgently requested baptism and received the sign of baptism …[210]

(95) The enmity between the Sultans of Egypt and Aleppo Meanwhile, the Sultan of Egypt, on learning that the French King was wintering on Cyprus, immediately set out on the march for the Damascus region and by way of the city of Jerusalem. His plan and aim thereby were to win over the Sultan of Aleppo, and those others who supported him, to make peace and an alliance, and to bring them to assist him. With this purpose the Caliph of Baghdad and the Old Man of the Mountain had sent envoys in order to reconcile them. But the Sultan of Aleppo, who recognized the trickery and cunning of the Sultan of Egypt, did not dare to trust him and was unwilling to make peace or a settlement with him. For this reason the Sultan of Egypt was roused to anger and had his forces invest the city of Ḥimṣ, which belongs to the Sultan of Aleppo; while he himself returned to Damascus. In the course of this siege, the Sultan is alleged to have suffered heavy losses among his men, goods and livestock, on account of the winter, the rains and Bedouin attacks. While the Egyptian army persisted in this investment, the Sultan of Aleppo made ready his forces and advanced in order to raise the siege. But the Caliph's ambassador joined him and advised him to make peace with the Sultan of Egypt, drawing to his attention the many dangers that threatened the Saracens at this juncture, inasmuch as the Christian army had come in order to destroy Mahomet's people and religion. If the Saracens thus directed their hostilities against themselves, it would result in damage and confusion for them and in success for their Christian enemies. When the Caliph's ambassador made these and many other representations and had discussed them on several occasions with the Sultan, the latter was in no way willing to entertain talk of peace, but said that as long as the Egyptians remained in his dominions he would on no account negotiate on this matter: unless they withdrew on the following day, he would certainly do battle with them. And so the ambassador saw that he would accomplish nothing in the peace negotiations and withdrew. He hastened to the Egyptian forces and induced them to raise the siege by informing them of the

---

210 There follow the account of Eljigidei's embassy, his letter and that of the Armenian Constable Smbat, the interrogation of Eljigidei's envoys, and the return embassy sent to the Mongols by King Louis (xxxii, 90–94). All this is taken from the report of the Legate Eudes [**doc. 56**].

imminent danger of attack. In the greatest disarray they fell back on Damascus, where the Sultan was residing, laid low by a grave illness ...[211]

On Cyprus, too,[212] he had small craft[213] manufactured which were necessary in order to occupy the enemy's territory. At this time certain men were captured who confessed that they and some others had been sent by the Sultan of Egypt to kill the King and the army leaders by poison.

(97) How the King captured the port of Damietta Finally, however, the ships and vessels arrived under escort. There also arrived from the islands ships in great numbers and many barons, knights and other pilgrims who had spent in the islands the winter just past. On the Saturday [8 May 1249] prior to[214] the Lord's Ascension, therefore, when the French King was already on board his ship, the leaders of the army assembled there, and on their advice a proclamation was made through the host that everyone should, with God's aid, head for Damietta. On Ascension Day [13 May], therefore, they embarked as had been ordered, but remained in harbour until the following Wednesday, because they lacked suitable weather for sailing and their men were not as yet completely ready. That day, then, the King set sail and left the port of Limassol with a great host of ships and vessels. But after they had gone some days with difficulty amid adverse winds, they arrived off Paphos, a city on Cyprus; and the weather was so very much against them that they were twice obliged to return to Limassol. At that point the Prince of Achaea, at the head of a great many of his vassals and subjects, came to join them in aid of the Holy Land, and with him likewise the Duke of Burgundy, who had been wintering in Romania. The pilgrims therefore waited at Limassol, and there reassembled their forces, which had been scattered by the adverse weather. At length, on the feast of the Holy Trinity [30 May], they hoisted sail and accomplished the voyage with fairly favourable weather, so that on the following Friday [4 June] they sighted Egypt and, after a short interval, the city of Damietta. So they drew in towards the city and entered the harbour, where they anchored their ships. That day, since they saw that the port was garrisoned by a great crowd of Turkish cavalry and foot, and that the mouth of the river, which was visible nearby, was defended by a great number of galleys, the King, in consultation with the leaders of the army, decided that they should land on the island at first light the following day in order to seize the terrain, namely at that spot which they had similarly occupied who had participated in the previous siege of Damietta, so that the river lay between them and the city.

The next day, then, the pilgrims, appropriately fitted out and armed, boarded the galleys and as many other small craft as could accommodate them, while the King

---

211 Omitted here are an account of the abortive negotiations with the Egyptians entered into by the Templar Master and the Marshal of the Hospital, and a narrative of events during the halt on Cyprus, all similarly taken from the Legate's report (xxxii, 95–6).

212 This is immediately preceded by the account of the dispute in Acre, which prevented Louis from receiving on schedule the additional vessels he had commissioned. The few details that follow are absent from the Legate's report, which suggests that they occurred in April 1249.

213 *parva quedam vasella*.

214 Reading *ante* for the *post* of the text, in view of the next date mentioned.

was in a vessel together with the Legate, who carried the holy triumphal Cross of the Lord, bare and on display, and the standard of the blessed martyr Denis was ahead in another vessel[215] close at hand, and the King's brothers, the rest of the barons, and the crossbowmen and knights accompanied them on all sides. Then they manfully advanced towards land in God's name, in the face of the enemy's ferocity, placing no little faith in God's mercy and the power of the Holy Cross, and launching heavy attacks with arrow-fire and other [projectiles]. Since the vessels that carried them were unable to reach dry land owing to the shallowness of the water, the Christian forces abandoned their boats in God's name and leapt into the sea, making it to dry land on foot with their weapons. The Saracens who had occupied the shore, in their efforts to defend the land, kept up a strong hail of arrows and other weapons against our men as they left the boats and approached, and struck at them with their swords. But our men gained the upper hand, landed and occupied the shore, repulsing the enemy. Almost none of our people were wounded or hurt, while several of the Saracens and a great many of their horses were killed or mortally wounded. Among them fell even some of the leaders, namely one who was in command of the town and two other amirs. The Sultan was not present, but had recently arrived from the direction of Damascus: at this point he was in a locality one day's journey from the city, where he was laid up with some illness. That day our galleys occupied the mouth of the river, and the Saracens' galleys retreated upstream. The King and the pilgrims pitched their tents on the shore, where they spent the night; and the next day, namely a Sunday [6 June], they remained there and arranged that [those of] their men and horses who were still on board ship could disembark and join the army.

(98) How the King entered and occupied the city after the enemy had been expelled and routed In addition to this auspicious beginning, Our Lord Jesus Christ gave yet more auspicious [things] to His catholic people. For the Saracens who were inside the city were struck with fear at the divine power, and suddenly that night the people, followed the next day, Sunday, by the chief men and all the rest, left the city, made off in flight and totally abandoned it after setting fire to it at all points. As soon as this was noticed, the troops were aroused, and many of our men rushed to enter the city by means of a bridge of boats that the Saracens had left reasonably intact apart from a gap which was forthwith repaired by our people. In addition the King, having ascertained the above, sent in some of his own men whom he had seen fit to choose for this purpose and had his troops garrison the entire city. Then he withdrew from the shore where he had been positioned, and that same day moved to the city's bridge, and there pitched his tents in front of the bridge, so that if it proved necessary he would be able to lend those inside the city timely assistance. Although a good deal of the garrison's provisions had been destroyed by fire, and much had been lost or pilfered, nevertheless much remained, since the city had been plentifully furnished by the Saracens for a long time [to come]. The city itself was also very well defended, both because of the course of the river and because it was surrounded by strong walls and towers; and it had been greatly reinforced since its

215 Reading, for *in alios vasallos*, *in alio vasallo*, as suggested by the text of Guillaume de Nangis.

earlier capture. For these reasons many asserted that it could in no way have been stormed or taken by force – unless God had miraculously brought it about through His power – as long as there were any inside who had sufficient foodstuffs and were willing to stay there.

The city was then cleansed of corpses and of the bodies of animals, and the fires extinguished; and the Legate, together with the Patriarch of Jerusalem and the archbishops and bishops who were present and a great many of the religious Orders, and King Louis and many others, accompanied by the King of Cyprus and several barons and others, entered the city in procession, barefoot. First of all the Legate reconciled the place where lay the Mosque,[216] which long before, at the time of the previous capture of the city, had been dedicated and appropriated as the Church of the Blessed Virgin. Then, when thanks had been given to the Most High for the blessings He had bestowed, Mass was solemnly celebrated by the Legate in honour of the Blessed Virgin Mary. The King further decided, should the Lord approve it, to install there prelates and canons who should constantly perform due service to the Lord. The city of Damietta was taken on the eighth day[217] after the feast of the Holy Trinity in the year of the Lord 1249.

The King remained there with the Christian army throughout the summer. For he did not wish to withdraw until the subsidence of the river, which at that juncture, so it was said, was due to cover the terrain, since on the previous occasion the Christian forces in those parts had suffered harm through its flooding. In this year, around the feast of St. John the Baptist [24 June 1249], King Louis's brother Alphonse, Count of Poitou, set out overseas, while their mother, Queen Blanche, stayed behind in sole charge of the realm. The Count put to sea at Aigues-Mortes with a large army on the day [25 August 1249] after St. Bartholomew, and landed at Damietta on the Sunday [24 October] before the feast of the Apostles Simon and Jude …[218]

216 *Machomeria.*

217 That is, seven days (6 June) after Trinity.

218 From this point onwards Vincent's narrative (xxxii, 99–102) closely follows the text of Louis's letter of August 1250 to his subjects [**doc. 70**], down to the departure from Acre of the King's two surviving brothers.

VI

Events in the Muslim Camp, and the Mamluk *Coup d'État*

The Arabic sources add little to our knowledge of the conduct of the campaign in Egypt, apart from details about minor skirmishing, the periodic arrival in Cairo of batches of Frankish prisoners and useful data on the numbers of the crusading army, particularly of the division which attacked Mansura. What they do furnish, however, that is lacking elsewhere is a wealth of information on the aftermath of the rapid fall of Damietta, on the tensions within the upper *échelons* of the regime both before and after the death of Sultan al-Ṣāliḥ Najm al-Dīn Ayyūb, and on the *coup d'état* that destroyed his son and ephemeral successor, al-Muʿaẓẓam Tūrān Shāh, early in May 1250. In the context of Egyptian politics, it should be noted, the Sibṭ and Ibn Wāṣil write from almost opposing standpoints, since the Sibṭ betrays some partiality for the Egyptian commander Fakhr al-Dīn Ibn al-Shaykh (a cousin of his informant, Saʿd al-Dīn),[1] while Ibn Wāṣil was a client and friend of Fakhr al-Dīn's rival, the viceroy of Egypt, Ḥusām al-Dīn.

The abandonment of Damietta, first by Fakhr al-Dīn and the field army, and then by the Banū Kināna garrison and the civil populace, was not simply a disgraceful episode, as Ibn Wāṣil makes clear, given the copious provisions and armaments stored in the city and its capacity accordingly to withstand a protracted siege (in sharp contrast with the situation in 1218–19); it also gave rise to tensions within the high command. The Sultan hanged the officers of the Banū Kināna, but was obliged to overlook the part played by Fakhr al-Dīn and his staff: had he survived, according to the Sibṭ, he would have put Fakhr al-Dīn to death. A section of the military wanted to kill the Sultan, but Fakhr al-Dīn restrained them on the grounds that Ayyūb could not live much longer.

Ayyūb's death on 22 November 1249 proved to be Fakhr al-Dīn's opportunity. He was summoned by the Sultan's widow Shajar al-Durr and the cavalry commander Jamāl al-Dīn Muḥassan, and the three agreed to keep Ayyūb's death secret and to continue to issue orders in his name; the grandees and principal military officers would be made to take an oath to Ayyūb, to his son al-Muʿaẓẓam Tūrān Shāh, and to Fakhr al-Dīn, as commander-in-chief of the armed forces. Messengers, including Fāris al-Dīn Aqṭāy, the commander of Ayyūb's Baḥriyya mamluk corps, were sent to fetch Tūrān Shāh from Ḥiṣn Kayfā in Mesopotamia, where Ayyūb had left him on coming south to take over Damascus after the death of his father al-Kāmil in 1238. During his lifetime, according to the viceroy Ḥusām al-Dīn ibn Abī ʿAlī, Ayyūb had

1 On the Banū Ḥamawiya family, which originated from Khurāsān, see H. L. Gottschalk, 'Awlād al-Shaykh', *EI*²; Cahen, 'Une source pour l'histoire ayyūbide', pp. 458–61.

refused to send for his son and had intended the government of Egypt to be entrusted to the ʿAbbasid Caliph; Ḥusām al-Dīn told the Sibṭ that Ayyūb had threatened to kill Tūrān Shāh if he appeared in Egypt.

Although the Sibṭ has Aqṭāy sent by the junta as a whole, Ibn Wāṣil hints that Fakhr al-Dīn was opposed to this but nevertheless had to acquiesce. Doubtless he believed, like others, that Tūrān Shāh would not in fact be able to get through to Egypt, in view of the danger of interception by the forces of Mosul or Aleppo; one observer, Ibn al-ʿAmīd, believed that the oath was taken to Fakhr al-Dīn in the event of Tūrān Shāh's failure to reach Egypt.[2] Despite the disclaimers issued by Fakhr al-Dīn, suspicion about his intentions appears to have been widespread. The Sibṭ claims that Muḥassan and others subsequently sent more mamluks who joined Tūrān Shāh at Damascus and made him fear that Fakhr al-Dīn aimed at the throne itself. In addition, the viceroy Ḥusām al-Dīn, having ascertained that the Sultan was dead and that the orders he was receiving were in fact forged, sent one of his own mamluks from Cairo to urge Tūrān Shāh to make haste in case Fakhr al-Dīn attempted to rule through a young scion of the Ayyubid dynasty: Ḥusām al-Dīn had the most likely candidate, Ayyūb's nephew, al-Mughīth ʿUmar, arrested and confined in the Jabal citadel.

By the time Tūrān Shāh reached Mansura on 25 February 1250, Fakhr al-Dīn was dead, a victim of the crusaders' surprise attack on the Muslim camp. But the new Sultan's mind had been turned against him: the Sibṭ claims that he had decided en route to eliminate Fakhr al-Dīn, and once in Egypt Tūrān Shāh repeatedly complained of the way in which the general had emptied the treasury. Tūrān Shāh's own acts of generosity, designed to win hearts, had already consumed the treasure at Damascus, and much of that from Kerak, during his halt in the Syrian capital. The discovery that the Egyptian treasury was virtually exhausted may have been a severe blow. It certainly meant that he was unable to extend his largesse to the amirs in Egypt, and that their hopes of being treated like their *confrères* in Damascus were sadly disappointed.

This situation may help to explain the Sultan's behaviour once he was ensconced at Mansura, such as his harassment of Shajar al-Durr for the jewellery she had received from his father. He was already suspicious of what had transpired prior to his arrival. In view of the dearth of resources at his disposal for winning over those currently in power, his need to replace them with men on whose loyalty he could depend was all the more pressing. Traditionally, every new monarch sought to install his own men in positions of authority; but the majority did so gradually and judiciously, perhaps replacing office-holders as they died or as an opportunity arose to transfer them elsewhere. It may in part have been in response to financial pressures that Tūrān Shāh, by contrast, acted precipitately, promoting the men who had accompanied him from Ḥiṣn Kayfā, a circumstance to which Joinville attributes the *coup* that overthrew him.[3] Especial mention should be made, perhaps, of the transfer of Fakhr al-Dīn's lucrative assignment to his own slave, Jawhar, and of his

2 Ibn al-ʿAmīd, p. 159 (trans. Eddé and Micheau, pp. 85–6).

3 Joinville, §§ 287-8, 348, pp. 158, 190 (trans. Hague, pp. 96, 111; trans. Shaw, pp. 236, 251).

reported intention to dismiss the qadis of Cairo and Miṣr and to promote the qadi of Ḥiṣn Kayfā in their place.

There were undoubtedly also other reasons for the new monarch's unpopularity with the military class. It is difficult to know how much weight to attach to the charges levelled at him by Fakhr al-Dīn's cousin, Saʿd al-Dīn, and by the Sibṭ, both surely hostile sources: that he was unstable, for instance; or that he engaged in acts of depravity with his father's mamluks and concubines. Although the Sibṭ alleges that he was less accessible to the people than his father, the markedly sympathetic account of Ibn Wāṣil suggests that Tūrān Shāh was temperamentally more attuned to the company of scholars (a trait which had won him the affection of his grandfather al-Kāmil); Ibn Wāṣil planned to dedicate to him a history he had compiled at an earlier date.

That said, Tūrān Shāh's provocative behaviour towards certain sections of the military was nothing short of foolhardy. The power of the Baḥriyya corps had grown substantially during his father's last years, when they had received many assignments confiscated from fallen amirs;[4] and they had saved the day, moreover, at Mansura. In the circumstances, to rehearse their execution, by slashing the heads off candles while drunk and calling out their names, was hardly the conduct of a sovereign who planned to retain the throne for more than a few weeks. He notably failed to make good his promise to their commander, Aqṭāy, who had journeyed to Mesopotamia at no small personal risk, of the *iqṭāʿ* of Alexandria. His demotion, too, of the viceroy Ḥusām al-Dīn, who had warned him of Fakhr al-Dīn's ambitions, appears to be another act of gross ingratitude. Actions of this kind would ensure that when the murderers struck Tūrān Shāh could not count upon anyone to display energy in his defence.

Tūrān Shāh was certainly no war-leader: the lack of energy with which he approached the reduction of Damietta did little to inspire confidence. On the other hand, the testimony of Bar Hebraeus (admittedly an author writing at a considerable distance from these events, in Mesopotamia, and wrong on a number of details) suggests that this may have represented conscious policy rather than mere indolence or ineptitude.[5] Had Damietta been taken by storm, the Sultan would have been obliged to distribute the plunder to the soldiery; but in the event of a negotiated surrender he could monopolize the city's resources himself. The author of the 'Rothelin' chronicle heard that Tūrān Shāh had been killed for the ransom money,[6] while Joinville depicts the murderers as anxious to act before the Sultan gained possession of Damietta and was no longer dependent on them.[7] If there is any truth in these tantalizing snippets of information, the *coup* takes on the appearance not simply of a defensive measure

4 R. Stephen Humphreys, 'The emergence of the Mamluk army', *Studia Islamica*, 45 (1977): 67-99 (here 96–9), does not seem to take this testimony on board in his assessment of their rise.

5 Bar Hebraeus (d. 1286), *Makhtebhânûth zabhnê*, trans. E. A. Wallis Budge, *The Chronography of Gregory Abû'l-Faraj, the Son of Aaron the Hebrew Physician, Commonly Known as Bar Hebraeus* (Oxford and London, 1932), vol. 1 (trans.), p. 415.

6 'Rothelin', p. 618 (trans. Shirley, p. 104); though this is just the kind of suspicion that would readily have occurred to many, including the ill informed.

7 Joinville, § 348, p. 190 (trans. Hague, p. 111; trans. Shaw, p. 251).

by the Baḥriyya, but also of a bid to appropriate the Frankish ransom money – and secure thereby the rewards that Tūrān Shāh had denied them.

DOCUMENTS 73–4

73. Ibn Wāṣil, Mufarrij al-kurūb fī akhbār banī Ayyūb, *Bibliothèque Nationale, Paris, ms. arabe 1703, fols 60v–66r, 74v–92r* passim

The year 646 [1248–9] ... [fol. 60v] *How al-Malik al-Ṣāliḥ's forces invested Ḥimṣ but then withdrew* ... [fol. 61r] Sultan al-Malik al-Nāṣir left Aleppo in mid-Ramaḍān of this year [early January 1249] for the siege of Ḥimṣ,[8] and encamped in the district of Kafr Ṭāb. The siege continued until the shaykh Najm al-Dīn al-Bādarā'ī[9] (God have mercy on him) arrived as the envoy of the Caliph al-Mustaʿṣim bi'llāh. He had come in order to make peace between the two Sultans, al-Malik al-Ṣāliḥ and al-Malik al-Nāṣir, the ruler of Aleppo, on condition that Sultan al-Malik al-Ṣāliḥ should withdraw from the attack on Ḥimṣ and that it should remain in the hands of al-Malik al-Nāṣir; and an agreement was made on these terms.[10] al-Malik al-Ṣāliḥ issued orders to his troops to move from Ḥimṣ, and they did so, after being on the point of taking it. Nevertheless, Sultan al-Malik al-Ṣāliḥ consented to make peace for two reasons. One was that he was ill; the other was that he had learned of the Frankish expedition and their invasion of Egypt in considerable strength from beyond the sea, and he believed that it was incumbent on him to make a peace and a settlement. While he was at Damascus, al-Malik al-Ṣāliḥ was visited by the shaykh Shams al-Dīn al-Khusrawshāhī, the envoy of al-Malik al-Nāṣir Dā'ūd,[11] accompanied by al-Malik al-Nāṣir [Dā'ūd]'s son, al-Malik al-Amjad Ḥasan. The object of the embassy was to ask al-Malik al-Ṣāliḥ to accept his surrender of Kerak in exchange for al-Shawbak[12] and an assignment in Egypt. al-Malik al-Ṣāliḥ agreed to this.

---

8 Both Ibn Wāṣil and Ibn ʿAbd al-Raḥīm, Bibliothèque Nationale ms. arabe 1702, fol. 354r, have here simply the phrase *wa'l-ḥiṣār ʿalā Ḥimṣ* ('and the siege of Ḥimṣ'), as if words have been inadvertently elided. I have reproduced the probable sense.

9 Najm al-Dīn ʿAbd-Allāh ibn Muḥammad al-Bādarā'ī (d. 1257), a distinguished teacher in Damascus: see Louis Pouzet, *Damas au VIIe/XIIIe siècle. Vie et structures religieuses d'une métropole islamique* (Beirut, 1988), p. 154.

10 For the war between al-Ṣāliḥ Ayyūb and al-Nāṣir Yūsuf over Ḥimṣ, see Humphreys, *From Saladin to the Mongols*, pp. 293–6.

11 Ayyūb's cousin, who had succeeded his father as ruler of Damascus (1227–29) until displaced by al-Kāmil; he had then been compensated with the principality of Kerak. Having taken Ayyūb prisoner in 1239, he had assisted him to gain the throne of Egypt in the following year, but went on to play a vacillating role in the conflicts between Ayyūb and his kinsmen: see Peter Jackson, 'The crusades of 1239–1241 and their aftermath', *Bulletin of the School of Oriental and African Studies*, 50 (1987): 32–60, reprinted in G. R. Hawting (ed.), *Muslims, Mongols and Crusaders* (London and New York, 2005), pp. 217–47.

12 The strategic fortress in the Transjordan known to the Franks as Montréal and in their hands until its capture by Saladin in 1187.

Sultan al-Malik al-Ṣāliḥ's return to Egypt Sultan al-Malik al-Ṣāliḥ set out for Egypt.[13] He was carried in a litter, since it was impossible for him to ride on a horse in view of his illness. [fol. 61v] When he had advanced two stages from Damascus, he ordered the amir Ḥusām al-Dīn[14] to go to Kerak in order to accept its surrender by al-Malik al-Nāṣir Dā'ūd and to hand over al-Shawbak. Ḥusām al-Dīn (God have mercy on him) told me, 'When the order reached me to this effect, I was unwilling to go to Kerak. I was aware of al-Malik al-Nāṣir's fickleness and that he did not abide by a single [undertaking]. I was afraid that he would seize me and go back on what he had agreed with the Sultan. So I wrote to the Sultan asking to be excused from this [duty], and the reply reached me that he had excused me from it and had sent Tāj al-Dīn ibn Muhājir to take charge of the affair … So al-Malik al-Ṣāliḥ directed Tāj al-Dīn ibn Muhājir to travel to Kerak, and the latter arrived there and met with al-Malik al-Nāṣir, asking him to fulfil the terms of the agreement. But al-Malik al-Nāṣir reneged on what had been settled with al-Malik al-Ṣāliḥ, the reason being that he had learned of the Frankish advance against Egypt' …

[fol. 62r] *The year 647 [1249-50]* began, and at its outset Ḥusām al-Dīn ibn Abī ʿAlī arrived in Cairo. His entry into the city occurred on Tuesday 3 Muḥarram [18 April 1249],[15] and he took up his quarters in the vizier's residence. The amir Jamāl al-Dīn Ibn Yaghmūr[16] travelled to Damascus to be governor there on Sultan al-Malik al-Ṣāliḥ's behalf. He left Cairo prior to Ḥusām al-Dīn's arrival, and so they met each other in the desert. He reached Damascus,[17] and remained there as governor…

[fol. 62v] Sultan al-Malik al-Ṣāliḥ arrived at Ushmūn Ṭannāḥ on Monday, three days having elapsed of Ṣafar of this year [= 17 May 1249]. Reports had continually reached him that Raydafrans, the leader of the French[18] among the Franks, who had left his own territory with a mighty host with the aim of attacking and conquering Egypt, had wintered on the island of Cyprus. And so the Sultan took up his position at Ushmūn Ṭannāḥ in order to confront the Franks if they arrived at Damietta. This Raydafrans was one of the most important Frankish kings and the most powerful. Afrans is one of the Frankish peoples, and the meaning of Raydafrans is 'King of Afrans': in their language, *rayd* means 'king'. He was a devoted adherent of the Christian faith, and so his spirit told him that he should recover Jerusalem for the Franks, since it is, they claim, the dwelling-place of the one they revere. But he knew

---

13 On Monday 4 Muḥarram [19 April 1249], according to Abū Shāma, pp. 182–3.

14 Ḥusām al-Dīn Abū ʿAlī ibn Muḥammad ibn Abī ʿAlī (d. 1260), of the Kurdish tribe of the Hudhbānī, was a high-ranking amir formerly in the service of the ruler of Ḥamā who had switched his allegiance to Ayyūb in the 1230s. There is an obituary in al-Yūnīnī, *al-Dhayl 'alā' Mir'āt al-zamān* (Hyderabad, A.P., 1374-80 H./1954–61), vol. 2, pp. 77–87; see also Humphreys, *From Saladin to the Mongols*, pp. 251, 253, 272 and index.

15 This was in fact a Sunday.

16 Jamāl al-Dīn Mūsā ibn Yaghmūr (d. 1265), who belonged to the Türkmen tribe of the Yürük (Yārūq), had formerly been in the service of the Sultan of Aleppo. There is a brief biography in al-Yūnīnī, vol. 2, pp. 330–32.

17 On 10 Rabīʿ I [23 June 1249], according to Abū Shāma, p. 183.

18 *al-Afransīsa.*

that he would achieve this only by conquering Egypt.[19] It was reported that his army, both horsemen and infantry, totalled more than 50,000. He had set out on campaign the previous year and had first made for the island of Cyprus. The Sultan learned that he would arrive in the country at the beginning of spring, and this is what induced him to hasten to reach a settlement with the people of Aleppo. Had it not been for this, he would not have left his troops and withdrawn from Ḥimṣ without first taking it.

al-Malik al-Ṣāliḥ set about assembling and building up provisions, men, armour and military equipment at Damietta. His order from Ushmūn Ṭannāḥ reached his viceroy, the amir Ḥusām al-Dīn ibn Abī ʿAlī, that he should fit out galleys[20] in the arsenal, fill them with men and money, and send them to him one at a time. Ḥusām al-Dīn saw to this diligently. al-Malik al-Ṣāliḥ also [ordered] the amir Fakhr al-Dīn Ibn al-Shaykh to take up position on the peninsula of Damietta with the troops under his command, so that they might confront the enemy when they arrived. Fakhr al-Dīn set out with his troops and made camp on the peninsula; between it and Damietta lay the River Nile.[21] [fol. 63r] The Sultan remained in his own position because of his illness.

How the Franks arrived in Egypt and gained possession of the port of Damietta During the second hour of the morning of Friday, nine days remaining of Ṣafar of this year [4 June 1249], the Frankish ships arrived, containing a mighty host. They had been joined by all the Franks of the coastlands. They anchored at sea, facing the Muslims; but on the following day, namely on the Saturday, they began to disembark onto the shore where the Muslims were. King Raydafrans pitched his tent, which was red. Some of the Muslims engaged in skirmishing with them, and there was martyred on this day the amir Najm al-Dīn, the son of the Shaykh al-Islam (God have mercy on him) … Another of the Egyptian amirs who was martyred was known as al-Wazīrī.[22] When evening came on, the amir Fakhr al-Dīn Ibn al-Shaykh set out with [the Muslim army] and took them across the bridge[23] to the eastern bank, on which lay Damietta, abandoning the western bank to the Franks. After Fakhr al-Dīn and his forces had crossed over to the eastern bank, he and they moved off in the direction of Ushmūn Ṭannāḥ. The troops were a prey to self-interest on account of the Sultan's illness; and there was nobody to stand in their way or keep them in check.

19 This is most interesting, reflecting as it does an awareness of the rationale behind the 'Egyptian strategy'.

20 *al-shawānī*.

21 For a succinct description of the topography of this area, see Hans L. Gottschalk, *Al-Malik al-Kāmil von Egypten und seine Zeit* (Wiesbaden, 1958), p. 60, citing al-Maqrīzī.

22 Ṣārim al-Dīn Uzbak al-Wazīrī, an amir formerly in the service of the Sultan of Aleppo who had gone over to Ayyūb in 1247–48: Ibn al-ʿAmīd, p. 158 (trans. Eddé and Micheau, pp. 82-3). The same author says that Najm al-Dīn, the son of the Shaykh al-Islām, was also killed at this juncture.

23 Gabrieli, *Arab Historians of the Crusades*, p. 285, translated this as 'cut the bridge', but the Frankish sources confirm that the Muslims left the bridge of boats intact.

Both the eastern and the western banks were devoid of Muslim forces, and the inhabitants of Damietta were afraid for their lives if they were besieged. There was a body of valiant Kināniyya in the city; but God (may He be praised) struck terror into their hearts, and they and the people of Damietta left and travelled throughout the night. Not a single person remained in Damietta: they left it empty of men, women and children and made their way in flight with the troops under cover of night as far as Ushmūn Ṭannāḥ. This action of theirs and of Fakhr al-Dīn and the troops was disgraceful. Had Fakhr al-Dīn only prevented [fol. 63v] the army from fleeing and stood his ground, Damietta would have been impregnable. When the Franks invested Damietta on the first occasion, during the reign of al-Malik al-Kāmil, there were few supplies or funds; and yet the Franks took a year to master it. It was besieged in the year 615 [1218] and taken in the year 616 [1219], and the enemy did not gain possession of it until its population was destroyed by pestilence and starvation. Had the Kināniyya and the people of Damietta only locked the gates and entrenched themselves within following the army's retreat to Ushmūn Ṭannāḥ, the Franks would not have overcome them, and the troops would have returned and defended them. They had provisions, equipment and funds in great abundance and would have held out there for two years or more. But when God desires an outcome, there is no resisting it. When the people of Damietta saw the troops in flight and knew of the Sultan's illness, they were afraid that the siege would be greatly prolonged and that they would perish of starvation, as had Damietta's inhabitants on the first occasion.

When dawn came on the Sunday, seven[24] days remaining of Ṣafar [6 June 1249], the Franks arrived at Damietta and found it devoid of people and its gates open; and they occupied it without a fight. They took possession of everything that was there by way of funds, weaponry, equipment, provisions and mangonels. This was a terrible disaster, the like of which had never happened. A note to this effect arrived on the Sunday for the amir Ḥusām al-Dīn when I was [staying] with him. Anxiety and fear mounted, and despair fell upon the whole of Egypt, especially since the Sultan was ill and was no longer strong enough to travel. He lacked the power to control his army, and their ambitions had grown [at his expense]. When the troops and the people of Damietta reached the Sultan, he was extremely angry with the Kināniyya and gave orders for them to be hanged; and hanged they all were. He was mortified by the conduct of Fakhr al-Dīn and the troops, but the moment did not permit anything but forbearance and overlooking what they had done.

How the Sultan al-Malik al-Ṣāliḥ [fol. 64r] *and the troops moved to Mansura and took up position there* After the events we have described, Sultan al-Malik al-Ṣāliḥ moved with his forces to Mansura, where he took up his position. This is the place where his father al-Malik al-Kāmil had made camp during the first Damietta campaign: it lies to the east of the Nile, opposite Jūjar, and the Ushmūn Ṭannāḥ river [flows] between it and the island on which stands Damietta. We have already told how al-Malik al-Kāmil[25] had ordered buildings to be constructed here and had laid

24 Reading *sab'* for the *tis'* of the ms.

25 Ibn ʿAbd al-Raḥīm's version (Bibliothèque Nationale, ms. arabe 1702, fol. 357r) substitutes al-Malik al-Ṣāliḥ Ayyūb himself.

a wall between it and the river; al-Malik al-Kāmil had a palace here on the River Nile. So al-Malik al-Ṣāliḥ made camp here and pitched his pavilion alongside it. The Sultan took up residence at Mansura on Tuesday, five days remaining of Ṣafar [8 June 1249], and the troops set about restoring the buildings and establishing bazaars and rebuilding the wall that lay along the river. He surrounded it with parapets. War-galleys large and small[26] arrived, complete with equipment and fighting men, and anchored below the wall; while infantry, common folk[27] and volunteers for the Holy War[28] arrived at Mansura from every other region in a great throng that could not be counted. Numerous groups of Bedouin came, and began to launch raids upon the Franks and to skirmish with them. The Franks strengthened the walls of Damietta and filled it with warriors.

On Monday, the last day of Rabīʿ I [= 12 July 1249], there reached Cairo 36 Frankish prisoners who had been captured by the Bedouin and others, including two horsemen. On Saturday, five days having elapsed of Rabīʿ II [= 17 July 1249], 39 prisoners arrived in Cairo who had been captured by the Bedouin and the Khwarazmians. Next, 22 of them entered Cairo who had been taken from Gaza; the date of their arrival was 7 Rabīʿ II [20 July 1249]. On Wednesday, 14 nights remaining of Rabīʿ II [28 July 1249], 35 captives arrived, including three horsemen. And on Friday, five days remaining of Rabīʿ II [6 August 1249], [news] came that the Sultan's forces at Damascus [fol. 64v] had gone out to Sidon and wrested it from the hands of the Franks. Thereafter a few of them would arrive in separate groups: 50 of them came when 12 nights remained of Jumādā I [29 August 1249].

While all this was happening, the Sultan's illness intensified, and his strength was on the wane and failing. The physicians who attended him night and day had succumbed to despair of the outcome. For all that, his spirit and his willpower were extremely strong. But two serious ailments were jointly at work upon him: a cancerous wound in the hollow of his knee and consumption.[29]

How Kerak was handed over to al-Malik al-Ṣāliḥ When al-Nāṣir Dā'ūd was reduced to straits at Kerak, he appointed as his deputy there his son al-Muʿaẓẓam Sharaf al-Dīn ʿĪsā, took what he prized most by way of jewels, and made his way across the desert to Aleppo in order to appeal to its ruler, Sultan al-Malik al-Nāṣir ibn al-Malik al-ʿAzīz, and to seek refuge with him … The mother of al-Malik al-Muʿaẓẓam,

26 *al-shawānī wa'l-ḥarārīq*. For *shawānī* (sing. *shīnī*) and the smaller *ḥarārīq* (sing. *ḥarrāqa*, originally a fire-ship, but later denoting a smaller war-vessel or even a transport ship), see Ali Mohamed Fahmy, *Muslim Naval Organization in the Eastern Mediterranean from the Seventh to the Tenth Century A.D.*, 2nd edn (Cairo, 1966), pp. 131–2, 134–6; Pryor, 'The crusade of Emperor Frederick II', p. 123.

27 *al-ḥarāfisha*.

28 *al-ghuzāt al-muṭṭawi'a*.

29 *al-jirāḥat al-nāṣūra fī ma'biḍihi wa'l-sill.* The Sultan's ailments are discussed by Felix Klein-Franke, 'What was the fatal disease of al-Malik al-Ṣāliḥ Najm al-Dīn Ayyūb?', in M. Sharon (ed.), *Studies in Islamic History and Civilization in Honour of Professor David Ayalon* (Jerusalem and Leiden, 1986), pp. 153–7, though he does not use Ibn Wāṣil's contemporary account. Joinville, §§ 144–5, p. 80 (trans. Hague, p. 60; trans. Shaw, p. 200), believed that Ayyūb was poisoned by an agent of the Sultan of 'La Chamelle' (Ḥimṣ, an error for Aleppo).

whom al-Nāṣir had left at Kerak as his deputy, was a Turkish concubine to whom al-Malik al-Nāṣir was extremely attached, and al-Malik al-Nāṣir loved him more than he loved any of his brothers. By the daughter of his uncle al-Malik al-Amjad Ḥasan ibn al-Malik al-ʿĀdil, he had two sons, who were older than al-Malik al-Muʿaẓẓam: al-Malik al-Ẓāhir Shādī and al-Malik al-Amjad Ḥasan. al-Malik al-Ẓāhir was the oldest of his sons, having been born in the citadel of Damascus before Damascus was taken from him … [fol. 65r] When al-Malik al-Muʿaẓẓam was promoted, the rest were aggrieved at this, and particularly the sons of his uncle's daughter … They agreed with their mother to seize their brother, al-Malik al-Muʿaẓẓam, and to take control of Kerak, and they resolved to hand it over to Sultan al-Malik al-Ṣāliḥ and receive compensation from him. And so al-Malik al-Amjad went to the army headquarters at Mansura, where he arrived on Saturday 9 Jumādā II of that year, namely 647 [= 18 September 1249]. He arranged with the Sultan to hand over Kerak to him, obtained guarantees from him for himself and his brothers, and asked for an assignment in Egypt that would maintain them. Sultan al-Malik al-Ṣāliḥ treated him with honour, showed the greatest concern for his interests, and sent to Kerak the cavalry commander Badr al-Dīn al-Ṣawābī, to receive its surrender and to act as his lieutenant there. All al-Malik al-Nāṣir's sons and his two brothers, al-Malik al-Qāhir ʿAbd al-Malik and al-Malik al-Mughīth ʿAbd al-ʿAzīz, with their wives, slave-girls, male slaves and retinues, arrived at the army headquarters, and were given important *iqṭā's* and assigned sizeable pensions. The elder of al-Malik al-Nāṣir's sons and his brothers made camp on the western side opposite Mansura. al-Malik al-Ṣāliḥ was overjoyed at the acquisition of Kerak, despite his sick condition. Cairo and Miṣr[30] were decorated, and the good news was proclaimed in the two citadels. The surrender of Kerak to al-Malik al-Ṣāliḥ took place on the evening of Monday, 12 nights remaining of Jumādā [fol. 65v] II [26 September 1249].

On Thursday, when 13 nights had elapsed of Rajab [22 October 1249], there arrived in Cairo as prisoners 47 Frankish foot-soldiers and 11 horsemen.

The death of Sultan al-Malik al-Ṣāliḥ Najm al-Dīn Ayyūb ibn al-Malik al-Kāmil (God have mercy upon him) Sultan al-Malik al-Ṣāliḥ's illness grew more intense. As we have said, he was suffering from two ailments: an ulcer in the hollow of the knee and consumption. He was unaware of the consumption, and continued to fancy that his incapacity and weakness arose from campaigning, whereas its cause was the wound [in the knee]. As the sickness neared its end, the growth diminished and dwindled, and the wound was alleviated. He wrote to the amir Ḥusām al-Dīn to give him the good news that he had recovered, that the wound was on the wane and that only riding and playing polo were beyond him. One of the physicians with him in the army camp was Rashīd, known as Abū Khalīfa, [who had been] physician to his father. He wrote to Ḥusām al-Dīn, asking him to send the doctor Muhadhdhab al-Dīn[31] Abū'l-Faḍl al-Ḥamawī, which he did. Then he sent to ask him to send the

30 This denotes the old city of Fusṭāṭ, founded by the Arab conquerors in the seventh century, as opposed to Cairo (al-Qāhira), which was built by the Fatimid Caliphs in the tenth.

31 Ibn ʿAbd al-Raḥīm (fol. 358v) calls him Muwaffaq al-Dīn.

doctor Fatḥ al-Dīn Ibn Abī'l-Ḥawāfir, the chief physician; and he sent him [too]. He arrived some days before his death. But [the Sultan's] strength had failed, and he had stopped taking food; and [the physician] was not admitted to his presence. When [the Sultan] died, he was admitted to take charge of washing him. The intention was to keep his death a secret, for had anyone else entered they would have had doubts about him and realized that he was dead.

al-Malik al-Ṣāliḥ went to the mercy and approval of God when he was confronting the Franks as a holy warrior in the path of God, and his death occurred on the evening of Sunday when 14 nights had elapsed of Shaʿbān of this year [22 November 1249]. His reign in Egypt had lasted for nine years, eight months and 20 days, and he was approximately 44 years old, since he was born in the year [fol. 66r] 603 [1206–1207].[32]

His character (God have mercy on him) … He bought more Turkish mamluks than had any other member of his family, until they became the major part of his army … On becoming ruler of Egypt, he began to cut down the amirs who had been with his father and his brother, and to arrest them; and whenever he severed an amir's assignment, he would appoint one of his own mamluks in his place, to the point where the majority of the amirs of the state were his mamluks. He purchased in Egypt a considerable number of Turks, and made them his retinue and the guards of his pavilion. They were known as the Baḥriyya.[33] They became a mighty force, of extreme courage and boldness, from which the Muslims derived the greatest benefit when the Franks fell upon the country, especially on the day of the surprise attack, as we shall relate.[34] On that occasion they were Islam's protectors, its instrument and bulwark; later they defended the Muslims against the Tatars[35] … During his final years he had only two wives. One, known as Bint al-ʿĀlima, was married after his death to the keeper of the polo-stick,[36] one of his mamluks. The other was Shajar al-Durr, Khalīl's mother, who was proclaimed Sultan for a time in succession to his son al-Malik al-Muʿaẓẓam and [later] married al-Malik al-Muʿizz ʿIzz al-Dīn Aybak al-Turkmānī: we shall speak of their careers later, God willing …[37]

[fol. 74v] He had three sons. The eldest, al-Malik al-Mughīth Fatḥ al-Dīn ʿUmar, returned with his father to Damascus from the East: what befell him – his imprisonment in the citadel at Damascus and his death there[38] – we have already

32 Forty years old, and born in 608 [1211–12], according to Ibn ʿAbd al-Raḥīm (fol. 359r).

33 See David Ayalon, 'Le régiment Bahriya dans l'armée mamelouke', *Revue des Études Islamiques*, 19 (1951): 133–41, reprinted in his *Studies on the Mamlūks of Egypt (1250–1517)* (London, 1977).

34 A reference to the crossing of the Ushmūn Ṭannāḥ and the attack on Mansura.

35 An allusion to the Mongols' defeat by the Mamluks under Sultan Quṭuz at ʿAyn Jālūt in September 1260, for which the credit was reaped by Quṭuz's murderer and successor, Baybars.

36 *jawkandār*. On this office, see H. Massé, 'Čawgān', *EI*^{2}.

37 The obituary continues for several more folios.

38 al-Mughīth fell into the hands of al-Ṣāliḥ Ismaʿīl when the latter seized Damascus in 1239, and was imprisoned in the citadel. His release was provided for during the negotiations

related … There came with him from the East [also] his infant son, entitled al-Malik al-Qāhir: al-Malik al-Ṣāliḥ left him in the citadel of Damascus with his son al-Malik al-Mughīth at the time of his journey to Nablus, and the news of [the boy's] death reached him when he was at Nablus[39] … He had left in the East his [other] son, al-Malik al-Muʿaẓẓam Tūrān Shāh, who resided at Ḥiṣn Kayfā.[40] He was interested in scholarship and studied science: his grandfather, Sultan al-Malik al-Kāmil (God have mercy on him) was very fond of him, since he saw in him signs of intelligence. [al-Malik al-Muʿaẓẓam] was [only] young during al-Malik al-Kāmil's lifetime…[fol. 75r] … al-Malik al-Ṣāliḥ used to love al-Malik al-Mughīth very much on account of his closeness to him in understanding, self-control and energy, and was training him to be his successor; but he greatly detested al-Malik al-Muʿaẓẓam. The amir Ḥusām al-Dīn ibn Abī ʿAlī told me what al-Malik al-Ṣāliḥ had enjoined upon him: 'When death comes upon me, do not summon Tūrān Shāh from Ḥiṣn Kayfā and do not entrust the country to him, for I know that nothing good will come from him; and do not entrust the country to any of my kinsfolk, but consign the government of the country to the Caliph, that he may set over it on his behalf whom he wishes.'

When al-Malik al-Ṣāliḥ was a prisoner in Kerak, a son was born to him by his wife, who was called Shajar al-Durr, and they named him Khalīl. He came to Egypt with his mother, and lived there for a time, but died in infancy. When the rulership devolved upon Shajar al-Durr, her title on documents and edicts was 'Khalīl's mother' …

What transpired after the death of al-Malik al-Ṣāliḥ (God have mercy on him) As we have said, al-Malik al-Ṣāliḥ was suffering from two ailments: one was a wound in the hollow of the knee, and the other was consumption. He was unaware of the consumption. His physician was his close friend al-Rashīd, known as Abū Khalīfa al-Naṣrānī, but he used to meet with him only rarely: he was stationed at the door, and a eunuch would go out and report on the Sultan's behalf how he was and would consult him as to what [treatment] was appropriate. When the growth diminished in size, the wound in the hollow of his knee was alleviated, and al-Malik al-Ṣāliḥ imagined that he had recovered. He wrote a letter to his viceroy, the amir Ḥusām al-Dīn, to say that the wound he suffered had improved and that the moisture in it had been reduced. All that remained was to ride and to play polo; 'insert [fol. 75v] this good news into your letters'. Ḥusām al-Dīn was delighted at this, and informed me of [the Sultan's] letter. I had learned the truth about his illness from one of the sons of the doctor Rashīd, the Sultan's physician: that his wound was improving only because of the disappearance of the moisture, and that his power to resist anything [else] was weakened. For that reason al-Malik al-Ṣāliḥ did not make a will, and left the situation unprovided for.[41]

---

between his father and al-Ṣāliḥ Ismaʿīl in 1243, but soon after these failed he died (of natural causes, it appears) in 1244: Humphreys, *From Saladin to the Mongols*, pp. 272–4, 276.

39 This was late in 1239/early in 1240: ibid., pp. 257–62.

40 Ibn ʿAbd al-Raḥīm (fol. 360v) adds that the amir Ḥusām al-Dīn was detailed to stay with him for a time.

41 What follows appears to be an indirect reference to the 'Testament' of al-Ṣāliḥ Ayyūb, preserved in a ms. of the encyclopaedic *Nihāyat al-arab* of al-Nuwayrī (d. 1332): it is edited

Had he left a will, he would not have omitted his viceroy, the amir Ḥusām al-Dīn, since he relied on nobody but him. He did not trust Fakhr al-Dīn Ibn al-Shaykh, even though he had promoted him to overall command of the army in view of his exalted status, his high rank under [al-Ṣāliḥ's] father al-Malik al-Kāmil, the obedience of the troops and the amirs towards him, his experience in governing the state and his skill in administration. Most recently, he had been pained by [Fakhr al-Dīn's] return from Damietta with the army and his neglect of it, to the point where the Franks captured it, which might have resulted in their conquest of Egypt and even (God forbid) of the whole of Islam.

When the death of Sultan al-Malik al-Ṣāliḥ occurred at such a critical juncture, his wife, Shajar al-Durr, recognized that nobody would be equal to this situation and to holding disorderly troops in check like the amir Fakhr al-Dīn; and she and the cavalry commander[42] Jamāl al-Dīn Muḥassan (he was the closest of the cavalry commanders to the Sultan and was in charge of the affairs of his *jamdāriyya* and Baḥriyya mamluks, who had grown to be a formidable force and wielded considerable power) agreed to summon the amir Fakhr al-Dīn. They informed him that the Sultan had died, and [the three of them] agreed to keep the event a secret from everyone in order that the Franks should not learn of the Sultan's death and so gain the upper hand over the Muslims, who might conceivably not withstand them since there was no one to hold them together. They [also] decided that the troops and the chief men of the country should be made to take an oath to Sultan al-Malik al-Ṣāliḥ and after him to his son, al-Malik al-Muʿaẓẓam Ghiyāth al-Dīn Tūrān Shāh, and to Fakhr al-Dīn Ibn al-Shaykh as commander-in-chief[43] and the man in charge of the government of the kingdom. Then they summoned the doctor Fatḥ [fol. 76r] al-Dīn Ibn [Abī']l-Ḥawāfir – he was one of the Sultan's physicians, and the Sultan had written to the amir Ḥusām al-Dīn to send for him, and he had sent him. He reached the camp at Mansura[44] when the Sultan was on the point of death. After his death, they sent for [Fatḥ al-Dīn] to wash him, to wrap him in a shroud and to say prayers over him at night, so that no suspicion[45] might be aroused through the entry of anyone else. So Fatḥ al-Dīn went in to his presence, washed him, wrapped him in a shroud and prayed over him, and he was placed in a coffin. The coffin containing the Sultan was

---

and trans. in Claude Cahen and Ibrahim Chabbouh, 'Le testament d'al-Malik aṣ-Ṣāliḥ Ayyūb', *BEO*, 29 (1977): 97–114; and for the text, see now also the full edition of al-Nuwayrī (Cairo, 1923–98), vol. 29, pp. 340–52. The prominence which this document gives to Fakhr al-Dīn, and to which Ibn Wāṣil apparently takes exception, is indeed one of the main grounds for doubting its authenticity, at least in the form in which it has reached us.

42 I have followed here the suggestion of Götz Schregle, *Die Sultanin von Ägypten* (Wiesbaden, 1961), p. 50, n. 1, that since Muḥassan appears as a commander of mamluks *ṭawāshī* here cannot have the usual meaning of 'eunuch'. It should be noted, however, that eunuchs are known to have been put in charge of the affairs of the mamluk corps in general, as opposed to holding military command over them.

43 *bi-atābakiya al-ʿaskar*. See D. Ayalon, 'Atābak al-ʿasākir', *EI*[2]. For *atabeg* (literally 'guardian'), a term first encountered in the Seljük era; see C. Cahen, 'Atabak', ibid.

44 Reading *al-manṣūra* for the *al-manṣūr* of the text.

45 Reading *rība* for the *ratba* of the text. Ibn ʿAbd al-Raḥīm (fol. 362r) has *laylā irtāba*.

then shut and conveyed in a galley[46] to the Jazīra citadel, where it was left until it was later taken to Cairo, as we shall describe, Almighty God willing.

Then the amirs and the military were summoned to the Sultan's pavilion, and were told that the Sultan had given orders for them to take an oath to himself, to his son al-Malik al-Muʿaẓẓam as heir-apparent after him and to the amir Fakhr al-Dīn Ibn Shaykh al-Shuyūkh as commander of the troops and the one in charge of the affairs of the realm. They consented to do this, and took the oath. And the *jamdāriyya* and the Baḥriyya swore likewise. Then a letter arrived in Cairo for the amir Ḥusām al-Dīn, which he was told was from the Sultan. Between the lines was written his well-known signature, which was 'Ayyūb ibn Muḥammad ibn Abī Bakr ibn Ayyūb'; but the writer was one of the Sultan's eunuchs, known as al-Suhaylī, who is still alive now and whose hand used to resemble that of al-Malik al-Ṣāliḥ. The gist of the letter that was sent to [Ḥusām al-Dīn] from the Sultan was that he should take an oath to the Sultan, to his son after him as heir-apparent, and to Fakhr al-Dīn as commander-in-chief and *atabeg*; that he should cause his lieutenants and any important men with him to take this oath; and that he should direct the preachers to make the Friday prayer, after the Sultan's name, in that of his son al-Malik al-Muʿaẓẓam.

The amir Ḥusām al-Dīn was joined by the chief Qadi, Badr al-Dīn Yūsuf ibn al-Ḥasan, the chief qadi of Cairo and what pertained to it in the direction of the sea, the lord Bahā' al-Dīn Zuhayr, the head of the secretariat[47] (the Sultan had been angry with him and had dismissed him, [fol. 76v] as we have described), the governor of Cairo, Shams al-Dīn Ibn Bākhil, and others among the military and the state grandees. The oath was taken in the form described, early on the morning of Thursday, 12 nights remaining of Shaʿbān [25 November 1249]; the death of al-Malik al-Ṣāliḥ had occurred on the evening of mid-Shaʿbān [22 November]. Next Bahā' al-Dīn was summoned to the army headquarters, and he made his way there and was restored to his office, though he later joined al-Malik al-Nāṣir, the ruler of Aleppo, as we stated earlier. The greatest efforts were made to conceal the death of al-Malik al-Ṣāliḥ from everyone in the state, great and small, right up to the amir Ḥusām al-Dīn ibn Abī ʿAlī, the viceroy of Egypt. Letters kept arriving for him thereafter from the army headquarters on matters relating to his duties, and on them was what resembled the Sultan's signature in the writing of the eunuch al-Suhaylī. He never imagined that the signature was not the Sultan's work on account of the close similarity between the two hands. But I had discovered the Sultan's death on the day the oath was administered, because one of the sons of the Sultan's physician al-Rashīd had arrived that day from the army headquarters and said, 'I had not yet left the headquarters when my father told me that [the Sultan] had completely stopped taking food and his pulse had faded, and there is no doubt that he has died'.

---

46 Douglas Haldane, 'The fire-ship of Al-Sālih Ayyūb and Muslim use of "Greek Fire"', in Donald J. Kagay and L. J. Andrew Villalon (eds), *The Circle of War in the Middle Ages: Essays on Medieval Military and Naval History* (Woodbridge, 1999), pp. 137–44, here understands *ḥarrāqa* in its original meaning of 'fire-ship': see note 26 above.

47 *kātib al-inshā'*. For Bahā' al-Dīn (d. 1258), a poet who had served al-Ṣāliḥ Ayyūb as vizier until his disgrace in 1248, see J. Rikabi, 'Bahā' al-Dīn Zuhayr', *EI*[2].

In addition to this, I had another piece of strong evidence, which was that al-Malik al-Ṣāliḥ did not repose in Fakhr al-Dīn the trust that would have led him to commit the affairs of state to him after his death; he was aware of Fakhr al-Dīn's far-reaching ambition … In reality al-Malik al-Ṣāliḥ did not rely upon anyone other than Ḥusām al-Dīn. We have already related what he ordered him [fol. 77r] to do at the time of his journey to Syria in respect of his brother al-ʿĀdil,[48] and that he should entrust Egypt to the Caliph and especially not to his son al-Malik al-Muʿaẓẓam or to any of his kinsfolk. Then there occurred Fakhr al-Dīn's withdrawal from Damietta with the troops, which caused the populace of Damietta to flee and leave it empty for the Franks so that they took it. The Sultan gave orders for the Kināniyya to be hanged for having abandoned Damietta; but he did not display his anger against Fakhr al-Dīn and the military at that difficult juncture. This serves as evidence that had al-Malik al-Ṣāliḥ made provision for anyone to exercise the government of the kingdom after him he would not have ignored Ḥusām al-Dīn, on account of the complete trust he placed in him. Now I put this idea that had occurred to me to the amir Ḥusām al-Dīn – I was constantly in his company for perhaps a month – and I conversed with him until the night had mostly passed. He was aghast at [my suggestion]. It so happened that a document reached him from the army headquarters concerning part of his responsibilities, and he drew my attention to it, having become suspicious about it. 'By Almighty God', I said, 'this signature is not in the Sultan's hand.' 'How do you know that?' he asked. 'Bring a document that contains his signature', I said. They brought it to me, and I compared the script with that of the other document. The differences between the two hands were evident, among them the fact that [the Sultan] used to write the *bā* in 'Ayyūb' in elongated form, whereas in this document it resembled a *rā*. When this became clear to him, he began making enquiries about it among the Sultan's close associates at the headquarters, and they informed him of [the Sultan's] death. And at that point his fear grew that Fakhr al-Dīn would gain control over the throne, by taking possession of it in person or by installing a boy from among the descendants of al-Malik al-Kāmil and [himself] acting as his *atabeg*.

Fakhr al-Dīn (God have mercy on him) was very ambitious, and his mind was set on the pinnacle of the affairs of state. He now began to release those who were in custody. He set free Muḥyī al-Dīn Ibn al-Jawzī and Sayf al-Dīn Ibn [fol. 77v] ʿAdlān; and then he released the leading men among those whom the Sultan had imprisoned. The Sultan had been angry with Jamāl al-Dīn Ibn Maṭrūḥ[49] and had dismissed him from the viceroyalty of Damascus and banished him; Fakhr al-Dīn brought him back and placed him close at hand. He sent for Bahī al-Dīn Zuhayr after the Sultan had banished him, and restored him to his office. He took control of the finances and disbursed an enormous sum; he bestowed robes of honour on

48 For the murder of Sultan al-ʿĀdil II (1238–40), al-Ṣāliḥ Ayyūb's half-brother and predecessor, see Ibn Wāṣil, vol. 5, pp. 379–80, though nothing is said there of any order issued to Ḥusām al-Dīn in this connection.

49 A poet and servitor of al-Ṣāliḥ Ayyūb, who after serving as vizier in Damascus fell from favour in 1248 and died in 1251: J. Rikabi, 'Ibn Maṭrūḥ', *EI*^{2}.

the leading amirs.[50] At this juncture the majority of the people became certain that the Sultan was dead; but nevertheless no one dared to utter a word [about it] out of fear, in view of the presence of the Franks in the country. And the *khuṭba*[51] and the coinage continued to be in al-Malik al-Ṣāliḥ's name and, after it, in that of his son al-Malik al-Muʿaẓẓam.

Then messengers were sent from the army headquarters to Ḥiṣn Kayfā on behalf of the cavalry commander Jamāl al-Dīn Muḥassan and Shajar al-Durr to summon al-Malik al-Muʿaẓẓam, and Fakhr al-Dīn could do nothing but acquiesce. Among those who went to summon [al-Malik al-Muʿaẓẓam] was Fāris al-Dīn Aqṭāy, the *jamdār*. His arrival from Ḥiṣn Kayfā was thought unlikely on account of the distance and the obstacles in the form of Badr al-Dīn Lu'lu', the ruler of Mosul, and the people of Aleppo. Ḥusām al-Dīn [too] despatched a messenger on his own behalf, one of his personal mamluks called Zayn al-Dīn al-ʿĀshiq, and sent with him a letter in which he urged him to set out in haste, from fear lest the country should escape from his grasp. Ḥusām al-Dīn did not trust those who had left the army headquarters to fetch him. Living with the Quṭbī princesses (the daughters of al-Malik al-ʿĀdil Sayf al-Dīn Abī Bakr ibn Ayyūb[52] and the [full] sisters of his son al-Malik al-Mufaḍḍal Quṭb al-Dīn) was a son of al-Malik al-ʿĀdil ibn al-Malik al-Kāmil,[53] namely al-Mughīth Fatḥ al-Dīn 'Umar. I was told by one of the people of Cairo that Fakhr al-Dīn Ibn al-Shaykh might perhaps send for him and entrust the kingship to him so that he [himself] might remain as *atabeg*. I reported this to the amir Ḥusām al-Dīn, who was disturbed by it because, in view of his [fol. 78r] close friendship with his master al-Malik al-Ṣāliḥ, he found it repugnant that the kingship should pass away from his progeny. al-Malik al-Mughīth, it is said, was approximately 14 years old. As soon as he heard this rumour from me, Ḥusām al-Dīn sent by night for Shams al-Dīn Ibn Bākhil, the governor of Cairo, and ordered him to convey al-Malik al-Mughīth from the house of the Quṭbī princesses early in the morning and take him up to the Jabal citadel. He did as he was bidden. Ḥusām al-Dīn went up into the citadel and ordered its governor to guard him, to keep a close watch on him, and not to hand [the prince] over to anyone who might ask him for him. Correspondence continued between Fakhr al-Dīn and Ḥusām al-Dīn, with Fakhr al-Dīn's letters headed 'The Servant Yūsuf Ibn Ḥamawiya' and Ḥusām al-Dīn's 'The Slave Abū ʿAlī'. Ostensibly it was all amiability between them. But Fakhr al-Dīn was aiming at sole and arbitrary rule should al-Malik al-Muʿaẓẓam find it impossible to come. He had acquired an impressive following[54] at headquarters: the amirs of the state all rode in attendance on him and dismounted for him; meals were laid out before them, and they came and ate and went.

Ḥusām al-Dīn's messenger reached Ḥiṣn Kayfā and met with al-Malik al-Muʿaẓẓam. He urged him to make haste to come to Egypt, telling him, 'If you delay,

50 Reading *al-umarā* for the *al-amr* of the text.

51 The sermon during the public Friday prayers, in which the ruler's name is mentioned: see A. J. Wensinck, 'Khuṭba', *EI*[2].

52 Sultan al-ʿĀdil I (d. 1218).

53 Sultan al-ʿĀdil II.

54 Reading, with Ibn ʿAbd al-Raḥīm (fol. 364r), *mawkib* for the *markab* of the ms.

the game is up:[55] Fakhr al-Dīn will have the country at his disposal, and may perhaps rule it in the name of your cousin, al-Malik al-Mughīth ibn al-Malik al-ʿĀdil.' There arrived also the messengers from the army headquarters and Fāris Aqṭāy, and they urged him to make haste to set out. It is reported that Fāris al-Dīn Aqṭāy asked him for Alexandria and that [al-Malik al-Muʿaẓẓam] promised him the place, but that when he arrived he did not keep his promise to him, did not treat him favourably, and barred him from his residence. Added to this was the fact that the aspirations of the rest of the *jamdāriyya* and Baḥriyya mamluks were disappointed, the result of which will be recounted later, Almighty God willing.

The journey of al-Malik al-Mu'aẓẓam ibn al-Malik al-Ṣāliḥ [fol. 78v] *to Egypt* When the messengers urged him to travel to Egypt in all haste, he set out with a group of his followers and close associates, including his secretary, the Egyptian Christian al-Nashū Ibn Ḥabshīsh, who was particularly intimate with him and managed all his affairs. The letters from al-Malik al-Muʿaẓẓam that reached Ḥusām al-Dīn during the lifetime of Sultan al-Malik al-Ṣāliḥ were[56] drafted in this secretary's handwriting. I read one of them, in which he praised his master and the virtues for which he was marked. The amir Ḥusām al-Dīn had been *atabeg* to al-Malik al-Muʿaẓẓam at Āmid.[57] He described him to me and listed his virtues, and said, 'When he comes, you will be closer to him than all other people, for he is different from his father in that respect.'

When al-Malik al-Muʿaẓẓam left Ḥiṣn Kayfā, he travelled at a rapid pace, from fear that Badr al-Dīn Lu'lu' and the people of Aleppo might prevent him from reaching his destination. He made his departure from Ḥiṣn Kayfā on the evening of Saturday when 11 nights had elapsed of the month of Ramaḍān of this year, namely 647 [18 December 1249], and he left at Ḥiṣn [Kayfā] his son al-Malik al-Muwaḥḥid ʿAbd-Allāh:[58] his age, I was told by al-Malik al-Muʿaẓẓam, was approximately ten, and he left with him people to conduct the government. Those of his close associates and companions who set out with him numbered approximately fifty horsemen. He reached Ḥīt [near] ʿĀna, which was part of the Caliph's territory. The ruler of Mosul and the people of Aleppo heard of his departure on the journey to Egypt, and they sent a detachment to seize him and make an agreement with him on terms of their own choosing. But they failed to overtake him, and he got to ʿĀna, where he crossed the Euphrates.

How the Franks advanced and took up position opposite the Muslim forces When the Franks ascertained that Sultan al-Malik al-Ṣāliḥ was dead, they came forth from Damietta with their cavalry and infantry, their galleys [moving] parallel with them

55 I take this to be the meaning of *fāta 'l-amr*.

56 Reading *kānat* for the *kātaba* of the ms.

57 From al-Ṣāliḥ Ayyūb's departure for Damascus late in 1238 until Ḥusām al-Dīn left Ḥiṣn Kayfā to join him there in 1239: Ibn Wāṣil, vol. 5, p. 189; Humphreys, *From Saladin to the Mongols*, p. 251.

58 He remained prince of Ḥiṣn Kayfā until his death, and his descendants continued to rule there until the fifteenth century.

on the river, and made camp at Fāraskūr. Then [fol. 79r] they advanced one stage beyond it. The date was Thursday, five days remaining of Shaʿbān [2 December 1249]. On the following day, which was a Friday, a letter arrived from the amir Fakhr al-Dīn, warning the entire population and ordering them to wage Holy War in the path of God. It contained an imitation of the Sultan's signature (God have mercy on him), and began, following the *bismillah:* 'Go forth, light and heavy! Struggle in God's way with your possessions and your selves; that is better for you, did you know.'[59] It was an eloquent letter, composed by the lord Bahā' al-Dīn Zuhayr (God have mercy on him) and containing numerous exhortations inciting [people] to fight the infidel. [It said that] the Franks (God curse them) had invaded the country in unprecedented numbers[60] and their hearts were greedy to conquer the country; it was incumbent on all Muslims to rush to arms against them and expel them from the land. This letter was read out to the people from the pulpit of the Prayer Mosque in Cairo. The populace wept copiously and were dismayed, and there set out from Cairo and the rest of Egypt a great throng. Fears were increased by the Sultan's death, the Franks' acquisition of a foothold by occupying the port of Damietta, and their numbers. They realized that if the army at Mansura were to be driven back just one stage to the rear the whole of Egypt would be conquered in the shortest time.

On Tuesday 1 Ramaḍān [= 7 December 1249] fighting took place between the Franks and the Muslims, in which the *amīr majlis*, known as al-ʿAlā'ī, and a number of troops with him were martyred;[61] and the Franks made camp at Sharamsāḥ. On Monday, seven days having elapsed of Ramaḍān [= 14 December], the Franks took up position at al-Baramūn; and their proximity to the Muslim forces gave rise to growing anxiety. On Monday, 13 nights having elapsed of Ramaḍān [20 December 1249],[62] the Franks advanced to the limits of the island of Damietta and began fighting with the Muslims: this was the position in which they had been encamped on the earlier occasion in the time of Sultan al-Malik al-Kāmil (God have mercy on him), when the Muslims had defeated them. They were here, while the main part of the Muslim army was in Mansura, which lay on the eastern bank. A number of the troops and the more senior sons of al-Malik [fol. 79v] al-Nāṣir Dā'ūd, namely al-Malik al-Ẓāhir Shādī, al-Malik al-Amjad Ḥasan, al-Malik al-Muʿaẓẓam ʿĪsā and al-Malik al-Awḥad Yūsuf, were on the western bank, facing the Franks with the River Nile between them. The number of al-Malik al-Nāṣir's sons, senior and junior, who had come to Egypt at that time was twelve. Also on the bank were al-Malik al-Nāṣir's two brothers, al-Malik al-Qāhir ʿAbd-al-Malik and al-Malik al-Mughīth ʿAbd al-ʿAzīz. When the Franks took up position with their forces at the edge of the island on which lies Damietta, and came face to face with the Muslims, they dug a trench around themselves, built a wall round their encampment, protecting it with

59 Qur'ān, ix, 41 (Arberry's translation).

60 I take this to be the significance of *bi-jaddihim wa-jadīdihim.*

61 'Rothelin', pp. 597–8 (trans. Shirley, p. 91), and Joinville, §§ 185–6, p. 102 (trans. Hague, p. 70; trans. Shaw, p. 211), mention the fighting on 7 December.

62 According to 'Rothelin', p. 597 (trans. Shirley, p. 91), supported by other Frankish sources [**docs 68 and 70**], the crusaders reached the edge of the 'island of Maalot' on 21 December.

screens, and set up mangonels to fire at the Muslims. Their galleys[63] were on the River Nile, opposite them, while the Muslims' galleys were opposite Mansura. A struggle broke out between the two sides on land and on the water. On Wednesday, 14 nights remaining of Ramaḍān [= 22 December 1249], six Frankish horsemen came over to the Muslims.[64] On the following day, the Thursday, al-Malik al-Muʿaẓẓam Tūrān Shāh reached ʿĀna; and he subsequently left ʿĀna on the journey to Damascus by way of al-Samāwa.

The arrival of al-Malik al-Mu'aẓẓam Ghiyāth al-Dīn Tūrān Shāh ibn al-Malik al-Ṣāliḥ at Damascus He left ʿĀna on Sunday, ten days remaining of Ramaḍān [= 26 December 1249]. Next, on Monday, three days remaining of Ramaḍān [3 January 1250], he reached al-Quṣayr in the pavilion that the amir Jamāl al-Dīn Ibn Yaghmūr (God have mercy on him), the viceroy of Damascus, had pitched for him; and he made his entry into Damascus on the following day, which was Tuesday.[65] The city was decked out, and the good news was proclaimed. He lodged in the citadel, and the amir Jamāl al-Dīn Ibn Yaghmūr was in attendance on him. The preacher Zayn al-Dīn ʿAbd al-Raḥmān Ibn Marhūb (God have mercy on him) arrived from Ḥamā as the envoy of its ruler, [fol. 80r] Sultan al-Malik al-Manṣūr (may God purify his soul), accompanied by the qadi Najm al-Dīn ʿAbd al-Raḥīm Ibn al-Bārzī (God have mercy on him); and the envoy of Sultan al-Malik al-Nāṣir ibn al-Malik al-ʿAzīz, the ruler of Aleppo, also joined him. All of them congratulated him on his arrival …

al-Malik al-Muʿaẓẓam celebrated the ʿĪd al-fiṭr[66] at Damascus. On that very same day a great Frankish count was captured, a kinsman of King Raydafrans. Fighting continued between the two sides on land and on water, and every day Franks were killed or a number of them were captured. They suffered great damage from the common folk among the Muslims, who would abduct and kill some of them. If they saw the Franks, they would hurl themselves into the water until they had left the Muslim side behind. They would employ every kind of trick to capture them. I was told that one man among them hollowed out a green water-melon and put it on his head. He then swam in the direction of the Franks until one of them fancied it was a water-melon carried along[67] on the water and came down to reach out for it, whereupon the man seized him and brought him as a prisoner to the Muslims.

On 4 Shawwāl [10 January 1250] the good news reached Cairo that al-Malik al-Muʿaẓẓam had arrived in Damascus and taken up residence in its citadel. This gave rise to the utmost rejoicing, and the good news was proclaimed in Cairo and in the army headquarters. On Wednesday 7 Shawwāl [= 12 January 1250] the Muslims captured [fol. 80v] a Frankish galley, containing 200 men and a great count.

---

63 *shawānī*.

64 Ibn ʿAbd al-Raḥīm (fol. 365r) adds: 'and they informed them of the Franks' straitened circumstances'.

65 The ms. has Monday in error. Abū Shāma, p. 183, says that he entered Damascus on Thursday 29 Ramaḍān [5 January 1250].

66 The celebration of the end of the Ramaḍān fast, on 1 Shawwāl (corresponding, in this year, to 7 January 1250).

67 Reading, with Ibn ʿAbd al-Raḥīm (fol. 365v), *sābiya* for *shā'ifa*.

And on Thursday mid-Shawwāl [= 20 January 1250] the Franks and the Muslims boarded [their ships], and the Muslims came over to [the Franks'] side of the river. A bitter struggle took place, and 40 Frankish horsemen were killed, as also were their horses.[68] On the next day, a Friday, 67 of them arrived in Cairo as prisoners, including three leading Templars. On Thursday, eight days remaining of Shawwāl [27 January 1250], the Muslims set light to a great Frankish ship[69] in the river, and they had gained a clear victory over them.

al-Malik al-Muʿaẓẓam's journey from Damascus to Egypt al-Malik al-Muʿaẓẓam set out from Damascus on his journey to Egypt,[70] having bestowed a robe of honour and a good deal of money on the amir Jamāl al-Dīn Ibn Yaghmūr and confirmed him as his viceroy there, and having given robes and a good deal of money also to the Qaymariyya amirs. He brought all the money out of the treasury and distributed it among the troops ... When al-Malik al-Muʿaẓẓam reached the desert, his chief secretary, Nashū al-Dawla Ibn Ḥabshīsh, accepted Islam at his hands and was given the style of Muʿīn al-Dīn.[71] [al-Malik al-Muʿaẓẓam] groomed him to be his vizier, just as Muʿīn al-Dīn Ibn al-Shaykh had been vizier to his father, al-Malik al-Ṣāliḥ.

How a surprise attack was made at Mansura and the amir Fakhr al-Dīn Ibn al-Shaykh (God have mercy on him) was killed; and how the Muslims were subsequently victorious We have described how the Franks entrenched themselves in their encampment opposite the Muslims and how there was constant fighting between the two sides, with the River Ushmūn between them. This is a narrow river, which has some shallow fords.[72] Some mischief-maker[73] guided the Franks to one of these fords, known as [fol. 81r] the Muslims' ford; and early in the morning of Tuesday 5 Dhū'l-Qaʿda [8 February 1250] the Franks mounted and made for that ford. The Muslims became aware [of their advance only] when they were in the middle of their encampment. The amir Fakhr al-Dīn Ibn Shaykh al-Shuyūkh was performing his ablutions in the bath when he heard shouts that the Franks had attacked the camp. In his consternation he took horse, unarmed and without escort; and a body of Franks

68 This conflict on St Sebastian's Day [20 January 1250] is described in 'Rothelin', p. 601 (trans. Shirley, pp. 93–4), and by Joinville, §§ 199–202, p. 110 (trans. Hague, pp. 73–4; trans. Shaw, p. 215).

69 'Rothelin', pp. 601–2 (trans. Shirley, p. 94), says that on the Saturday before Candlemas [29 January] the Muslims set alight four barges, which they launched in the direction of the Frankish ships in an unsuccessful bid to destroy them. I am unsure what kind of ship is meant by *maramma*.

70 On Monday 26 Shawwāl [1 February 1250], according to Abū Shāma, p. 183.

71 Ibn al-ʿAmīd, p. 160 (trans. Eddé and Micheau, pp. 86–7), calling him Muʿīn al-Dīn Hibat-allāh ibn Abī'l-Zuhr ibn Ḥashīsh, says that on 1 Dhū'l-Qaʿda/5 February 1250 Tūrān Shāh sent him to secure the treasury at Kerak.

72 Reading *riqāq* for the *rifāq* of the ms.

73 *baʿḍ al-mufsidīna.*

chanced upon him. He was martyred (God have mercy on him) and his life came to a fine end.[74]

Raydafrans entered Mansura,[75] and penetrated as far as the Sultan's palace, which lay on the river. The Franks dispersed through the narrow streets of Mansura, and everyone there, whether soldiers or the general population or the bazaar folk, scattered to right and left. Islam was on the verge of being torn up by the roots, and the Franks were confident of their victory. But it was fortunate for the Muslims that the Franks dispersed through the narrow streets, so that [their] situation became critical and dangerous. The Turkish mamluk regiment of the Sultan (God have mercy on him), consisting of the *jamdāriyya* and the Baḥriyya – lions in battle and champions of cut and thrust[76] – turned[77] and launched a single mighty charge against the Franks, which shook their foundations, shattered their entire edifice and turned their crosses upside down. The swords and maces of the Turks set about them, inflicted[78] on them death and wounds, and strewed them in the narrow streets of Mansura. The number of their dead was not far off 1500 of their horsemen and their leading warriors.

Now their infantry had advanced as far as the bridge of al-Manṣūb over the River Ushmūn in order to cross it. Had there been any remissness [at that point] and had the infantry crossed over to the Muslims' bank, it would have completed a critical situation: the infantry would have protected their cavalry, since they were extremely numerous. Had it not been for the restricted scope of the fighting, which was taking place among the narrow streets and alleys, [the cavalry] would have been totally annihilated; but [as it was] some survivors escaped, made their way to the locality called Jadīla and sought refuge there. It was impossible to attack them, and nightfall separated the two sides.

[The Franks] threw up a wall and dug a trench around themselves at Jadīla. Some stayed on the eastern [fol. 81v] bank, but the majority were at the end of the island leading to Damietta, patrolling the trench and the wall.[79] This battle was the prelude to success and the key to victory. When battle was joined, messengers arrived in Cairo after dawn on the aforementioned Tuesday, and the amir Ḥusām al-Dīn was given the news and passed it on to me. The gist was that carrier-pigeons had been released and the enemy had attacked Mansura; a bitter battle was in progress between the Muslims and the Franks. This was all the messengers had to say. This information alarmed us, as it alarmed all the Muslims, and everyone imagined the ruin of Islam. Fugitives from the Muslim forces arrived towards dusk. The Naṣr Gate stayed open all that Tuesday night, and soldiers, common folk, secretaries and functionaries entered by [that gate] as refugees, in ignorance of what had transpired

74 Ibn ʿAbd al-Raḥīm (fol. 365v) has at this point a few sentences praising Fakhr al-Dīn's personal qualities (though admitting that his ambition reached as far as the throne itself): this eulogy, significantly, is not found in Ibn Wāṣil's original text either here or in the obituary later. According to Abū Shāma, p. 184, the Shaykh al-Fāḍil Ḍiyā' al-Dīn Muḥammad ibn Abī'l-Ḥajjāj, the Controller of Finance of the army, was also killed in this attack.

75 An error, of course. Ibn Wāṣil has confused Louis with his brother, Robert of Artois.

76 *al-ṭa'n wa'l-ḍarb.*

77 Reading *intiḥat* for the *intikhat* of the ms.

78 Reading *ittijanū* for the *ittiḥanū* of the ms.

79 I take this to be the sense of *'alā'l-ṭā'ifa mina'l-khandaq wa'l-sūr.*

since the Franks had penetrated Mansura. One of those who arrived that night was the qadi Tāj al-Dīn, known as Ibn Bint al-Aʿazz, who was at this time director of the Dīwān al-Ṣuḥba … He visited the amir Ḥusām al-Dīn in the vizier's residence, and told him how the enemy had entered Mansura but that he did not know what had happened thereafter. People's hearts remained disturbed until sunrise on the Wednesday, when the good news of the victory arrived. The two cities of Cairo and Miṣr were decorated, and great was the rejoicing and exhilaration that God had made victory possible. This was the first battle in which the Turkish lions were victorious over the polytheist dogs. The good news reached al-Malik al-Muʿaẓẓam while he was on his way, and he redoubled his efforts to reach Egypt speedily. The amir Fakhr al-Dīn (God have mercy on him) was taken to al-Ghirāfa, where the grave of al-Shāfiʿī (God have mercy on him) is to be found, and was buried there (may God's mercy approve of him).

…[80]

[fol. 83r] *The arrival of al-Malik al-Mu'aẓẓam at the camp at Mansura* When a succession of reports came in of the approach of al-Malik al-Muʿaẓẓam, the first to go out to meet him was the qadi Badr al-Dīn, who met him at Gaza.[81] Then the viceroy, the amir Ḥusām al-Dīn, went out to meet him, and I accompanied him … We reached al-Ṣāliḥiya, where we halted. Then, on Saturday, 14 nights remaining of Dhū'l-Qaʿda [= 20 February 1250], we met him at Masāfa, near al-Ṣāliḥiya. The amir Ḥusām al-Dīn bent down to dismount, but [the Sultan] prevented him. al-Malik al-Muʿaẓẓam spoke with him and embraced him, and gave him the warmest welcome. Ḥusām al-Dīn made a sign to me to kiss the Sultan's hand, and I dismounted, approached him and kissed his hand. He spoke of Ḥusām al-Dīn in his presence in the highest terms, and he welcomed me and ordered me to mount. I mounted, and the Sultan continued [his journey], with the amir Ḥusām al-Dīn on his right hand and the qadi Badr al-Dīn on his left. After we had halted [later], the amir Ḥusām al-Dīn told me that qadi Badr al-Dīn had said to him, 'I have not seen anyone who resembles our master the Sultan in refinement, learning, wit and [skill at] debate in every field'.

[fol. 83v] al-Malik al-Muʿaẓẓam took up his quarters in his father's palace at al-Ṣāliḥiya, and was joined from the army headquarters by a great number of his father's amirs and mamluks. From that point onwards al-Malik al-Ṣāliḥ's death was made public: it had been concealed for about three months, during which the *khuṭba* had been read for al-Malik al-Ṣāliḥ and for al-Malik al-Muʿaẓẓam as his heir-apparent. And on that day the amir Ḥusām al-Dīn was given a splendid robe of honour, a sword embossed with gold, one of the choicest horses with its saddle decorated in gold, and 3000 *dīnārs* …

80 There follows a lengthy obituary of Fakhr al-Dīn Ibn al-Shaykh.

81 Reading *ghaza* (confirmed by Ibn ʿAbd al-Raḥīm's version, fol. 367r) for the *'izza* of the ms.

[fol. 84v] [al-Malik al-Muʿaẓẓam] reached Mansura on Thursday, nine[82] days remaining of Dhū'l-Qaʿda [= 25 February 1250], and was met by his father's Baḥriyya and *jamdāriyya* amirs and mamluks, and took up residence in his father's palace. Had he only treated them favourably and behaved towards them as his father had done, showing them kindness and being accessible to them, they would have given him their help and support. But he completely rejected them and treated them harshly, giving precedence over them to those who were unfit to take precedence over them. And so his situation deteriorated just as had that of his uncle, al-Malik al-ʿĀdil, following [the reign of] his father al-Malik al-Kāmil.

al-Malik al-Muʿaẓẓam now rode forth with the troops to confront the Franks. He skirmished with them and invested the position they had occupied. Meals were served in public every day and were attended by amirs and the principal figures from among the turbanned folk. A number of scholars came to the encampment … [fol. 85r] … Fakhr al-Dīn Ibn al-Shukrī and the preacher Aṣīl al-Dīn al-Isʿirdī were in the encampment. They, and others who are ranked among men of culture and letters and the poets, gathered in the Sultan's camp because they discovered in al-Malik al-Muʿaẓẓam a market where excellence was in demand. They would be present at the meals, and the Sultan questioned them on intellectual matters and engaged in discussion with them … I did not cease to attend his court until I entered Cairo with the amir Ḥusām al-Dīn. I decided to compose a book in his name and to go back to him; but circumstances prevented it.

How the Muslim fleet attacked the [fol. 85v] *Frankish fleet and cut their supply-lines, and how the Franks were weakened* Once the Franks were entrenched in their position, supplies used to reach them from Damietta by way of the River Nile. The Muslims had recourse to ships which they might load with men, and they carried them on camels to the Baḥr al-Maḥalla, and launched them:[83] it contained water from the time of the Nile floods which was stagnant, though it communicated with the Nile. And when the Frankish ships that were on their way from Damietta passed the Baḥr al-Maḥalla, the Muslim ships which were lying there in ambush moved out against them and a fight took place between the two sides. Muslim ships coming downstream from Mansura arrived and joined the fleet of ships that were lying in ambush, and they surrounded and captured [the Frankish ships] by hand-to hand fighting.[84] The number of Frankish ships captured was 52, and about 1000 men on board were killed or taken prisoner. The supplies that were on board were seized [too]. The prisoners were carried on camels to the army headquarters. As a result of this the Franks' supply-lines were severed, and they were considerably weakened.[85]

82 Reading *tisʿ* for the *sabʿ* of the ms. Abū Shāma, p. 183, dates his arrival in Mansura on 18 Dhū'l-Qaʿda [22 February].

83 'Rothelin', p. 610 (trans. Shirley, p. 99), gives the number as 50.

84 I have translated thus the phrase *akhadhūhum akhdh*[an] *bi'l-yad*.

85 See Joinville, § 292, p. 160 (trans. Hague, p. 97; trans. Shaw, p. 237), for the severance of the supply-lines and the capture of 80 Frankish vessels. 'Rothelin' (as in note 83) mentions only the interception of two convoys.

At this time I was in Mansura, and I rode out with the qadi ʿImād al-Dīn ibn al-Quṭb, qadi of Miṣr, and the Sharīf ʿImād al-Dīn, who had married his sister. We halted on the western bank, where were to be found the sons and the two brothers of al-Malik al-Nāṣir, and one crosses over to it from the Mansura side by means of a great bridge of ships[86] at a locality called Janjir. Between us and the Frankish position lay the River Nile. The stones from the mangonels were flying from their side towards the Muslim fleet. It was a day to be remembered, on which God strengthened Islam and sapped the power of the polytheists. From that day onwards high prices and a lack of provisions increased among them,[87] and they were blockaded and could neither stay put nor leave. The Muslims had the upper hand over them and were emboldened against them.

On 1 Dhū'l-Ḥijja [7 March 1250] the Franks captured seven [smaller] galleys[88] belonging to the Muslim flotilla that lay on the Baḥr al-Maḥalla, but the [fol. 86r] Muslims on board escaped. On 2 Dhū'l-Ḥijja al-Malik al-Muʿaẓẓam ordered the amir Ḥusām al-Dīn to enter Cairo and stay in the vizier's residence, where he was to operate in his customary fashion as viceroy. I was given a robe of honour, as were a group of lawyers who had come to attend on him. His generosity extended to all who passed through his gate. We entered Cairo two days later. On Monday 9 Dhū'l-Ḥijja [15 March], the Day of ʿArafat,[89] the Muslim galleys moved out against the [Frankish] ships. They came upon them loaded with provisions, and the clash occurred near the Mosque of Victory. The Muslim galleys captured 32 Frankish ships, including nine [larger] galleys.[90] The Franks grew still weaker and more disheartened, and prices in their camp rose higher. At that time they began to correspond with the Muslims and asked them for a truce. The Frankish envoys arrived and were met by the *amīr jāndār*, the amir Zayn al-Dīn, and the chief qadi, Badr al-Dīn. The Franks' demand was that they should hand over to the Muslims the port of Damietta and should receive in exchange Jerusalem and part of the coast; but this did not meet with acceptance.[91] On Friday, three days remaining of Dhū'l-Ḥijja [1 April] the Franks set fire to all their timber and destroyed[92] their ships; and they resolved to fall back on Damietta. When this year ended, they were still in their position, facing the Muslims.

---

86 This is presumably the bridge of boats across which Joinville would be taken to Mansura following his capture: Joinville, § 332, p. 180 (trans. Hague, p. 107; trans. Shaw, p. 246).

87 Ibid., § 293, p. 160 (trans. Hague, p. 97; trans. Shaw, p. 237), specifying that by Easter 1250 an ox cost 80 *livres*, a sheep or a pig 30, a barrel of wine 10, and an egg 12 *deniers*.

88 *ḥarārīq*.

89 The most important day of the annual pilgrimage to Mecca.

90 *shawānī*: Pryor, 'The crusade of Emperor Frederick II', p. 123, suggests that these were escorting the other boats, and that they may have represented the total number of Louis's war-galleys. Ibn ʿAbd al-Raḥīm (fol. 368v) gives the number as seven.

91 According to Joinville, §§ 301–2, pp. 164, 166 (trans. Hague, pp. 99-100; trans. Shaw, p. 239), these negotiations foundered on the question whether Louis or one of his brothers should be left as a hostage.

92 The ms. has *aqabū*, but possibly in error for *afanū*, the reading in Ibn al-Furāt (Lyons, *Ayyubids, Mamlukes and Crusaders*, vol. 1, p. 34).

…

[fol. 86v] *The year 648 [1250–51]* began …

[fol. 87r] *How the Franks were routed and annihilated through death or capture and how their king was taken prisoner* When what we have described occurred, and the Franks' resistance was impaired and all that was left for them was an excess of hunger and the suspension of the wherewithal to hold out on the spot, they made preparations to retreat. On the evening of Wednesday, three nights having elapsed of Muḥarram [= 6 April] – a glorious evening which unveiled a mighty victory and a great triumph – the Frankish cavalry and infantry moved out on the march towards Damietta in order to seek its protection. Their ships were taken downstream along the River Nile, in parallel with them. The Muslims crossed over to their bank, and rode in pursuit hard on their heels. Dawn arrived on the Wednesday aforementioned, and the Muslims had surrounded them, set about them with their swords and overwhelmed them, killing [some] and taking [others] prisoner. Only the leaders escaped, and so it was reported that the number killed that day reached 30,000. In that engagement al-Malik al-Ṣāliḥ's Baḥriyya and *jamdāriyya* mamluks had the decisive influence and the largest role.[93]

The accursed King Raydafrans and his principal followers withdrew to a hill there in capitulation and seeking quarter. It was granted by the cavalry officer Jamāl al-Dīn Muḥassan al-Ṣāliḥī, who gave them a guarantee; and so they complied with the surrender. They were surrounded, and Raydafrans and the others were taken to Mansura. Shackles were put on the legs of Raydafrans, and he was confined in the house where the head of the secretariat, Fakhr al-Dīn Ibn Luqmān, used to live. He was guarded by the cavalry officer Ṣabīḥ al-Muʿaẓẓamī, one of the servitors of al-Malik al-Muʿaẓẓam Tūrān Shāh: he was particularly close to him and had accompanied him from Ḥiṣn Kayfā, and so [the Sultan] had promoted him and raised him in rank and power, appointing him to be commander of his guard.[94] Similarly he promoted [another] of his followers, called al-Ṭūrī. A Kurdish jurist named Shams al-Dīn al-…,[95] who was the qadi of Ḥiṣn Kayfā, had similarly come with him from Ḥiṣn Kayfā: he gave him honours, and had a tent pitched for him [fol. 87v] close to his own pavilion. It was widely rumoured among the people that he would dismiss the chief qadi, Badr al-Dīn, qadi of Cairo, and the qadi ʿImād al-Dīn ibn al-Quṭb al-Ḥamawī, qadi of Miṣr, and combine the two districts in [the hands of] this Kurd. He had likewise raised in rank the head of his secretariat, al-Nashū al-Miṣrī, who had accepted Islam at his hands at the point when they had entered the desert: it was said that he would obtain the vizierate. He was a young man, with a handsome face and of good address; and while we were at Mansura he had gone backwards and forwards on the business between the Sultan and the amir Ḥusām al-Dīn. The amir known as …[96] was *atabeg* to al-Malik al-Muʿaẓẓam at Āmid. He was an Egyptian and had

93 Ibn ʿAbd al-Raḥīm (fol. 369v) calls them 'Islam's Templars [*dāwiyyat al-Islām*]'.

94 *amīr jāndārhu.*

95 The ms. has the indecipherable reading *K..L.TY.*

96 Most of the name is missing in the ms., which has only the first three letters (LMA).

relatives in Egypt, and he was an excellent secretary: after al-Malik al-Muʿaẓẓam was murdered, he joined Sultan al-Nāṣir and became one of the chancery scribes in Damascus.

The lord Jamāl al-Dīn Ibn Maṭrūḥ (God have mercy on him) says regarding this battle:

> Give the Frenchman, if you love him, a true statement from those who offer sound advice:
> 'May God requite you for the slaughter that has befallen the worshippers of Jesus the Messiah!
> You came to Egypt, thirsting to conquer it and reckoning the drumbeat but a gust of wind;
> And so Time has carried you to a disaster which has made narrow what was broad in your eyes;
> While through your fine strategy you have brought all your men to the inside of the tomb:
> Of fifty thousand not one is to be seen who is not dead or a wounded prisoner.
> God grant you [more] triumphs of this ilk, that Jesus may perhaps find relief from you .
> If the Pope was satisfied with this, perchance fraud has emanated from the counsellor!'
> And tell them, if they think of coming back to take revenge or for some sound purpose:
> 'Ibn Luqmān's house is still there; the chains and the officer Ṣabīḥ have not gone away.'

After these events, al-Malik al-Muʿaẓẓam and the army set out for Damietta and made camp at Fāraskūr, which lay in the Damietta province. Here the Sultan's pavilion was set up, and beside it [fol. 88r] was erected a wooden tower, in which he would go up at intervals.[97] The good news was sent to Miṣr, Cairo, Damascus and the other regions. al-Malik al-Muʿaẓẓam stayed [here], displaying no energy for the capture of Damietta. Had he only made haste to get there and take up position before it, and had he required its surrender by King Raydafrans, who was in his power, it would have been his in the shortest possible time. But he was kept from doing this by the flawed policy that foreordained destiny had decreed.

On Friday 5 Muḥarram [= 8 April 1250] there reached the amir Ḥusām al-Dīn ibn ʿAlī a decree from al-Malik al-Muʿaẓẓam that he should go to him and that al-Malik al-Muʿaẓẓam had appointed as viceroy the amir Jamāl al-Dīn Aqush al-Najmī al-Ṣāliḥī, one of al-Malik al-Ṣāliḥ's amirs. And so Ḥusām al-Dīn left Cairo for the army camp at Fāraskūr. He told me en route, when he was a prey to conjecture and fancy: 'Had I only known that this youth' – he meant al-Malik al-Muʿaẓẓam – 'would inevitably suffer what befell his uncle, al-Malik al-ʿĀdil, namely being arrested and supplanted, and that the sequence of events, and what he determined in his mind, and how his career ended would be similar to his uncle's case!' He travelled on, and halted at Fāraskūr. He did not find the reception that befitted him, and did not meet [the Sultan] except at mealtimes; nor did [the Sultan] consult him on any business. This was likewise the case with every one of his father's great amirs. And in the same way he repudiated his father's *jamdāriyya* and Baḥriyya mamluks, especially

97 The pavilion complex and the tower are described by Joinville, §§ 345-6, p. 188 (trans. Hague, pp. 110–11; trans. Shaw, pp. 250–51).

their commander, Fāris al-Dīn Aqṭāy the *jamdār*, who had gone to him at Āmid and summoned him to his capital: he had promised to grant him Alexandria as his *iqṭā'*, but he did not keep this promise or gratify him. There was with him a group of prominent amirs on whom his father had relied and whom he had raised in rank, such as Sayf al-Dīn al-Qaymarī, ʿIzz al-Dīn al-Qaymarī, Fakhr al-Dīn Ibn Abī Zakarī, and the amir Fakhr al-Dīn Ibn Ḥashrīn, among others [fol. 88v] (ʿIzz al-Dīn was not one of the Qaymariyya themselves, but was a dependant of theirs and so was ascribed to them). Similarly, there were with him great amirs whose association with his father was of long standing, such as Shihāb al-Dīn Ibn Kamshā and his father Saʿd al-Dīn, who was the sister's son of the great al-Malik al-ʿĀdil; or like Zayn al-Dīn the *amīr jāndār* and Shihāb al-Dīn al-ʿArs. All these he repudiated and shunned. They would stay in their tents, and he did not see them except at the public meals; and when the meal ended they returned to their tents. The people who were in attendance on him were the crowd who had accompanied him from Ḥiṣn [Kayfā]. They had made no impression on the people's minds; and nevertheless he wanted his regime to be placed on a new footing in this situation,[98] before his position was securely established and he was settled on the throne of his kingdom in his citadel. When his father had wanted to overhaul his regime, he had done it step by step and over a long period. But when Almighty God desires an outcome, he puts in place the means to do it. There were further reasons in addition, among them that he allegedly wanted to send Fāris al-Dīn Aqṭāy to Mosul and later give orders for his elimination; and other things about which there were a great many reports. And so the Baḥriyya were alienated from him and feared for their lives. We shall recount what happened.

How al-Malik al-Mu'aẓẓam Ghiyāth al-Dīn ibn al-Malik al-Ṣāliḥ was killed (God have mercy on him) When what we have described transpired – the estrangement of the Baḥriyya, the isolation of his father's amirs and close associates, and the promotion of contemptible persons over them – a number of his father's mamluks agreed to kill him. And in the early morning of Monday, one evening remaining of Muḥarram of this year, namely 648 [= 2 May 1250], the public meal was laid out in his pavilion in accordance with his past custom; and all the people [fol. 89r] were in his presence and he ate with them. When the meal was over and the amirs dispersed to their tents, he rose from his seat with the intention of going to his tent and being alone; and he was approached by Rukn al-Dīn Baybars, known as al-Bunduqdārī, one of his father's *jamdāriyya*. He it was who would later rule the country, as we shall describe, and would bear the title al-Malik al-Ẓāhir.[99] He was a mamluk of the amir ʿAlā' al-Dīn Aydigīn al-Bunduqdār, one of Sultan al-Malik al-Ṣāliḥ's mamluks

98 I have conjectured this as the meaning of *fī yād hī al-amr*; though even the precise reading is uncertain.

99 It may be significant that all the sources which ascribe the first blow to Baybars (in contrast, therefore, with the Sibṭ) were composed during his reign. Possibly propaganda on the new Sultan's behalf credited him with the murder of Tūrān Shāh in 1250, just it did in the case of his immediate predecessor, the Mamluk Sultan Quṭuz in 1260: on this see Peter Holt, 'Three biographies of al-Ẓāhir Baybars', in D. O. Morgan (ed.), *Medieval Historical Writing in the Christian and Islamic Worlds* (London, 1982), pp. 19–29, and note 104 below.

and great amirs who had been with him in the East, had stuck by him when he was deserted by his people, stayed with al-Malik al-Nāṣir Dā'ūd until al-Malik al-Ṣāliḥ emerged from confinement, and entered Egypt with him and were made amirs. It so happened that al-Malik al-Ṣāliḥ was once angry with ʿAlā' al-Dīn and put him in prison and confiscated his mamluks: among them was this Rukn al-Dīn, who became one of his *jamdārs*.

Rukn al-Dīn Baybars drew his sword, rushed at al-Malik al-Muʿaẓẓam and struck him with it. The blow fell between two of al-Malik al-Muʿaẓẓam's fingers, wounding him slightly. Rukn al-Dīn Baybars [then] threw away the sword in fear, and fled, while al-Malik al-Muʿaẓẓam withdrew and sat down on a couch. His men and the Baḥriyya gathered in his presence, and said, 'Has something happened?' He replied, 'One of the Baḥriyya has wounded me.' 'Perhaps it was the work of an Ismāʿīlī,'[100] said one of them. But [the Sultan] said, 'Nobody else but the Baḥriyya did this to me.' From that moment the Baḥriyya were afraid of him and were on their guard. [The Sultan] then rose and went up into the wooden tower which stood alongside his pavilion. He sent for the surgeons to treat his hand, and drank something. The Baḥriyya gathered in fear for their lives. They realized that thereafter he would not spare them, and they resolved to kill him, reinforcing what was already in their minds. They drew their swords and surrounded the tower, under the command of the aforesaid Fāris al-Dīn Aqṭāy – the one who had gone to Ḥiṣn Kayfā and endured daunting trials in order to bring him [fol. 89v] to his throne, and had hoped to be closer to him than anyone else and that he would give him Alexandria as his *iqṭāʿ*.

al-Malik al-Muʿaẓẓam opened the windows of the tower, and called on the people for help. But nobody responded; nor did any of the amirs come to his assistance, for in every case he had exhausted their good will. They also feared for their lives, since the Baḥriyya were standing by and were a redoubtable force and possessed of extreme courage. Then [the Baḥriyya] brought fire with which to burn down the tower, and Fāris al-Dīn called out to him, 'Come down, and you have nothing to fear; but if you do not come down, we shall burn down the tower'. And so he came down from the tower. The siege of the tower had lasted some time, and when the news reached the amir Ḥusām al-Dīn he mounted with his squadron; and the Qaymariyya and their squadrons mounted [too]. The Baḥriyya were afraid lest the amirs arrive and they would not see the business through;[101] and so they sent word to Ḥusām al-Dīn and the amirs, saying, 'He has already been killed, and the matter is finished: do not embark upon a conflict that will bring about the destruction of Islam'; and so they paused. The envoy of the Caliph was in the camp, and took horse, but they compelled him to return to his tent, threatening to kill him if he did not yield. The men of the *ṭablkhāna* had begun beating the drums for the *Ḥalqa*[102] and the [rest of the] troops to take horse. But [the Baḥriyya] threatened them if they did not cease doing this, and they stopped.

---

100 That is, one of the Assassins, or Bāṭiniyya as they are often termed in the Muslim sources. Their headquarters were in northern Syria; the Franks called their Master the 'Old Man of the Mountain'.

101 *ya'tuhum al-umarā wa-lā yutamm lahum amr^un^*.

102 An élite corps of guards: see D. Ayalon, 'Ḥalḳa', *EI*[2].

When al-Malik al-Muʿaẓẓam came down to join them, Fāris al-Dīn Aqṭāy reproached him,[103] or so I was told, and al-Malik al-Muʿaẓẓam appealed to him for help, saying, 'I shall stand by my promise to you of the *iqṭāʿ* of Alexandria, and shall do for you whatever you wish'. But [Aqṭāy] did not trust his word. At that point Rukn al-Dīn Baybars attacked him a second time with a sword in his hand, and he ran all the way to the banks of the River Nile, where some galleys lay, with the aim of seeking refuge on one of them. Those in the galleys saw him and came in towards land to take him up. Had they only reached [land], he would have escaped. [fol. 90r] But Rukn al-Dīn followed him, struck him with his sword, and killed him.[104] He remained abandoned on the bank of the river for two days, in which nobody dared to approach him. [Then] a group of dervishes[105] came and took him across to the western bank, where they buried him (God have mercy on him).

His character (God have mercy on him) ... When the amir Ḥusām al-Dīn journeyed to the army headquarters I lingered behind in order to produce a remarkable book in the name of al-Malik al-Muʿaẓẓam ... I appended it to a book which I had written in the name of al-Malik al-Ṣāliḥ (God have mercy on him) and in which I recounted the history of the Prophets (peace be upon them), the Caliphs and the kings, ending with the entry of al-Malik al-Ṣāliḥ into Damascus when he made his way there from the East in the year 636 [1238–39].[106] I travelled to the army headquarters, taking with me the two books in order to present them to al-Malik al-Muʿaẓẓam, on Sunday, three days remaining of Muḥarram [1 May 1250], which was the day preceding his murder. I spent the night at Qalyūb, and then went on from there on Monday to Marṣafā, which is a large village [fol. 90v] adjoining the *iqṭāʿ* of the amir Ḥusām al-Dīn ibn Abī ʿAlī ... [In] a town on the river, called Mīna al-Ghabrī, I encountered a Kurd from the military, who had come from the headquarters in the direction of Cairo. He was weeping, and I asked him for news. 'The Sultan was killed yesterday', he replied. I recited Qur'ān, ii, 151.[107] I was much afflicted by this news and was afraid that if I went on I should be stopped; and so I turned back in the direction of Cairo, where I arrived as the day ended.

How the Sultanate was conferred on Shajar al-Durr, the wife of al-Malik al-Ṣāliḥ, and how 'Izz al-Dīn al-Turkmānī was appointed commander-in-chief Following the murder of al-Malik al-Muʿaẓẓam, which we have described, the amirs and the Baḥriyya assembled at the Sultan's pavilion and discussed whom they should install

103 Reading *i'tanafahū* for the *i'tanaqahū* ('he embraced him') of the ms.

104 Abū Shāma, p. 185, likewise attributes the final blow to Baybars. Ibn ʿAbd al-Raḥīm, fol. 371v, in a much briefer account, says that the Sultan was trying to board a galley and that Aqṭāy followed him to the river-bank and finished him off with a sword-blow. According to Joinville, § 353, p. 192 (trans. Hague, pp. 112-13; trans. Shaw, p. 252), Aqṭāy cut out the dead Sultan's heart.

105 *fuqarā*.

106 This must be the *Ta'rīkh Ṣāliḥī*: see Claude Cahen, 'Sur le *Ta'rīkh Ṣāliḥī* d'Ibn Wāṣil: notes et extraits', in Sharon, *Studies in Islamic History and Civilization*, pp. 507–16.

107 I take this to be the meaning of *istarja'tu*. The verse is designed to be read in time of affliction: 'Surely we belong to God, and to Him we return' (Arberry's translation).

as *atabeg* of the troops once they had agreed that Shajar al-Durr, the mother of al-Malik al-Ṣāliḥ's son Khalīl, should assume the office of Sultan and ruler and that the Sultan's mandates should be issued in her name and under her signature. They [first] offered the post of *atabeg* to the amir Ḥusām al-Dīn, telling him, 'Sultan al-Malik al-Ṣāliḥ relied on you, and you are the most deserving [fol. 91r] of this office'. But he refused and advised them that the cavalry officer Shihāb al-Dīn al-Kabīr would fill the post well. So they offered it to him, but he refused [also]. Then they offered it to the amir Khāṣṣ Turk al-Kabīr, who was one of the leading Ṣāliḥī amirs, but he would not do it. [Finally] they agreed on ʿIzz al-Dīn Aybak al-Turkmānī al-Ṣāliḥī, and they swore allegiance to Shajar al-Durr as Sultan and to ʿIzz al-Dīn as *atabeg* and commander-in-chief of the troops. The amir ʿIzz al-Dīn al-Rūmī al-Ṣāliḥī returned to Cairo and went up into the citadel, where he informed the Lady, Khalīl's mother, of all this. All the business of state began to be attributed to her and documents began to be issued in her name and to bear her own signature in the form 'Khalīl's mother'. The *khuṭba* was read in Cairo, Miṣr and the rest of Egypt in her name as Sultan. An event like this was not known to have occurred previously in Islam.[108] Admittedly, authority and executive power had been in the hands of Ḍayfa Khātūn, the daughter of al-Malik al-ʿĀdil, in Aleppo and its territories from the death of her son, al-Malik al-ʿAzīz, until she died;[109] but the *khuṭba* had been made for her grandson al-Malik al-Nāṣir (God have mercy on him) as Sultan.

The capture of Damietta When the amirs and the military had taken the oath and the situation was stabilized, as we have recounted, they entered into negotiation with the captive King Raydafrans regarding the surrender of Damietta to the Muslims. The amir Ḥusām al-Dīn ibn Abī ʿAlī was chosen as spokesman by universal agreement because he was a model of good judgement and counsel, because they knew him to be experienced, and because of the trust that their master, Sultan al-Malik al-Ṣāliḥ, had placed in him. Discussions took place between him and Raydafrans until agreement was reached that Damietta should be surrendered and that [Raydafrans] and his companions [fol. 91v] among the princes and nobles should be set free.

Ḥusām al-Dīn told me that [Raydafrans] was a thoughtful and intelligent man. 'In one of my conversations with him', he said, 'I asked him, "How did it ever occur to someone of Your Majesty's wisdom, refinement and sound intellect to go on board [a] wood[en] [vessel] and travel across this sea to get to this country, which is full of Muslim troops, in the conviction that you would conquer it and become its ruler? What you did involved extreme risk for yourself and your coreligionists." [Raydafrans] laughed but made no reply. "Some jurists", I told him, "are of the

108 In fact, there had been a female sovereign in the Yemen in the eleventh–twelfth centuries: Farhad Daftary, 'Ṣayyida Ḥurra: the Ismāʿīlī Ṣulayhid queen of Yemen', in Gavin R. G. Hambly (ed.), *Women in the Medieval Islamic World: Power, Patronage, Piety* (New York, 1998), pp. 117–30. More recently, in 1236, a group of Turkish mamluks in Delhi had enthroned as sultan Raḍiyya, the daughter of their old master, Iltutmish: Peter Jackson, 'Sulṭān Raḍiyya bint Iltutmish', ibid., pp. 181–97.

109 Ḍayfa Khātūn was regent of Aleppo for her grandson al-Nāṣir Yūsuf from 1236 to 1242.

opinion that if a man travels by sea more than once, risking both his person and his possessions, his testimony should not be accepted, because it is inferred from this that he is weak-minded and the testimony of the man of weak mind is not accepted." He laughed,' he said, 'and observed, "Whoever said that was right and his conclusion did not miss the mark."' 'One opinion within our school [of law]', I told him,[110] '[is] that repeated journeys by sea do not entail rejection of testimony, because the majority of those who travel by sea remain unharmed. Regarding whether the Pilgrimage is obligatory when it is possible only by sea, there are two points of view. One is that it is not, since a sea voyage carries danger and risk to life; the other is that it is, because the majority return safe.'

When agreement was reached between the Muslims and Raydafrans for the surrender of Damietta, Raydafrans sent to the people in Damietta to order them to hand over the city to the Muslims. After some objection and going to and fro between him and them, they agreed to do this, and the Sultan's standard entered Damietta on Friday 3 Ṣafar of this year, namely 648 [= 6 May 1250], and was hoisted on the walls, and Islam was proclaimed there. Raydafrans was set free, and he and his men were transferred to the western bank. Then, on the following day, he and his men set sail for Acre. [fol. 92r] He stayed on the coast for a time, and fortified Caesarea,[111] and then he returned to his own country. [Thus] God cleansed Egypt of them.

This victory was greater than the earlier one, namely in the year 618 [1221] during the time of al-Malik al-Kāmil, in view of the fact that many times more of them were killed or taken prisoner. The jails in Cairo were filled with Franks. The good news of this [victory] was transmitted to the rest of the Islamic world, where there were public displays of gladness and rejoicing.[112]

74(a). Sibṭ Ibn al-Jawzī (Shams al-Dīn Abū'l-Muẓaffar Yūsuf ibn Qizūghlī) (d. 1256), Mir'āt al-zamān fī ta'rīkh al-a'yān, *vol. 8/2 (Hyderabad, A.P., 1372 H./1952), pp. 772–4*

The year 647 [1249–50] In this year, on 4 Muḥarram [19 April 1249], al-Ṣāliḥ Ayyūb set out from Damascus for Egypt in a litter owing to his grave illness. Those who were with him announced to the people: 'We have money: come, then, and take what belongs to you.' And the people went up to the citadel and took what belonged to them.

[p. 773] In this year al-Nāṣir Dā'ūd went from Kerak to Aleppo …

In this year Ḥasan, son of al-Nāṣir, went from Kerak to Egypt, and handed over Kerak to al-Ṣāliḥ Ayyūb in Jumādā II [11 September-9 October 1249]. He [the Sultan]

110 The speaker now seems to be Ibn Wāṣil rather than Ḥusām al-Dīn.

111 Louis in fact restored the fortifications of Jaffa and Sidon also, prior to returning to France in 1254.

112 There follows a brief account of Louis's attack on Tunis during the Eighth Crusade (1270), wrongly dated 660 H./1262, and of the arrival of the news in Egypt during Baybars's reign.

granted them stipends, and removed from there the dependants of al-Muʿaẓẓam,[113] his sons and daughters, and al-Nāṣir's mother and everyone to be found there. He sent him 1,000,000 *dīnārs*, jewels, treasure and many things [besides].

In this year, in Rabīʿ I [14 June–13 July 1249], the Franks broke into Damietta. Fakhr al-Dīn Ibn al-Shaykh and the army were there: they abandoned [the city], and its inhabitants left too. al-Ṣāliḥ was at Mansura, and he had sixty of the chief men hanged. The survivors fled in fear lest they should suffer what had happened on the first occasion. When he issued orders for them to be hanged, they asked what they had done wrong: when his troops and the amirs took flight and set fire to the arsenal, what could they do? Among those hanged was a decent man, of the Kināna, who had a son who was the handsomest of men in appearance. His father said, 'By God, hang me before him'. al-Ṣāliḥ was told and said, 'No, hang the son first.' And they did so.

Disturbances broke out among the troops, and they cursed Ayyūb. I was told that his mamluks wanted to kill him, but that Ibn al-Shaykh said to them, 'Be patient with him. [p. 774] He is on the brink [of death]: if he dies, you will be rid of him; if not, he will be in your hands.' Najm al-Dīn, the son of the Shaykh al-Islām, had been killed. al-Ṣāliḥ Ayyūb said to Fakhr al-Dīn and the troops, 'Were you not able to stand your ground before the Franks for one hour, when none of the troops was slain except that weakling (namely the son of the Shaykh al-Islām)?'[114] … Had he [the Sultan] lived, he would have put Ibn al-Shaykh and the others to death. When the Franks attacked by one gate and Ibn al-Shaykh and the troops left by another, they imagined it to be a trap and held back. Then they realized for certain the weakness of the Muslims and the departure of the populace of Damietta – barefoot and unclad, hungry and thirsty, in poverty and disarray, women and children – and that they had been granted what would support them, and they plundered them on the road to Cairo.

On the evening of 15 Shaʿbān [23 November 1249], al-Ṣāliḥ Ayyūb died at Mansura. Khalīl's mother[115] was with him, and she took over the direction of affairs. She altered nothing in the state of the [royal] pavilion. Every day the table was laid and the amirs were in attendance, while she would say, 'The sultan is ill; nobody is to approach him.' They sent to al-Ṣāliḥ Ayyūb's son, al-Muʿaẓẓam Tūrān Shāh, at Ḥiṣn Kayfā, Aqṭāy, a mamluk of al-Ṣāliḥ Ayyūb. [Tūrān Shāh] left Ḥiṣn Kayfā with him and made his way across the desert, at risk to his life, since he almost died of thirst. He reached Damascus towards the end of Ramaḍān [end of December 1249-beginning of January 1250]. He gave robes of honour to the men of Damascus, bestowed sums of money on them and treated them with favour: no request was made to which he gave a negative answer. I was told that there were 300,000 *dīnārs* in the citadel of Damascus: he brought it [all] out, and [then] sent to Kerak for [more] money, which he spent.

113 al-Muʿaẓẓam ʿĪsā, ruler of Damascus (1218–27), the younger brother of Ayyūb's father al-Kāmil.

114 The Sibṭ's account here seems to be derived from Saʿd al-Dīn Ibn Ḥamawiya: see al-Dhahabī, *Ta'rīkh al-Islām*, [vol. 5:] *641-650 H.*, pp. 370–71.

115 Shajar al-Durr, so called from the name of the son whom she had borne to Ayyūb but who died in infancy.

74(b). Shams al-Dīn Muḥammad ibn Aḥmad al-Dhahabī (d. 1348), Ta'rīkh al-Islām, *ed. 'Umar 'Abd-al-Salām Tadmurī, [vol. 5:]* 641–650 H. *(Beirut, 1419 H./1998), p. 45*[116]

The year 647 [1249–50] Ibn al-Sā'ī says: At the beginning of this year the Franks captured Damietta. They had attacked it, and al-Ṣāliḥ Najm al-Dīn sent troops to assist those who were in [the city]. But he was ill. The Franks were repulsed, but then they gained the upper hand over them. Two amirs showed spirit, namely the son of the Shaykh al-Islām and al-Jawlānī, and charged at [the Franks]. The son of the Shaykh al-Islām was killed, but al-Jawlānī survived. The gates of Damietta were locked. They sent a slip of paper. The Sultan had drunk a narcotic remedy, and the physician told them not to disturb him. The message arrived, but the servant hid it. Then a second [message] came, but no reply was sent back to them, and the Sultan knew nothing of it. In Damietta it was being said that the Sultan was dead, and they lost spirit. The populace of Damietta resolved on flight. They set fire to the gates and went out. Troops were sent to bring them back, but did not catch up with them.[117] The troops came back and plundered the city.

74(c). al-Dhahabī, Ta'rīkh al-Islām, *pp. 358, 373*

Obituaries for the year 647 [*1249–50*]

…

Obituary of al-Ṣāliḥ Ayyūb [p. 358] Sa'd al-Dīn told how his cousin, the viceroy Fakhr al-Dīn, entered the Sultan's tent the day after [his death] and arranged with the cavalry officer Muḥassan for an announcement to be made that the Sultan had ordered the people to take an oath of allegiance to his son al-Malik al-Mu'aẓẓam and to Fakhr al-Dīn as his lieutenant. This was settled, and they summoned the [chief] people, who took the oath except the sons of al-Nāṣir.[118] They hesitated and said, 'We want to see the Sultan.' A servant went in and [then] came out, and said, 'The Sultan greets you.' [Fakhr al-Dīn] said, 'Why are you eager to see him in such circumstances, when he has ordered [you] to swear an oath?' And so they took the

116 The following passages from al-Dhahabī are included here because they retail information derived from contemporary authors, and in particular extracts from the lost memoirs of Sa'd al-Dīn Ibn Ḥamawiya al-Juwaynī which are not to be found in the history produced by the Sibṭ (see introduction, pp. 5–6). Most of these passages are translated in Cahen, 'Une source pour l'histoire ayyūbide', pp. 474–8.

117 Joinville, § 163, p. 90 (trans. Hague, p. 64; trans. Shaw, p. 204), heard that the Muslim forces withdrew because they had received no response to the carrier-pigeons they had sent to Ayyūb to warn him of the Frankish landing. It should be noted that, in contrast with other authors, Ibn al-Sā'ī corroborates the statement in Sultan Ayyūb's 'Testament' (Cahen and Chabbouh, text p. 100, trans. p. 107) that the populace abandoned Damietta before the military, who attempted without success to bring them back.

118 al-Nāṣir Dā'ūd, Ayyūb's cousin and the former ruler of Kerak.

oath … And Fakhr al-Dīn had copies of the oath sent to the provinces, so that they might swear allegiance to al-Muʿaẓẓam.

…

Obituary of Fakhr al-Dīn Ibn al-Shaykh … [p. 373] When al-Ṣāliḥ died, Fakhr al-Dīn took charge of the government. He treated the people with favour, and abrogated some uncanonical taxes. He gathered a bodyguard.[119] If Fate had only given him time, he would have been our sovereign master.

He sent al-Fāris Aqṭāy to Ḥiṣn Kayfā to fetch the Sultan's son, al-Malik al-Muʿaẓẓam Tūrān Shāh. And he brought him, and he was made ruler.

al-Muʿaẓẓam had it in mind to kill [Fakhr al-Dīn]. The mamluks who went to Damascus to urge al-Muʿaẓẓam to hurry made him suspect that Fakhr al-Dīn had caused the oath to be taken to himself as king …

74(d). Sibṭ Ibn al-Jawzī, Mir'āt al-zamān, *vol. 8/2, pp. 774–7*

In Dhū'l-Qaʿda there was a great battle at Mansura. The Franks penetrated as far as the pavilion, and Fakhr al-Dīn Ibn al-Shaykh came out and fought, but was killed. The troops fled to escape their hands. [But] then the Muslims rallied and turned upon the Franks, conducting a mighty slaughter [p. 775] among them.

After staying in Damascus for twenty-seven days, al-Muʿaẓẓam Tūrān Shāh set out for Egypt. It is said that he had arrived [in Damascus] on 20 Ramaḍān [27 December 1249] and left on 17 Shawwāl [23 January 1250]; and certainly he reached Egypt towards the end of the year [647, that is, the late winter of 1249–50]. He had determined to eliminate Ibn al-Shaykh, since he had learned that he had designs on the kingship and that the people all wanted him. [But Ibn al-Shaykh] died a martyr and was given rest (Almighty God have mercy on him) …

[Obituary of al-Ṣāliḥ Ayyūb] … Khalīl's mother, a freed slave of Ayyūb, would write documents in a hand that resembled his: she was an expert on signatures. His wound had turned septic and had spread to his right leg and foot, and his body wasted away. A litter was made for him to be carried in, and he used to suffer patiently. Not a soul was informed of what had befallen him. His coffin was conveyed to the Jazīra [fortress] and suspended in chains until he was buried in his grave alongside his college in Cairo …

[p. 776] *[Obituary of Fakhr al-Dīn Ibn al-Shaykh]* In this year died Fakhr al-Dīn Yūsuf Ibn Shaykh al-Shuyūkh. He was wise and generous, and a leader qualified to rule and beloved of the people … When Ayyūb died, Fakhr al-Dīn Ibn al-Shaykh took over the government of the realm and treated the people with kindness. A group sent to Ḥiṣn [Kayfā] and summoned Tūrān Shāh. The soldiers were jealous of Fakhr

---

119 I take this to be the sense of *rakkaba 'l-shāwushiyya*. For *shāwush* (= Turkish *chavush*, 'guard', 'man-at-arms'), see R. Dozy, *Supplément aux dictionnaires arabes* (Leiden, 1881; repr. Beirut, 1968), vol. 2, pp. 717–18.

al-Dīn and determined to kill him and plunder his house. But he summoned the amirs and nobles, and said, 'I have no designs on the kingship: I am only guarding my master's house until his son comes and takes over the country.' So they made promises on oath. But this made the servitor Muḥassan and a number [of others] suspicious, and they sent some of al-Ṣāliḥ's mamluks to Damascus, on al-Muʿaẓẓam's arrival there, to urge him to make haste and come to Egypt. Some of the mamluks who were joining him made him suspect that the army had sworn an oath to Fakhr al-Dīn personally: how long would it be before he was [himself] murdered? So he lingered and disbursed the treasure at Damascus among the troops in order thereby to win the support of the Egyptian army. The mamluks whom Fakhr al-Dīn had sent to him had already sworn to kill Fakhr al-Dīn.

It happened that the Franks advanced on the Muslim army and crossed the ditches and the river, and the Muslims rushed headlong among them. It was a terrible day. Fakhr al-Dīn mounted at daybreak to investigate the news, accompanied by some of his mamluks and troopers, and chanced to encounter a squadron of Templars. They charged [p. 777] upon him, and those with him fled. He was pierced in the side and fell from his horse; and they struck him two sword-blows the length and breadth of his face, and slew him. His mamluks went to his house, broke open his coffers, and looted most of the contents. They took his treasure and his horses. al-Jawlānī Qudūr appropriated his baths, and al-Dumyāṭī the gates of his house. It was of no advantage that he had reared his mamluks kindly … Then they took him in [just] a shirt from the battlefield and conveyed him in a galley to Cairo. His house was destroyed as if the previous day it had not existed. It was destroyed by the amirs who used to ride every day to wait upon him and to stand at his door. There were more than seventy of them: they used to count themselves fortunate if he glanced at one of them, and [now] they destroyed his house … At the time of his death he was 36 years old.

When Tūrān Shāh reached the army headquarters, he took Fakhr al-Dīn's lesser mamluks and some of his cloth at half their value, and did not give them a *dirham*. Nor did he pay his heirs anything in compensation. The value was 15,000 *dīnārs*. Whenever he sat at table, he would turn Fakhr al-Dīn's virtues into vices, saying: 'He freed [from tax][120] the cotton and the sugar, disbursed the treasure and threw open the prisons. What did he leave for me?' Yet [Fakhr al-Dīn] had preserved the throne for him, maintaining discipline among the troops and confronting the enemy – these were in fact his greatest offences.

74(e). al-Dhahabī, Ta'rīkh al-Islām, *pp. 373–4*

[Fakhr al-Dīn's] cousin, Saʿd al-Dīn, said: It was a terribly misty day. They fired [arrows] at him, pierced him, and struck him two sword-blows in the face. The only other person [of his entourage] killed with him was the keeper of his wardrobe.[121] al-Jawlānī appropriated the baths that he had built in Mansura, and al-Dumyāṭī the gates of his house. That day were slain [p. 374] Najm al-Dīn al-Bihisnī, al-Shujāʿ Ibn

---

120 The sense as taken in Ibn al-Furāt, trans. Lyons, *Ayyubids, Mamlukes and Crusaders*, vol. 2, p. 26.

121 *jamdār*.

Bawsh and al-Taqiyya al-Kātib, and all the tents of the left wing were pillaged. Then the Muslims rallied and attacked the Franks, of whom 1600 horsemen were killed. The Franks pitched their tents on this bank of the river, and set about digging a trench around themselves. He continued: Then we washed Fakhr al-Dīn, who was wearing only a shirt. As for the house he had built in Mansura, that day it was reduced to a state of ruin, to the point where they say, 'This is the house where only yesterday the standards of seventy amirs were arrayed at its gates to witness his going out'. Praise be to Him who neither changes nor ceases.

74(f). Sibṭ Ibn al-Jawzī, Mir'āt al-zamān, *vol. 8/2, pp. 778–9*

[p. 778] *The year 648* [*1250–51*] On the first night of the year, a battle took place between the Franks and the Muslims at Mansura after al-Malik Tūrān Shāh had advanced against the dreadful Frenchman.[122] A hundred thousand Franks were slain. A letter arrived [at Damascus] from al-Muʿaẓẓam Tūrān Shāh, saying: 'Praise be to God, who has taken away our misery and from whom alone comes victory. "This day let the faithful rejoice in God's help; God helps whom He will,"[123] and He is the mighty judge. "As for your Lord's blessing, declare it,"[124] and "If ye count up God's blessings, ye cannot number them."[125] We send to the august court of Jamāl [al-Dīn Ibn Yaghmūr], nay to the whole of Islam, the good news of what a victory God has granted the Muslims over the enemy of the faith; how his position had grown menacing and his evil had taken root; how the worshippers [of God] had despaired for their wives and offspring. There was announced to them the verse, "Do not despair of God's comfort; of God's comfort no man despairs."[126] On the arrival of Wednesday, the first day of the blessed year [5 April 1250], God brought Islam's blessings to fruition. We opened up the treasury, disbursed the funds, distributed the arms, and mustered the Arabs and the volunteers – and there gathered a vast host whom none but Almighty God could count, and they came from every deep valley [p. 779] and every far distant locality. When the enemy beheld this, he sent to sue for peace on the basis of what was agreed between them and al-Malik al-Kāmil; but this we rejected. When night fell, they abandoned their tents, their baggage and their money, and set out in flight for Damietta. We followed on their tracks in pursuit; nor did the sword cease its work among their backsides throughout the night. Shame and disaster were their lot, and when dawn arrived on Wednesday we slew 30,000 of them, not counting those who threw themselves into the depths [of the river]. As for the prisoners, tell of the sea and you will not be far out. The Frenchman took refuge in al-Munya and asked for quarter, which we granted him. We took him and treated him with honour, and we took possession [of Damietta] through the aid and power and glory and might of God.' His letter continued at length.

But on 28 Muḥarram, al-Muʿaẓẓam Tūrān Shāh was slain …

122 *al-Faransīs*.

123 Qur'ān, xxx, 4.

124 Qur'ān, xciii, 11.

125 Qur'ān, xiv, 34.

126 Qur'ān, xii, 87.

74(g). al-Dhahabī, Ta'rīkh al-Islām, *pp. 387–8*

Obituary of al-Mu'aẓẓam Tūrān Shāh … [p. 387] Sa'd al-Dīn Ibn Ḥamawiya says: al-Mu'aẓẓam arrived, and everyone who was insignificant in his father's time had their say. He was found to be lacking in wisdom and poor in resolve. He transferred the appanage of Fakhr al-Dīn Ibn al-Shaykh, with its revenues, to the slave Jawhar for his womenfolk. The amirs expected that he would bestow gifts upon them as he had done to the amirs of Damascus; but they saw no hint of it. His left shoulder and half of his face, particularly where the beard joins it, were constantly convulsed. When he was drunk, [p. 388] he would slash at candles with his sword, and say, 'This is what I want to do to my father's slaves!' And he threatened the amirs with death. He disturbed everybody's spirits, and people loathed him – not to mention [his] greed.[127]

74(h). al-Dhahabī, Ta'rīkh al-Islām, *pp. 50–51*

Events of the year 648 [*1250–51*] … [p. 50] Sa'd al-Dīn says in his history: If the Frenchman had only wished to save himself, he could have taken refuge in Jabal Sabaq or Ḥarāfa. Yet he stayed in the thick of it to protect his followers. The prisoners [p. 51] included princes and counts. A tally was made of the number of captives, and there were more than 20,000; those who had drowned or been killed numbered 7000. I saw the dead, and they covered the face of the earth in their profusion … It was a day of the kind the Muslims had never seen; nor had they heard of its like. Of the Muslims, there were slain no more than a hundred.

al-Malik al-Mu'aẓẓam sent more than fifty robes to the Frenchman, the princes and the counts. All donned them except [the Frenchman], who said, 'My country is larger than that of the ruler of Egypt: how can I wear his robes?' The next day the Sultan gave a great feast. The Accursed One likewise declined to attend, and said, 'I will not eat his food. He has only invited me so that I may be a laughing-stock to his soldiery. [This way] that will not be possible.' He was a man of wisdom, constancy and faith (in their fashion), and they put their trust in him. He was of fine appearance.

al-Mu'aẓẓam sorted the prisoners. He took the nobles and craftsmen, and ordered the ordinary mass to be beheaded.[128]

---

127 I have followed here the rendering of *ṣādif dhālika bukhl^{an}* given by Cahen, 'Une source pour l'histoire ayyūbide', p. 477.

128 Joinville, § 334, p. 182 (trans. Hague, p. 107; trans. Shaw, p. 246), claims that the prisoners were given the choice of conversion to Islam or death. According to Ibn al-'Amīd, p. 160 (trans. Eddé and Micheau, p. 88), the Sultan deputed one of his associates from the East, Sayf al-Dīn Yūsuf al-Ṭūrī, to take charge of the execution of the Frankish prisoners, and they were killed at the rate of 300 per night.

74(i). Sibṭ Ibn al-Jawzī, Mir'āt al-zamān, *vol. 8/2, pp. 781–3*

[*Obituary of al-Mu'aẓẓam Tūrān Shāh*] [p. 781] In this year died Tūrān Shāh, son of al-Malik al-Ṣāliḥ Ayyūb, whose title was al-Muʿaẓẓam. We have already related his journey to Syria and his entry into Egypt. The defeat of the Franks coincided with his arrival, and the people saw his appearance as a good omen and rejoiced to see him, until reasons emerged for their hearts to turn from him and they agreed to kill him. One [reason] was that he was of a frivolous disposition … [p. 782] Another was that he hid himself from the people more than his father [had done]. He gave himself over, so they say, to depravity with his father's mamluks – they were not accustomed to that from his father – and similarly with his father's concubines.[129] When he was drunk, he gathered candles and would slash at the heads [of the candles] with his sword and lop them off, saying, 'Thus shall I do with the Baḥriyya,' and he would mention his father's mamluks by name. The base-born were exalted and those of quality removed. He treated his father's chief mamluks with contempt. He had promised Aqṭāy that he would make him an amir, but he did not keep his word, and so Aqṭāy became alienated from him. When [Tūrān Shāh] reached Jerusalem, Khalīl's mother had moved to Cairo, but he sent threats to her, demanding the treasure and the jewellery. She grew afraid of him and, so they say, mentioned it in her letters.[130]

How he was slain When Monday, 27 Muḥarram [1 May 1250] came, he took his seat at table. One of the Baḥriyya mamluks struck at him with his sword. [The Sultan] met [the blow] with his hand and some of his fingers were severed. He rose and went into the tower and shouted, 'Who wounded me?' 'The Assassins,' was the reply. 'No, by God,' he said: 'it was the Baḥriyya. By God, I shall not leave one of them alive.' He sent for the barber, who stitched his hand. He was [still] uttering threats against them, and so they said to one another, 'Finish him off, or he will destroy you.' So they went in after him. He fled to the top of the tower, and they lit fires around it and fired arrows at him. Then he threw himself out and fled towards the river, saying, 'I have no desire to rule. Send me back to Ḥiṣn [Kayfā]. Oh Muslims, is there none among you who will aid and stand by me?' All the soldiers were standing there, but not one answered, while the arrows overwhelmed him. So [runs one version. Another is that] when he went up into the tower they fired arrows at him, and he clung to Aqṭāy's skirts; but they would not protect him, and cut him to pieces. His swollen body remained on the river bank for three days, while no one dared give him burial, until the Caliph's ambassador interceded for him and he was carried to the other bank and buried.

---

129 The printed text does not make sense at this point: some words are garbled and several clearly omitted. I have therefore used the phrasing supplied by al-Jazarī, *Ḥawādith al-zamān*, Forschungs- und Landesbibliothek Gotha, ms. Orient. A 1559, fol. 125v, who here claims to be citing the Sibṭ verbatim.

130 Again, the text needs to be corrected from that of al-Jazarī, thus reading *kātabat* for *kānat* as proposed by Schregle, *Die Sultanin*, p. 57, n. 3. Ibn al-Furāt (in *Ayyubids, Mamlukes and Crusaders*, vol. 1, p. 39) similarly uses the Sibṭ here but adds, after 'wrote about it', 'to her husband's mamluks'.

When they had killed him, they entered the Frenchman's tent with their swords and said, 'We want the money.' And he [p. 783] agreed. Then they released him, and he went to Acre in accordance with the agreement they made with him.[131]

Those who carried out the murder were four. Saʿd al-Dīn Masʿūd ibn Tāj al-Dīn Shaykh al-Shuyūkh[132] said: I learned from a trustworthy source that his father al-Malik al-Ṣāliḥ Ayyūb said to the servant Muḥassan, 'Go to my brother al-ʿĀdil[133] in prison, and take with you some of the mamluks to strangle him.' Muḥassan put this proposal to all of the mamluks, but they declined the charge, except these four, who went with him and strangled [al-ʿĀdil]. So as a punishment God brought them to put his son to a more shameful death and to do to [his son] as he had done unto his brother.

I was told by the amir Ḥusām al-Dīn ibn Abī ʿAlī[134] that Tūrān Shāh was irresponsible and unfitted to rule. [Ḥusām al-Dīn] used to say to al-Ṣāliḥ Najm al-Dīn, 'Do not delay, but summon him here'. But [al-Ṣāliḥ] would say, 'Leave me alone.' [Ḥusām al-Dīn said,] 'One day we pressed him, and he said, "If I agree to [his coming] here, I shall kill him" ...'

Three things were associated in his death: the sword, fire and water. They slew him when he had sought refuge in the river. The prayers were recited from the pulpit in Cairo and Miṣr in the name of Khalīl's mother.

74(j). al-Dhahabī, Ta'rīkh al-Islām, *pp. 53, 55–6*

[p. 53] Saʿd al-Dīn says in his history: They reached an agreement that the Frenchman should surrender Damietta; that he and the counts should pay 800,000 *dīnārs* as compensation for the revenues while they occupied Damietta; and that they should release the Muslim prisoners. They swore [to do] this. The army set out on 2 Ṣafar [5 May 1250]. We made camp before Damietta until around dawn. The people entered, and plundered and killed some of the Franks who remained [there],[135] so that the amirs drove them out with blows. The balance of the revenues there was assessed at 400,000 *dīnārs*. They accepted 400,000 *dīnārs* from the Frenchman, and in the afternoon he and a group [of his people] were released and embarked in a galley. He sent a messenger to the amirs, to say: 'What I have seen [reflects] how little wisdom or faith you have – how little faith, because you killed your Sultan; how little wisdom, because a king from overseas like myself fell into your hands and you

131 According to al-Dhahabī, pp. 52–3 (whether on Saʿd al-Dīn's authority, we cannot know), Ḥusām al-Dīn warned his colleagues that Louis had seen all their weak points and should be kept a prisoner; but Aybak (the future Sultan) refused to countenance such treachery.

132 This is Fakhr al-Dīn's cousin Saʿd al-Dīn, a member of the Banū Ḥamawiya family: see above, page 125 and note 1.

133 al-ʿĀdil II, Sultan of Egypt (1238–40); murdered in prison in 1248.

134 Viceroy (*nā'ib*) of Egypt and friend and patron of the historian Ibn Wāṣil. This is the only mention of him in the Sibṭ's account of these events.

135 Joinville, § 369, p. 200 (trans. Hague, p. 117; trans. Shaw, p. 256), says that after entering Damietta the Muslim troops got drunk. One of them later told Joinville and his companions that he had killed six of their people: ibid., § 370, p. 202 (trans. ibid.).

demanded [only] 400,000 *dīnārs*. Had you demanded my kingdom, I should have made you a present of it in order to gain my release.'[136]

…

[p. 55] … Saʿd al-Dīn says: The Turks appeared at the Sultan's pavilion and swore allegiance to Shajar al-Durr and her deputy, the amir ʿIzz al-Dīn al-Turkmānī. During Ṣafar [4 May–1 June 1250] the lady Shajar al-Durr began to bestow robes on the amirs and gave them gold and horses. 500 Frankish prisoners were released, including 100 horsemen. [p. 56] On 1 Rabīʿ I [2 June 1250] they conferred on al-Fāris Aqṭāy, the keeper of the wardrobe,[137] the assignment[138] of Fakhr al-Dīn Ibn al-Shaykh, with the addition of three villages …

136 Improbable sentiments from King Louis's mouth.

137 *jamdār*.

138 Reading *khubz* for the *khabar* of the printed text.

VII

The Reaction to Failure: Criticism and Rational Explanation

The sources which would enable us to gauge the reaction to the failure of 1250 are possibly fuller than they are for any crusading disaster since the outcome of the Second Crusade in 1149. We certainly possess at least as much evidence as we have for the distress that greeted the less spectacular collapse of the Fifth Crusade in Egypt in 1221.[1]

Pope Innocent IV, who had summoned the crusade, was a tempting target for reproach – not least, predictably, for his great enemy, the Emperor Frederick. In a letter to the Castilian King, Frederick blamed the Pope for having chosen to wage war against fellow Christians rather than against the infidel, and having thus left the Holy Land isolated. Had Innocent been willing to negotiate with him, the Emperor and his sons could have led an army to the East in order to retrieve the disaster; as it was, however, he had been forced to defend his royal rights against papal encroachment [**doc. 79**].[2] In another letter (probably of a similar date), to his son-in-law, the Emperor John III Ducas Vatatzes of Nicaea, Frederick was more outspoken, blaming the Pope directly for the slaughter in the Nile delta.[3] The southern French troubadour Austorc d'Aurillac, lamenting the disaster, similarly attacked the Pope, but associated him also with 'false clerics' who, merely in order to raise money, sought to bring so many folk down [**doc. 82**] – evidently another allusion to the 'political crusade'.

The French King was not totally above criticism. A German annalist saw Louis's failure to divide up the plunder at Damietta as symptomatic of his conceit [**doc. 80**]. This seems to echo complaints made by Joinville and others at the time of the city's capture, when the King had refused to share out provisions and the rest of the plunder in the manner required by the custom of the kingdom of Jerusalem, but had kept them all in his own hands, to be distributed as and when need arose.[4] For Matthew Paris, the way in which Louis had scraped an infinite sum of money from

1 For the Fifth Crusade, see Powell, *Anatomy of a Crusade*, pp. 195–6; J. Van Moelenbroek, 'Het klaaglied over het debacle van de kruistocht in Egypte (1221) in de kroniek van Ryccardus van San Germano', *Millennium. Tijdschrift voor middeleeuwse studies*, 14 (2000): 42–57.

2 He had made a similar claim in relation to the threat from the Mongols in 1241: Huillard-Bréholles, vol. 5/2, p. 1152 = Matthew Paris, *Chronica Majora*, vol. 4, p. 116 (trans. Giles, vol. 1, p. 345); Jackson, *The Mongols and the West*, p. 67.

3 Huillard-Bréholles, vol. 6/2, p. 774.

4 Joinville, §§ 168–9, p. 92 (trans. Hague, pp. 65–6; trans. Shaw, pp. 206-7).

his realm for the crusade had incurred God's disapproval, as was manifest in the crusade's failure.[5] At another point, Matthew delivers himself of the verdict that the Holy Land, as Christ's patrimony, was the only valid objective for a crusade[6] (thus ignoring the whole rationale behind the 'Egyptian strategy').

Joinville subscribes to the now well-established view that the defeat had been brought about by the crusaders' sins: they had been unmindful of their Saviour; they had angered the Virgin and her Son.[7] But it was also a commonplace for crusading disasters to be ascribed to the sins of Christians in general (*peccatis exigentibus*).[8] For the Pope, writing to Queen Blanche and to the Archbishop of Rouen, Louis had been guilty of no neglect or shortcomings, but had dedicated himself and his resources to the crusade, at risk to his own interests; God must have been offended, rather, by the sins of the people [**docs 75–6**]. The same theme of widespread sinfulness is touched on also by the Legate Eudes de Châteauroux, in two sermons composed in memory of Louis's brother Robert of Artois, probably therefore in February 1251 [**docs 77–8**].[9] In the first of these, he exonerates the dead crusaders, who had been engaged in a Just War. God was showing Christians at large, rather, how much they had sinned and offended Him; He was trying to strike fear into their hearts, because if even those who had responded to the crusading appeal had met with death and suffering, how much worse might it be for those who had not bestirred themselves to go out east in the first place?

The Pope drew Queen Blanche's attention to the way in which Louis and his brothers had not merely undergone their tribulations for Christ's sake, but through them, were also imitating Him. The Legate's first sermon reminded his audience that the death suffered by the fallen crusaders was martyrdom, a proof, in fact, of how much God loved them. And the two men drew comfort from the fact that God had preserved the King and his barons. For Eudes, this was both the result of intercession by the martyred crusaders and a demonstration of divine power, since Louis and his colleagues had been freed, not through some victory in battle, but at the point when the situation was utterly desperate; whereas the triumphant Sultan had been cut down by his own officers. Jean de Garlande, too, saw Louis's release as a miracle [**doc. 81**].

What effect, then, did the collapse of the crusade have on public opinion in Western Europe? Some, like Jean de Garlande, writing within two years of the event,

---

5 Matthew Paris, *Chronica Majora*, vol. 5, p. 102 (trans. Giles, vol. 2, p. 330; trans. Vaughan, p. 205).

6 Ibid., vol. 5, p. 88 (trans. Giles, vol. 2, p. 320; trans. Vaughan, pp. 193-4).

7 Joinville, §§ 166, 598, pp. 90, 328 (trans. Hague, pp. 65, 178; trans. Shaw, pp. 207, 314). See Philippe Ménard, 'L'esprit de la croisade chez Joinville. Etude des mentalités médiévales', in Yvonne Bellenger and Danielle Quéruel (eds), *Les Champenois et la croisade. Actes des quatrièmes journées rémoises 27–28 novembre 1987* (Paris, 1989), pp. 131–47 (here pp. 138–42).

8 Elizabeth Siberry, *Criticism of Crusading 1095–1274* (Oxford, 1985), pp. 81–9.

9 These two sermons have been analysed in Penny Cole, D. L. d'Avray and J. Riley-Smith, 'Application of theology to current affairs: Memorial sermons on the dead of Mansurah and on Innocent IV', *BIHR*, 63 (1990): 227–47, where it is suggested that the second may have been delivered to a clerical audience (231).

could take heart from the fact that many more martyrs had found a welcome in Heaven, and could express confidence that the crusaders' defeat would be avenged. But others were less sanguine. There was clearly a sense that the Muslims now held the Christians in contempt and derision [**docs 76, 78 and 81**],[10] and in some measure it may have translated into feelings of abject inferiority on the part of Christians. Matthew Paris three times inserts into his narrative a reference to widespread apostasy in the West once news came through that the invasion of Egypt had ended in disaster.[11] It would be easy to dismiss such claims; but they seem to be corroborated elsewhere – by an incidental reference in Jean de Garlande's poem [**doc. 81**], by the troubadour Austorc [**doc. 82**], by the Franciscan Salimbene [**doc. 83**], and even in a sermon of the Legate Eudes [**doc. 78**]. The impact of the failure of 1250 on crusading enthusiasm is not easily discernible. But we might logically surmise that hopes of success had now paled, given the failure of a king who was known to be a man of high moral character and unswerving Christian intent: he had been spared by God after a mortal illness, as if singled out for the task of recovering Christ's own territory,[12] and he had headed what was believed to be the best-prepared and best-organized expedition to have left Western shores. It is possible that the *débâcle* of 1250 provoked a genuine crisis in crusading history.

DOCUMENTS 75–83

75. Pope Innocent IV to Queen Blanche, [August 1250], in Hans Martin Schaller, 'Eine kuriale Briefsammlung des 13. Jahrhunderts mit unbekannten Briefen Friedrichs II.', Deutsches Archiv für Erforschung des Mittelalters, *18 (1962): 171–213; reprinted in Schaller,* Stauferzeit. Ausgewählte Aufsätze *(Hanover, 1993), pp. 283–328 (no. 15) (page references are to the reprinted version)*

[p. 326] To you in your sadness we in ours send you words of sorrow, written in misery; and since enormous grief has completely taken hold of our thoughts, we can barely express to you what is in our mind, nor will you be able to read what we write without a host of tears – nay rather, we believe, the most bitter weeping will prevent you [even] from beginning to read. The mourning is indeed shared, and we grieve along with you, for the terrible misfortune of your sons afflicts your heart with suffering and twists our spirit with a similar torment. It is the same sword that transfixes the innards of [us] both; the whole of Christendom, too, shares in tribulation of this kind, and this situation strikes at all the faithful. For what Catholic, on hearing that such a grave crisis has befallen our dearest son in Christ, the illustrious King of France, his brothers, and the Christian army, will not be excessively cast down and

10 Matthew Paris, *Chronica Majora*, vol. 5, p. 331, where words are put into the mouth of the Bishop of Ely (trans. Giles, vol. 2, p. 524).

11 Ibid., vol. 5, pp. 169–70, 254; and see (citing the Bishop of Ely) 332 (trans. Giles, vol. 2, pp. 387, 451, 524; the first of these passages also in the Vaughan trans., p. 256).

12 Ibid., vols 4, p. 488, and 5, pp. 1–2 (trans. Giles, vol. 2, pp. 116, 252; the latter passage also in the Vaughan trans., p. 129). *Les chansons de croisade*, ed. Bédier and Aubry, p. 252 [**doc. 3**].

burst into lamentation? Who of the faithful, on learning of their unhappy lot, will not straightway cast himself on the ground, sigh bitterly, and give vent to sorrowful mourning? How great is the Church's grief, how loud its groans, and how great its cries! It bemoans, indeed, the grievous death of so many great warriors for the Faith, and most especially of [p. 327] R[obert], Count of Artois, of happy memory, whom it reared in love in the depths of its bosom; it mourns, in addition, the outlay of so much expense and so much effort which [remain] fruitless and stillborn. But even if this is the gravest disaster, we should nevertheless not grieve inconsolably, lest the Divine Kindness be offended, particularly since no small means of comfort [stems] from the fact that the King does not appear to have been guilty of neglect or inadequacy in the business of the Cross, to which he devoted himself and his possessions completely in preference to his own interests. Wherefore some transgressions on the part of the people have offended in the sight of the Almighty, on account of which He has allowed so heavy a loss to occur for the correction of His own. It ought, moreover, to be no small antidote to such great sorrow that the King and his brothers are known to be undergoing such suffering (healthily recalling their Lord's) on behalf of Christ, Who raised them up especially among the world's princes in prestige, power and wealth. But it can particularly assuage the bitterness of the current crisis that the Divine Mercy has preserved safe and sound the persons of the King and his brothers, our beloved sons the Counts of Poitou and Provence, being unwilling for His Church and the Catholic Faith to remain bereft of the guardianship of such great princes. Since they survive safe and unharmed in their persons, they will be able to rise up magnificently at all times, both for the completion of the affairs of Jerusalem and for the performance of everything that has to do with the promotion of the Christian religion; everything necessary is available to them in abundance, while the Church stands ever ready to promote their advantage and renown. For this reason we ask Your Excellency, with the greatest possible affection, to think on these matters and accept consolation in the Lord Jesus Christ, Who stands alongside those who are afflicted at heart, and Who after weeping and lamentation brings forth exaltation, expressly calling to mind the patience of Job. For he, through many great tribulations, was steadfast and [p. 328] humble, in all things blessing the Lord's name, and earned the grant of relief and receipt of twofold blessings at His hands. In your comfort the Catholics of the realm of France and those of other realms will find relief from their current sadness; and, thriving in the sight of the Most High, you will pour forth prayers and will cause others most devoutly to beseech Him that in His mercy He does not delay to provide for these matters or to apply in good time the remedy of consolation amid so great a misfortune.

76. Pope Innocent IV to Eudes Rigaud, Archbishop of Rouen [second half of August 1250], in Historiae Francorum Scriptores*, ed. Du Chesne, vol. 5, pp. 415–17*

[p. 416] … It is not surprising, then, if the entire Church mourns such an adverse outcome, when a graver disaster could scarcely have befallen her, through which her body is greatly afflicted and in her distress her spirit wets her cheeks with constant tears, for she has no grief comparable to this. She bemoans the deaths of so many sons, even though they are not to be counted as dead but rather as reborn to a better life. She also sighs over the waste of so much expense and effort, which proved to be so fruitless when what had been gloriously gained thereby was disgracefully lost. And in addition she laments bitterly over the boasts of those races who, perhaps glorying in these worldly losses of the faithful, revile and taunt them, saying, 'Where is their God?[13] Where is their helper, in whose aid they trusted?'[14] All the sons of the Church grieve also, and in public places and highways give common voice to misery. No cheerful face is to be seen. Each and every one turns his eyes towards the ground in shame. One mourns with another, and they rehearse the sadness they feel by passing on the tale of such a tragic event. Scarcely a word is heard from anyone's mouth that is not sad; nor is there anyone who may console another …

We do not believe that in this affair either the Church or the King was guilty of any negligence or fault, since the Church devoted to its success all the care and concern of which she was capable, and in addition incurred heavy expenditure; while the King had so taken the business to heart that for its sake he had left his wealthy, splendid and renowned kingdom and with fervent passion travelled to those regions with his brothers and the rest of the magnates of that kingdom – indeed he set it above his own comfort and totally dedicated to it himself and his possessions. Perhaps, therefore, some sins on the part of the people gravely offended the eyes of the Divine Majesty [p. 417], on account of which the Lord is provoked and has allowed this disaster to come about for the correction of His people, whom He longs to save. For He does not hate whom He reproves, nor is He unmindful of the salvation of him whom He chastises. But rather does He strike him whom He loves. He demonstrates this in that He assiduously prepares the rod for the son whom He loves, and does not, in His wrath, restrain His mercy. Nor, when He is angry, is He forgetful of compassion; and thus,[15] after administering the beating, He is at once felt to be a kindly comforter. Wherefore expressions of thanks are due to Him both in prosperity and in misfortune, and His name is to be blessed in all things, that the tongue of His people should in no eventuality and at no time refrain from praising Him. Under His powerful right hand must the great and the petty alike be humbled, so that in time of need they are worthy to be raised up by His mercy, since this is the Lord Who humbles and Who lifts up; Who looks kindly on the meek and gazes from afar at those who are highly placed; Who deals both wound and remedy, and in the wake of sadness brings rejoicing. For these reasons we must hope firmly that following the pain of this chastisement He will, in His mercy, apply the healing of timely consolation …[16]

---

13 Cf. Psalm xli, 4 and 11 (in the Vulgate; otherwise xlii, 3 and 10).

14 Cf. Psalm cxliii (in the Vulgate; otherwise cxliv), 2.

15 Reading *sic* for the *si* of the text.

16 The Pope continues by ordering prayers and preaching throughout Eudes's province.

77. Eudes de Châteauroux, Sermo in anniversario Roberti comitis Attrabatensis et aliorum nobilium qui interfecti fuerunt a Sarracenis apud Mansuram in Egipto *('Sermon on the anniversary of Robert, Count of Artois, and of other nobles who were killed by the Saracens at Mansura in Egypt') [1251?]: Penny J. Cole,* The Preaching of the Crusades to the Holy Land, 1095–1270 *(Cambridge, MA, 1991), appendix D, pp. 235–9*[17]

[p. 237] … We must take thought as to the reasons why the Lord allowed such a tragic event to befall the Christian people … How, then, did He tolerate it that bought slaves – indeed, what is worse, slaves of the Devil, full of all foulness – killed such noble men, such mighty friends of God and champions of the entire Christian people?

The aforesaid nobles were waging a just war, with the aim of recovering the land which the ungodly Saracens had wrested from the Christians; while the Saracens were waging an unjust war. How, then, did God permit that unrighteousness should conquer righteousness and impiety piety? Those nobles also fought with the intention of snatching the ungodly Saracens from an infidel death – and a death in Hell – and bringing them to salvation,[18] just as a shepherd strives to snatch his sheep from the jaws of the lion or the wolf. How great [an act] of impiety, then, was it that the ungodly Saracens should put to the sword and to death those who were striving to rescue them? … In this fashion Christians who were present at this slaughter, and even those who were not, have been able to reproach the Saracens that they unjustly killed those who had arrived in those regions for their salvation.

But if we give close attention to this matter, we shall be in a position to see that in this the Lord was just and loved righteousness. For the Lord allowed this to happen for the very purpose of showing the Christian people how gravely they had offended Him and how serious were the sins they had committed against Him, just as the Lord showed our first parents how gravely they had sinned in disobeying the Lord's command, when they saw their son Abel, a righteous man, killed by his godless brother. And so when they realized this, they persisted in their mourning for thirty years, as Josephus relates,[19] and throughout that time abstained from intercourse because they recognized that this murder would never have occurred had it not been for their transgression. Thus Christians will be able to understand that had it not been for their sins this shocking disaster would never have arisen. And thus God's Son was willing to die a most shameful death in order to demonstrate how grave were our sins, for the expiation of which He underwent such suffering.

---

17 The sermon is preached on II Kings (in the Vulgate; otherwise II Samuel), i, 18–19: 'Take thought, O Israel, for them that have died, wounded upon thy heights. The beauty of Israel are slain upon her high places. How are the mighty fallen.'

18 By this Eudes meant, presumably, that one aim of the crusade was to secure the conditions (that is, the restoration of Christian rule in Egypt) that might facilitate the conversion of Muslims. It is worth noting that this was certainly Louis's chief purpose, during the Eighth Crusade (1270), in heading for Tunis after reports that its Muslim king desired baptism: Siberry, *Criticism of Crusading*, pp. 17–18.

19 There appears to be no trace of this story in the Latin Josephus.

Another purpose of the Lord in allowing this disaster was that we wretched folk might be struck with fear. And the Lord can say to us what we read He said to the women who wept for Him, in Luke, xxiii: 'Daughters of Jerusalem, weep not for me, but weep for yourselves and for your children',[20] and (a few lines later) 'For if they do these things on a green tree what shall be done in the dry?';[21] and I Peter, iv, 'The time is come that judgement must begin at the house of the Lord. And if it first begin at us, what shall the end be of them that obey not the Gospel of God? And if the righteous scarcely be saved, where shall the ungodly and the sinner appear?'[22] ... We wretches ought to bear in mind that if the aforesaid nobles, who had already undergone so much on so many occasions on Christ's behalf, had become drunk on this most bitter draught, what then will become of us? If the chastisement and whipping of the cub strikes fear into the lion, much more must the killing and tearing to pieces of the lion strike fear into the cub. [p. 238] The nobles we have spoken of were noble lions in birth, steadfastness and fearlessness, who were so brutally torn to pieces; whereas we are paltry cubs. What, then, can we expect?

There is a third reason why the Lord allowed it. We read in Genesis, xxii, that the Lord said to Abraham, 'Now I know' (that is, I have caused you and others to know) 'that thou fearest God and hast not spared thine only-begotten son on my account.'[23] In this fashion the Lord, through that affair, caused the aforesaid nobles and other Christians to know that these nobles feared God, by the fact that they did not spare their sons, wives or other dear ones, leaving them behind exposed, as it were, to any enemies they had. But neither did they spare themselves or certain of their dear ones besides, whom they had taken with them, exposing both themselves and [these others] to death.

There is a fourth reason why the Lord allowed this: that if there was anything within those nobles we have often mentioned that they had contracted through human frailty, and that had to be cleansed, He might cut it out with the sickle of martyrdom, so that just as by his own blood He 'entered into the holy place',[24] so they too might enter through their own blood. In the Old Testament, the perfect and final cleansing was made through blood. For they, like Judah (Genesis, xlix), washed in blood 'his garments', and 'his clothes in the blood of grapes'.[25] For if the penalty is paid by punishment, and no punishment is greater than the pain of violent death, it is a fact that by paying the penalty of death, namely by suffering death willingly for Christ's sake, they are relieved of every other punishment.

The fifth reason, furthermore, why the Lord allowed it was to show them and everyone else how much He loved them. For Joseph demonstrated how much he loved Benjamin above the rest by giving him a larger share, such that 'it was five times so much' (Genesis, xliii).[26] Similarly Jacob demonstrated that he loved Joseph

20 Luke, xxiii, 28.
21 Luke, xxiii, 31.
22 I Peter, iv, 17–18.
23 Genesis, xxii, 12.
24 Cf. Hebrews, ix, 12.
25 Genesis, xlix, 11.
26 Genesis, xliii, 34.

more than all his other sons when he gave him 'one portion above his brethren which he took out of the hand of the Amorite with his sword and his bow' (Genesis, xlviii).[27] Thus the Lord in this affair has shown that He loved the aforesaid nobles above others by granting them that they should undergo the sacrifice of death for His sake. And thus the Lord has demonstrated that He loved those nobles above others by granting not only that they should believe in Him but that they should also suffer for Him … As a sign of love the Lord gave them to drink from His own cup,[28] so that they might recompense Him for all the things with which the Lord had requited them, according to the verse of the Psalm: 'What shall I render unto the Lord for all his [p. 239] benefits towards me? I will take the cup of salvation.'[29] For they drank of the cup of the Lord and have become God's friends. They have drunk of the same wine as He did, and are clothed in the same purple as He[30] …

The Lord further allowed this to happen in order that through the instrumentality of their deaths the remainder might be rescued from the danger of death, as became clear in the amazing release of the King and his men. For had they found their freedom through battle, it would not have been wonderful, since many are frequently defeated by a few and we also often see the victor overcome by the vanquished. But this is the wonderful thing, that the Saracens, who had in their hands the King and all the other warriors, killed their lord, the Sultan, who had given them great rewards following the King's capture,[31] and [then] released the King and his men, especially since the Christians could in no way keep Damietta, for the few who were there were planning to flee[32] – and flee they would have done had not the King been so swiftly released. Nor did they have any provisions, or anything else necessary for defending the city, and nothing could be brought to them either by land or by river …

78. Eudes de Châteauroux, Sermo in eodem anniversario *['Sermon on the same anniversary'] [1251?]: Cole,* Preaching of the Crusades*, Appendix D, pp. 240–43*[33]

[p. 242] … through the tragic disaster that occurred this day [of the year] at Mansura in Egypt, when a man renowned and of happy memory, Robert, Count of Artois, the son of a King of France, Raoul, Count of Coucy, Roger, lord of Roset, the lord Robert de Courtenay and many other nobles – or, in a word, almost the entire flower

27 Cf. Genesis, xlviii, 22.

28 Cf. Mark, x, 38–9; Matthew, xx, 22–3.

29 Psalm cxv (in the Vulgate; otherwise cxvi), 12–13.

30 References to the purple garment in which the soldiers clothed Christ and to the wine mixed with myrrh He was offered on the Cross: Mark, xv, 17, 23.

31 This does not appear to have been true, in fact: Tūrān Shāh's failure to reward his father's officers and mamluks was one of the reasons for his murder. See Ibn Wāṣil [**doc. 73**], pp. 146, 148–50 above.

32 This confirms the sparse details in Joinville, § 399, p. 218 (trans. Hague, p. 125; trans. Shaw, p. 263), who tells us that the Pisans, Genoese and 'those of the other communes' were on the point of deserting the town when the Queen took steps to hold them back.

33 Preached on Zechariah, viii, 19: 'Thus saith the Lord of hosts: The fast of the fourth month, and the fast of the fifth, and the fast of the seventh, and the fast of the tenth, shall be to the house of Judah joy and gladness and cheerful feasts.'

of the Christian army who accompanied the most Christian King of the French, Louis, son of Louis, son of Philippe – were slaughtered by the swords of the ungodly Saracens. And we ought to mourn because of the reproach to the Christian people, who because of this disaster are held cheap and are deemed paltry and contemptible, so that already the Saracens do not regard the Christians as of any significance. For this reason we can lament with the prophet: 'We are become a reproach to our neighbours, a scorn and derision to them that are round about us';[34] or again: 'Oh God, how long shall the adversary reproach? Shall the enemy blaspheme thy name for ever?';[35] 'God, thou hast repulsed and destroyed us.'[36] We ought also to mourn and grieve on account of the blasphemy against God's name, as if the God of the Christians was unable to free them. For this reason they have been able to say, 'Their God hath forsaken them; come and take them';[37] 'their God has sold them and shut them up';[38] 'let your God rise up and help you and only be your protection in need'.[39] And again, on account of the contempt for the standard of the holy Cross, since wherever they encountered it they spat upon it, threw it on the ground and trampled it. And likewise on account of the boldness that the godless Saracens have derived from it and the futile[40] fear of the Christians. And so too there are many weak in their faith who, on hearing of this disaster, apostatized; others blasphemed against God, Who allowed it to happen. But yet again we must weep for this catastrophe while imputing it to our sins. For the nobles we have mentioned did not deserve to be slaughtered so vilely. But just as in the Old Testament they were killed on account of sins they had not committed, so too these men were killed – and so, furthermore, was Christ. Let us, then, take the advice of the prophet, that we should love 'peace and truth' and in this way the Lord would convert this grief and misery into 'joy and gladness' … [p. 243] … Let us not mourn, then, for the nobles named above, but for ourselves, who have not been worthy to undergo such things as they underwent. And if there is anything else to be cleansed within them, let us then ask God to show them indulgence and bring them to eternal rest and to make us partners in their glory and reward, Who lives for ever and ever. Amen.

79. Frederick II to [Ferdinand III], King of Castile, [May or June 1250]: Huillard-Bréholles, vol. 6/2, pp. 769–71

Weighing the depth of the love which we have always had towards you until now, and have [still] unimpaired, we firmly believe that, just as we willingly embrace your honour and advantage, so you in return cherish ours, which very much impinge directly upon your cause and that of other kings and princes and in which you have

34 Psalm lxxviii (in the Vulgate; otherwise lxxix), 4.

35 Psalm lxxiii (in the Vulgate; otherwise lxxiv), 10.

36 Psalm lix, 3 (in the Vulgate; otherwise, lx, but this verse is omitted).

37 Cf. Psalm lxx (in the Vulgate; otherwise lxxi), 11.

38 Cf. Deuteronomy, xxxii, 30.

39 Cf. Deuteronomy, xxxii, 38.

40 Perhaps we should read here *incessum* for the *incassum* of the text, and translate 'the fear that has come over Christians'.

no less at stake than we ourselves. We do not believe that it has perhaps escaped your notice how papal ambition, to the detriment of the imperial honour and of other secular ranks, has until now constantly endeavoured to violate our rights and to crush the limbs of our power, bringing about the destruction of the Roman Emperor in order to make easier progress in his greed against other kings and princes. The Pope, indeed, giving no thought to how many great upheavals may arise in the world from this kind of disorder, contrives incessantly to stir up our enemies against us in the temporal sphere and to detach our vassals [p. 770] from their devotion to us. But if he were guided by a spirit of righteousness and matters developed in an orderly fashion, he ought to put aside arms against Christians and call for assistance from Christ's faithful in every quarter to relieve the Holy Land, which we see is deprived of any assistance whatsoever. For apart from other crises which virtually the whole world could now have avoided were we and the Supreme Pontiff at one and our discord lulled, sensible and careful precautions might perhaps have been taken against the recent disaster which we have heard, not without some cost to our faith, has transpired overseas, since he could, to good effect, have gained our presence there and that of our sons, which we have willingly offered on several occasions, had he only been ready to choose the negotiated peace that we so often sought. For we, who from respect for the Catholic faith revere the holy Roman Church in all respects as a mother, would willingly attend to the Supreme Pontiff as a father if he would treat us with due regard as a son. But in this affair we are defending our rights in such a way that we shall win the laurels for our defence not only for ourselves but for you and other princes.

You, however, whose cause is at stake here no less than ours, and on whom an affair of this kind could easily rebound, appear openly to be so unmindful of the current situation, or rather to be sleeping through it, as if it had no impact upon you at any point and you had no concern for our honour. For what kind of security would you and other kings have left in a parallel situation were the cause to be abandoned by the Roman Augustus? Or whose shoulders would be strong enough to bear these burdens if we were prepared to draw back our neck from carrying them? But since this incumbent of the see of Rome, turning aside, perhaps, from the piety he preaches, strives to harm Our Majesty both in the Empire and in our kingdoms in whatever way he can (though his power will not prove adequate against us), we cannot hold back our impulses from manfully defending our own cause and the injury to others. We request and keenly beg Your Benevolence, therefore, that you carefully consider how the Supreme Pontiff, who ought to have nothing to do with the sword, is not content with his own powers but makes so bold as to wield his sickle on the harvest of others, and how – not to seek an illustration too far removed from you – in the kingdom of Portugal [p. 771] he usurped the [royal] prerogative for himself;[41] and that you keep your concern and spirit alert.

For in the wake of the splendid army that we have sent ahead victorious into Italy, we should have gone there in person without hesitation to crush the necks of those who rebel against us and to undo the snares that through papal cunning are

41 A reference to Innocent's judgement at Lyons in 1245 against Sancho II of Portugal, who was obliged to accept his brother Alfonso as joint ruler.

being set in the way of our progress. But on hearing of the fate of our beloved friend, the illustrious King of France, we at once saw the advisability of withdrawing into our own kingdom, where we are arranging to make our vessels, men and support available in such impressive force for the overseas enterprise that he will rapidly find himself benefiting from Our Puissance's right hand, which we profusely extend towards him. We do not, however, as a result of this neglect such concerns, but shall take steps mightily and manfully to crush the remnants of those who are in rebellion. Let Your Benevolence believe without doubt whatever N. de …, our devoted vassal, tells you is of service to us in this regard, and be so well-disposed as to put it into effect.

80. 'Annales Erphordenses', MGHS, *vol. 16, pp. 37–8*

In this year [1250] all those of the army of the Faithful had been established in Damietta (or so they thought), for the King of France had set up there a bishopric, prebends and canons for the Divine worship. But since no man can serve different masters, namely God and the flesh[42] – for the King of France, puffed up with empty glory, had wanted the victory in warfare to be ascribed to himself alone and his men, to the exclusion of the rest of the pilgrims, [p. 38] nor that the booty of those who fought should be distributed equally – on that account, when on the Friday [8 April][43] after the Octave of Easter the army of the Lord faithfully engaged the Saracens, it was defeated through the hidden judgement of God, the King of France was captured and his brother Robert was killed.[44] And, as was announced by Eberhard, Master of the Teutonic Knights in Alemannia, who was present at this engagement, 36,000 were slain and 15,000 taken prisoner. He said further that 4000 apostatized and went over to the infidel owing to lack of provisions. Thus Damietta was surrendered; the King ransomed himself for 100,000 marks, and swore in addition an oath that he would not attack the Saracens again in his lifetime.

*81. Jean de Garlande [*c. *1252],*[45] De triumphis ecclesiae libri octo*, ed. Thomas Wright (London, 1856), pp. 135–9* passim

Fortune's sportive tricks are at hand, which raise up some there and bring down others here, and offer enticing gifts, only to snatch them away. Damietta, freely given, it takes back; it sets against us the disarmed Sultans, and once again strengthens and arms them. Why, oh God, hast Thou allowed the just to yield to the unrighteous? Thou art just, and Thou givest Thy kingdoms to the righteous … Whether they are victors or vanquished, they gain their reward, by the increase of faith and holy martyrdom.

42 Matthew, vi, 24: 'No man can serve two masters'. Cf. also Luke, xvi, 13.

43 This is only approximately correct. Louis's own letter [above, **doc. 70**] suggests that he was captured on 5 April; the letter of the Patriarch of Jerusalem found in the Burton annals [**doc. 68**] indicates Wednesday 6 April.

44 Again misleading: Robert of Artois had of course been killed on 8 February 1250 in the attempt to take Mansura.

45 See Introduction to this volume, note 24.

Through martyrdom does fortunate France send her choice leaders to Heaven, and the King of Heaven enriches them: Robert, Count of Artois, and William, surnamed Longsword, distinguished in their excellence. Blood floods forth around William as he plies his sword, and a thick pile of heads dyes the ground purple … [p. 136] … Some are strewn in battle who are raised above the stars; it is the luckless who have not merited suffering. Their bodies will rise up from the dust at the hour of Judgement, when glory will be awarded to the good and punishment to the wicked … Why do you rejoice, wretched Sultan? Your gladness will be brief, and will be followed by God's abundant vengeance … [p. 139] … Let nobody ever think to deny God in this way or that: such frenzy will be death to body and soul. Oh grief – oh worse than grief, oh anxious death, through which justified complaint inspires elegies with tears! The title, combined with the metre, is indeed fitted to deep wailing; and yet I did not fear such terrible things – that the King should fail, that right be brought low, that Babylon should overwhelm the glorious standards of the Cross. [But] it is not thus that Heavenly reckoning decrees that the Ark should, when but a short time has elapsed,[46] be captured by the wicked. A shepherd lad conquers Goliath; Israel stretched out her freed neck from Babylon's yoke. The King of England and the King of Spain add to the Church's forces; on every side fresh bands renew her strength. Their achievements require other poets who will sing of them when the time comes.[47] God has granted that through a miracle the King survives in safety.

82. Austorc d'Aurillac,[48] Sirventés*, ed. A. Jeanroy, 'Le troubadour Austorc d'Aurillac et son sirventés sur la septième Croisade', in* Mélanges Chabaneau. Festschrift Camille Chabaneau zur Vollendung seines 75. Lebensjahres 4 märz 1906 dargebracht von seinen Schülern, Freunden und Verehrern, *Romanische Forschungen, vol. 23 (Erlangen, 1907), pp. 81–7*

[p. 82] Oh God, why did you bring this great misfortune on our generous and courtly French King, when you allowed him to suffer such humiliation – him, who laboured to serve you with all his power, [p. 83] and by night and day devoted his heart and mind to your service, and strove to do and say what would please you? For this you have given him but a poor recompense.

Ah! You fine folk, gracious and courtly, who crossed the sea so well fitted out, we shall never see you return to this land! For this has great grief spread throughout the world. May Alexandria be cursed! Cursed be all the clergy, and cursed too the Turks who have caused you to remain there! God has done badly in so empowering them.

---

46 Reading *passo* for the *passa* of the text.

47 Both Henry III and Ferdinand III of Castile had taken the Cross. Jean clearly anticipates that he will not live long enough to witness their exploits in the East.

48 A member of a noble family in the Toulouse region, which is attested during the thirteenth century. This Austorc died in 1259/60. His son and namesake was then a minor and hence cannot have been the author: the work must accordingly date from the 1250s (Jeanroy, pp. 86–7; and see also note 51 below).

I see Christendom completely shamed. It has never suffered such a loss. This is the reason why men disbelieve in God and why we worship Bafomet[49] in his stead, and Tervagan and his company,[50] for God and Holy Mary will it that we be vanquished, contrary to all justice, and that the infidel carries off the honours.

I would that the Emperor had taken the Cross and that the Empire had been left to his son;[51] and that the French nation had rallied to him against the false clerics in whom Faithlessness holds sway, and who have slain Worth and Chivalry, slain all Courtliness, and care little for what afflicts others, provided only that they can lie amid luxury.

Ah! Valiant King, if you had the greatness of Alexander, who conquered the whole world, you would avenge the humiliation you have suffered. Ah, remember Charles,[52] remember the Marquis Guillem, remember Gerard and his victories.[53] Ah, noble King! If you call these to mind, the wicked Turks will be at your mercy, for God lends ready aid to a firm resolve.

Saint Peter held to the right path, but the Pope has strayed from it – he and the false clerics whom he holds in his power and who, just for money's sake, wish evil upon so many folk …[54]

83. Salimbene de Adam, Cronica *[c. 1285], ed. Giuseppe Scalia (Turnhout, 1998–99), vol. 2, pp. 672–3*

So[55] the French who had remained behind in France were at this juncture angered against Christ, to the point where they dared to blaspheme the name of Christ, which is blessed [p. 673] above all names. When in those days the Franciscan and Dominican Friars asked for alms in Christ's name, they would 'gnash upon them with their teeth';[56] and when they saw them, they would call over some poor man and give him money, saying, 'Take this in the name of Mahomet, who is mightier than Christ'. Thus the words of the Lord in Luke viii were fulfilled in them: 'For a while they shall believe, and in time of temptation fall away.'[57]

---

49 Mahomet, that is, the Prophet Muḥammad.

50 Tervagant sometimes appears as one of Mahomet's companions, e.g. in the York cycle: see Rosalind Hill, 'The Christian view of the Muslims at the time of the First Crusade', in Holt, *The Eastern Mediterranean Lands*, pp. 1–8 (here pp. 5–6).

51 For Jeanroy (pp. 84–5), this is fairly conclusive evidence that the piece refers to the Seventh Crusade and Louis's captivity, rather than to the Eighth and his death (as earlier scholars had assumed), since in 1270 there was as yet no Emperor.

52 Charlemagne.

53 Guillaume d'Orange (the 'Marquis') and Gérard de Roussillon are heroes of epic fiction, whose names and exploits would have been familiar throughout Western knightly and noble circles.

54 In the unique manuscript which includes it, the *sirventés* is incomplete.

55 For the passages that precede and follow this extract, see **doc. 95**.

56 Cf. Psalm xxxvi [in the Vulgate; otherwise xxxvii], 12: 'The wicked plotteth against the just and gnasheth upon him with his teeth.'

57 Luke, viii, 13.

VIII

The 'Crusade' of the *Pastoureaux* (1251)

One indirect consequence of the *débâcle* in Egypt was the so-called 'Crusade of the *Pastoureaux*', which began as a bid to bring assistance to the beleaguered French monarch. Participation by non-military folk in the Holy War against the Muslims had been discouraged since the Third Crusade, and one of Pope Innocent III's purposes in fostering redemptions of the crusade vow had been to associate non-combatants more closely in an effort that was designed to draw in and represent the entire *populus Christianus*. 'Popular' crusading, as it has been termed, had thus become increasingly divorced from the campaigns waged in the East by the military élite, whether serving as *crucesignati* or as mercenaries; but on occasions official crusade preaching sparked off just the kind of response from the non-military classes that ecclesiastics and secular princes alike were keen to discourage. The 'Children's Crusade' of 1212 is a case in point; so too is the mass movement in France in 1251 led by an obscure figure known as the 'Master of Hungary'. The term *Pastoureaux* means strictly 'shepherds', but it is probably as inadequate a description of the participants as is the phrase 'Children's Crusade' applied to the earlier *émeute*.[1]

The course of the movement has been studied, on the basis of an in-depth analysis of the sources, by Professor Malcolm Barber.[2] As in 1212, we are dealing here with agitation on the part of mostly younger folk, of whom the majority had doubtless not yet left the parental home and represented one of the most vulnerable groups in society. One theme of the preaching that had rallied them was the claim that God had transferred the task of recovering the Holy Land from the rich and powerful, who had failed, to the poor and simple [**docs 88 and 93**]. Shepherds, as those to whom Christ's birth had first been announced, were especially qualified for this task.[3]

But the movement was swiftly distracted from its original purpose, and degenerated into violence against fellow Christians, as the hostility of the crowds turned against the clergy at large. One reason for this appears to have been that the leaders harboured anti-clerical sentiments in any case, questioning clerical morality and privilege, challenging the validity of the sacraments and arrogating to

---

1 See Peter Raedts, 'The Children's Crusade of 1212', *JMH*, 3 (1977): 279–323; Gary Dickson, 'The genesis of the Children's Crusade (1212)', in his *Religious Enthusiasm in the Medieval West*.

2 Malcolm Barber, 'The Crusade of the Shepherds in 1251', in J. F. Sweets (ed.), *Proceedings of the Tenth Annual Meeting of the Western Society for French History, 14–16 October 1982, Winnipeg* (Lawrence, KS, 1984), pp. 1–23, and reprinted in Barber, *Crusaders and Heretics, 12th–14th Centuries* (Aldershot, 1995). The older study by Reinhold Röhricht, 'Die Pastorellen (1251)', *Zeitschrift für Kirchengeschichte*, 6 (1884): 290–96, is still useful.

3 'Annales S. Benigni Divionensis', in *MGHS*, vol. 5, p. 50.

themselves the right to administer them, in a manner reminiscent of certain twelfth-century heretical groups. They also sought to administer the Cross to would-be crusaders. In the specific context of the crusade, the clergy were perhaps also seen as unwilling to disgorge further sums on Louis's behalf. The Friars in particular suffered the unwelcome attentions of the Shepherds, because they were associated both with the preaching of the ill-fated crusade to Egypt and with the renewal of the campaign against the Hohenstaufen; in Tours, at least, their houses were singled out for violent attack, and a number of Friars suffered injury [**docs 90, 94 and 95**]. Although the Jewish community at Bourges suffered attacks [**docs 84–6 and 88**], the movement exhibits no previous symptoms of antisemitism and the victims seem in this case to have been selected because the clergy and the Mendicants in the city had gone into hiding.[4] Queen Blanche, who had initially responded favourably to the Shepherds' leaders, had to issue orders for their suppression.

The origins of the movement – in the French-Imperial borderlands, a region traditionally highly susceptible to crusade preaching and religious ferment[5] – have been elucidated by Professor Gary Dickson, who suggests that the return of the Count of Flanders from the East and the dissemination of King Louis's own letter of August 1250 appealing to his subjects for reinforcements [**doc. 70** above] do not in themselves suffice to explain the outbreak. It was in large part provoked, rather, by the preaching of the crusade in this region, during late March–early April 1251, on behalf of William of Holland and against Frederick's son and successor, Conrad IV.[6] Given the crusaders' predicament in the East, the revival of the anti-Hohenstaufen crusade aroused especially bitter resentment, and William's attempts to encroach on Flemish territory may have won him enemies. Some elements of this hypothesis has been challenged; and it may be that the 'Shepherds' were reacting primarily against the practice of vow redemption that could be deemed to have underlain the French King's failure in Egypt.[7]

A high proportion of the sources translated below convey the sense of what Barber has termed 'a kind of reverse-image of a crusade'.[8] The leaders are accused of being agents of the Egyptian Sultan – or possibly of other enemies of Christendom [**docs 87, 92 and 97**]; some authors allege that just before his death the Master called upon 'Mahomet' [**docs 90, 93–4**].[9] A similar claim appears in Thomas of Sherborne's account (where one of the leaders, who had made for Bordeaux following the dispersal of the Shepherds, was allegedly found to have carried letters written in Arabic and 'Chaldaean').[10] However convenient the ecclesiastical authorities may have found such a charge, at least two Franciscans, one of them the Englishman

4 Barber, 'The Crusade of the Shepherds', pp. 5, 9.

5 Ibid., p. 2.

6 Dickson, 'The advent of the *Pastores*', pp. 258–64.

7 Maier, *Preaching the Crusades*, pp. 153–5.

8 Barber, 'The Crusade of the Shepherds', p. 10.

9 This allegation is also found in 'Annales monasterii de Theokesberia', in *Annales Monastici*, vol. 1, p. 145.

10 Matthew Paris, *Chronica Majora*, vol. 5, pp. 246, 252 (trans. Giles, vol. 2, pp. 452, 456–7; the earlier section also trans. in L. and J. Riley-Smith (ed.), *The Crusades: Idea and Reality*, p. 140).

Roger Bacon, seem seriously to have entertained it. Such paranoia was far from being a new phenomenon. Back in the 1190s, some observers had entertained the possibility of collusion between the Muslims and Patarene heretics (Cathars) within Western Europe;[11] and in 1241 the Jews, similarly, had been suspected of acting as fifth-columnists for the advancing Mongols.[12] But these parallel accusations against the Pastoureaux in 1251 take on a broader significance, given the growth of a sense that Islam might be destined to triumph over Christianity and a perception that many were going over to the rival faith.[13]

DOCUMENTS 84–97

84. Guillaume de Nangis, 'Gesta sanctae memoriae Ludovici regis Franciae', RHGF, *vol. 20, p. 382*

In the year of grace of Our Lord 1251 began the crusade[14] of the shepherds and of numerous children, of whom some pretended to have seen several visions and often claimed that they performed miracles and that God had sent them to avenge King Louis of France on the Saracens who had captured him. Among these shepherds were some who had called themselves Masters: in the city of Paris they consecrated holy water after the fashion of bishops, and conducted and dissolved marriages at will. They perpetrated many murders and [other] outrages against clerks, religious and lay persons, because there were none who opposed them; and they crossed and uncrossed many people just as they wished. The man who led them was known as the Grand Master of Hungary. While passing with a great host through the city of Orléans, he had killed some clerks. And he arrived in Bourges and there did much evil: he entered the homes of the Jews and destroyed all their books and confiscated all their possessions. But after he had left Bourges and arrived at a river between the town called Mortemer and Villeneuve, some of the citizens who were pursuing him killed him there. When the Master of Hungary was slain in this way, the other masters of the shepherds scattered in different directions and were killed or hanged for their wrongdoing; and then all the rest fled and disappeared like smoke.

85. 'Chronique de Primat, traduite par Jean du Vignay', RHGF, *vol. 23, pp. 8–10*

In the year of Our Lord 1251 there arose evil deceivers of the people, who were known as the Masters of the Shepherds and who said that they had assumed the duty of preaching the Cross at the orders of Our Lord Himself. Some of them claimed that they had previously been enjoined to do so by a vision of the Blessed Virgin Mary,

11 Marjorie E. Reeves, 'History and prophecy in medieval thought', *Medievalia et Humanistica*, 5 (1974): 51–75 (here 61).

12 Sophia Menache, 'Tartars, Jews, Saracens and the Jewish-Mongol "plot" of 1241', *History*, 81 (1996): 319–42.

13 The connection made explicitly in Matthew Paris, *Chronica Majora*, vol. 5, p. 254 (trans. Giles, vol. 2, p. 458).

14 *cruce signatio*; in the French version, *croiserie*.

and for this reason they had standards and banners carried before them like the prince of an army. They had the banners painted with images of this vision they pretended to have seen (though they lied), so that by this deceitful sign of truth they might lure into error the lowly and the simple among the people. This disgraceful falsehood thereupon became a foul growth, for the shepherds left their livestock in the pasture and went off without a farewell to father or mother. They came rushing from all the different parts of the realm alike: from Brabant, from Flanders, from Hainault and from Picardy, and they would gather in groups wherever they heard that other groups and the chief [spreader] of this falsehood had arrived. Thus their numbers increased daily, and within a short time they became a great multitude of folk.

Among them there appeared those who, though outwardly in the garb of sheep, were inwardly ravening wolves,[15] namely wicked and perverse men, such as thieves, rapists and murderers, who mingled with them – not for the sake of any good they might do them, nor from any humanity, but in order to plan thefts and rape under their cover whenever they should see a convenient [p. 9] opportunity to do their mischief, as subsequent events will show. Just like the greater leaders of this most execrable gathering, the simple folk were at their bidding. They saw that they were enriched with great plenty, to the point that, whenever they passed by towns and fortresses, there were scarcely any who did not fear them on beholding them puffed up with great pride and possessing all kinds of weaponry. They moved in groups, carrying various weapons – swords, scimitars,[16] and a kind of weapon which is known in France as a Danish axe and is like a dagger and a pick in front and like a mallet behind. And then they gradually began to move into new heresies and to embroil the people in the most execrable falsehood. For they joined nine men to one woman as if in matrimony, so that no one knew to whom she belonged. It is certain that marriage can be conducted only by a priest, and that banns are three times solemnly published in a church, as is the custom. And they further administered the Cross, moreover, with their own hands, and absolved of all their sins those who accepted it. They boasted that they would restore sight to the blind, and heal the lame and the enfeebled, and bring back to health those afflicted with every sickness. It was a marvel! For the lay folk were most ready to believe in the vanities of this false religion and subscribe to its erroneous opinions. So entrapped were they in this vile delusion that they called them holy men; and when they had them to dine with them, there were some who did not blush to declare that the food on their table was not at all consumed but increased.

The clerics and most wise doctors, who regarded as nothing their follies and vanities, had pity on the delusion and error of the people, and thus opposed their endeavours to stir up the common folk. But the people, who would not tolerate their representations, grew so heated in their anger against the clergy that they asserted roundly that these evildoers were good men and that it was from envy that the clergy said they were evil and despised what was good. And then in this deceitful manner they reached Paris; and because this was the seat of the royal majesty and contained

15 Matthew, vii, 15: 'Beware of false prophets, who come to you in sheep's clothing but inwardly are ravenous wolves.'

16 *fauchons*.

the greatest power of the secular arm, they were afraid lest their conduct would be examined and they would meet with greater opposition to their crimes than in those other cities, for they had heard that here flowed the fountain of the seven liberal arts and a great abundance of wise men of the faculty of theology. But it so happened that Queen Blanche, who at that time was governing the realm alone with marvellous wisdom, did not recognize their errors, or else she let them proceed in this way, perhaps, because she hoped that they would bring help to King Louis, her son, who was still overseas. And when they had passed through Paris, they thought they had evaded all danger, and boasted that they were good men, arguing this on the grounds that when they were in Paris – the fount of faith and wisdom – nobody had opposed them. They then began to spread their errors more strongly and to plan among themselves looting and theft more enterprisingly. After entering the city of Orléans, they did battle with the clerks of the University, with the result that several of this crowd were killed, as were also several clerks.

After this, having entered Berri, they split up in different directions throughout the region. Since they were openly committing theft and murder, 12 of the Masters who had duped the simple were taken in the acts of theft and murder at a town called Cone and were hanged on a gibbet as their actions merited. A Master who was from Hungary made for the city of Bourges with a great crowd of his [followers], and they began cruelly to rave against the Jews and tore up their books and looted their money and their silver. Then, when the commonalty of the town saw this – that in this fashion they were annihilating [p. 10] the Jews, who were under the King's protection – they closed the gates of the city, to avenge the injury done to the King through the Jews. But [the shepherds] broke the locks and bolts on the gates, and made for the open country, while the burgesses followed them on horseback. One of these burgesses fell upon the Master, who had drawn his sword and prepared to defend himself. The burgess struck him with the [sword-]hilt and wounded him in the side; but he did not fall until another burgess made haste to come upon him and pierced his entrails with a thrust from a lance. Then, when the Master lay on the ground, they tore him limb from limb. His companions were killed with the sword, apart from those who had escaped death by flight. In such manner, then, did this bogus crusade gradually revert to nothing: all those who had supported them were disappointed, and those who had put their hope in them were cheated of their hope.

86. Giovanni de Columna, 'E Mari Historiarum', RHGF*, vol. 23, pp. 123–4*

In the following year [1251], almost all the shepherds of France, duped by I know not what trickery, gathered together. Under the leadership of one whom they called their Master, they claimed that it would be revealed to them by an angel that the Promised Land was due to be liberated by them from the hands of the pagans in the near future. They came together in a great multitude, and under the pretence of fervour and zeal for justice they especially persecuted clerics and the religious, who opposed their crimes and immoral actions. For they performed and dissolved marriages; they absolved at will sins committed or even yet to be committed; and certain of them, who wore rings in the style of bishops, used to give their blessing to the people. In order to fabricate miracles they would open churches and ring bells, claiming that they saw visions of angels and conversed with [p. 124] them. So when the clergy gainsaid them, they raged against them as if they were criminals and harassed them to the point of drawing blood. For at Orléans, Chartres and other places that they passed through, they killed many clerics and laymen who opposed them. But when their Master arrived at Bourges with a host of his shepherds, he began for the first time to persecute the Jews, plundering all their possessions and burning their books; and when he had perpetrated numerous outrages there, he left. As he withdrew, the citizens followed him; and coming upon him between Villeneuve and Mortemer,[17] they killed him together with many of his people. Once he was dead, the rest dispersed in all directions. Many of them were slain; some were hanged for the evil deeds they had committed, and their bands disappeared.

87. 'Extraits des Chroniques de Saint-Denis', RHGF, *vol. 21, pp. 115-16*

Another episode occurred in the year of Grace 1251 in the kingdom of France. For a Master, who knew the magic arts, made a compact with the Sultan of Babylon that he would by means of magic bring him all the young people aged 25 or 30 or 16, on condition that he should receive for each head 4 gold *besants*;[18] this compact was made when the King was in Cyprus. He told the Sultan that he had learned in his wizardry that the King of France would be defeated and would fall captive into the hands of the Saracens. The Sultan was very greatly cheered by what he said, for he was deeply apprehensive about the King of France's coming. And so he begged him to make haste to accomplish what he promised, giving him gold and silver in great quantities, and kissed him on the mouth as a sign of his great love.

The Master departed from Outremer and came to France. Upon his arrival, he bethought himself as to where he should work his magic. And so he made straight for Picardy, and took a powder that he carried, and threw it up in the air among the fields, as a sacrifice to the Devil. Having done this, he came to the shepherds and the children who were tending the animals, and told them he was a man of God: 'Through you, my sweet children, will Outremer be delivered from the enemies of the Christian faith.' As soon as they heard his voice, they abandoned their livestock and went after him, and began to follow him wherever he wished to go. All those he encountered set out after the others, with the result that his company grew so numerous that in less than eight days they were more than 30,000. They reached the city of Amiens, and the whole city was full of shepherds.

The people of the town handed over to them wine and meat and whatsoever they demanded; for they were so bewitched that they thought no holier folk could exist. They asked them who their leader was, and they showed them. And he appeared before them with a long beard, as if he was a penitent, and he had a pale and thin

17 Apparently Morthomiers, not far from Villeneuve-sur-Cher.

18 Cf. **doc. 92** below, where the figure is 5 *besants*. Is this a confused echo of the reward of 10 *besants* offered by Sultan Ayyūb, during the summer of 1249, to any of his troops who brought in the head of a Frankish crusader? See 'Rothelin', p. 592 (trans. Shirley, p. 88). Joinville, § 177, p. 98 (trans. Hague, p. 68; trans. Shaw, p. 209), has the reward as 1 gold *besant*.

face. When they saw the look of his face, they begged him to take their homes and possessions just as he wished. Some of them even knelt before him, as though he were the body of a saint, and they gave him whatever he asked.

From there he left, and began to travel round the whole region and to take all the children of the country, so that they numbered more than 60,000. When he saw that he had attained such state, he began to preach and to dissolve marriages and to do all things at will; and he claimed that he had the authority to absolve all manner of sins. The priests and clerks, hearing what they were doing, opposed them and showed them that they could not do this. For this reason the Master conceived so great a hatred for them that he ordered the shepherds to kill all the priests and all the clerks they might encounter. And thus he went off through the country until he came to Paris.

Queen Blanche, who was aware of their arrival, ordered that no one should dare to gainsay them in anything; for she believed, as did others, that these were good people [working] on behalf of Our Lord. She had the Grand Master brought before her, and asked him what his name was. He replied that he was known as the Master of Hungary. The Queen showed him great honour and gave him large gifts. He left the Queen and entered Paris with his companions, who were well aware of his wickedness. He asked them to seek to kill as many priests and clerks as [p. 116] they could find; for he had so beguiled the Queen and all her people that she would take in good part whatever they did.

The Master grew so arrogant that he dressed like a bishop in the church of St Eustache at Paris and preached with a mitre on his head like a bishop, and had himself shown great honour and service. The rest of the shepherds went through Paris and killed all the clerks they found there. It was arranged that the gates of the Petit-Pont should be closed, for fear that they might kill the scholars who had come from several countries for the purpose of learning.

When this Master of Hungary had plucked Paris of whatever he could, he left and divided his shepherds into three groups, for there were so many that they could not find any town that could house or sustain them all. Thus he sent one group to Bourges, ordering those who were to lead them that they should take whatever they could seize and extract from the region; and when they had done this, they should rejoin him at the port of Marseilles, where he would await them. And so they took their leave, one group making for Bourges and the other for Marseilles.

When the clerks of Bourges learned of the arrival of such people, they were afraid; for they had been informed that they [the shepherds] did quite some damage. So they went to speak to the justices and those whose duty was to guard the town, and told them that this movement of children and shepherds had come about through evil means, through the Devil's arts and through witchcraft: if they were willing to make the effort, they could arrest the Masters of the shepherds as proven evildoers and in the act of theft. The provost and the *bailli* agreed to what they proposed, and everyone was privy to the business.

The shepherds entered Bourges and spread through the town, only to find no clerks or priests. So they began to work their mischief, just as they had done in Paris and in other fine towns, and everything was handed over to them to do as they wished. When the Masters of the shepherds saw the people totally obedient to their wishes, they took to breaking open chests and coffers and seizing gold and silver. And in addition they seized the young ladies and maidens, and sought to lie with them. They acted in such a way that the justices, who were on the alert to recognize their faces, perceived their wickedness. And so they arrested them and made them confess all their wrongdoing and how they had beguiled the entire country with their witchcraft. Thus the Grand Masters were judged and hanged, and the children returned quite dismayed, each to their own region.

The *bailli* of Bourges sent off three messengers, whom he ordered to travel by night and by day to Marseilles and who carried for the *viguier*[19] letters containing all the evil done by the Master of Hungary. And so he was immediately seized and hanged from a high gibbet, and the shepherds who followed in his wake made their way back as impoverished beggars.

88. 'E Chronico Sancti Laudi Rotomagensis', RHGF, *vol. 23, pp. 395–6*

In the year 1251 there occurred a wretched agitation of shepherds, who announced that they were setting out for the Holy Land. For there were among them those who imposed the Cross on others as though they were masters, and lyingly claimed to work signs and miracles. In order to deceive the simple, these chiefs of robbers made out that they had seen visions of angels and that the Blessed Virgin Mary had appeared to them and ordered them to assume the Cross and to gather an army of shepherds and simple folk, who had been chosen by God to go to the aid of the Holy Land and of King Louis who was staying there. They had reproduced this vision on the standard that they carried before them.

While these robbers were passing through the towns and countryside of Flanders and Picardy, they led astray the shepherds and simple folk with bogus appeals. And when they reached France, they had already grown to such a number that they formed thousands and hundreds like an army. While they were moving through [p. 396] the rural districts, the shepherds would leave behind their beasts without consulting their kinsfolk. As they passed through towns and cities, they carried aloft swords, axes and other weapons, with the result that they inspired fear among the population and the judicial authorities. They reached such a degree of error that they conducted marriages, signed people with the Cross and gave absolution from sins. And in addition they had so hoodwinked the people that several believed that the foodstuffs and other things that were laid before them did not diminish with eating or drinking but were increased. But because the clergy sought to speak against this error, they met with great hatred from them, to the point that they killed several [clerics] whom they encountered in the countryside.

Yet by Queen Blanche, the regent of the kingdom, who believed that through them help would reach her son King Louis in the Holy Land, they were allowed to pass through the city of Paris without obstacle. As a result, their boldness in wrongdoing increased very considerably; and when they arrived, thieving and looting, in the city of Orléans they entered into a battle with the clerks of the University, killing several and several of their own being slain. At length they reached the city of Bourges,

19 Mayor.

whereupon their leader and chief, who was known as the Master of Hungary, entered the Jews' synagogue, destroyed their books and plundered their possessions. But when he withdrew from the city with his followers, the people of Bourges, who had armed and made ready, manfully pursued them and killed the aforesaid Master along with several of his accomplices, making a great slaughter.

Since the outset, their wrongdoing had grown to such a pitch that during the Pentecost synod they expelled the Archbishop of Rouen[20] from the church in Rouen, together with all the priests who had assembled for the synod. But after the slaughter I have mentioned, they scattered through different localities. Some of them were killed or hanged for their crimes; others perished in boats, while [yet] others returned to their own homes. And thus they were reduced to nothing.

89. 'Chronique anonyme des rois de France finissant en 1286', RHGF, *vol. 21, p. 83*

In this same year [1251] the shepherds of Picardy[21] and of the whole of France gathered under a shepherd named Roger, who was their Master and who gave the Cross to all those who wished to take it, to women as well as children and men. He did this without the counsel of Holy Church, as a result of which he and his enterprise came to a bad end. This Roger arranged that each group of ten should have its own master and banner. They all gathered in France, and then moved off through the town of Bourges, committing many outrages against good people. In the end Master Roger was taken and hanged, and many of the rest were killed or thrown into gaol; so that their entire movement came to nought.

90. Actus pontificum Cenomannis in urbe degentium *[1255–72], ed. G. Busson and A. Ledru (Le Mans, 1901 =* Archives Historiques du Maine, *vol. 2), pp. 500–501*

In his time [that of Bishop Geoffroi de Laudun], the Devil kindled his wrath against the Church. For certain accursed shepherds arose, who were violently stirred up by a demoniacal spirit. They chose as their masters boys, who perpetrated many shameful things against the faith, claiming that they healed the sick: rogues and vagabonds would lyingly allege that they were sick, and would then falsely claim to have been healed by them. As countless shepherds, thieves and murderers gathered together, then, they set up masters for their deception and wrongdoing, and also commanders of ten and a hundred. And thus, at the Devil's instigation in order to destroy the Church and abolish Christ's name, they assembled through the cities and settlements, deluding the inhabitants by claiming that they had been sent by God and were to set out overseas to aid the Holy Land.

They reached Tours, where they were received with honour by the citizens, for a fickle and credulous folk is easily drawn into error. There they perpetrated false

---

20 Eudes Rigaud (d. 1276).

21 This indication that the movement originated in Picardy (see also **doc 87**) is at variance with the testimony of other sources, and Dickson, 'The advent of the *Pastores*', p. 256, n. 33, suggests that Roger may have been merely the leader of the Picard shepherds.

and dishonourable marriages and many other things contrary to the faith. At length, accompanied by the citizens themselves, they wrecked the houses of the Dominican Friars, carrying off the spoils they found and taking and – alas! – mishandling the vessels of the Lord. The Friars, in their weakness and bewilderment, fled into hiding.

They arrived in Orléans, where they harshly intimidated the clergy and scholars, [p. 501] and inflicted on them many kinds of injury and harassment. One day, when their Master – a man of no faith, most wicked and benighted, whom they called the Hungarian – was walking on the bridge over the Loire and saw a scholar passing, he drew his sword, butchered him and threw [his body] into the water.

They came to Paris, where on seeing so wild, so fearful and so numerous a mob, unheard-of in times gone by, the scholars and clerics shut their doors and hid in their houses until they were delivered by the royal power.

They arrived in Bourges. Here, when they had inflicted unspeakable injuries on the clergy and citizens, a certain knight, surrounding himself with a band of warriors, fell on the aforesaid Hungarian and transfixed him with a lance; and the latter, who was heard by the bystanders to call upon Mahomet, forthwith expired. The rest scattered in flight. They reached a fortress called Malamors, where the inhabitants, who were already fully aware of the shepherds' infidelity and wrongdoing, attacked that accursed host, killing some and hanging others. The survivors fled in confusion, and in this way the storm passed.

91. 'Richeri Gesta Senoniensis ecclesiae', MGHS, *vol. 25, pp. 310–11*

Not long after [the Mongol invasion], therefore, it happened that there arrived in the regions of Lorraine, Burgundy and Francia certain magicians, who joined to themselves all the shepherds of various sorts, with the result that no shepherd could be found in the surrounding tracts who on simply hearing of this gathering did not at once hurry [to join it]. For they alleged that it was their duty to cross the sea [p. 311] and that through them the Holy Land would be delivered from the Saracens' yoke. And so such a great crowd of shepherds massed together that when they entered cities and towns they took by force whatever they were not given for nothing. They claimed that several ships awaited them on the sea-coast. But when they reached the coast, the leaders of these shepherds were put in chains by the inhabitants of that region and thrown into prison; and when force was applied they disclosed everything in order. These magicians alleged that their intention was to delude such shepherds, who are believed to be simpler folk, by their arts in such a way, and that they were trying to lead them overseas and aiming to sell them to the peoples of those parts, just as we noticed earlier with the children.[22] On hearing this, the magnates of the land condemned the magicians to be hanged. Of the shepherds, too, who saw this and concluded that they had been duped, some returned to their own homes, while others dispersed through various regions in order to be able to live. And in just the same way as the blessed Gamaliel, the teacher of the blessed Apostle Paul, witnessed concerning the Apostles when they were detained in Jerusalem by the Jews, saying,

22 A reference to the 'Children's Crusade' (1212).

'If they had been apostles from God, their kingdom would have held firm, but since it was not it would be put asunder',[23] so it was with these shepherds: because their actions did not come from God, as we have said above, it collapsed at once.

92. 'Balduini Ninovensis chronicon', MGHS, *vol. 25, p. 544*

In that same year [1251] the shepherds assembled from different parts of the world and set out for Jerusalem. The reason for this was as follows. A certain apostate and magician, who had renounced the Christian faith and gone over to paganism, promised the King of the Saracens that he would bring him an infinite number of Christians on condition that he would receive from him for every Christian five besants.[24] He soon crossed to France, where both personally and through his accomplices he gathered such a great host of shepherds from various regions that they could scarcely be counted. Bringing them together in one mass throughout the whole of France, he caused them to follow him until he arrived with them at Bourges, where his villainy was recognized by a citizen and he was put in chains with some of his colleagues, condemned by the archbishop of the city, and died by hanging. Of the rest of the host, some perished when trying to defend themselves, while others escaped by flight; and thus that enormous army of shepherds almost totally dispersed.

93. 'Chronica universalis Mettensis', MGHS, *vol. 24, p. 522 (from ms. 'A')*

In this year [1250] a great crowd of shepherds assembled in France, in the hope that the Holy Land, which so many knights of France were unable to regain, would be surrendered to shepherds. But their simple minds were led astray by the crowd of evil people who were associated with them – namely thieves, outlaws, apostates, pagans, heretics and prostitutes – who with the approval of lay people killed clerics and even drowned many in the city of Paris in the Seine. They drove all [clerics] out of Orléans; while in Tours they preached in public that the sacraments of the Church were nothing, and that whoever killed a clerk or a priest would receive absolution for a drink of good wine. When the Dominican Friars preached in opposition [to this], they severely wounded four Dominicans; and after breaking up the seats in the choir and plundering their church, they whipped eleven Friars through the middle of the city in the sight of all, and sought to kill them outside the city. But from fear of the King and Queen, the citizens would not allow this. When as many as 60,000 had gathered while perpetrating so many crimes, their leaders were hanged – of whom one called upon Mahomet at the moment of death – and the rest were killed; very few secretly escaped.

---

23 Acts, v, 38–9.

24 Cf. **doc. 87** above (4 *besants*).

94. 'Annales monasterii de Burton', pp. 290–93[25]

A letter concerning the shepherds Friar ..., known as warden of the Order of Friars Minor at Paris, to his venerable brothers in Christ, Adam de Marsh[26] and the Friars Minor of Oxford, greetings. Recently, on the feast of the Resurrection [16 April 1251], when we were hoping that peace had now been restored to the Holy Church and that the hammer of the whole earth had been smashed to pieces,[27] there arose a trouble we had not foreseen. A certain heretic or pagan arrived, remarkable for his lifestyle and teaching but a false prophet, like a wolf in his hypocrisy, not entering the sheep-pen through the gate,[28] but nevertheless clad in sheep's clothing; and under the pretext of the crusade and the appearance of piety, he made himself leader of the shepherds, claiming that he had received revelations from God that he should cross the sea to fight against the Saracens and wield the sword in war along with Christian shepherds. In combination with I know not what, but with God's permission on account of our sins, such foolishness spread abroad that everywhere, within a very short space of time, shepherds from different parts of the world converged in a throng and follow this damned man. [p. 291] He and his accomplices grew so popular among the common people, too, that they were able to say and do whatever they wished. When this damned man saw that he was surrounded by such a large crowd and had the support of the people, he could no longer hold in the poison that he had generated, but began to profane the dignity of the Church by cursing the sacraments, blessing the people, preaching, giving out the Cross, sprinkling [holy] water in a novel fashion, fabricating miracles and going around, moreover, massacring churchmen.

At length, when he, his forerunners and his followers reached Paris, there was such a strong agitation by the people against the clergy that within a few days several clerics were killed, some being thrown into the river, while more were wounded; even a parish priest in the Mass was deprived of his chasuble and made a laughing-stock by being crowned with roses. [Their] spite reached the point that had it not been for the Saviour's mercy they would have uprooted the University from Paris, at the cost of shedding churchmen's blood and to the shame of Christians. In Rouen they wrecked the church and the Archbishop's house. In Orléans, similarly, they killed several clerics and forced the community of clergy, who had long resided there, to leave. At Tours, among other things they attacked the school-house of the Dominicans, in great force, wounding some and dragging others behind them like prisoners, without even the decency of their habits, and they deprived them of the provisions and the rest of the things in the city that pious Christians had bestowed on them. What is dreadful to hear and to recount – though more dreadful to witness – is that, when they entered a church where the undefiled and most sacred sacrament

25 There is also an incomplete text in *Chartularium universitatis Parisiensis*, ed. Heinrich Denifle, vol. 1 (Paris, 1889), pp. 224–5 (no. 198).

26 Adam forwarded this letter to Robert Grosseteste, Bishop of Lincoln: 'Adae de Marisco epistolae', no. 24, in *Monumenta Franciscana*, vol. 1, p. 109.

27 Presumably the Emperor Frederick, who had died in December 1250.

28 John, x, 1.

of the Body of Christ had been reverently placed upon the altar, they reprehensibly hurled it down [on the floor]; they hacked off the nose from the image of the glorious Virgin and gouged out the eyes; they carried off in their criminal hands whatever took their fancy. At length[29] they carried away [the belongings] of our Friars, things that[30] God had given them, amid violence to them. [p. 292] They even burst into our Friars' little house by force, and left the fathers[31] distressed and terrified by the injuries they had inflicted.[32] But – alas – none of this was of any concern to the French. What more can I say? I lack the capacity to describe the blasphemies of these scoundrels, the people's contempt for the divine word of God, the injuries inflicted on the religious and the clergy – and, among other things, the madness of the common folk, offering the sick to be cured by men like this, namely murderers, assassins and thieves, and, when they were not cured or did not even improve, preaching the virtues of [these] wretched men.

And yet God, in His overflowing goodness and through no merit of ours, decreed that this son of Perdition should meet his end as follows. When he arrived at Bourges, he took to spreading more widely the poison he had generated, and began to tell all the bystanders that they ought not to believe what the clergy said, on the grounds that their teaching was not in keeping with their way of life and therefore they embellished [it] with all [kinds of] folly. At these words a certain remarkable phoenix, afire with zeal for the Most High, began to challenge the statement of this mighty and wise man, asserting that, although in some respects their lives did not correspond to their teaching, what the clergy and religious said was well-founded and confirmed by the scriptures of the Old and New Testaments, whereas that man's words had no support whatsoever. On hearing this, the son of Perdition in his pride could no longer contain himself, but rushed at this man of Christ, struck him with his sword and killed him. When they saw this, the dead man's fellow citizens took up arms and, with considerable casualties among their own people, they killed the son of Perdition as he defended himself and, it is alleged, called upon Mahomet, together with some of his accomplices, hacking him to pieces and putting the rest to flight.

It is said that their design had been first to exterminate the clergy from the country, secondly to eliminate the religious, and later to turn against the knights and nobility, so that the land would thus be bereft of all protection and would more easily be exposed to the errors and attacks of the pagans. This seems close to the truth, especially since a host of unknown knights, dressed in white, [p. 293] began to appear in German regions. This is the state of affairs as of today and as far as has been learned from reliable sources.

Dated Paris, in the year of the Lord 1251.

29 Reading, with Denifle, *demum* for the *domum* of Luard's edition.

30 Reading, with the ms. and Denifle, *que* for the *quam* adopted by Luard.

31 Reading *patres*, with Denifle, for the *fratres* of Luard's edition.

32 Denifle's edition omits the remainder of this paragraph.

95. Salimbene de Adam, Cronica, *vol. 2, pp. 672, 673*

In the year of the Lord 1251 a countless multitude of shepherds gathered in France, claiming that it was their duty to cross the sea to kill the Saracens and avenge the King of France. Many from different cities in France followed them, and nobody dared to resist them; they were given provisions and whatever they desired. For this reason even the shepherds were abandoning their flocks in order to join them. For their leader claimed that it would be revealed to him by God that the sea would be opened up and that he was to lead that multitude to avenge the King of France. I myself said, on hearing such things, 'Woe to the shepherds who have left their flocks![33] What will they be able to do where the King of France, with the armed knights of France, has been able [to achieve] so little?' The common people of France believed in them, and turned in a fearful manner against the religious, especially the Preachers and Minors, on the grounds that they had preached the Cross and had signed men with it to sail overseas with the King, who had [then] been vanquished by the Saracens … [p. 673] … Where the King of France did not grow angry but was long-suffering, they raged in a terrible fashion. This multitude of shepherds so destroyed a single house of the Friars Preachers in a certain city that one stone did not remain upon another – and this merely because they had dared to make some remark against them. But in these [people] there was fulfilled what Paul's wise master Gamaliel said in the Acts of the Apostles, [namely] that 'if their counsel or this work be of men',[34] it would not be able to stand but would be dispersed. He spoke the truth, because in that same year they were reduced to nothing and almost the entire movement was destroyed.

96. Thomas de Cantimpré, Bonum Universale de Apibus, *liber II, iv, 15, ed. Georgius Colvenerius (Douai, 1627), vol. 1, pp. 140–41*

We have also[35] seen recently, in the year 1251 since the Lord's Incarnation, a host of Shepherds assembled from various regions, in an amazing and unheard-of madness, who in the name of the Cross were led by very wicked men to such evil conduct that they tried to assault and destroy towns, cities and [their] inhabitants in many parts of Gaul – to the point where they attempted this in Paris and Orléans, most distinguished cities, killing several clerics. And behold, O reader, a wretched and outstanding sinful act! The lay folk, from hatred of the clergy, cheered on those who perpetrated these things, and greater offences would have been committed had not a common plague eventually engulfed the laity themselves along with the clergy. These [the Shepherds] too, at God's instigation, very rapidly perished in different localities and by [different] punishments. Reflect, therefore, on the basis of what has been narrated, [p. 141] how numerous a crowd Antichrist, when he arrives, will gather to himself from among the Christian people.

33 Cf. Jeremiah, xxiii, 1.

34 Acts, v, 38.

35 Thomas has just been speaking of the Children's Crusade.

97. Roger Bacon, Opus Majus *[1267], ed. John Henry Bridges (Oxford and London, 1897–1900), vol. 1, pp. 401–2*

It is greatly to be feared lest the Tartars and the Saracens, while remaining in their own territories, send to the Christians men through whom they may, by means of astrology, spread misfortune and provoke dissension among princes, for the Christians' enemies make the greatest efforts to arouse war and dissension among them. This kind of thing has many times occurred, although the foolish multitude does not reflect whence it originates. You have perhaps seen or heard for a fact that at one time boys in the kingdom of France gathered in a countless throng in the wake of an evil man, with the result that their fathers and mothers and friends could not restrain them, and they were embarked on ships and sold to the Saracens; sixty-four years have not yet passed since [that event].[36] Similarly in our own time the Shepherd Master stirred up the whole of Germany[37] and France. A multitude of people hurried in his wake, and he enjoyed the favour of the whole of the common lay folk in despising the clergy and [bringing] confusion upon the Church. He told the Lady Blanche that he would go overseas to her son, deceiving with these words the most sagacious of women. The wise are in no doubt that these men were agents of the Tartars or the Saracens, and that they possessed some device whereby they mesmerized the people. I saw with my own eyes [the Master] carrying openly something in his hand as if it were some holy [p. 402] object, just as a man would transport relics, and he went with bare feet; and although there was around him a multitude of armed men, they were dispersed through the countryside in such a way that it was possible for all who encountered him to see what he was carrying in his hand so flamboyantly.

36 Another reference to the Children's Crusade. The figure 64 is clearly an error for 54, since Bacon was writing in 1267.

37 Strictly speaking, only the north-western borderlands – Brabant and Hainault.

IX

Efforts to Send Assistance to King Louis from the West

One of Louis's avowed aims in remaining in the East in 1250, as we have seen, was to act as a magnet for crusading reinforcements [**doc. 70** above]. Yet during the next four years, it seems, relatively few came out to assist him. As early as August 1250 some Scottish knights who had taken the Cross were planning to sail to the Holy Land, but it is not clear whether they ever fulfilled their vows.[1] The King's brother, Alphonse of Poitou, took the Cross a second time in 1252, in the wake of a serious illness, with the intention of re-joining Louis [**doc. 108**]. From March 1253 Innocent IV was certainly ordering funds to be assigned to him from various sources.[2] But although the Pope in October still expected him to leave for the East, and although evidence exists that at least fifty of his knights had arrived in Palestine on his behalf by the autumn of 1252,[3] the Count himself remained at home. We learn of a few other arrivals from Joinville. Philippe de Toucy, a baron from the Latin Empire of Constantinople, spent some time in Palestine from 1251.[4] The Count of Eu (a son of Jean de Brienne) joined the King at Jaffa at some point in 1252, accompanied by the lord of Guînes and two of his brothers.[5] Lesser crusaders included a certain Elinard ('Alenard') of Seninghem, of a noble family in the vicinity of Saint-Omer.[6] In a letter dated 29 March 1253, the Pope speaks of 'some men from the kingdoms of France and Navarre as well as the counties of Toulouse, Provence and Poitou' having taken the

---

1 Registrum Vaticanum, Innocent IV, annus 8, fol. 13v (no. 66); summary in Berger, no. 4814. For Scottish *crucesignati* in 1250–51, see generally Macquarrie, *Scotland and the Crusades*, pp. 49–51.

2 *Layettes*, vol. 3, pp. 176–8 (nos 4042–7, March 1253), 196–7 (no. 4081, 17 October 1253) [see **docs 109–12**].

3 *Layettes*, vol. 3, pp. 171–2 (no. 4032).

4 Joinville, § 495, p. 272 (trans. Hague, p. 150; trans. Shaw, p. 289). No date is given, but he appears at Caesarea in July 1251, when Louis assumed a debt on his behalf: *Layettes*, vol. 3, p. 138 (no. 3954).

5 Joinville, § 521, p. 286 (trans. Hague, p. 157; trans. Shaw, p. 296).

6 Ibid., § 493, p. 270 (trans. Hague, p. 149; trans. Shaw, p. 289). Joinville says that his ship had been commissioned in Norway, and he is consequently taken to be a Norwegian by Purcell, *Papal Crusading Policy*, p. 111 and n. 58, and by Jordan, *Louis IX and the Challenge of the Crusade*, pp. 33, 69; though correctly identified by Richard, *Saint Louis*, p. 143 (French edn, p. 256). On the Elinards of Seninghem, see Hans Eberhard Mayer, 'The crusader principality of Galilee between Saint-Omer and Bures-sur-Yvette', in Curiel and Gyselen, *Itinéraires d'Orient*, pp. 157–67 (here p. 164).

Cross [**doc. 111**].[7] But again we cannot be certain how many (if any) of them left for the East. Doubt has recently been cast, lastly, on Matthew Paris's statement that Louis's cousin, King Ferdinand III of Castile and Leon, took the Cross for the East in 1250, with the result that his death two years later came as a bitter blow to the French king.[8] It has been suggested instead that Ferdinand's plans prefigured those of his son and successor, Alfonso X, for an expedition against Muslim North Africa.[9]

It is clear that this dearth of support cannot be ascribed to any lack of appeals by the Pope. Once he learned of the disaster in Egypt, Innocent authorized crusade preaching, at least in the archdiocese of Rouen [**doc. 76**]. From November 1250, apparently, he was again seeking to recruit Frisian crusaders for the war in the eastern Mediterranean [**doc. 100**] – to the detriment, of course, of the crusade against the Hohenstaufen. He was still endeavouring to whip up enthusiasm for the crusade to the East in April 1253, when he ordered the Dominican Prior in Paris to have the Cross preached throughout the kingdoms of France and Navarre and in Provence, Brittany and Burgundy [**doc. 107**]. A notable juridical development of these years was the Pope's extension of the plenary crusading indulgence: to the wives of English *crucesignati* (1252)[10] and to the proctors whom Alphonse nominated to care for his interests in Toulouse during his absence (1253) [**doc. 109**].

Most importantly, perhaps, the news of Louis's failure had led Innocent to exert pressure upon the English King Henry III [**docs 102–4**], who had taken the Cross in March 1250. This step represents something of a *volte-face* by the Pope, since in April of that year – as it happened, just a few days following the collapse of Louis's operations in Egypt – he had been trying to persuade Henry to postpone his departure, evidently from fear that the simultaneous absence of the French and English Kings would benefit Frederick in his struggle with the papacy [**doc. 54** above].[11]

The most convincing analysis of the English King's thinking has been advanced by Dr. Simon Lloyd.[12] Henry took the vow most probably in response to the news of Louis's capture of Damietta and from a desire not to be outshone by his neighbour and rival. At this point, his representatives duly made a new truce with the French government, to last for five years [**doc. 63** above]. But in view of the need for lengthy preparations (like Louis's own) he set a date of June 1256 for his departure: in other words, at this point he did not envisage his own expedition overlapping with that of the French. Then – in the summer of 1250, presumably – came reports of the failure

---

7 See also Berger, no. 6419 (14 March 1253), where he speaks merely of 'some men from the kingdom of France and the county of Poitou'.

8 Matthew Paris, *Chronica Majora*, vol. 5, pp. 170, 311 (trans. Giles, vol. 2, pp. 387, 505–6; the first passage trans. in Vaughan, pp. 256–7), calling him 'Alfonso' in error.

9 See García, 'Henry III', pp. 101–2. But Jean de Garlande was similarly under the impression that Ferdinand had taken the Cross to go to Louis's assistance [above, **doc. 81**].

10 Berger, no. 5980. Purcell, *Papal Crusading Policy*, pp. 57-9. This had been foreshadowed in 1247 by the grant of the indulgence to the widow of a *crucesignatus* for as long as she remained a widow: Berger, no. 2665.

11 Lloyd, *English Society and the Crusade*, pp. 91, 211.

12 Ibid., pp. 210–25; also Lloyd, 'King Henry III, the Crusade and the Mediterranean', in Michael Jones and Malcolm Vale (ed.), *England and Her Neighbours, 1066–1453: Essays in Honour of Pierre Chaplais* (London and Ronceverte, 1989), pp. 97–119 (here pp. 98–113).

of Louis's assault on Egypt and of his withdrawal to Palestine. Henry wrote to Louis, expressing his sympathy and assuring him of his own eagerness to move to the relief of the French crusaders and the Holy Land. But this transformation of the situation in the East opened up new possibilities for the English King. However sincere his intentions regarding the Holy Land (and they are by no means transparent), he was also only too ready to exploit Louis's predicament with an eye to recovering his lost patrimony in France. A letter he wrote to the French monarch in 1252, offering to bring forward his passage overseas if his lands were restored [**doc. 106**], was nothing short of blackmail. Henry sought to build up the pressure upon the French King by despatching similar letters to Queen Blanche and to several important figures in the East, in which he informed them of his intention to leave within four years of 24 June 1252 and his readiness to bring the date forward should Louis satisfy his territorial demands.[13]

For some years Innocent certainly took Henry's professions at face value. Despite friction arising from the English King's apparent insistence on the grant of vow redemptions and other sources of funding, regardless of papal undertakings given to other crusaders [**doc. 104**], he was assigned the residue of crusade monies collected in Scotland [**doc. 98**]. In February 1251 the Pope was taking steps to suppress unrest in Gascony which might have impeded Henry's preparations [**doc. 101**]; and although he had issued instructions for the tenths to be made available to Henry two years prior to his departure, he extended this period to three years [**doc. 102**]. In 1252 he gave orders for *crucesignati* in England, Ireland and Gascony to be compelled to accompany the King to the Holy Land [**doc. 105**]. Yet notwithstanding all this papal support, Henry never did leave for the East, and from 1255 he was involved in negotiations with Innocent's successor, Pope Alexander IV, for participation in a crusade against the Emperor Frederick's bastard son Manfred in Sicily and the conferment of its crown upon his younger son Edmund.

DOCUMENTS 98–112

98. Pope Innocent IV to the Bishops of St Andrews and Aberdeen,[14] *17 October 1250: Berger, no. 4868*

Since our dearest son in Christ, [Henry], the illustrious King of England, is making preparations to cross the sea in splendid force, as befits so great a prince, and is obliged to shoulder a very great burden of expense for this purpose, we order you faithfully to collect, in person or through others, the legacies, offerings and [sums] left or made over in any other manner for the relief of that country [the Holy Land] in the kingdom of Scotland. Having first satisfied all those to whom any undertakings have been given regarding this [money] by the Apostolic See, you should assign all

13 For these letters, see *Foedera*, vol. 1/1, p. 167. Henry's letters to the East, dated 6 June, were addressed to, among others, the Patriarch of Jerusalem, the King of Cyprus, Bohemond V of Antioch-Tripoli, the King of Armenia, and the consuls and communes of Genoa, Pisa and Venice.

14 St Andrews: David de Bernham (1240–53). Aberdeen: Peter de Ramsey (1247–56).

the residue, insofar as we have not thought fit to grant it to native crusaders, to the aforesaid King, when we have sent word and he sets out overseas. Those who resist, etc.

Dated Lyons, the 16th Kalends of November, in the eighth year of our pontificate.

99. Pope Innocent IV to the Bishops of Paris, Évreux and Senlis,[15] *29 November 1250: Berger, no. 4926*

Since at this time the Holy Land has need of military assistance, we order that, both in person and through others whom you deem fit, you assiduously urge, and effectively persuade, in keeping with the wisdom given you by God, all those who have taken the Cross in Provence, the county of Toulouse, the neighbouring ports and in the entire kingdom of France, as well as those who have been so bold as to lay aside the Cross without the Church's authority, to sail to the relief of the Holy Land in the next passage to be determined by you at the pleasure of our dearest daughter in Christ, B[lanche], illustrious Queen of France; compelling them, if necessary, to do so through ecclesiastical censure without [right of] [p. 161] appeal. Notwithstanding etc. If all [of you] etc.

Dated Lyons, the 3rd Kalends of December, in the eighth year of our pontificate.

100. Pope Innocent IV to the Dominican Prior and the Franciscan Minister of the province of Germany, 29 November 1250: Berger, no. 4927; also in Rodenberg, vol. 3, pp. 15–16 (no. 20)

Since at this time the Holy Land has need of military assistance, and bearing in mind that many Frisians, kindled with the zeal of devotion and faith, have received the sign of the Cross and that Frisians have usually acquitted themselves well overseas,[16] we order that both in person and through others whom you deem fit you assiduously urge, and effectively persuade, in keeping with the wisdom given you by God, all those who have taken the Cross in Frisia and Norway to sail to the relief of the Holy Land by the next passage to be determined by you at the pleasure of our dearest daughter in Christ, B[lanche], illustrious Queen of France; compelling them, if necessary, to do so through ecclesiastical censure without [right of] appeal. Notwithstanding etc. If both [of you] etc.

Dated [Lyons, the 3rd Kalends of December, in the eighth year of our pontificate].

---

15 Paris: Renaud de Corbeil (1250–68). Evreux: Jean de la Cour d'Aubergenville (1244–56). Senlis: Adam de Chambly (1227/28–58).

16 A reference to the prominent role played by Frisians in the Fifth Crusade. See p. 51 and note 12

101. Pope Innocent IV to the Bishop of Angoulême,[17] *1 February 1251: Berger, no. 5028*

[Having been informed of the turbulent situation in Gascony by Simon de Montfort, orders the Bishop to ensure that the peace of the region is not disturbed]

102. Pope Innocent IV to the archbishops and bishops in the English kingdom, 16 February 1251: Berger, no. 5106

[Informs them that the funds collected for Henry III's crusade are to be made over to him three years prior to his departure, rather than two years in advance as previously arranged]

103. Pope Innocent IV to Henry III, King of England, 18 October 1251: 'Annales monasterii de Burton', in Annales Monastici, *vol. 1, pp. 293–5*

The unhappy tract of Jerusalem, in a position of dire straits, cries urgently to us for swift aid – it cries, I say, and, assailed by constant trials, chastised by harsh scourgings, and borne down by the yoke of too shameful subjection, it repeats and raises its cries of grief more bitterly in accordance with the great number of its woes. Behold, that sad region is oppressed, it sighs with anxiety and, bound with the enemy's chains, it laments and groans without remission. Where will its sighs and sobs go unnoticed? Where will its shrieks and groans go unheard? For its grief is known to all, and its powerful cries have reached the ears of the whole world. Who, then, of the faithful who loves [it] cannot mourn at the sound of that unhappy, plaintive voice? Who, I say, can feel no compassion with its bitter suffering? Whose heart is not stirred to go to [its] assistance by the shedding of so many tears? Whose mind is not stung to aid it by its manifest need? Yet surely Mother Church opens her ears to hear the pitiful cries [p. 294] of that land, kindly turns in bitter reflection to its grievous condition, commiserates with it on such great troubles with a tender heart, and strives to come kindly and swiftly to its assistance with whatever means of relief she can. And while she recalls that the land has been provided many times with aid but that it failed to yield the hoped-for results, and while she deems the countless expense and effort of Christ's faithful have availed to protect nobody but have virtually gone to waste, she burns all the more fiercely to help it because she discerns that the enemy's strength is growing against it.

You also, on hearing the groans of that land and moved all too greatly to pity it, as a distinguished prince and especial champion of God, have from the first roused your mind to helping it. Taking the sign of the Cross, you have at once begun to make splendid preparations for the fulfilment of your vow. Wholly aflame with this desire, you have, as we learn from his envoys, sent a letter to our dearest son in Christ, the illustrious King of France, [saying] that the lamentable outcome which unfortunately befell him and his men by way of the slaughter of so many captives, and the devastation of that land, have transfixed your inmost heart with the shaft of

17 Pierre (1247–52).

enormous grief; and at length, overjoyed at the King's miraculous release, you have pressed ahead to good effect with the fulfilment of the vow, altogether longing to see the King in person in that country and there to bring him relief from his distress. He for his part, vastly cheered by this, has written back to you in affectionate terms, praising, as he ought, your kindly intention in this regard and making known his fervent hopes of relieving that land's wretchedness jointly with you and, reinforced by your strength, of delivering it from the hands of the infidel. He awaited your arrival more eagerly than any other, particularly since a conflict has arisen among the infidels themselves and through the Divine providence their strength is now diminished, so that he will now more easily be able to bring modest aid to that land. He further indicated that unless the condition of the land improves he was not planning to return to his own, calling to mind nevertheless the many splendid things [done] by your predecessors and his, who in that land had acted together in this business.[18]

Oh, if the outcome for that land were so happy, if it were attended by such great and favourable fortune as to be bolstered by the presence of two such princes, to benefit in equal measure from the protection of both, and to experience at once the strong right arm of each of them, how much will it be strengthened [p. 295] by healing comfort, how greatly will it rejoice, and to what pitch of confidence will it surely be able to rise that it will be wrested from the pagans' grasp and be plucked from the jaws of those who rend it. Oh, if that wretched [land] beheld this deliverance, if in its affliction it found such a refuge, if the inflammation of its wounds were soothed by the application of such healing remedies as to be aided by the power of these two [princes] in succession, the might of each would be joined and the strong arms of both would be raised against those who blaspheme Christ. How easily would that land have respite from its tribulations, gain relief from such heavy oppression, and find release from the bonds of such prolonged slavery! Surely, dearest son, if you reinforce that land with the strength of your valour while the aforesaid King is staying there to defend it, in such a way as jointly to champion its cause – since the might of each one of you is great and renowned throughout the whole world, inasmuch as you are anointed – the greatest victories will spring from this alliance and will form an irreversible bulwark against the enemy, since that land will manifestly seize on the awaited[19] outcome, it will completely satisfy the daily longings of the faithful, and with God's help the hoped-for and peaceful result of so much effort and expense will easily follow.

And so we keenly beseech and urge Your Highness, and we entreat you in the Lord Jesus Christ, that you mercifully heed that land's pressing need, bear in mind that the assistance which is applied at this juncture will assuredly yield a greater return than if it were given at some other time, and piously reflect, moreover, how steadfastly the aforementioned King persisted in aiding that land and that he earnestly desires to be your collaborator in recovering it, for which reason he anxiously awaits your mighty host. Remember too that your aforesaid predecessors together brought

---

18 An allusion to the activity of Richard I of England and Philippe Augustus of France in the years 1190–92, during the Third Crusade.

19 Reading *expectatum* for the *expectare* of the text.

aid to that land and prosecuted its business in splendid fashion. Do not delay going to its assistance, but – just as we believe that you have firmly decided to do – bring that help swiftly. Rise up with a ready heart and, surrounded by an estimable and mighty force, go there in all haste to avenge the injury to Christ, Who has sought there to bring about your salvation and that of all people, and through Whom you gain the throne of the realm in order, with God's help, to brandish the sword of triumph. For as a result of this, in addition to an eternal reward, you will obtain outstanding glory here and will fill with enormous joy the entire Christian people. If you are unable to set out overseas swiftly at this time, permit the *crucesignati* in your realm who wish to set sail to fulfil their vows, in reverence for God.

Dated Rome, the 15th Kalends of November, in the ninth year of our pontificate.

104. Pope Innocent IV to Henry III, King of England, 1252: 'Annales monasterii de Burton', in Annales Monastici, *vol. 1, pp. 298–9*

We want you to know, dearest son, and to be in no doubt that since we regard you, among all the world's other kings and princes, as an outstanding and special defender of the faith and the Church, we readily desire to accommodate your wishes in all matters, as far as we are able with God. But since it befits Your Highness that, preserving our honour, you moderate your desires regarding what you have demanded, or are to demand, in such a way that no scandal will arise from them, and it is not inappropriate to listen to us, who would not willingly prove fickle, you ought in kindness to attend to our feelings and mildly excuse [our] failure in your conscience. Thus is the mutual affection of friends preserved and enhanced by reciprocal sentiments.

Since, therefore, you have recently written to us regarding the assignment to Your Magnificence of the redemptions of vows in your territories, and of other [sums] destined for the relief of the Holy Land and not yet collected, though granted to others, and since it does our reputation no good and neither should you, who are zealous for the Church's dignity, wish us (who, albeit undeserving, by the Lord's dispensation preside over the universal government) to disappoint, like a laughing-stock, those who have put their hopes in our grace, we have seen fit to ask [Your] Royal Excellency in affectionate terms that (reflecting carefully how disgraceful it is for any [p. 299] honest man, least of all the Supreme Pontiff, whom the rest ought to take as a model and a pattern, to be charged with inconsistency and broken promises) you hold us excused from [acceding to] your requests, which on those grounds alone we have not granted.

In order that you may, in greater might and magnificence as befits so great a prince and as the magnitude of the task demands, pursue the business of the Cross, which through the wretched disaster that is said to have lately befallen the Christian army overseas lies exclusively on your shoulders, and since the resources and manpower of a single king or realm are inadequate for the purpose, given that at one time in the past Frederick, Emperor of the Romans, King Philippe of France and King Richard of England, of happy memory – assuredly energetic men, who excelled in [the number of their] soldiers, their wealth and their power – assembled together with many other barons and nobles from other realms, not without forethought, to deal with such a great business; it is advisable – indeed vital – that for so pious and needful a cause the kings and princes of the whole of Christendom, and everyone else who, we firmly believe, will prove susceptible, be most urgently persuaded by the Apostolic See; and that you exercise that forbearance and mildness towards the prelates, barons and other nobles and the entire clergy and laity of your realm, who will be of greater use to you than any of the rest, completely refraining from [giving] them [grounds for] complaint or offending them, so that you will be in a position to find them even readier and more disposed in heart than in body to [carry out] your wishes and orders, and the business will thus, in your arms supported by your own men and others, and with God's aid, be able to flourish and to confront whatever new danger arises. But if, God forbid, you approach the business putting your trust instead in your own resources, while it is at such a low ebb, as the sins of the Christian people require, it is to be feared, and justifiably so, that Christendom and the faith will be vanquished, since the eyes of all are raised in this matter towards you, as a champion, and they hope to be delivered from such upheaval by your good offices. Wherefore we beg you, reflect and consider that, since the cause you have taken up is rendered much harder and more burdensome by disaster, you proceed with it at the proper pace, persuading the barons, nobles and others by whatever means you can, so that you may set out overseas in Christ's name to wipe out Christendom's disgrace well supported, having assembled a great host of nobles and people from different parts of the world, and secure in the knowledge that we are ready to furnish for the purpose, personally and through others, as much aid and effort as we are able.

Dated etc. in the year of the Lord 1252.

105. Pope Innocent IV to the archbishops and bishops of England, Ireland and Gascony, 3 September 1252: Berger, no. 5979

[Instructs them to persuade *crucesignati* and those yet to take the Cross in Henry III's territories, and if necessary to compel them by means of excommunication and interdict, to delay no longer and to prepare to accompany the English King overseas]

106. Henry III, King of England, to Louis IX, 8 June 1252: Foedera, *vol. 1/1, p. 167*

To the excellent prince, Louis, by God's grace illustrious King of France, Henry, by the same grace King of England etc., greetings.

You have long asked in your letters that we should hasten our arrival in aid of the Holy Land; and we recall having written back to Your Serenity that, were you to be guided by sound policy and return to us our territories which were seized by you and your forebears, we should expedite our passage and put our person and our resources at the service of the Crucified One, to the enhancement of your prestige. And although our passage is a matter on oath and fixed for a set date, we shall even so bring that passage forward, making mighty preparations to aid the aforesaid land, provided that you are so kind as to restore to us what has been taken. This would be conducive to the abiding vigour of your royal authority and to the high esteem of your good name.

In the King's presence, at Westminster, the 8th day of June.

107. Pope Innocent IV to the Prior of the Dominican Order in Paris, 2 April 1253: Berger, no. 6469

[Orders him to have the crusade to the Holy Land preached throughout the realms of France and Navarre and in Provence, Brittany and Burgundy, as well as the counties, lands, lordship, castellanies and fiefs of Alphonse of Poitou][20]

108. Philippe, chaplain to Alphonse, Count of Toulouse, to Louis IX, [before 28 November] 1252: Layettes, *vol. 3, pp. 170–71 (no. 4030)*

[Informs the King that Alphonse, after being afflicted by a serious illness,[21] has taken the Cross and is eager to return to the Holy Land]

109. Pope Innocent IV to [Philippe,] treasurer of the Church of Saint-Hilaire at Poitiers, 19 March 1253: Berger, no. 6440

[Orders him to grant to the proctors whom Alphonse appoints to deal with his affairs in the county of Toulouse the same pardon for their sins as is enjoyed by those who cross the sea to aid the Holy Land]

110. Pope Innocent IV to [Philippe,] treasurer of the Church of Saint-Hilaire at Poitiers, 21 March 1253: Layettes, *vol. 3, p. 176 (no. 4043); also in Berger, no. 6466*

[Orders him to urge the executors of those in the kingdom of France and in Alphonse's own territories who have died since he took the Cross, or will have died by the time of his return, to assign to Alphonse's crusade any bequests made for unspecified pious purposes]

---

20 This is in large measure a reissue of Innocent's letter of 28 February 1250 to French prelates [**doc. 18**], though it naturally substitutes for the triumph at Damietta the disaster that had since befallen Louis's army, and Alphonse's preparations to go to his assistance. Preaching in the kingdom of Navarre had not been envisaged in the earlier letter.

21 Matthew Paris, vol. 5, p. 311 (trans. Giles, vol. 2, p. 506), says that Alphonse succumbed to a paralytic illness in 1252, which enables us to date this letter to that year; cf. also vol. 5, p. 354 (trans. Giles, vol. 3, p. 6). But it cannot be much later than 28 November, when Blanche (the Queen referred to in this letter) died. For Matthew, Alphonse's disease was divine retribution for his failure to return to Louis's aid.

111. Pope Innocent IV to [Philippe,] treasurer of the Church of Saint-Hilaire at Poitiers, 29 March 1253: Layettes, *vol. 3, pp. 177–8 (no. 4047); partially edited in Berger, no. 6459.*

[Orders him to compel any in the kingdoms of France and Navarre and the counties of Toulouse, Provence and Poitou who have taken the Cross on condition that, if unable or unwilling, they may send instead a specified sum of money, to assign to him these funds, which are to be transmitted to Alphonse at his departure; they are to be given the usual pardon for their sins]

112. Pope Innocent IV to Alphonse, Count of Poitou and Toulouse, 17 October 1253: Layettes, *vol. 3, pp. 196–7 (no. 4081)*

Innocent, Bishop, servant of the servants of God, to his beloved son, the noble A[lphonse], Count of Poitou and Toulouse, *crucesignatus*, greetings and apostolic benediction. At one time, as has been represented before us on your behalf, we ordered you, when you had taken the Cross in aid of the Holy Land, to be assigned, on certain conditions, the proceeds of the redemption of the vows of crusaders, bequests for pious purposes unspecified, and monies extorted and confiscated illicitly through wicked usury should nobody appear to whom they ought to be restored, in the kingdom of France and in your counties, demesne lands, castellanies or fiefs, and other favours to be conferred [on you] in connection with the [Holy] Land. And so, consenting to your requests, we grant you, by the authority of this [p. 197] letter, that no disadvantage may accrue to you through favours conferred by us, in similar circumstances, on others in this same realm, counties, demesne lands, castellanies or fiefs belonging to you directly or indirectly. Nobody shall be permitted to contravene these terms of our grant or to be so bold as to challenge it; but if any person shall presume to make the attempt, he should know that he will incur the wrath of Almighty God and of His Apostles, the Blessed Peter and Paul.

Dated the Lateran, the 16th Kalends of November, in the eleventh year of our pontificate.

X

The Second Phase: King Louis's Four-year Stay in Palestine

One reason that King Louis imagined that he might benefit the Christian cause by remaining in the Holy Land in August 1250 was the conflict that was looming between the new regime in Cairo and the Sultan of Aleppo, al-Nāṣir Ṣalāḥ al-Dīn Yūsuf. Muslim authors simply do not mention the Franks during this period (a fact which surely indicates that the crusaders were now a negligible quantity), and so are of no direct value for the operations of Louis and his forces. Indeed, we could be forgiven for inferring from the majority of these sources that Louis and his staff had embarked for France in the autumn of 1250: Ibn Wāṣil's account of the crusaders' defeat in Egypt ends with the briefest reference to Louis's fortification work at Caesarea and his departure, followed by a paragraph about his attempt to conquer Tunis during the Eighth Crusade several years later. Even if Ibn Wāṣil had not left Egypt on a pilgrimage to Mecca with his patron Ḥusām al-Dīn early in 1252, therefore, and so bequeathed us a highly laconic account of the events of the ensuing year, he probably would still have had nothing to say about the intruders on the coast.

It is, however, impossible to understand King Louis's optimism regarding the situation in the Muslim world without an awareness of the complexity of events following Tūrān Shāh's murder. The letters written from Palestine in 1250–51, beginning with Louis's own appeal of August 1250 to his French subjects to come to his assistance [**doc. 70** above], refer only to the outbreak of hostilities between Cairo and Aleppo. We derive a much fuller picture from the Arabic sources – and from Ibn Wāṣil in particular.

Firstly, two other Ayyubid princes, al-Mughīth Fatḥ al-Dīn ʿUmar (the son of Ayyūb's brother, Sultan al-ʿĀdil II) and al-Saʿīd ibn al-ʿAzīz, seized control respectively of the Transjordanian strongholds, Kerak and al-Shawbak, and of al-Ṣubayba in Syria. And secondly, it is clear that the situation in Cairo during the few months following the coup was highly volatile and that events moved with almost bewildering rapidity. The news on 23 July 1250 that al-Nāṣir had taken Damascus with the complicity of the Kurdish amirs there prompted the arrest of a number of Kurdish amirs in the Egyptian capital and the realization that a female sultan was inadequate to meet the crisis: Shajar al-Durr was deposed in favour of the Mamluk commander, al-Muʿizz ʿIzz al-Dīn Aybak, who promptly married her. Then, says Ibn Wāṣil, on the very day of Aybak's enthronement (31 July 1250) reports reached Cairo of the loss of Transjordan and of al-Ṣubayba, and the amirs decided that only a sovereign from the Ayyubid dynasty would furnish the legitimacy they lacked and serve as a counterblast. They duly enthroned as sultan a young and insignificant prince, al-Ashraf Mūsā, on 5 August, while demoting Aybak to be his *atabeg* or guardian/commander-in-chief. Within the space of just over three months, therefore, Egypt had witnessed three changes of monarch.

The precise date given by Ibn Wāṣil for the news of the loss of the fortresses renders it extremely likely that the crusaders heard of these developments at some point during August, if not necessarily before King Louis wrote to France;[1] and the fact that messengers are said to have arrived daily at Acre with fresh news for the King[2] suggests that the Franks were informed of events relatively promptly. At this juncture, it must have seemed as if the once-mighty Ayyubid empire was on the brink of dissolution into several warring principalities. It may not be altogether fanciful to imagine that Louis and his advisers felt they were being offered a second chance – with greatly depleted forces at their disposal, it is true, but confronted by an enormously weakened Muslim enemy. The King's reason for mentioning in his letter only the imminent conflict between the Egyptians and the Sultan of Aleppo may well have been reluctance to paint too sanguine a picture and hence undermine his appeal for reinforcements.

As it transpired, the crusaders were unable to profit from inter-Muslim rivalry. To the new masters of Egypt, al-Naṣir Yūsuf of Aleppo undoubtedly appeared a major threat. Even his name and titles were programmatic: they were those borne by his great-grandfather, the famous conqueror Saladin. Unfortunately, however, he was not destined to vindicate them. In October 1250 he fell ill, and he did not recover until December, thus forfeiting a vital opportunity for a strike against Egypt. When he did advance into Egypt in January 1251, the campaign was a fiasco. Early in February, his forces were initially victorious over the Egyptians near al-ʿAbbāsa, and fugitives reaching Cairo reported that all was lost; there was even a short-lived coup in Cairo on his behalf. But a small division headed by Aybak himself rallied and charged straight at al-Nāṣir Yūsuf's own position, driving him in headlong flight. When his scattered forces regrouped after advancing a great distance in pursuit of the fleeing Egyptian forces, they had little choice but to follow their master back northwards to Damascus.

al-Nāṣir Yūsuf remained a potential menace to the regime in Cairo even after the failure of this attempt on Egypt. But Louis was initially in no position to benefit, because the Egyptians held so many crusaders prisoner. Not until the middle of 1251 were these all released, but only as the result of an agreement which committed Louis to joint action with the Egyptians against al-Nāṣir Yūsuf. The confrontation between the Egyptian and Syrian forces persisted for two years without any engagement worth mentioning, until in 1253 the Caliph's envoy, Najm al-Dīn al-Bādarā'ī, finally engineered a peace agreement between them. This was not the first occasion on which al-Bādarā'ī had intervened effectively in Syrian affairs. Back in 1248 he had brought about a truce in the war between al-Ṣāliḥ Ayyūb and al-Nāṣir Yūsuf which had freed the Egyptian army to return home and confront the imminent invasion by King Louis [**doc. 73** above]. Whatever verdict be entered regarding the administrative efficiency and diplomatic skill of the caliphal regime in Baghdad during the few years prior to its

1 His letter, dated simply August 1250, must have been written before 10 August, when his brothers, who carried it to France, left Palestine: **doc. 70** and note 185 above.

2 'Rothelin', p. 625 (trans. Shirley, p. 109).

destruction by the Mongols in 1258, one great service it certainly did render the Islamic world was to induce the Near Eastern princes to close ranks in the face of the threat from the crusaders both in 1248 and in 1253.

All that Louis achieved during his four years in Palestine, therefore, was the fortification of a number of strongholds: the Montmusard suburb of Acre and the walls of Haifa, Caesarea, Jaffa and Sidon. He was also the first crusading leader to recognize in a practical way the desperate need of the Holy Land for a permanent garrison force, leaving in Acre a body of 100 French knights under Geoffrey de Sargines.[3] The circumstances of Louis's final departure for France in April 1254 are a trifle obscure. Clearly it was not a direct response to the news of his mother's death (28 November 1252),[4] which must have reached him at Jaffa (that is. prior to the spring of 1253), a full year before he embarked.[5] On the other hand, the decision had clearly been taken well in advance of the King's departure: the Papal Legate told Joinville that Louis had decided to return to France at the coming Easter even prior to completing work on the fortifications at Sidon.[6] What other considerations influenced him? According to Joinville, when Louis had completed the construction work at Sidon the Patriarch and the barons of the kingdom of Jerusalem approached him and told him somewhat bluntly that his further stay would not benefit the kingdom.[7] But this story seems hardly credible, given that in September 1254, only a few months after Louis's embarkation, the most prominent figures in the kingdom wrote to Henry III, imploring him to come to their assistance and claiming that the French King's departure had left the Holy Land bereft [**doc. 122**]. Louis's confessor Geoffrey de Beaulieu claims that he had heard news of a possible renewal of conflict with the English King.[8] This again is improbable, because – as we have seen [**doc. 63** above] – Henry had in fact renewed the truce between the two monarchs for five years in the spring of 1250, shortly after himself taking the vow. The most likely explanation for Louis's departure is surely a growing sense that his presence was not in fact serving to attract further reinforcements from Western Europe and that the active phase of the crusade was at an end. In fact, the 'Rothelin' chronicle, in the context of the King's decision to leave, refers simply to the dearth of news that any help was on its way.[9] One wonders whether the sentiments that Joinville puts into the mouths of the Patriarch and the barons were not, rather, King Louis's own.

---

3 See generally Christopher J. Marshall, 'The French regiment in the Latin East, 1254–1291', *JMH*, 15 (1989): 301–7; also p. 230, note 90, below.

4 As stated, for instance, by the Minstrel of Reims, § 430, p. 220 (trans. Levine, p. 100; trans. Stone, p. 346).

5 Geoffrey de Beaulieu, 'Vita Ludovici noni', p. 17, confirms that Louis was at Jaffa when the news arrived. The statement by Joinville, § 603, p. 330 (trans. Hague, p. 179; trans. Shaw, p. 315), that he was at Sidon is less reliable.

6 Ibid., § 610, p. 334 (trans. Hague, p. 180; trans. Shaw, p. 317).

7 Ibid., §§ 615–16, p. 336 (trans. Hague, p. 182; trans. Shaw, p. 318).

8 Geoffrey de Beaulieu, 'Vita Ludovici noni', p. 17: he speaks of danger from both England and Germany.

9 'Rothelin', p. 629 (trans. Shirley, p. 112).

DOCUMENTS 113–22

113. Guillaume de Châteauneuf, Master of the Hospital, to the Dominican Walter de St Martin [1251], in Matthew Paris, Chronica Majora, *vol. 6:* Additamenta, *pp. 204–5*[10]

To the Hospital's very dear and particular friend, the religious and honourable Friar Preacher Walter de St Martin, [from] Brother Guillaume de Châteauneuf, by God's grace humble Master of the holy Order of the Hospital of Jerusalem and Guardian of Christ's poor: greetings and a ready will to do his pleasure.

Since we are aware that Your Grace has always had a sincere affection for the house and brethren of the Hospital, and has in good faith looked kindly on its desires, we offer Your Liberality our abundant thanks for this, and assure you that henceforward we and all the brethren of the Hospital are in your debt and you hold us under an everlasting obligation to do whatever you please. In case you are glad to hear it, we give you news of ourselves, namely that through God's grace we, together with thirty of our brethren and many other religious and laymen, have been freed from a Babylonian prison by the agency of the lord King of France,[11] and on 17 October we entered the city of Acre; we left behind an immense crowd of the faithful in captivity in Egypt, who we hope will, with [p. 205] God's aid, soon be released. A mighty dispute is raging between the Sultans of Babylon and Aleppo; and through this we are confident that, if military reinforcements arrive from overseas, the Holy Land will flourish and the pride of the enemy will be crushed. Farewell.

114. Guillaume de Châteauneuf, Master of the Hospital, to the Dominican Walter de St Martin [1251], in Matthew Paris, Chronica Majora, *vol. 6:* Additamenta, *pp. 203–4*

To my dear and special friend, the religious, outstanding and wise Friar Preacher Walter de St Martin, [from] Brother Guillaume de Châteauneuf, by God's grace humble Master of the holy Order of the Hospital of Jerusalem: greetings and a total disposition to do his pleasure.

In the hope that you will be glad to hear news from the Holy Land – such as it is – we have seen fit to pass it on to you. It is that following that inexplicable disaster which the lord King of the French and the entire Christian army suffered in Egypt, when defeated and captured by the enemy, through the Divine clemency the King was miraculously released and arrived in the city of Acre, along with his brothers and some noble princes, whose lives God had preserved from death during the crisis.

---

10 I have reversed the order of these first two letters, since in the one given here in second place the Master is sceptical that the dispute between Egypt and Aleppo will have beneficial consequences for the Christian cause. That such sentiments are not found in the letter given at pp. 204–5 suggests it was written earlier.

11 He had been a prisoner in Egypt since the battle of La Forbie in October 1244. His release, along with 25 Hospitallers, 25 Templars, 10 Teutonic Knights, 100 secular knights and 600 other prisoners, both male and female, is mentioned in 'Rothelin', p. 625 (trans. Shirley, p. 110).

And since in the absence of a truce he could not leave Syria in peril of being lost without a reduction in the royal dignity, he sent back his brothers and all the other nobles to France [p. 204] for reinforcements, planning to stay until, with assistance from his own people and the rest of Christ's faithful, he might be in a position to crush the pride of the heathen, or by means of a truce establish the Holy Land on a favourable footing. But although at the time of writing a mighty dispute was under way between the Sultans of Aleppo and Babylon, which might give rise to hope that a satisfactory truce is due to come about, it did not seem to us, as one who has experience of the heathens' cunning, that at the instigation of some – or the many who share this view – the outcome will be as is hoped. When with the passage of time, however, matters become clearer, we shall take care to inform Your Prudence of their outcome. Farewell.

115. Robert, Patriarch of Jerusalem, to Queen Blanche, [summer 1251]: 'Annales monasterii de Burton', in Annales Monastici*vol. 1, p. 296*

Letter of reassurance addressed to the Queen of France by the Patriarch In our desire to give Your Benevolence some small respite from rumours, let us inform you that the lord King of France, my lady the Queen, their two sons Jean of Damietta[12] and Pierre,[13] born in Chastel Pèlerin[14] in June on the feast of Saints Peter and Paul [29 June 1251], and the lord King's council, are – like ourselves – in flourishing bodily health, and desire to hear the same of you. The King with his forces pitched his tents before Caesarea-in-Palestine on 1 April and has restored[15] it in the finest fashion with three walls and ditches;[16] and there we are [at present] with the rest of the Christians from this side of the sea. But as we believe you have heard, the Sultan of Aleppo[17] suffered a major defeat near Egypt at the hands of the Egyptians on the Feast of the Purification of the Virgin last [2 February 1251], though he escaped with a few men and fled to Damascus. The Egyptian army, for its part, under the leadership of Feres Cerataye,[18] took up its position at Nablus shortly after we reached Caesarea, and remained there until the end of July: for then the Sultan of Aleppo, who had regathered his forces, moved against him with no small host, and they [the Egyptians] therefore turned tail and withdrew from there in flight towards Egypt. Nor is this to be wondered at, since they were few compared with the men of Aleppo, who were pursuing them. We believe that

12 Jean 'Tristan', born at Damietta in April 1250: see Joinville, §§ 398–9, pp. 216, 218 (trans. Hague, pp. 124–5; trans. Shaw, pp. 262-3). He died near Tunis on crusade with his father in 1270.

13 Later Count of Alençon (d. 1283).

14 The great Templar fortress (also known as Athlit), where Queen Marguerite was currently staying while Louis superintended the fortification of Caesarea and where she gave birth to their son Pierre: Joinville, § 514, p. 282 (trans. Hague, p. 155; trans. Shaw, p. 294); also **doc. 121** below.

15 The printed text reads *restitit*, evidently in error for *restituit*.

16 For the fortification work done at Caesarea in 1251–52, see Joshua Prawer, *Histoire du royaume latin de Jérusalem* (Paris, 1969–70), vol. 2, pp. 344–5.

17 al-Nāṣir Yūsuf.

18 Fāris al-Dīn Aqṭāy.

they will yet endeavour to seize the Egyptian borders by some means. We shall notify you of what happens depending on time and place.

Dated etc.[19]

116. Louis IX to Alphonse, Count of Poitou and Toulouse, Caesarea, 11 August 1251: Layettes, *vol. 3, pp. 139–40 (no. 3956)*

Louis, by God's grace King of the French, to his dearest brother and vassal, Alphonse, Count of Poitou and Toulouse, greetings and fraternal love. Since the departure of our envoys whom we despatched overseas, namely Bartholomew, our chaplain, and Jean de Domibus, knight, the events [p. 140] that are recounted below have occurred among us here and around the Holy Land. An amir – one of the chief men of Egypt – called Feres Katay,[20] as we have already written to Your Highness, had arrived in the territory of the kingdom of Jerusalem with around 2000 Turks, with the aim of making war on the Sultan of Aleppo and of recovering the kingdom of Damascus, which the said Sultan had seized following the murder of the Sultan of Egypt. He took up permanent position at the city of Nablus, which is around nine leagues distant from Caesarea, and for some time waited there for reinforcements, while some gradually joined him from Egypt. Now the Sultan of Aleppo gathered numerous warriors whom he had collected from various quarters, and despatched a large and far superior force through the aforesaid region to destroy these Egyptians; while the latter, mounting many sallies against the army of Aleppo, lay in wait for them. On some occasions, as the columns drew near to one another in this or that direction, it was often rumoured among us, and believed for a fact, that they were due to do battle; but for all that they kept at a distance from one another. And indeed we sometimes received envoys from either side, whom they sent to us at Caesarea. But what they had to say was too imprecise and carried no weight, and so did not form the basis for concluding a truce.

Since we arrived in Caesarea, indeed, the Christian army has enjoyed peace and quiet and has not been harassed or injured by Saracens from any quarter – not even by the Bedouins, as is so often the fate of armies on this side of the sea. Through God's grace, moreover, there has regularly been a fairly full supply of provisions and other necessities among the troops, and the route between Acre and Caesarea has been clear and safe from harassment by Saracens or anyone else whatever; except that on occasions pirates, as they have tended to do along the coasts, have inflicted some losses on some of those who sail the seas, even though we were keeping galleys and armed vessels at sea at our own expense. Recently, however, these captured a vessel full of such corsairs;[21] and since it suffered the rigours of the law, this event

19 The date is not given in the mss., but the letter clearly belongs to the late summer of 1251.

20 Fāris al-Dīn Aqṭāy.

21 This incident is referred to in a letter of King Louis to the members of the Genoese commune in Syria, Caesarea, August 1251: Pierre-Vincent Claverie, 'Un nouvel éclairage sur le financement de la première croisade de saint Louis', *Mélanges de l'École Française de Rome, Moyen Age*, 113 (2001): 621–35 (here 634, annexes, no. 1).

has instilled great terror into the rest, so that the sea route will henceforth be clearer and safer.

Recently, the army of the Sultan of Aleppo, which we mentioned, crossed the river and approached Nablus, where the Turks of Egypt were stationed, while the Sultan himself stayed behind at Damascus with a few men. Finally, on the Saturday [29 July 1251] following the feast of St Mary Magdalene the aforementioned Egyptian amir, together with his Turks, learned of their advance and did not wait for their great numbers, which he was in no position to resist since his strength was greatly inferior: he struck camp and suddenly withdrew from that locality, heading for Gaza. Thereupon the men of Aleppo pushed through that region in pursuit. The Egyptians moved ahead of them; and finally, when they reached Gaza, and the men of Aleppo were on their heels and drew near that place, the Egyptians took to flight and made across the desert towards Egypt.

This rivalry and warfare, which has lasted until now and still continues, through God's providence, among the enemies of the Christian faith, has proved – and can be in the future – very useful and vital to Christendom, if God so grants. For it is plausibly believed and hoped that if we were to receive reinforcements at once from some quarter, we could win from one of the parties – or perhaps both – a good truce and one that was to the advantage of Christendom. For this reason, it is vital, especially at this moment, that some measure of aid should reach us swiftly and contribute greatly to bringing matters to a head and to the aid and relief of ourselves and the country.

As regards our own situation, we wish you to know that through God's grace we are safe and sound, quartered in the camp at Caesarea-in-Palestine together with the Christian army, and are busy with strengthening the fortifications of that city. And since work on the walls is already for the most part far advanced, we are now making ceaseless efforts day after day with a view to completing the task, by having work done on the walls and the ditches alike.

Lastly, keep us informed of the health of our dearest lady and mother, of your own, of that of our dearest and faithful Charles, Count of Anjou and Provence, and of our dearest sister,[22] of which we constantly aspire to hear favourable reports, and of the news from our country, as often as the chance to send envoys arises.

Dated in the camp near Caesarea-in-Palestine, in the year of the Lord 1251, on the day after that of St Laurence the Martyr.

---

22 Isabelle (d. 1269).

117. Joseph de Cancy[23] *to Walter de St Martin, 6 May 1252, in Matthew Paris,* Chronica Majora, *vol. 6:* Additamenta, *pp. 205–7*[24]

To the venerable, beloved in Christ, Brother Walter de St Martin, [from] Brother Joseph de Cancy, humble treasurer of the holy Order of the Hospital of Jerusalem at Acre: greetings, and may his desires have a happy outcome.

Regarding news from the Holy Land, Your Benevolence should not be unaware that the illustrious King of France has now completed a year's stay at Caesarea-in-Palestine, causing it to be surrounded by a line of walls and ditches, operations that at the time of writing were almost finished. Although envoys have again been frequently despatched to the lord King both by the Sultan of Aleppo and by those who appear for the moment to be in charge and control of Egypt, with a view to negotiating the confirmation of a truce with one another, the King would not agree to any truce with the Sultan of Aleppo; and in the Easter week that has passed he made a truce with the Egyptians for fifteen years, entailing a corporal oath on both sides on the following terms: 'Together with the rest of the prisoners who still survive and whom they promised to hand over in the previous truce when they held the lord King, the said Egyptians have surrendered to the lord King all the territory this side of the River Jordan, [p. 206] whichever Saracen may be in possession, except Gaza, Gibelin,[25] Grand Gérin[26] and Darum, which shall according to the truce remain in Egyptian hands.' It was determined in addition that unless the Egyptians had their troops at Gaza by the middle of the May following the date of this letter, and the King should, by the same date, have led his army from Caesarea to the region of Jaffa, the alliance in the truce should be void.

The Sultan of Aleppo, however, the declared enemy of these Egyptians, was halted at Damascus at the time of writing and occupied the entire territory as far as a locality called Cascy between Gaza and Darum, with 12,000 warriors against the Egyptians and a further 3000 expected to arrive shortly to join these 12,000; while the total strength of the Egyptians did not exceed 6000 or 7000 armed men, part of whom they persisted in keeping back within Egypt in order to guard it against the Bedouin and other natives, and the lord King's forces are not so redoubtable that they could bring timely aid to the Egyptians should it prove necessary, since, even including the hundred knights it was hoped he could recently recruit, he had, between religious and secular warriors, only 200 knights and 400 mounted Turcopoles. For this reason we and very many others feared that the Egyptians would find no means of getting through and thus the aforesaid truce would be worthless.

23 A Hospitaller known from other letters, including one to Edward I in 1282: see W. B. Sanders, 'A Crusader's letter from the Holy Land', in *Palestine Pilgrims' Text Society*, vol. 5/5 (London, 1888), p. 7.

24 Matthew inserts at the head of the letter: 'These reports of circumstances in the Holy Land reached us on the natal feast of St John' [24 June 1252]. He gives a summary of its contents *ad annum* 1252: *Chronica Majora*, vol. 5, pp. 305–6 (trans. Giles, vol. 2, p. 501).

25 Beth Gibelin (to the Muslims: Bayt Jibrīn), at one time a Hospitaller possession.

26 The Muslims' Jinīn.

We wish you furthermore to be aware that the whole of the territory on this side of the sea which is inhabited by Christians – with the exception of Armenia, whose condition is satisfactory, thanks to the truce which the king of that country has made with the Sultan of Iconium[27] – is now in a worse state than we have ever known it. For the land of Antioch, long the scene of the raving savagery of certain infidels known as Turcomans, is completely devastated, with the result that it is feared the city of Antioch itself [p. 207] is in danger of soon being lost and its inhabitants in apprehension are abandoning it and taking flight.[28] Of this wicked race, a band of 10,000 has already advanced as far as a place called Caesarea the Great, where they have pitched their tents in order to stay. They overran our territory of Crac[29] and that of others towards Tripoli, burned many villages, drove off with them 4000 of our bigger [livestock], slaughtered many people and dragged off with them a host of prisoners, before returning to the aforesaid Caesarea the Great. There they are staying, until they have ravaged the entire country unless the Lord is appeased. It is believed that they will move against us in order to help the Sultan of Aleppo, at whose appeal all these things have been perpetrated.

Dated the 2nd Nones of May.[30]

118. Ibn Wāṣil, Mufarrij al-kurūb, *Bibliothèque Nationale, Paris, ms. arabe 1703, fols 92v–98v, 102r–106r, 107v, 108v, 111r*

The army's return to Cairo and new developments After the capture of Damietta, the troops marched to Cairo, which they entered on Thursday 9 Ṣafar [13 May 1250]. The preacher Aṣīl al-Dīn al-Isʿirdī, one of the imams of al-Malik al-Ṣāliḥ (God have mercy on him), travelled to Damascus as an envoy to administer an oath to the amir Jamāl al-Dīn ibn Yaghmūr, the viceroy of Damascus, and the amirs who were with him. There were, among others, a number of al-Ṣāliḥ's mamluks there. When Aṣīl al-Dīn entered Damascus, he required from the amirs an oath to Shajar al-Durr, Khalīl's mother, as Sultan, and to ʿIzz al-Dīn Aybak al-Turkmānī as *atabeg* and commander of the army, and the performance of the *khuṭba* in the name of Khalīl's mother. But Jamāl al-Dīn was rude to him and would not consent to it. Letters had previously gone from the Qaymariyya[31] to Sultan al-Malik al-Nāṣir, the ruler of Aleppo, inviting him to come to them so that they might surrender Damascus to him.

27 This truce between Lesser Armenia and the Seljük Sultanate of Rūm does not appear to be mentioned in other sources.

28 The Franciscan William of Rubruck was to comment on the city's gravely weakened condition in 1255: *Itinerarium*, xxxviii, 18, p. 329 (trans. Jackson and Morgan, p. 275).

29 The celebrated Hospitaller stronghold of Krak des Chevaliers.

30 Matthew adds that this news circulated on the Assumption of the Blessed Mary [15 August 1252], which is at variance with his rubric at the head of the letter.

31 A Kurdish group who had fled from Mesopotamia along with the Khwarazmians in 1244, at the time of the Mongol advance, and had entered Ayyūb's service: Humphreys, *From Saladin to the Mongols*, p. 275; Anne-Marie Eddé, *La principauté ayyoubide d'Alep (579/1183–658/1260)*, Freiburger Islamstudien, 21 (Stuttgart, 1999), pp. 261–3, for greater detail on the leaders.

On Monday, 13 nights having passed of Ṣafar [16 May 1250], robes of honour were given to the amirs in Cairo and maintenance grants bestowed upon them. And on this day news arrived that al-Malik al-Saʿīd ibn al-Malik al-ʿAzīz ʿUthmān ibn al-Malik al-ʿĀdil had seized the money that was to be found in Gaza and had fled. This al-Malik al-Saʿīd used to hold the fortress of al-Ṣubayba, which is near Bānyās, and ruled it following the death of his brother al-Malik al-Qāhir ibn al-Malik al-ʿAzīz, as we have previously said; but subsequently he handed it over to his cousin, Sultan al-Malik al-Ṣāliḥ, who bestowed on him a grant in Egypt.[32] He remained in al-Ṣāliḥ's service until the latter's death, and [then] served his son al-Malik al-Muʿaẓẓam; and when al-Malik al-Muʿaẓẓam was killed at Fāraskūr, al-Malik al-Saʿīd fled to Gaza and did what we have described. A guard was put on his house in Cairo. [fol. 93r] But then al-Malik al-Ṣāliḥ's lieutenants at al-Ṣubayba surrendered it to al-Malik al-Saʿīd, who took possession of it …

How al-Malik al-Mughīth ibn al-Malik al-ʿĀdil ibn al-Malik al-Kāmil took control of Kerak and al-Shawbak When, as we have recounted, the amir Ḥusām al-Dīn ibn Abī ʿAlī learned that Fakhr al-Dīn ibn Shaykh al-Shuyūkh might possibly produce al-Malik al-Mughīth Fatḥ al-Dīn ʿUmar ibn al-Malik al-ʿĀdil ibn al-Kāmil and make him ruler of Egypt (he was with his paternal aunts, the Quṭbī princesses), Ḥusām al-Dīn sent him up into the Jabal fortress and imprisoned him there.[33] When al-Malik al-Muʿaẓẓam arrived at Mansura, he gave orders for him to be taken to al-Shawbak, where he was imprisoned. After al-Malik al-Muʿaẓẓam's murder, the amir Badr al-Dīn al-Ṣawābī al-Ṣāliḥī, who was al-Ṣāliḥ's lieutenant at Kerak and had responsibility for al-Shawbak, made [al-Mughīth] ruler of Kerak and al-Shawbak, while remaining in control of the government …

How Sultan al-Malik al-Nāṣir Ṣalāḥ al-Dīn Yūsuf ibn al-Malik al-ʿAzīz marched on Damascus and took possession of it Sultan al-Malik al-Nāṣir had received a letter from al-Malik al-Muʿaẓẓam in which he announced the good news of his victory over the Franks and his capture of Raydafrans, and the glad tidings were inserted in the sermons. Then, after a few days, came the report that he had been murdered, and this was followed by the arrival of envoys from the Qaymariyya at Damascus, inviting [al-Nāṣir] to join them so that they might surrender Damascus to him. Sultan al-Malik al-Nāṣir left Aleppo to march on Damascus. He arrived there, and the troops surrounded Damascus on Saturday 8 Rabīʿ II [fol. 93v] of this year, namely 648 [9 July 1250].[34] Then he moved against [the city] on Monday 10 Rabīʿ II. The Qaymariyya opened the gate of the city for him, and al-Malik al-Nāṣir and his men entered Damascus and took possession of it without a fight. He gave robes of honour to the amir Jamāl al-Dīn ibn Yaghmūr and the Qaymariyya, and treated them with favour. But he arrested the group of Egyptian mamluk amirs of al-Malik al-Ṣāliḥ, and put them in prison; and his rule over Damascus grew secure. Aṣīl al-Dīn al-Isʿirdī,

---

32 Humphreys, *From Saladin to the Mongols*, p. 292.

33 See Ibn Wāṣil [**doc. 73**], p. 139 above..

34 8 Rabīʿ II was in fact a Sunday [10 July 1250]; compare the date given by Ibn al-ʿAmīd [**doc. 120** below].

the envoy of the Egyptians, was in Damascus, but he offered no resistance, and left for Egypt. Baʿlabakk, ʿAjlūn, Ṣarkhad and Shumaymīsh defied al-Malik al-Nāṣir for a time, but later they all surrendered to him.

When news arrived of al-Malik al-Nāṣir's march from Aleppo to take Damascus, the amirs and the troops assembled at the Jabal fortress and the oath to Khalīl's mother and to the amir ʿIzz al-Dīn al-Turkmānī was administered to them once more. Then the officials set about the troops' departure from Cairo and their march into Syria. That was on Thursday 6 Rabīʿ II [7 July 1250]; and on Wednesday, 12 nights having elapsed of Rabīʿ II [13 July 1250], orders were issued to the amir Ḥusām al-Dīn to proceed into Syria with the troops as their commander. But then news arrived on Sunday, 14 nights remaining of Rabīʿ II [17 July 1250], that al-Malik al-Nāṣir and his forces had encamped before Damascus, and in Cairo there was urgency about the departure of the troops so that they might enter Damascus before al-Malik al-Nāṣir took it and prevent him doing so.

The arrest of a number of amirs in Cairo When Sunday, 9 days remaining of Rabīʿ II [= 23 July 1250], arrived, news reached Cairo that al-Malik al-Nāṣir had occupied Damascus and had taken up residence [fol. 94r] in its citadel; that the Qaymariyya were those who had corresponded with him, invited him in and made him ruler of Damascus, having opened the city's gate for him and surrendered it; and that he had arrested and imprisoned [the Egyptian mamluks'] comrades,[35] the Ṣāliḥiyya amirs. This was painful for the Ṣāliḥiyya and Baḥriyya amirs who were in Cairo, and they came to an agreement to seize and put to death the non-Turkish amirs – the Kurds and others – from fear that they might play the hypocrite towards them, as the Qaymariyya had done in Damascus. A group of mamluks took horse, halted at the house of Sayf al-Dīn al-Qaymarī, seized him and conveyed him to the fortress, where they imprisoned him. Next they seized ʿIzz al-Dīn al-Qaymarī and a number of [other] amirs.[36] Disorder broke out in Cairo, and the amir Ḥusām al-Dīn was afraid for his life.[37] A group of chamberlains came to him and said, 'The amir ʿIzz al-Dīn sends his greetings and informs you that your authority is the same as it was previously, because you were the chief man in the regime of our master al-Malik al-Ṣāliḥ; and so let your mind be at rest, but do not challenge what has happened'. They later seized the qadi Najm al-Dīn ibn Shams, qadi of Nablus, and whoever was suspected of partiality for al-Malik al-Nāṣir…

35 *khushdāshūn*. Strictly speaking, this term denotes slaves (or former slaves) of the same master: see David Ayalon, 'L'esclavage du Mamelouk', *Israel Oriental Notes and Studies*, 1 (1951): 1–66 (here 29–31, 34–7), reprinted in his *The Mamlūk Military Society* (London, 1979). I have translated it, and the noun *khushdāshiyya* used later, as 'comrade[s]' in every case.

36 Named by al-Dhahabī, p. 58, as Sayf al-Dīn al-Qaymarī, Jamāl al-Dīn Hārūn, al-Sharaf al-Shayzarī, al-ʿIzz al-Qaymarī, ʿAlāʾ al-Dīn ibn al-Shihāb, al-Ḥusām ibn al-Qaysī, Quṭb al-Dīn ruler of Āmid, Quṭb al-Dīn ruler of al-Suwaydā, Nāṣir al-Dīn al-Tibnīnī, Shams al-Dīn ibn al-Muʿtamid (who had been in command of the citadel of Damascus), Shams al-Dīn ibn al-Bakā (former governor of Damascus), and al-Shujāʿ the chamberlain (*al-ḥājib*).

37 Since he too was a Kurd.

[fol. 94v] *The conferment of the Sultanate of Egypt on 'Izz al-Dīn al-Turkmānī and his adoption of the title of al-Mu'izz* Following the events we have recounted – the conquest of Damascus by Sultan al-Malik al-Nāṣir and the arrest of certain of the amirs in Cairo – the Baḥriyya and the Turkish amirs assembled and consulted among themselves. They said that it was impossible to defend the country when the ruler was a woman and that there was no alternative to a male ruler. By common consent they agreed to entrust the sovereignty to ʿIzz al-Dīn Aybak al-Turkmānī, and they did so. The name of Shajar al-Durr, Khalīl's mother, was removed [from the *khuṭba*], and [ʿIzz al-Dīn] was styled al-Malik al-Muʿizz.[38] And on Saturday the last day of Rabīʿ II [31 July 1250] al-Malik al-Muʿizz ʿIzz al-Dīn Aybak rode under the royal standards, and the amirs of the state carried the *ghāshiya*[39] in their hands … [fol. 95r] … But towards the end of that day arrived the reports that al-Malik al-Mughīth Fatḥ al-Dīn ʿUmar ibn al-Malik al-ʿĀdil had gained control of Kerak and al-Shawbak and that al-Malik al-Saʿīd ibn al-Malik al-ʿAzīz had gained control of al-Ṣubayba, as we have already described.

The conferment of the Sultanate of Egypt on al-Malik al-Ashraf ibn al-Malik al-Mas'ūd ibn al-Malik al-Kāmil The amirs and the Baḥriyya now met together and agreed that there was no alternative to installing as ruler someone from the Ayyubid dynasty so that all might unite in obeying him. This came about because the amir Fāris al-Dīn Aqṭāy (he commanded the *jamdāriyya* and the Baḥriyya and they looked up to him), the amir Rukn al-Dīn Baybars al-Bunduqdārī (who was to become ruler, as we shall see), Sayf al-Dīn al-Rashīdī and Sunqur al-Rūmī – these were the leading Ṣāliḥī *jamdāriyya* – rejected [the idea] that ʿIzz al-Dīn al-Turkmānī should be Sultan, and preferred that a child from among the Ayyubids should have the royal title while they [themselves] should be in charge of the affairs of state and devour the world in his name … [fol. 95v] al-Malik al-Ashraf Muẓaffar al-Dīn Mūsā ibn Yūsuf ibn Muḥammad ibn Abī Bakr ibn Ayyūb[40] was living in the Ghazalī palace with his paternal aunts, the Quṭbī princesses, the daughters of al-Malik al-ʿĀdil. When the Baḥriyya agreed on the enthronement of a child from among the Ayyubid dynasty, they sent for this boy, invested him with the Sultanate, and appointed al-Malik al-Muʿizz ʿIzz al-Dīn al-Turkmānī as his *atabeg*. [al-Ashraf] was at that time approximately ten years old… This occurred when five days had elapsed of Jumādā I [5 August 1250],[41] five days after the accession of al-Malik al-Muʿizz …

How a group of the military and the amirs agreed to enter the service of al-Malik al-Mughīth, ruler of Kerak, and to put him on the throne, and how their design was

38 Ibn al-ʿAmīd, p. 161, says that Aybak married Shajar al-Durr on this same day, 29 Rabīʿ II. al-Dhahabī, p. 58, dates Aybak's accession on 28 Rabīʿ II [30 July].

39 The ceremonial cushion.

40 Ibn Wāṣil explains (fols 95r–v) that the child's grandfather, al-Malik al-Masʿūd, had been ruler of the Yemen and had died in the lifetime of his father al-Kāmil. His son in turn had died during Sultan Ayyūb's reign. The genealogy given in the rubric above is therefore incorrect

41 According to al-Dhahabī, p. 58, Aybak's resignation and the accession of al-Ashraf occurred on 2 Jumādā I [1 August].

frustrated [fol. 96r] The amir Rukn al-Dīn Khāṣṣ Turk, one of the more exalted of the Ṣāliḥī amirs, had advanced to Gaza, accompanied by a large military force. They were met by the army of al-Malik al-Nāṣir Ṣalāḥ al-Dīn Yūsuf, and retired precipitately before them, falling back in the direction of Egypt and making camp at al-Sanā'ij. At al-Sanā'ij were a group of amirs, who agreed to write to al-Malik al-Mughīth, ruler of Kerak, and they had the *khuṭba* read in his name at al-Ṣāliḥiya on Friday 4 Jumādā II of this year [= 3 September 1250]. So al-Malik al-Muʿizz ordered a proclamation to be made in Cairo and Miṣr that the country belonged to the Caliph al-Mustaʿṣim bi'llāh and that al-Malik al-Muʿizz ʿIzz al-Dīn Aybak was his deputy there. This was on 5 Jumādā II, and on the following day hasty preparations were made to despatch the army to al-Sanā'ij, and the oath to al-Malik al-Ashraf as Sultan and to al-Malik al-Muʿizz as *atabeg* was renewed. On that day there fled from al-Sanā'ij[42] the cavalry officers Shihāb al-Dīn Rashīd the Greater, Shihāb al-Dīn Rashīd the Lesser, Rukn al-Dīn Khāṣṣ Turk and Aqīsh the *musharrif*, who were among those who had agreed to enthrone al-Mughīth ibn al-Malik al-ʿĀdil, ruler of Kerak. But then the slaves[43] of Shihāb al-Dīn Rashīd the Lesser seized him and took him with them to Cairo, where he was imprisoned. The rest gave themselves up. Robes of honour were sent out to those who had taken the oath at al-Sanā'ij, and they were forgiven and were put at their ease; they were [also] sent the wherewithal to maintain themselves. And when it was Thursday 10 Jumādā II [= 9 September 1250], al-Ashraf Muẓaffar al-Dīn Mūsā rode forth with the royal banners, with al-Malik al-Muʿizz accompanying him on horseback and the amirs carrying the *ghāshiya* for him, each one in turn, until they went up into the citadel. On Sunday 10 [fol. 96v] Rajab [= 9 October 1250] the amir Fāris al-Dīn Aqṭāy, commander of the *jamdāriyya* and the Baḥriyya, set out for Syria with an army of 1000 horsemen. He reached Gaza, where there was a corps of al-Malik al-Nāṣir's men. He fell on them, and they fled precipitately before him ...[44]

[fol. 97r] In the latter part of Rajab of this year [mid-to-late October 1250] Fāris al-Dīn Aqṭāy returned from Gaza to al-Ṣāliḥiya, where he halted before arriving in Cairo on 4 Shaʿbān [1 November 1250]. On the next day Zayn al-Dīn, the Ṣāliḥī *amīr-jāndār* and one of the great men of the Ṣāliḥī regime, was arrested and imprisoned. Similarly [fol. 97v] the qadi Ṣadr al-Dīn, known as the qadi of Āmid, was arrested: he was prominent in the regime of al-Malik al-Ṣāliḥ and was a relative of Shams al-Dīn, qadi of Nablus ...[45]

How Sultan al-Malik al-Nāṣir fell ill in Damascus and [then] recovered When Sultan al-Malik al-Nāṣir gained possession of Damascus, he resolved to move with his army against Egypt with a view to conquering it. This was not, as far as I learned, his own notion. Rather, the amir Shams al-Dīn Lu'lu' al-Amīnī,[46] who directed his government,

---

42 Ibn ʿAbd al-Raḥīm (fol. 376v) reads al-Ṣāliḥiya.

43 *ghilmān*.

44 Here follows an account of the removal of al-Ṣāliḥ Ayyūb's coffin to Cairo.

45 There follows an account of the destruction of Damietta by the Egyptian government, in order that it might not again afford a base for the Franks.

46 A slave of Armenian origin, who had risen to be one of al-Nāṣir Yūsuf's amirs: see Eddé, *La principauté ayyoubide d'Alep*, pp. 273–4.

put pressure on him and egged him on to do it, belittling the condition of the Egyptian army and making light of the enterprise. 'If you advance on Egypt,' he told him, 'you will win over to yourself all its troops and the country will be reduced without a struggle.' And so he decided to head a campaign there.

al-Malik al-Nāṣir had sent the lord Kamāl al-Dīn ʿUmar ibn Abī'l-Ḥarāda, known as Ibn al-ʿAdīm,[47] as envoy to al-Malik al-Muʿaẓẓam when the latter was at Mansura. Having set out, Kamāl al-Dīn learned en route of the defeat of the Franks; and when he reached Fāqūs he heard that al-Malik al-Muʿaẓẓam had been murdered. He reached the army headquarters and entered Cairo, where he took up residence and had discussions with a number of amirs regarding their sympathy towards his master Sultan al-Malik al-Nāṣir. They came to an agreement about this, and promised him that they would assist in [al-Malik al-Nāṣir's] victory. He was asked on behalf of al-Malik al-Muʿizz, 'Tell us what you have brought with you on your embassy'. He displayed the letter that he had brought with him, and said, 'My embassy was to a man who has died, and the letter was for him: I did not bring it on an embassy to you.' [al-Malik al-Muʿizz] dismissed him with a robe of honour, and he returned to Damascus, which he reached prior to the arrival of al-Malik al-Nāṣir. He was detained there for some days, but was then released and travelled to Aleppo. The Qaymariyya amirs had written to al-Malik al-Nāṣir summoning him to Damascus …[fol. 98v] Then al-Malik al-Nāṣir reached Damascus, which he took through the Qaymariyya opening the gate for him to enter, as we have related. While al-Malik al-Nāṣir was planning to move on Egypt, he was afflicted by a grave illness. It brought him to the point of death, and people almost despaired of his life. Accompanying him were al-Malik al-Ṣāliḥ ʿImād al-Dīn Ismaʿīl ibn al-Malik al-ʿĀdil[48] and al-Malik al-Nāṣir Dā'ūd. It is reported that, at the time when there was despair of al-Malik al-Nāṣir Yūsuf's life, al-Malik al-Nāṣir [Dā'ūd] endeavoured to secure his own possession of Damascus, and this was the reason why al-Malik al-Nāṣir Yūsuf turned against him, to the point of imprisoning him, as we shall relate, Almighty God willing. al-Malik al-Nāṣir Yūsuf (God have mercy on him) subsequently recovered from his illness in the latter part of Shaʿbān of this year [second half of November 1250] …[49]

[fol. 102r] *How Sultan al-Malik al-Nāṣir Ṣalāḥ al-Dīn Yūsuf advanced on Egypt with his forces in order to conquer it* When al-Malik al-Nāṣir recovered his health, the amir Shams al-Dīn Lu'lu' began [again] to instigate him to attack and conquer Egypt. And so he set out from Damascus with his army on the march towards Egypt. The date of his departure was Sunday mid-Ramaḍān of this year, namely 648 [11 December 1250] … Sultan al-Malik al-Manṣūr (may God purify his soul), the ruler of Ḥamā, had sent reinforcements to al-Malik al-Nāṣir, and they marched with him; and there marched with him also al-Malik al-Ashraf Muẓaffar al-Dīn Mūsā ibn al-Malik al-Manṣūr, the

47 The celebrated historian of Aleppo (d. 1262): see B. Lewis, 'Ibn al-ʿAdīm', *EI*².

48 The former ruler of Damascus (1239–45).

49 Here lengthy poems by Shaykh Sharaf al-Dīn ʿAbd al-ʿAzīz ibn Muḥammad al-Anṣārī and by Bahā' al-Dīn Zuhayr, former head of al-Ṣāliḥ Ayyūb's secretariat, congratulating al-Nāṣir Yūsuf on his recovery, are followed by an account of the incarceration of al-Nāṣir Dā'ūd at Ḥimṣ.

ruler of Ḥimṣ, in whose possession at that time were Tall Bāshir, al-Raḥba and Tadmur; al-Malik al-Muʿaẓẓam Fakhr al-Dīn Tūrān Shāh ibn al-Malik al-Nāṣir Ṣalāḥ al-Dīn and his brother, Nuṣrat al-Dīn; of the sons of al-Malik al-Nāṣir Dā'ūd, al-Malik al-Ẓāhir Shādī and al-Malik al-Amjad Ḥasan; and other princes of the dynasty. His troops were under the command of the amir Shams al-Dīn Lu'lu' al-Amīnī, who, as we have described, was the prime mover behind the expedition and its chief instigator, since he believed that the enterprise would be easy, that most of the Egyptian troops would go over to him and that the remainder would not stand their ground at all… The expedition was not the brainchild of al-Malik al-Nāṣir, for he inclined towards conciliation and did not approve of confrontation. [fol. 102v] On this campaign he was like one disgusted by it.

al-Malik al-Nāṣir moved through the coastal regions at the head of a mighty army, [including] his mamluks, the Nāṣiriyya, and those of his father, the ʿAzīziyya.[50] These were a large group of Turks, and some of them were hostile towards the commander of the army, Shams al-Dīn Lu'lu', from what I learned, because of the way he conducted himself towards them, spurning them and displaying no concern about them. At heart they were inclined towards the Turks in Egypt, for this reason and through racial solidarity;[51] and we shall describe what happened, Almighty God willing.

When news reached Egypt of the advance of Sultan al-Malik al-Nāṣir, al-Malik al-Muʿizz and the Baḥriyya who were with him were alarmed and assembled in order to meet al-Malik al-Nāṣir, do battle with him [fol. 103r] and repel him from the country. A number of amirs were arrested under suspicion of favouring al-Malik al-Nāṣir. Their arrest occurred on Wednesday 2 Shawwāl [28 December 1250], and on that same day al-Malik al-Nāṣir arrived with his forces at Gaza, where he took up his position. al-Malik al-Muʿizz issued orders to the Egyptian troops to prepare for an engagement. The following day false rumours multiplied, and instructions were given to bring up the livestock from the spring [pastures]. On Monday 8 Shawwāl [= 2 January 1251], which corresponded to 2 Kānūn II,[52] the amir Ḥusām al-Dīn ibn [Abī] ʿAlī and the rest were ordered to go forth from Cairo. On Tuesday 9 Shawwāl the amir Fāris al-Dīn Aqṭāy the *jamdār*, commander of the Baḥriyya and the *jamdāriyya*, emerged with a great mass of troops and advanced towards Syria. He halted at al-Sanā'ij in al-Ṣāliḥiya. The amir Ḥusām al-Dīn came forth as far as Mashhad al-Taban [?], and then on Thursday 11 Shawwāl [= 5 January 1251] he reached al-Ṣāliḥiya, where he too made camp. On Saturday 13 Shawwāl [= 7 January 1251] al-Malik al-Muʿizz appointed as viceroy in Egypt the amir ʿAlā' al-Dīn al-Bunduqdār …

On this day [27 Shawwāl = 22 January] false reports multiplied that al-Malik al-Nāṣir had halted with the Syrian army at Dārūm and that he was intending to enter the desert. On Monday 29 Shawwāl [= 23 January 1251] al-Malik al-Muʿizz

---

50 Named after their master, al-Nāṣir Yūsuf's father and predecessor at Aleppo, al-ʿAzīz Muḥammad (d. 1236): see Eddé, *La principauté ayyoubide d'Alep*, pp. 274–6.

51 *li'l-jinsiyya.*

52 A rare reference by Ibn Wāṣil to the Syrian/Coptic Christian calendar: Kānūn II is January. Ibn ʿAbd al-Raḥīm (fol. 381r) has Kānūn I [December] in error.

presented robes of honour to al-Malik al-Manṣūr Nūr al-Dīn Maḥmūd ibn al-Malik al-Ṣāliḥ ʿImād al-Dīn Ismaʿīl and his brother al-Malik al-Saʿīd ʿAbd al-Malik, who had both been under arrest since the days of al-Malik al-Ṣāliḥ Najm al-Dīn, as we said earlier. He did this in order to arouse suspicion that their father al-Malik al-Ṣāliḥ, who was with al-Malik al-Nāṣir, was secretly in league with al-Malik [fol. 103v] al-Muʿizz and the Baḥriyya and that this would alienate al-Malik al-Nāṣir from him. And on Tuesday 1 Dhū'l-Qaʿda [= 24 January 1251] there was announced the conclusion of a peace between al-Malik al-Mughīth Fatḥ al-Dīn ʿUmar ibn al-Malik al-ʿĀdil, the ruler of Kerak, and al-Malik al-Muʿizz and the Baḥriyya. Here too the purpose was to mislead al-Malik al-Nāṣir so that when he learned of this he would hesitate to enter the desert. On Thursday 3 Dhū'l-Qaʿda [= 26 January 1251] al-Malik al-Muʿizz moved with the rest of the Egyptian army to al-Ṣāliḥiya, where the whole of the Egyptian forces were united. al-Malik al-Ashraf Muẓaffar al-Dīn Mūsā remained as Sultan in the citadel.

On Saturday 5 Dhū'l-Qaʿda [= 28 January 1251] the news came in that Sultan al-Malik al-Nāṣir had arrived at Qaṭayyā, and on Monday 7 Dhū'l-Qaʿda [= 30 January 1251] Sultan al-Malik al-Nāṣir and his forces reached Kurāʿ, which is in the vicinity of al-ʿAbbāsa and al-Darīr [?]. The two armies were now close to one another. The notion had gained hold of their minds that the Syrian army would be victorious in view of their numbers and the secret partiality towards them of some of the Egyptian troops. al-Malik al-Nāṣir was accompanied, as we have described, by a numerous corps of the mamluks of his father al-Malik al-ʿAzīz and also of his own mamluks. The majority of them secretly favoured the Turks who were from Egypt by reason of their racial solidarity and their dislike of the amir Shams al-Dīn Lu'lu', who was in charge of the government, as we have previously mentioned. We shall describe what transpired.

The rout of the Syrian forces and the withdrawal of Sultan al-Malik al-Nāṣir to Damascus When al-Malik al-Nāṣir halted at Kurāʿ, al-Malik al-Muʿizz advanced from al-Ṣāliḥiya with the Egyptian forces and made camp at Samūṭ, facing al-Malik al-Nāṣir. On Thursday 10 Dhū'l-Qaʿda [= 2 February 1251] the Syrian army mounted. The right and left wings, the centre and the two flanks were drawn up, and the Egyptian forces [fol. 104r] were drawn up similarly. The two armies approached one another, and then the battle began during the fourth hour of this day. The Syrian forces launched a formidable charge against the Egyptian troops, who were shattered and turned in flight, capable of doing nothing. The Syrian troops followed on their heels. But al-Malik al-Muʿizz, with a small force of Baḥriyya, among others, stood his ground and withdrew to one side. He had decided to flee, it is alleged, to the neighbourhood of al-Shawbak, and with him the amir Fāris al-Dīn Aqṭāy.

al-Malik al-Nāṣir remained beneath the royal standards at the head of a small force. The movement of troops created a distance between him and his forces who were pursuing the fleeing Egyptians, until they were far away from him, and on the heels of the fugitives they reached al-ʿAbbāsa, where they pitched Sultan al-Malik al-Nāṣir's pavilion. They had no knowledge of what was happening to their rear. The amir Ḥusām al-Dīn ibn Abī ʿAlī (God have mercy on him) told me that at the moment of the [Syrian] charge his horse collapsed under him and he fell to the ground. A soldier found him on the ground and helped him to remount, saying, 'There is no doubt that the Egyptians are completely routed and that they are no longer able to put up any further resistance'. 'I saw a squadron halted not far from me', said [Ḥusām al-Dīn], 'and I made towards them and saw that their colours were those of the Egyptians. And when I drew near them, I found al-Malik al-Muʿizz and Fāris al-Dīn Aqṭāy, accompanied by a small force totalling not more than 70 horsemen. I greeted al-Malik al-Muʿizz and Fāris al-Dīn and took up my position with them. al-Malik al-Muʿizz asked me, "Do you see that group there in front of you?" I replied that I did. "That", he said, "is al-Malik al-Nāṣir and his troops, beneath the standards."' Then [said Ḥusām al-Dīn] al-Malik al-Muʿizz and the Turks with him charged at the squadron that included the Sultan, who turned in flight towards Syria. His standards were broken; what he had with him was plundered; some [of his men] were taken prisoner and others gave themselves up; while some of the ʿAzīziyya joined forces with [fol. 104v] al-Malik al-Muʿizz.

The pursuit of the Egyptian troops by the Syrian army and their abandonment of the Sultan, alone with just a small force, came about through the mismanagement of Shams al-Dīn Lu'lu'. It was his duty, when the Egyptians turned [in flight], to restrain the troops from moving far from al-Malik al-Nāṣir, so that they advanced to the halting-place to take up position there and then set out [back] on the next day in full strength. Had events only followed this course, they would most certainly have conquered the country. But what God wills and ordains is not to be resisted. That day were captured al-Malik al-Ṣāliḥ ʿImād al-Dīn Ismaʿīl; al-Malik al-Ashraf, ruler of Ḥimṣ; al-Malik al-Muʿaẓẓam Tūrān Shāh ibn Ṣalāḥ al-Dīn; and his brother Nuṣrat al-Dīn. The amir Shams al-Dīn Lu'lu' was told of al-Malik al-Nāṣir's flight, and said, 'This will not disadvantage us when we have been victorious: he will rejoin us, since he has conquered the country.' Shams al-Dīn had a number of troops with him; and when al-Malik al-Nāṣir took flight, Shams al-Dīn Lu'lu' saw [it ?]. al-Malik al-Muʿizz had returned with a body of troops. [Shams al-Dīn] underestimated them and wanted to attack them. 'Leave them be,' he was told; 'we have no need to fight them.' 'We have no choice but to attack them', he said, and fell upon them. They fought back, and routed the force that accompanied Shams al-Dīn, capturing him and the amir Ḍiyā' al-Dīn al-Qaymarī. Shams al-Dīn was brought before al-Malik al-Muʿizz, who ordered him to be beheaded ... When Ḍiyā' al-Dīn al-Qaymarī was brought in, he was [also] beheaded ...

[fol. 105r] As for the Egyptian troops who had fled, they continued to flee and had no inkling of what had happened since. They reached Cairo on the following day, which was Friday, while some of them fled towards Upper Egypt. The main part of the Syrian army made camp at al-ʿAbbāsa, where they remained. One of al-Malik al-Nāṣir's amirs who were with them was the amir Jamāl al-Dīn Ibn Yaghmūr. Their only idea was that the Egyptians had been routed and that their fortunes were completely at an end. But then the news reached them of al-Malik al-Nāṣir's flight, the killing of Shams al-Dīn Lu'lu' and of Ḍiyā' al-Dīn al-Qaymarī, and the capture of the princes, among others. Their opinions varied as to their [next] objective. Some of them advised entering Cairo: if they once entered the city, it would be theirs, for al-Malik al-Muʿizz did not have a large force and the majority of the Baḥriyya and others had scattered in all directions.[53] [If they had entered Cairo, they would have taken possession of the Jabal citadel and the Jazīra citadel and both cities. Others among them advised retreat.] Among them was Tāj al-Mulūk ibn al-Malik al-Muʿaẓẓam ibn Ṣalāḥ al-Dīn, who was wounded [and died of his wounds. Had Shams al-Dīn Lu'lu' not been killed but been with them, he would have entered Cairo at their head.] They stayed overnight at al-ʿAbbāsa. Most of the ʿAzīziyya and Nāṣiriyya had gone over to al-Malik al-Muʿizz. Their commander, who has been mentioned, was the amir Jamāl al-Dīn Aydughdī al-ʿAzīzī, who swore to me that he joined al-Malik al-Muʿizz only after he had learned of al-Malik al-Nāṣir's flight. This engagement was one of the strangest and most unusual of all battles …[54]

[fol. 105v] *The events that occurred in Cairo on the day of the battle* When the day following the battle arrived, which was Friday 11 Dhū'l-Qaʿda [= 3 February 1251], the fugitives from the Egyptian army reached Cairo, following on each other's heels and with dejected faces. Some of them went into hiding in Cairo, and some [fol. 106r] fled on into Upper Egypt. The populace of the two cities, Cairo and Miṣr, were convinced that al-Malik al-Nāṣir was master of Egypt and did not doubt that al-Malik al-Muʿizz and those with him had fled. The *khuṭba* was read for al-Malik al-Nāṣir in the Jabal citadel and likewise in the mosque of ʿAmr ibn al-ʿĀṣ[55] in the city of Miṣr. But in Cairo the *khuṭba* was not made in the mosque; they suspended it until they discovered the truth of the matter … And one hour after the prayers had ended, reports came that al-Malik al-Muʿizz and the Baḥriyya were victorious and that al-Malik al-Nāṣir had fled. The good news was made public, and some troops arrived, bringing Nuṣrat al-Dīn ibn Ṣalāḥ al-Dīn, who was taken up into the citadel and incarcerated there. In the citadel were Nāṣir al-Dīn Ibn Yaghmūr, major-domo to al-Malik al-Ṣāliḥ Ismaʿīl, and Amīn al-Dawla, the latter's vizier; the two of them had been prisoners there since the days of al-Malik al-Ṣāliḥ Najm al-Dīn (God have mercy on him). When they had learned of the rout of the Egyptians, they had emerged from their cells and publicly rejoiced, issuing orders and prohibitions. But then, when the news came of al-Malik al-Nāṣir's flight and the Egyptians' victory, they were returned to prison …

al-Malik al-Muʿizz and those with him, the Baḥriyya and those of the ʿAzīziyya and Nāṣiriyya who had joined them after deserting their master, marched towards Cairo by a route that avoided al-ʿAbbāsa, from fear of the troops of Aleppo who were encamped there. They reached Cairo early in the morning of Saturday 12 Dhū'l-Qaʿda [= 4 February 1251] and made their entry …[56]

53 The two short passages in square brackets that follow within this paragraph are taken from Ibn ʿAbd al-Raḥīm (fol. 383r), since ms. arabe 1703 appears to be incomplete at this point, omitting to mention the second opinion that was expressed among al-Nāṣir Yūsuf's troops.

54 Ibn Wāṣil proceeds to describe two similarly bizarre engagements, one from the ninth century, and the other, involving the rulers of Irbil and Mosul, from the thirteenth.

55 The Arab conqueror of Egypt in 640–42, and its first caliphal governor.

56 Here follow accounts of the killing of Nāṣir al-Dīn Ibn Yaghmūr, Amīn al-Dawla and their master al-Ṣāliḥ Ismaʿīl, together with an obituary of the latter prince.

[fol. 107v] On Saturday 27 Dhū'l-Ḥijja [22 March 1251],[57] the amir Fāris al-Dīn Aqṭāy the *jamdār* advanced at the head of 3000 horsemen to Gaza, which he occupied together with the neighbouring district. He then returned to Cairo. Sultan al-Malik al-Nāṣir returned to Damascus, and his associates and his troops followed in close succession …[58]

[fol. 108v] In this year [649 = 1251–52], al-Malik al-Nāṣir's troops took up a position at Tall al-ʿAjūl, to do battle with the Egyptians. Command of the army was given to the amir Sayf al-Dīn Baktūt, major-domo[59] to al-Malik al-Nāṣir. al-Malik al-Muʿizz and Fāris al-Dīn Aqṭāy thereupon set out with the Egyptian army and made camp at al-Ṣāliḥiya, facing the Syrian troops. But the shaykh, the Imam Najm al-Dīn ʿAbd-Allāh ibn Muḥammad al-Bādarāʾī arrived from the Caliph al-Mustaʿṣim bi'llāh with the aim of making peace between al-Malik al-Nāṣir and the Egyptians. He passed backwards and forwards from Damascus to Egypt and from Egypt to Syria in order to make peace between them. When the year [649] came to an end, this was still the situation …[60]

[fol. 111r] The year 650 [1252–53] began. The army of al-Malik al-Nāṣir, under the amir Sayf al-Dīn Baktūt the *ustād-dār*, was encamped at Tall al-ʿAjūl, while the Egyptian army was encamped at al-Ṣāliḥiya, facing the army of Damascus; and Najm al-Bādarāʾī passed to and fro on embassies between them. Circumstances remained the same, without peace being arranged between them, when this year continued until its completion. The year 651 [1253–54] began, and the situation was as we have described; but in this year peace was established and an agreement made that al-Malik al-Muʿizz and the Baḥriyya should have Egypt, Gaza and Jerusalem, while the rest of Syria should belong to al-Malik al-Nāṣir. An alliance was sworn on these terms. al-Malik al-Muʿizz, Fāris al-Dīn Aqṭāy and the troops re-entered Cairo, and al-Malik al-Muʿaẓẓam Fakhr al-Dīn Tūrān Shāh ibn Ṣalāḥ al-Dīn, his brother Nuṣrat al-Dīn, and al-Malik al-Ashraf Muẓaffar al-Dīn Mūsā ibn al-Malik al-Manṣūr, the ruler of Ḥimṣ, were released from confinement and made their way to Syria.

119. Sibṭ Ibn al-Jawzī, Mirʾāt al-zamān, *vol. 8/2, pp. 779–81, 785, 789*

In this year [648/1250] the son of al-Malik al-ʿAzīz, ruler of Bānyās,[61] arrived in flight from Egypt, having been banished by Tūrān Shāh. When he reached Damascus, he went to ʿAzzatā, where he was detained. At the beginning of Rabīʿ II [July 1250] al-Malik al-Nāṣir Yūsuf ibn al-Malik al-ʿAzīz, ruler of Aleppo, arrived at Qārā in his design on Damascus. Jamāl al-Dīn ibn Yaghmūr and the Qaymariyya sent word to ʿAzzatā, and they brought al-Malik al-ʿAzīz's son to Damascus and installed

57 This was actually a Wednesday.

58 Here follows an account of various embassies headed by Kamāl al-Dīn Ibn al-ʿAdīm on al-Nāṣir Yūsuf's behalf.

59 *ustād-dār*.

60 There follow obituaries of men who died in this year, some verses by Jamāl al-Dīn Ibn Maṭrūḥ (who was among them), and an account of the pilgrimage made by Ḥusām al-Dīn ibn Abī ʿAlī to Mecca, accompanied by the author.

61 The former Ayyubid ruler of al-Ṣubayba, al-Saʿīd Ḥasan: see above, pages 205, 214.

him in the house of Farrukhshāh. The Aleppan army reached al-Quṣayr and took up position there. They moved to Dārayyā on Sunday 7 Rabīʿ II [9 July 1250], and on Monday 8 Rabīʿ II they marched up to the Lesser Gate. Nāṣir al-Dīn al-Qaymarī had been entrusted with it,[62] and al-Mujāhid Ibrāhīm was in the citadel. When [the Aleppan forces] arrived at the two gates, the locks were broken from within, and the gates were opened. They entered and plundered the houses of Jamāl al-Dīn ibn Yaghmūr and Sayf al-Dīn al-Mushidd and of the troops of Egypt and Damascus. Their property was seized, whether their stables or money or furnishings from their houses. Ibn Yaghmūr entered the citadel, but then an amnesty was proclaimed. [p. 780] The era of al-Ṣāliḥ Ayyūb[63] at Damascus was finished: his second reign had lasted five years minus a few days.

Then al-Malik al-Nāṣir entered the citadel, and the people's spirits recovered and they were not anxious about a single thing. al-Malik al-Nāṣir Dā'ūd was stationed at al-ʿUqayba, and al-Malik al-ʿAzīz came and stayed with him that night. al-ʿAzīz's son fled to al-Ṣubayba. One of his eunuchs, to whom he had written, was there, and when he arrived [the eunuch] let him in and he entered. al-Malik al-Nāṣir took Baʿlabakk from al-Ḥumaydī, and Buṣrā and Ṣarkhad, among other places …

In this year died Jamāl al-Dīn ibn Yaghmūr at al-ʿAbbāsa.[64] Carrier pigeons were sent to al-Malik al-Nāṣir, and preparations were made for him to stay there. al-Malik al-Nāṣir was on the way to Kurāʿ, and he was not informed of this. He was stationed with his standards, his kinsmen and his followers. When the Egyptians suffered [p. 781] defeat, ʿIzz al-Dīn Aybak al-Turkmānī and Aqṭāy were in headlong flight towards Syria with 300 horsemen. En route they came upon al-Shams Lu'lu' and al-Ḍiyā' al-Qaymarī.[65] Shams al-Dīn Lu'lu' charged towards them, and they fell upon him and took him prisoner. They killed Ḍiyā' al-Dīn al-Qaymarī, and handed over Shams al-Dīn Lu'lu' to ʿIzz al-Dīn al-Turkmānī.[66] I was told that Ḥusām al-Dīn ibn Abī ʿAlī said, 'Do not kill him, so that we may conquer Syria through him'. But Aqṭāy said, 'This is the man who would gain victory with 200 veiled women.[67] He

62 al-Jazarī, *Ḥawādith al-zamān*, fol. 121r, and al-Dhahabī, p. 56, who otherwise follow the Sibṭ here, seem to have had access to a better text, since they state that Ḍiyā' al-Dīn al-Qaymarī was in charge of the Lesser Gate, while Nāṣir al-Dīn al-Qaymarī had been entrusted with the Jābiya Gate.

63 al-Jazarī, fol. 121v, adds 'and the line of al-ʿĀdil', which surely makes more sense.

64 The printed edition is extremely corrupt at this point, rendering it impossible to understand the sequence of events. Again al-Jazarī, fols 121v–122r, and al-Dhahabī, p. 59, appear to be following a fuller text. The version they give is that the Egyptians were routed and that in response the following day the *khuṭba* was read in Cairo, in the citadel, and throughout Egypt in al-Nāṣir Yūsuf's name; Ibn Yaghmūr, who was with al-Nāṣir's advance forces, took up his quarters at al-ʿAbbāsa and was endeavouring to notify the Sultan of this victory. al-Dhahabī, p. 62, also refers to the reading of the *khuṭba* for al-Nāṣir; and cf. Ibn Wāṣil [**doc. 118**], p. 222 above.

65 al-Dhahabī, p. 59, adds *'alā ghayr ta'bi'a*, 'unprepared'.

66 The text has ʿIzz al-Dīn Lu'lu' in error. I have reconstructed this passage with the aid of al-Dhahabī, p. 60.

67 This boast by Lu'lu' is not previously mentioned in the printed text of the Sibṭ's work, but is found in the account given by al-Nuwayrī, vol. 29, p. 377; Eddé, *La principauté*

took us for effeminates!' And they cut off his head, and prevented the Sultan from demanding him.

Some of the ʿAzīziyya, [al-Nāṣir's] father's mamluks, betrayed him, and a number of them went over to ʿIzz al-Dīn and Aqṭāy, saying, '[Move] to where the Sultan is stationed'. They fell upon[68] the division, and the ʿAzīziyya shattered the Sultan's standards, broke open his coffers, plundered his property, and fired arrows at him. Nawfal al-Badawī[69] and a group of his mamluks and attendants seized him and made off with him to Syria. The Egyptians fell upon al-Malik al-Muʿaẓẓam Tūrān Shāh ibn Ṣalāḥ al-Dīn, and took him prisoner, after they had wounded him.[70] They wounded [also] his son, Tāj al-Mulūk, and captured his brother al-Nuṣrat, al-Ashraf the son of the ruler of Ḥimṣ, [the latter's] uncle al-Ẓāhir, al-Ṣāliḥ Ismaʿīl, and Aleppan leaders. Tāj al-Mulūk ibn al-Muʿaẓẓam died of the wounds he had received: they conveyed him to Jerusalem, where he died ...[71]

[p. 785] *The year 649* [*1250–51*] In this year al-Malik al-Nāṣir Ṣalāḥ al-Dīn withdrew from Gaza, the coastlands and Nablus, and governed the country according to the principles of the Sharīʿa. al-Malik al-Nāṣir made ready his forces which had come to his assistance, and the Turks retreated into Egypt. The troops remained at Gaza for two years and some months, while envoys passed to and fro between them. The year ended with what will be [related] subsequently.

In this year al-ʿĀdil's son[72] seized Kerak and al-Shawbak, which had been handed over to him by the cavalry officer.[73] Aqṭāy had left Cairo with 1000 horsemen and had encamped at Gaza ...

In this year the Turks demolished Damietta and carried its gates off to Cairo. They [also] destroyed the Jazīra [citadel], and it is said that they abandoned it ...

[p. 789] *The year 651 [1253–54]* In this year Najm al-Dīn al-Bādarāʾī intervened between the two armies and engineered a settlement for the parties. The fighting had hit both sides [hard],[74] especially the Syrian army, but Almighty God upholds Islam and its affairs proceed along the most magnificent lines. al-Bādarāʾī and al-Niẓām ibn al-Mawlā went to Cairo, and the ruler and the amirs took an oath and released the amirs al-Muʿaẓẓam, his brother al-Nuṣrat, the son of the ruler of Ḥimṣ and the others, al-Ashraf's daughter and the sons of al-Ṣāliḥ Ismaʿīl.

---

ayyoubide d'Alep, p. 151, n.200. Strictly speaking, *qināʿ* denotes a woman's headgear.

68 Reading, with al-Jazarī, fol. 122r, *ʿaṭafū* for the *qaṭaʿū* of the text.

69 al-Jazarī gives him the additional *nisba* of al-Zubaydī.

70 Reading here and in the next line *ajraḥūhū* for the *akhrajūhū* of the printed text: al-Jazarī has the simple form *jaraḥūhū* twice. This was al-Muʿaẓẓam Tūrān Shāh, a son of Saladin. He commanded Aleppo for al-Nāṣir Yūsuf at the time of the Mongol invasion in 1260.

71 al-Jazarī, who otherwise follows the Sibṭ's wording, states that Tāj al-Mulūk was conveyed to Jerusalem while dying and that Ḥusām al-Dīn al-Qaymarī, who was also wounded, died there. There follows at this juncture the passage concerning Tūrān Shāh's murder, translated above [**doc. 74(i)**].

72 al-Mughīth ʿUmar.

73 Named in other sources as Badr al-Dīn al-Ṣawābī al-Ṣāliḥī.

74 Read *ḍarabat* for the meaningless *ḍarasat* of the text.

120. Ibn al-'Amīd (al-Makīn ibn Jirjīs), Kitāb al-Majmūʿ al-mubārak, *ed. Claude Cahen, 'La "Chronique des Ayyoubides" d'al-Makīn b. al-'Amīd',* BEO, *15 (1955–57): 161–4* passim

The beginning of the regime of the Turks and their dominance over Egypt: the first of their rulers, 'Izz al-Dīn Aybak al-Turkmānī al-Ṣāliḥī He began to reign over Egypt on Saturday 29 Rabīʿ II 648 [31 July 1250]. They set up alongside him in the government[75] al-Malik al-Ashraf ibn Ṣalāḥ al-Dīn ibn al-Malik Masʿūd ibn al-Malik al-Kāmil, who was at that time six years old. Diplomas and decrees were written in the names of the two rulers, but al-Muʿizz [ʿIzz al-Dīn Aybak] was in control of the country and its administration. The child [associated] with him had nothing but the title; and after a time [Aybak] placed him in confinement and assumed sole rule.

[The historian][76] says: In this year al-Malik al-Nāṣir Ṣalāḥ al-Dīn Yūsuf ibn al-Malik al-ʿAzīz, ruler of Aleppo, attacked Damascus with his army. He reached it on Sunday 8 Rabīʿ II [10 July 1250], and took control of it at the behest of the Qaymariyya amirs. This came about because the viceroy there, the amir Jamāl al-Dīn Mūsā ibn Yaghmūr, entered into an agreement with the Ṣāliḥī mamluk amirs, and they made common cause. The Qaymariyya feared for their lives, and wrote to al-Nāṣir, the ruler of Aleppo, to come and take Damascus, posing as a condition that their stipends should be increased. al-Nāṣir advanced, and arrived early in the morning of the aforementioned Sunday. The amir Ḍiyā' al-Dīn al-Qaymarī opened to them the Lesser Gate, which had been entrusted to his charge, and his judgement was shared by his followers. That day the Aleppan forces entered Damascus by this gate and took control of it without bloodshed. al-Nāṣir took up his quarters in the tent that had been set up for him in the Green Hippodrome,[77] where he waited for some days until the astrologers chose the day for him to make his way to the citadel of Damascus and take control of it, its treasury [p. 162] and the goods it contained. He arrested Jamāl al-Dīn ibn Yaghmūr, but then released him from confinement and treated him with favour. He [also] arrested a number of Ṣāliḥī mamluk amirs, and subsequently despatched them to [various] fortresses. He conferred their stipends on the Qaymariyya amirs in addition to what they already had, in accordance with the agreement between them; he gave them robes of honour and made over sums of money to them …

In this year, namely 648 [1250–51], al-Nāṣir, the ruler of Aleppo, decided to attack Egypt at the prompting of the *atabeg* Shams al-Dīn Lu'lu' and with the agreement of the Qaymariyya amirs. He made ready and set out with his army for Egypt. al-Muʿizz, the ruler of Egypt, came forth with the Egyptian army, and they met at al-Kurāʿ,[78] near al-Khashabī in the desert, and fought a bitter engagement. Initially the battle went against the Egyptians, and the majority fled towards Cairo and Miṣr and, from what we have been told, they went as far as Upper Egypt. But at that juncture

75 Not immediately, but five days later, and in fact Aybak was at that point demoted to be merely the child Sultan's *atabeg*: see Ibn Wāṣil [**doc. 118**], p. 216 above..

76 Ibn al-ʿAmīd's source is unidentified.

77 *al-Maydān al-akhḍar*.

78 A village near al-ʿAbbāsa.

a number of the ʿAzīziyya, the mamluks of al-Nāṣir's father, abandoned his service and, with their squadrons and their retinues, went over to al-Muʿizz and entered into obedience to him: these were Jamāl al-Dīn Aydughdī al-ʿAzīzī, Shams al-Dīn al-Turkī, Shams al-Dīn Āqūsh al-Ḥusāmī and a number of others. They advised [al-Muʿizz] to attack al-Nāṣir's standards in the hope that they might overwhelm and kill him [as he stood] beneath them and annihilate his army. al-Muʿizz, with a body of his troops numbering 300 horsemen, charged towards al-Nāṣir's standards in the belief that the latter was beneath them and that he might seize and kill him. But al-Nāṣir had moved out from beneath his standards and had taken up a position at a distance from the battle, out of fear for his life. Unable to overwhelm him, [al-Muʿizz] withdrew with his men.

Fancying themselves victorious, the Qaymariyya maliks and amirs, among others, had gathered to plunder various groups [of the enemy]. Their followers had dispersed in search of booty, and there remained with them only a few of their mamluks. al-Muʿizz chanced upon them on his way back from [the position] beneath al-Nāṣir's standards, and he and his men did battle with them. Those killed included Shams al-Dīn Lu'lu', Ḥusām al-Dīn al-Qaymarī, Ḍiyā' al-Dīn al-Qaymarī, Tāj al-Mulūk ibn al-Muʿaẓẓam Tūrān Shāh ibn Ṣalāḥ al-Dīn, Sayf al-Dīn the *jamdār*, Nūr al-Dīn al-Zarzārī, and a number of al-Nāṣir's principal amirs. Leading men in his government were captured, including al-Muʿaẓẓam Tūrān Shāh ibn Ṣalāḥ al-Dīn, his brother Naṣīr al-Dīn,[79] al-Ṣāliḥ Ismaʿīl ibn al-Malik al-ʿĀdil,[80] al-Ashraf the son of the ruler of Ḥimṣ, Shihāb al-Dīn al-Qaymarī, Ḥusām al-Dīn Ṭurunṭāy al-ʿAzīzī and a number of ʿAzīziyya amirs who were his comrades. As for al-Nāṣir, when he saw how the situation had turned out, he took with him Nawfal al-Zubaydī and ʿAlī al-Saʿīdī, and fled towards Damascus.

The rest of al-Nāṣir's amirs were unaware of all this, but were hot on the heels of the Egyptian troops who had fled, until they [p. 163] reached al-ʿAbbāsa. [Here] they pitched their tents around the royal pavilion. But subsequently they heard what had happened, and they agreed to retreat into Syria. They withdrew to Damascus with their baggage and whatever plunder they had. Having overwhelmed the [other] group, killing some and taking others prisoner, al-Muʿizz moved with his troops to al-ʿAbbāsa with the aim of overtaking them. But he saw al-Nāṣir's pavilion and how his army had pitched their tents at al-ʿAbbāsa, and he turned aside to take the road to al-ʿAlāqima.[81] He reached Bilbays at daybreak on the Friday [of the] aforementioned [week]; but he did not find there a single Egyptian soldier. He and his companions made camp at Bilbays, where he was joined by the amirs who had fled before al-Nāṣir's forces, with their men. It was an engagment the likes of which had never been heard, and than which no historian has narrated a stranger one: that each of two armies should be in part victorious and in part defeated, and that those who were triumphant on each side should plunder those who had earlier been vanquished on the other!

79 *Recte* Nuṣrat al-Dīn.

80 The former ruler of Damascus (1239–45).

81 Twenty kilometres or so north of Bilbays.

He says: When al-Muʿizz was certain that al-Nāṣir's forces had withdrawn into Syria, he set about consolidating his power … He learned that the amir Sayf al-Dīn al-Qaymarī had proposed having the Friday *khuṭba* read for al-Malik al-Nāṣir. [Sayf al-Dīn] was a prisoner in the Fortress, and a number of [other] prisoners agreed to this because they had heard that [al-Nāṣir] had taken control of the country.[82] This infuriated [al-Muʿizz], who had Nāṣir al-Dīn Ismāʿīl ibn Yaghmūr, a slave of al-Malik al-Ṣāliḥ Ismaʿīl, and Amīn al-Dawla al-Sāmirī, [al-Ṣāliḥ Ismaʿīl's] vizier, both of whom were among the prisoners who had agreed regarding the *khuṭba*, hanged. He [also] wanted to destroy the amir Sayf al-Dīn al-Qaymarī, but was advised not to get involved with him; and so he let him be and after a time expelled him from Egypt to Syria.

He says: al-Muʿizz was informed that a group of al-Nāṣir's troops and slaves had got through to Cairo. He gave orders for them to be driven out into Syria, and they were expelled on 28 Dhūl'-Qaʿda [21 February 1251]. They totalled roughly 3000 men. They were mounted on asses, and the only ones who were riding horses were their commanders, the amir Nūr al-Dīn al-Aktaʿ,[83] Shihāb al-Dīn ibn ʿAlam al-Dīn, and Badr al-Dīn Uzdumur al-ʿAzīzī, together with five or six of their comrades …

[The historian] says: In this year [649/1251–52] occurred the murder of al-Malik al-Ṣāliḥ Ismaʿīl ibn al-Malik al-ʿĀdil ibn Ayyūb. al-Malik al-Muʿizz, ruler of Egypt, had taken him prisoner on the occasion of [the battle of] al-Kurāʿ, as was related above, and confined him in the Fortress of al-Jabal. al-Muʿizz and his closest aides agreed to kill him, and al-Muʿizz ordered his comrade, the amir ʿIzz al-Dīn Aybak al-Rūmī al-Ṣāliḥī, to put him to death. The latter took with him a group of men, and they proceeded with [al-Ṣāliḥ Ismaʿīl] as far as al-Qarāfa, where they killed and buried him …

[p. 164] He says: In this year al-Nāṣir, ruler of Syria, was told that al-Muʿizz, the ruler of Egypt, planned to attack him. So al-Nāṣir deployed his forces at Gaza, that they might confront the Egyptian army and defend the country. al-Muʿizz moved out with the Egyptian army and made camp at al-Bārida, on the borders of his territory. They remained in this position for almost two years. Then al-Nāṣir went off with those of his mamluks and closest aides who remained with him, and took up his quarters at ʿAmtā in the Ghawr,[84] where he pitched his tents and stayed for almost six months. There arrived from Baghdad the shaykh Najm al-Dīn al-Bādarā'ī, the Caliph's ambassador, who negotiated a peace between them. It was agreed that al-Malik al-Muʿizz should receive, from al-Malik al-Nāṣir's lands, Jerusalem and Gaza and their territories, together with the entire coastal region as far as the borders of Nablus, and that al-Muʿizz should release every one of the maliks and amirs whom he held prisoner and whom, as we mentioned, he had captured at al-Kurāʿ.

---

82 A reference to the events immediately following the initial victory of al-Nāṣir Yūsuf's army over the Egyptian forces: see page 222 and note 64 above.

83 *al-aktaʿ*, 'the one-armed'.

84 The Arabic name for the Jordan valley. ʿAmtā is approximately seventy kilometres from Tiberias. See Guy Le Strange, *Palestine under the Moslems* (London, 1890; reprinted Beirut, 1965), p. 393.

The shaykh Najm al-Dīn made them swear an oath to this effect, and each of them returned to his capital.

121. Guillaume de Saulx and Hugues de Bordeaux to Louis IX, Chastel-Pèlerin, 31 October 1251: Pierre-Vincent Claverie, 'Un nouvel éclairage sur le financement de la première croisade de saint Louis', Mélanges de l'École Française de Rome, Moyen Age*, 113 (2001): 621–35, annexes, no. 2*

[p. 635] To their most excellent lord, Louis, by God's grace King of the French, Guillaume de Saulx[85] and Hugues de Bordeaux, knights, greetings and a readiness to serve him in all matters.

We are informing Your Excellency that, since you had given us instructions through your letters patent that we should have the garrison of knights, squires and serjeants stationed at your expense in Chastel-Pèlerin paid their wages up to the octave [16 October 1251] of St. Denis last, and we did not have the money to pay them, we have borrowed from Opizzino Marioni, citizen of Genoa and the bearer of this letter, 520 *livres tournois*, for which we promised the aforesaid citizen that reimbursement would be arranged through Your Excellency without delay, and we have sealed this letter with our seals as testimony that we have received the money.

Dated at the above-mentioned Chastel-Pèlerin, on the eve of All Saints, in the year of the Lord 1251.

122. The magnates of the kingdom of Jerusalem to Henry III, King of England, [late] September 1254: 'Annales monasterii de Burton', in Annales Monastici*, vol. 1, pp. 368–9*

To the outstanding and most excellent lord Henry, by God's grace illustrious King of England, Jocelin, Archbishop of Caesarea; H[enry], Archbishop of Nazareth; the consecrated Archbishop-elect of Tyre;[86] R[enaud], Master of the Knights of the Temple; G[uillaume], Master of the Hospital of Saint John; P[eter], Marshal and Vice-master of the Teutonic Knights;[87] John of Ibelin, Count of Jaffa and lord of

85 Recently arrived in the East, since he was among the passengers of the Saint-Victor, who are known to have been still at Messina in July 1250: Claverie, 'Un nouvel éclairage', pp. 627–8.

86 This was Gilles de Saumur, the former Archbishop of Damietta, elected Archbishop of Tyre in 1253: 'Estoire de Eracles', p. 441 (trans. in Shirley, *Crusader Syria*, p. 139).

87 I have followed here the identifications given in *Regesta Regni Hierosolymitani (MXCVII–MCCXCI)*, ed. Reinhold Röhricht (Innsbrück, 1893), p. 322 (no. 1221): Renaud de Vichiers, Master of the Temple (1250–1256) and Guillaume de Châteauneuf, Master of the Hospital (1242–58). But his reading 'Poppo', for 'P.', Marshal and Vice-Master of the Teutonic Knights, is incorrect, as is clear from a near-contemporary letter from Peter, Marshal of the Teutonic Knights, to Alfonso X of Castile: see José Manuel Rodríguez García and Ana Echevarría Arsuaga, 'Alfonso X, la Orden Teutónica y Tierra Santa. Una nueva fuente para su estudio', in Ricardo Izquierdo Benito & Francisco Ruiz Gómez (eds), *Las Órdenes Militares en la Península Ibérica*, vol. 1 *Edad Media* (Cuenca, 2000), pp. 489–509 (here p. 509)..

Ramleh, *bailli* of the kingdom of Jerusalem;[88] Philip of Montfort, lord of Tyre and Toron; John of Ibelin, lord of Arsur and Constable of the kingdom of Jerusalem; Julian, lord of Sidon and Beaufort; Geoffrey of Sargines, Seneschal of the kingdom of Jerusalem; and John Aleman,[89] lord of Caesarea – in their own names and in that of all the people of the kingdom of Jerusalem: Greetings and may your good fortune abound.

We have thought fit to inform Your Royal Majesty by this letter of the condition of the kingdom of Jerusalem. Your royal greatness should know, therefore, that in view of the departure of the most pious, Christian and illustrious King of France, by whose presence the said kingdom was sustained and by whose aid it was defended – and still is defended – against the faithless Saracens, the Holy Land is left extremely bereft and deprived of help and counsel.[90] That desolation has increased enormously with the death of the venerable father, the lord Robert, late Patriarch of Jerusalem,[91] by whose foresight, judgement and advice we were guided, as well as by the departure of our reverend father, the lord O[do],[92] bishop of Tusculum, legate of the Apostolic See,[93] from whom we derived great counsel and assistance; and we have been left like fatherless orphans and like sheep in the midst of wolves, without either shepherd or guide. The Sultans of Aleppo and Babylonia are on good terms and of one mind and more than they have ever previously been wont, it is reliably claimed, against those who profess the Christian faith. They have no interest in making an agreement or truce with Christendom, and have broken off and completely abandoned negotiations for a truce. This is at the instigation of the Babylonians, who, it is said, have several times asked the Sultan of Aleppo to lay siege to one of the greater Christian strongholds, while they [themselves] were ready to invest another stronger one. Of this we and the whole of Christendom are wondrously afraid, since although by gathering together in one direction we can resist the Saracens, we fear that with our forces split we may be unable to withstand their strength and numbers, owing to the small numbers of the Christian people.

Because, however, we cannot fully explain to you in writing what relates to the affairs of the Holy Land, we are sending to Your Highness Brother Robert of Arras, [p. 369] of the Order of Friars Preachers, and Brother Ralph of the Order of Friars

---

88 He had become *bailli* earlier in 1254: 'Estoire de Eracles', p. 441 (trans. in Shirley, *Crusader Syria*, p. 140). See Hans Eberhard Mayer, 'Ibelin *versus* Ibelin: the struggle for the regency of Jerusalem, 1253–1258', *Proceedings of the American Philosophical Society*, 122 (1978): 25–57, reprinted in his *Probleme des lateinischen Königreichs Jerusalem* (London, 1983).

89 The text reads *Asa magnus*, clearly an error for *Alamannus*. On him, see Mayer, 'Ibelin *versus* Ibelin', p. 29.

90 Peter, Marshal of the Teutonic Knights, complaining similarly of the parlous state of Holy Land as a result of Louis's embarkation, says that he had left 500 crossbowmen in addition to the 100 knights: García and Arsuaga, 'Alfonso X', p. 509.

91 He died on 8 June: 'Estoire de Eracles', p. 441 (trans. in Shirley, *Crusader Syria*, p. 140).

92 The text reads 'C' in error for 'O'.

93 Eudes had embarked in mid September 1254: 'Estoire de Eracles', p. 442 (trans. in Shirley, *Crusader Syria*, p. 140).

Minor, religious, discreet and honest men, who will explain the condition of the country to you more fully on our behalf: Your Sublimity may without doubt see fit to place confidence in what they say. We, on the other hand, your devoted [servants], learning that you have taken the sign of the Cross to aid the said land, now some time ago, are turning to Your Royal Majesty, in whom, among all the other princes of the world, we and the rest of the Christians this side of the sea place our hope after God as a refuge and shelter. And we beg you to open to us the inmost depths of your compassion and to deign in such a fashion to see to all the said matters, by hastening your fortunate arrival in order to relieve the several needs of this land, so that this tiny remnant of Christendom in the kingdom of Jerusalem can be defended by your aid and counsel against the faithless Saracens, and the Holy Places, which were distinguished by the conception, birth, actions and teachings of the Saviour and sanctified by His passion and resurrection, may no longer be hammered by the heathen. May the Almighty preserve you safe and sound for His Church for many years to come.

Dated Acre in the year of the Lord 1254, Wednesday …,[94] in the month of September.

---

94 No day of the month is given, but the letter was clearly written after Eudes's departure.

Bibliography

PRIMARY SOURCES

Abū Shāma, Shihāb al-Dīn Abū'l-Qāsim, *al-Dhayl 'alā'l-rawḍatayn*, ed. M. Z. al-Kawtharī as *Tarājim rijāl al-qarnayn al-sādis wa'l-sābi'* (Cairo, 1366 H./1947; reprinted Beirut, 1974)

Actus pontificum Cenomannis in urbe degentium, ed. G. Busson and A. Ledru (Le Mans: G. Fleury and A. Dangin, 1901 = *Archives Historiques du Maine*, vol. 2)

al-Dhahabī, Shams al-Dīn Abū ʿAbd-Allāh Muḥammad, *Ta'rīkh al-Islām*, ed. ʿUmar ʿAbd al-Salām Tadmurī, [vol. 5:] *641–650 H.* (Beirut: Dār al-Kutub al-ʿArabī, 1419 H./1998)

al-Jazarī, Shams al-Dīn Muḥammad, *Ḥawādith al-zamān*, Forschungs- und Landesbibliothek Gotha, ms. Orient. A 1559

al-Nuwayrī, Shihāb al-Dīn Aḥmad, *Nihāyat al-arab fī funūn al-adab* (33 vols, Cairo, 1923–98)

al-Yūnīnī, Quṭb al-Dīn Abū'l-Fatḥ Mūsā, *al-Dhayl 'alā' Mir'āt al-zamān* (4 vols, Hyderabad, A. P.: Dairatu'l-Maʿarifi'l-Osmania, 1374–80 H./1954–61)

'Annales de Terre Sainte', ed. R. Röhricht, *AOL*, 2 (1884), documents: 427–61

'Annales Erphordenses', in *MGHS*, vol. 16, pp. 26–40

Annales Ianuenses, ed. Luigi Tommaso Belgrano and Cesare Imperiale de Sant'Angelo, *Annali Genovesi di Caffaro e de' suoi continuatori dal MXCIX al MCCXCIII*, Fonti per la Storia d'Italia, vols 11–14*bis* (5 vols, Genova: Istituto sordo-muti, and Rome: Tipografia del Senato, 1890–1929)

'Annales monasterii de Burton', in *Annales Monastici*, vol. 1, pp. 181–500

'Annales monasterii de Theokesberia', in *Annales Monastici*, vol. 1, pp. 41–180

Annales Monastici, ed. Henry Richards Luard, Rolls Series, no. 36 (5 vols, London: Longman, 1864–69)

'Annales S. Benigni Divionensis', in *MGHS*, vol. 5, pp. 37–50

'Annales S. Rudberti Salisburgenses', in *MGHS*, vol. 9, pp. 758–810

Bacon, Roger, *Opus Majus*, ed. John Henry Bridges (3 vols, Oxford: Clarendon Press, and London: Williams and Norgate, 1897–1900)

'Balduini Ninovensis chronicon', in *MGHS*, vol. 25, pp. 515–46

Baudouin d'Avesnes, 'Chronicon Hanoniense', in *MGHS*, vol. 25, pp. 414–67

Bédier, Joseph and Aubry, Pierre (ed.), *Les chansons de croisade* (Paris: Honoré Champion, 1909)

Cahen, Claude, and Chabbouh, Ibrahim, 'Le testament d'al-Malik aṣ-Ṣāliḥ Ayyūb', *BEO*, 29 (1977): 97–114

'Chronica minor auctore minorita Erfordiensi', in *MGHS*, vol. 24, pp. 172–204

'Chronica universalis Mettensis', in *MGHS*, vol. 24, pp. 502–26

'Chronique anonyme des rois de France finissant en 1286', in *RHGF*, vol. 21, pp. 80–102

'Chronique de Primat, traduite par Jean du Vignay', in *RHGF*, vol. 23, pp. 1–106

Claverie, Pierre-Vincent, 'Un nouvel éclairage sur le financement de la première croisade de saint Louis', *Mélanges de l'École Française de Rome, Moyen Age*, 113 (2001): 621–35

Codex Diplomaticus Hungariae Ecclesiasticus ac Civilis, ed. György Fejér (11 vols in 40 parts, Buda, 1829–44)

'Continuation de Guillaume de Tyr, de 1229 à 1261, dite du manuscrit de Rothelin', in *RHC HOcc.*, vol. 2, pp. 485–639; trans. in Shirley, *Crusader Syria in the Thirteenth Century*, pp. 11–120

Dawson, Christopher (ed.), *The Mongol Mission: Narratives and Letters of the Franciscan Missionaries in Mongolia and China in the Thirteenth and Fourteenth Centuries* (London and New York: Sheed and Ward, 1955)

de Nangis, Guillaume, 'Gesta sanctae memoriae Ludovici regis Franciae', in *RHGF*, vol. 20, pp. 309–465

Decrees of the Ecumenical Councils, vol. 1: *Nicaea I to Lateran V*, ed. Norman P. Tanner SJ (London: Sheed and Ward, and Georgetown, DC: Georgetown University Press, 1990)

Delorme, Ferdinand M., 'Bulle d'Innocent IV pour la Croisade (6 février 1245)', *AFH*, 6 (1913): 386–9

—— 'Bulle d'Innocent IV en faveur de l'empire latin de Constantinople (29 sept. 1245)', *AFH*, 8 (1915): 307–10

Diplomatarium Norvegicum, ed. C. C. A. Lange and Carl R. Unger, vol. 1 (Christiania: P.T. Mallings Forlagshandel, 1849)

Documents historiques inédits tirés des collections manuscrites de la Bibliothèque Royale et des archives ou des bibliothèques des départements, ed. M. Champollion-Figeac (2 vols, Paris: Firmin Didot frères, 1841–43)

'E Chronico Sancti Laudi Rotomagensis', in *RHGF*, vol. 23, pp. 395–7

'Extraites des Chroniques de Saint-Denis', in *RHGF*, vol. 21, pp. 103–23

Foedera, Conventiones, Literae et Cuiuscumque Generis Acta Publica inter Reges Angliae et Alios Quosvis Imperatores, Reges, Pontifices, Principes vel Communitates ab Ineunte Saeculo Duodecimo, viz. ab Anno 1101 ad Nostra usque Tempora Habita aut Tractata, ed. T. Rymer, 3rd edn (10 vols, The Hague: Joannes Neaulme, 1739–45; reprinted Farnborough: Gregg, 1967)

Gabrieli, Francesco, *Arab Historians of the Crusades*, trans. E. J. Costello (London: Routledge and Kegan Paul, 1969)

García, José Manuel Rodríguez, and Arsuaga, Ana Echevarría, 'Alfonda X, la Orden Teutónica y Tierra Santa. Una nueva fuente para su estudio', in Ricardo Izquierdo Benito & Francisco Ruiz Gómez (eds), *Las Órdenes Militares en la Península Ibérica*, vol. 1. *Edad Media* (Cuenca, 2000), pp. 489–509.

Geoffrey de Beaulieu, 'Vita Ludovici noni', in *RHGF*, vol. 20, pp. 5–40

Georgios Akropolita, *Khronike syngraphe*, ed. Immanuel Bekker, *Georgii Acropolitae Annales* (Bonn: Weber, 1836)

Giovanni de Columna, 'E Mari historiarum', in *RHGF*, vol. 23, pp. 107–24

Hauréau, J. B., 'Quelques lettres d'Innocent IV extraites des manuscrits de la Bibliothèque Nationale (N° 1194–1203 du fonds Moreau)', in *Notices et extraits des manuscrits de la Bibliothèque Nationale*, vol. 24/2 (Paris: Imprimerie Nationale, 1876), pp. 157–246

Historia Diplomatica Friderici Secundi, ed. J. L. A. Huillard-Bréholles (6 vols in 11 parts, Paris: Henri Plon, 1852–61)

Historiae Francorum Scriptores ab Ipsius Gentis Origine, ed. André Du Chesne, vol. 5 (Paris: sumptibus Sebastiani Cramoisy, 1649)

Ibn ʿAbd al-Raḥīm, revised version of Ibn Wāṣil, *Mufarrij al-kurūb*, Bibliothèque Nationale, Paris, ms. arabe 1702

Ibn al-ʿAmīd (al-Makīn ibn Jirjīs), *Kitāb al-majmūʿ al-mubārak*, ed. Claude Cahen, 'La "Chronique des Ayyoubides" d'al-Makīn b. al-ʿAmīd', *BEO*, 15 (1955–57): 108–84; trans. Anne-Marie Eddé and Françoise Micheau, *Al-Makīn ibn al-ʿAmīd. Chronique des Ayyoubides (602–658/1205–6–1259–60)*, DRHC, vol. 16 (Paris: Académie des Inscriptions et Belles-Lettres, 1994)

Ibn al-Furāt, *Taʾrīkh al-duwal waʾl-mulūk*, extracts ed. and trans. U. and M. C. Lyons, with introduction and commentary by J. S. C. Riley-Smith, *Ayyubids, Mamlukes and Crusaders* (2 vols, Cambridge: Heffer, 1971)

Ibn Wāṣil, Jamāl al-Dīn Abū ʿAbd-Allāh Muḥammad, *Mufarrij al-kurūb fī akhbār banī Ayyūb*, partial edn by Jamāl al-Dīn al-Shayyāl et al. (5 vols, Cairo, 1953–77); Bibliothèque Nationale, Paris, ms. arabe 1703

Jal, Auguste, 'Pacta naulorum des années 1246, 1268 et 1270', in *Documents historiques inédits*, ed. Champollion-Figeac, vol. 1, pp. 507–615

Jean de Garlande, *De triumphis ecclesiae libri octo*, ed. Thomas Wright (London: Roxburghe Club, 1856)

Jeanroy, A., 'Le troubadour Austorc d'Aurillac et son sirventés sur la septième Croisade', in *Mélanges Chabaneau. Festschrift Camille Chabaneau zur Vollendung seines 75. Lebensjahres 4 märz 1906 dargebracht von seinen Schülern, Freunden und Verehrern*, Romanische Forschungen, vol. 23 (Erlangen, 1907), pp. 81–7

Joinville, Jean de, *Vie de saint Louis*, ed. Natalis de Wailly (Paris: Firmin Didot frères, 1874); trans. René Hague, *The Life of Saint Louis by John of Joinville* (London and New York: Sheed and Ward, 1955); trans. M. R. B. Shaw, *Joinville and Villehardouin: Chronicles of the crusades* (Harmondsworth: Penguin, 1963)

Kohler, Charles, 'Deux projets de croisade en Terre-Sainte composés à la fin du XIIIe siècle et au début du XIVe', *Revue de l'Orient Latin*, 10 (1903–1904): 406–57

Layettes du Trésor des Chartes, ed. Alexandre Teulet, H. De la Borde et al. (5 vols, Paris: Henri Plon, 1863–1909)

Les registres d'Innocent IV, ed. Elie Berger (4 vols, Paris: Thorin et fils, 1884–1921)

'L'estoire de Eracles empereur et la conqueste de la terre d'Outremer', in *RHC HOcc.*, vol. 2, pp. 1–481; partial translation in Shirley, *Crusader Syria in the Thirteenth Century*, pp. 121–43

Marino Sanudo Torsello, *Istoria del Regno di Romania*, in *Chroniques gréco-romanes*, ed. Charles Hopf (Berlin: Weidmann, 1873)

'Menkonis Chronicon', in *MGHS*, vol. 23, pp. 523–61

'Minstrel of Rheims', ed. Natalis de Wailly, *Récits d'un ménestrel de Reims au treizième siècle* (Paris: Librairie Renouard, 1876); trans. Edward Noble Stone, *Three Old French Chronicles of the Crusades* (Seattle, WA: University of Washington, 1939); trans. Robert Levine, *A Thirteenth-century Minstrel's Chronicle* (Lewiston, NY, Queenston, Ontario, and Lampeter: Edwin Mellen, 1990)

Monumenta Franciscana, ed. J. S. Brewer, Rolls Series, no. 4, vol. 1 (London: Longman, 1858)

Onze poèmes de Rutebeuf concernant la croisade, ed. Julia Bastin and Edmond Faral, DRHC, vol. 1 (Paris: Geuthner, 1946)

Paris, Matthew, *Chronica Majora*, ed. Henry Richards Luard, Rolls Series, no. 57 (7 vols, London: Longman etc., 1872–83); trans. J.A. Giles, *Matthew Paris's English History from the Year 1235 to 1273* (3 vols, London: Bohn's Library, 1853); partial translation by Richard Vaughan, *Chronicles of Matthew Paris: Monastic Life in the Thirteenth Century* (Gloucester: Alan Sutton, and New York: St Martin's Press, 1984)

Plano Carpini (Giovanni di Pian di Carpine), *Ystoria Mongalorum quos nos Tartaros appellamus*, ed. Enrico Menestò *et al.*, *Storia dei Mongoli* (Spoleto: Centro italiano di Studi sull'alto medioevo, 1989); trans. in Dawson, *The Mongol Mission*, pp. 3–72

Preußisches Urkundenbuch, ed. Rudolf Philippi, Max Hein et al. (6 vols, Königsberg: Hartung, and Marburg: Elwert, 1882–1986)

Qaraṭāy al-ʿIzzī al-Khazāndārī, *Ta'rīkh majmū' al-nawādir*, Forschungs- und Landesbibliothek Gotha, ms. Orient. A 1655

Qur'ān, trans. Arthur J. Arberry, *The Koran Interpreted* (London: Allen and Unwin, 1955)

Regesta Regni Hierosolymitani (MXCVII–MCCXCI), ed. Reinhold Röhricht (2 vols, Innsbrück: Wagner'sche akademische Buchhandlung, 1893–1904; reprinted New York: Burt Franklin, [1960])

Regestrum Visitationum Archiepiscopi Rothomagensis. Journal des visites pastorales d'Eude Rigaud, archevêque de Rouen. MCCXLVIII–MCCLXIX, ed. T. Bonnin (Rouen: Auguste le Brument, 1852)

Registrum Vaticanum, Innocent IV: microfilm in the Seeley Historical Library, Cambridge

Riant, Comte [Paul], 'Six lettres relatives aux croisades', *AOL*, 1 (1881): 383–92

—— 'Déposition de Charles d'Anjou pour la canonisation de saint Louis', in *Notices et documents publiées par la Société de l'histoire de France à l'occasion du cinquantième anniversaire de sa fondation*, ed. C. Jourdain (Paris: Honoré Champion, 1884), pp. 170–76

Richard, Jean, 'La fondation d'une église latine en Orient par saint Louis: Damiette', *BEC*, 120 (1962): 39–54; reprinted in Richard, *Orient et Occident au Moyen Age: contacts et relations (XIIe–XVe s.)* (London: Variorum Reprints, 1976)

—— 'La lettre du Connétable Smbat et les rapports entre Chrétiens et Mongols au milieu du XIIIème siècle', in Dickran Kouymjian (ed.), *Études arméniennes in memoriam Haïg Berbérian* (Lisbon: Calouste Gulbenkian Foundation, 1986), pp. 683–96; reprinted in Richard, *Croisades et États latins d'Orient* (Aldershot: Variorum Reprints, 1992)

'Richeri Gesta Senoniensis ecclesiae', in *MGHS*, vol. 25, pp. 249–345

Riley-Smith, Louise and Riley-Smith, Jonathan (ed.), *The Crusades: Idea and Reality, 1095–1274*, (London: Edward Arnold, 1981)

Saint-Bris, T., 'Lettre adressée en Égypte à Alphonse, comte de Poitiers, frère de saint Louis', *BEC*, 1e série, 1 (1839–40): 389–403

Salimbene de Adam, *Cronica*, ed. Giuseppe Scalia, Corpus Christianorum Continuatio Mediaevalis, vols 125–125A (2 vols, Turnhout: Brepols, 1998–99)

Sayous, André-E., 'Les mandats de saint Louis sur son trésor et le mouvement international des capitaux pendant la septième croisade (1248–1254)', *Revue Historique*, 167/2 (1931): 254–304

Schaller, Hans Martin, 'Eine kuriale Briefsammlung des 13. Jahrhunderts mit unbekannten Briefen Friedrichs II.', *Deutsches Archiv für Erforschung des Mittelalters*, 18 (1962): 171–213; reprinted in Schaller, *Stauferzeit. Ausgewählte Aufsätze*, Schriften der Monumenta Germaniae Historica, vol. 38 (Hanover: Hahn, 1993), pp. 283–328

Shirley, Janet, *Crusader Syria in the Thirteenth Century*, CTT, vol. 5 (Aldershot: Ashgate, 1999): see 'Continuation de Guillaume de Tyr, dite du manuscrit de Rothelin' and 'L'estoire de Eracles'

Sibṭ Ibn al-Jawzī (Shams al-Dīn Abū'l-Muẓaffar Yūsuf ibn Qizūghlī), *Mir'āt al-zamān fī ta'rīkh al-a'yān*, vol. 8/2 (Hyderabad, A.P.: Dairatu'l-Maʿarifi'l-Osmania, 1372/1952)

Simon de Saint-Quentin, *Historia Tartarorum*, excerpts (from Vincent de Beauvais) ed. Jean Richard, *Simon de Saint-Quentin. Histoire des Tartares*, DHRC, vol. 8 (Paris: Geuthner, 1965)

Spicilegium sive Collectio Veterum Aliquot Scriptorum Qui in Galliae Bibliothecis Delituerant, ed. Luc D'Achéry, new edn by Étienne Baluze and L. F. J. de la Barre (3 vols, Paris: Montalant, 1723)

Thomas de Cantimpré, *Bonum Universale de Apibus*, ed. Georgius Colvenerius (2 vols, Douai: ex typographia Baltazaris Belleri, 1627)

Vetera Monumenta Historica Hungariam Sacram Illustrantia, ed. Augustin Theiner (2 vols, Rome: Typis Vaticanis, 1859–60)

Vincent de Beauvais, *Speculum Historiale*, ed. Johann Mentelin (Straßburg, 1473)

William of Rubruck, *Itinerarium*, in *Sinica Franciscana*, vol. 1, *Itinera et relationes Fratrum Minorum saeculi XIII et XIV*, ed. Anastasius Van den Wyngaert (Quaracchi-Firenze, 1929); trans. Peter Jackson and David Morgan, *The Mission of Friar William of Rubruck: His Journey to the Court of the Great Khan Möngke 1253–1255*, 2nd series, vol. 173 (London: Hakluyt Society, 1990)

William of Tyre, *Historia*, ed. R. B. C. Huygens, *Guillaume de Tyr. Chronique*, Corpus Christianorum Continuatio Mediaevalis, vols 63–63A (Turnhout: Brepols, 1986); trans. Emily Atwater Babcock and A. C. Krey, *A History of Deeds Done Beyond the Sea, by William Archbishop of Tyre* (2 vols, New York: Columbia University Press, 1943, reprinted New York: Octagon, 1976)

SECONDARY MATERIAL

Abulafia, David, *Frederick II: A Medieval Emperor* (London: Allen Lane Penguin Press, 1988)

Alexandrescu-Dersca, M. M., 'Babylone d'Égypte', *Revue Historique du Sud-Est Européen*, 20 (1943): 190–201

Amitai-Preiss, Reuven, 'Mamluk perceptions of the Mongol-Frankish rapprochement', *MHR*, 7 (1992): 50–65

Ayalon, David, 'Le régiment Bahriya dans l'armée mamelouke', *Revue des Études Islamiques*, 19 (1951): 133–41; reprinted in Ayalon, *Studies on the Mamlūks of Egypt (1250–1517)* (London: Variorum Reprints, 1977)

—— 'L'esclavage du Mamelouk', *Israel Oriental Notes and Studies*, 1 (1951): 1–66; reprinted in Ayalon, *The Mamlūk Military Society* (London: Variorum Reprints, 1979)

Barber, Malcolm, 'The Crusade of the Shepherds in 1251', in J. F. Sweets (ed.), *Proceedings of the Tenth Annual Meeting of the Western Society for French History, 14–16 October 1982, Winnipeg* (Lawrence, KS, 1984), pp. 1–23; reprinted in Barber, *Crusaders and Heretics, 12th–14th Centuries* (Aldershot: Variorum Reprints, 1995)

Berger, Elie, *Histoire de Blanche de Castille reine de France* (Paris: Thorin et fils, 1895)

Blochet, Edgar, 'Les relations diplomatiques des Hohenstaufen avec les sultans d'Égypte', *Revue Historique*, 80 (1902): 51–64

Boyle, John Andrew, *The Mongol World-Empire 1206–1370* (London: Variorum Reprints, 1977)

Cahen, Claude, *La Syrie du Nord à l'époque des croisades et la principauté franque d'Antioche* (Paris: Geuthner, 1940)

——, 'Saint Louis et l'Islam', *Journal Asiatique*, 257 (1970): 3–12; reprinted in Cahen, *Turcobyzantina et Oriens Christianus* (London: Variorum Reprints, 1974)

—— 'Une source pour l'histoire ayyūbide: Les mémoires de Saʿd al-Dīn Ibn Ḥamawiya Djuwaynī', in his *Les peuples musulmans dans l'histoire médiévale* (Damascus: Institut Français de Damas, 1977), pp. 457–82

Cole, Penny J., *The Preaching of the Crusades to the Holy Land, 1095–1270* (Cambridge, MA: Medieval Academy of America, 1991)

—— D'Avray, D. L. and Riley-Smith, J., 'Application of theology to current affairs: Memorial sermons on the dead of Mansurah and on Innocent IV', *BIHR*, 63 (1990): 227–47

Curiel, Raoul and Gyselen, Rika (ed.), *Itinéraires d'Orient: Hommages à Claude Cahen*, Res Orientales, 6 (Bures-sur-Yvette: Groupe pour l'étude de la civilisation du Moyen-Orient, 1994)

Delaborde, H.-F., 'Joinville et le conseil tenu à Acre en 1250', *Romania*, 23 (1894): 148–52

Delaruelle, Étienne, 'L'idée de croisade chez saint Louis', *Bulletin de Littérature Ecclésiastique*, 61 (1960): 241–57; reprinted in Delaruelle, *L'idée de croisade au Moyen Age* (Torino: Bottega d'Erasmo, 1980), pp. 189–207

de Rachewiltz, Igor, *Papal Envoys to the Great Khans* (London: Faber and Faber, 1971)

Dickson, Gary, 'The advent of the *Pastores* (1251)', *Revue Belge de Philologie et d'Histoire*, 66 (1988): 249–67; reprinted in Dickson, *Religious Enthusiasm in the Medieval West*

—— *Religious Enthusiasm in the Medieval West: Revivals, Crusades, Saints* (Aldershot: Ashgate, 2000)

Dozy, R., *Supplément aux dictionnaires arabes* (2 vols, Leiden: Brill, 1881; reprinted Beirut: Librairie du Liban, 1968)

Eddé, Anne-Marie, *La principauté ayyoubide d'Alep (579/1183–658/1260)*, Freiburger Islamstudien, vol. 21 (Stuttgart: Franz Steiner, 1999)

Edbury, Peter W., *John of Ibelin and the Kingdom of Jerusalem* (Woodbridge: Boydell, 1997)

Fahmy, Ali Mohamed, *Muslim Naval Organization in the Eastern Mediterranean from the Seventh to the Tenth Century A.D.*, 2nd edn (Cairo: National Publication and Printing House, 1966)

Forey, A. J., 'The Crusading vows of the English King Henry III', *Durham University Journal*, 65 (1973): 229–47; reprinted in Forey, *Military Orders and Crusades* (London: Variorum Reprints, 1994)

Foulet, Alfred, 'Joinville et le conseil tenu à Acre en 1250', *Modern Language Notes*, 49 (1934): 464–8

García, José Manuel Rodríguez, 'Henry III (1216–1272), Alfonso X of Castile (1252–1284) and the crusading plans of the thirteenth century (1245–1272)', in Björn K. U. Weiler (ed., with Ifor Rowlands), *England and Europe in the Reign of Henry III (1216–1272)* (Aldershot: Ashgate, 2002), pp. 99–120

Gottschalk, Hans L., *Al-Malik al-Kāmil von Egypten und seine Zeit* (Wiesbaden: Harrassowitz, 1958)

—— 'Awlād al-Shaykh', *EI*[2]

Haldane, Douglas, 'The fire-ship of Al-Sālih Ayyūb and Muslim use of "Greek Fire"', in Donald J. Kagay and L. J. Andrew Villalon (ed.), *The Circle of War in the Middle Ages: Essays on Medieval Military and Naval History* (Woodbridge: Boydell, 1999), pp. 137–44

Hambis, Louis, 'Saint Louis et les Mongols', *Journal Asiatique*, 258 (1970): 25–33

Hardy, Ineke, '"Nus ne poroit de mauvaise raison" (R1887): a case for Raoul de Soissons', *Medium Aevum*, 70 (2001): 95–111

Holt, P. M. (ed.), *The Eastern Mediterranean Lands in the Period of the Crusades* (Warminster: Aris and Phillips, 1977)

Holt, Peter, 'Three biographies of al-Ẓāhir Baybars', in D. O. Morgan (ed.), *Medieval Historical Writing in the Christian and Islamic Worlds* (London: School of Oriental and African Studies, 1982), pp. 19–29

Housley, Norman, *The Italian Crusades: The Papal-Angevin Alliance and the Crusades Against Christian Lay Powers, 1254–1343* (Oxford: Oxford University Press, 1982)

Humphreys, R. Stephen, *From Saladin to the Mongols: The Ayyubids of Damascus, 1193–1260* (Albany, NY: State University of New York Press, 1977)

—— 'The emergence of the Mamluk army', *Studia Islamica*, 45 (1977): 67–99

Irwin, Robert, *The Middle East in the Middle Ages: The Early Mamluk Sultanate 1250–1382* (London and Sydney: Croom Helm, 1986)

—— 'The image of the Byzantine and the Frank in Arab popular literature of the late Middle Ages', in Benjamin Arbel, Bernard Hamilton and David Jacoby (ed.), *Latins and Greeks in the Eastern Mediterranean after 1204* (London: Frank Cass, 1989 = *MHR*, 4/1), pp. 226–42

Jackson, Peter, 'The end of Hohenstaufen rule in Syria', *BIHR*, 59 (1986): 20–36

—— 'The crusades of 1239–41 and their aftermath', *Bulletin of the School of Oriental and African Studies*, 50 (1987): 32–60; reprinted in G. R. Hawting (ed.), *Muslims, Mongols and Crusaders* (London and New York: Routledge Curzon, 2005), pp. 217–47

—— 'Eljigidei', *Encyclopaedia Iranica*

—— *The Mongols and the West, 1221–1410* (Harlow: Pearson Education, 2005)

Jacoby, David , 'The kingdom of Jerusalem and the collapse of Hohenstaufen power in the Levant', *Dumbarton Oaks Papers*, 40 (1986): 83–101

Jordan, William Chester, *Louis IX and the Challenge of the Crusade: A Study in Rulership* (Princeton, NJ: Princeton University Press, 1979)

—— '"Amen!" cinq fois "Amen!". Les chansons de la croisade égyptienne de saint Louis, une source négligée d'opinion royaliste', in Laurence Moulinier and Patrick Boucheron (ed.), *Hommes de pouvoir: individu et politique au temps de saint Louis* (Saint-Denis: Presses Universitaires de Vincennes-Paris VIII, 1998 = *Médiévales*, 34, Spring 1998), pp. 79–90

Kedar, Benjamin Z., 'The passenger list of a crusader ship, 1250: towards the history of the popular element on the Seventh Crusade', *Studi Medievali*, 3a serie, 13 (1972): 267–79; reprinted in Kedar, *The Franks in the Levant, 11th to 14th centuries* (Aldershot: Variorum Reprints, 1993)

—— *Crusade and Mission: European Approaches to the Muslims* (Princeton, NJ: Princeton University Press, 1984)

Klein-Franke, Felix, 'What was the fatal disease of al-Malik al-Ṣāliḥ Najm al-Dīn Ayyūb?', in M. Sharon (ed.), *Studies in Islamic History and Civilization in Honour of Professor David Ayalon* (Jerusalem: Cana, and Leiden: Brill, 1986), pp. 153–7

Labande, Edmond-René, 'Saint Louis pèlerin', *Revue d'Histoire de l'Église de France*, 57 (1971): 5–18

Le Goff, Jacques, *Saint Louis* (Paris: Gallimard, 1996)

Le Strange, Guy, *Palestine under the Moslems* (London: Alexander P. Watt for the Palestine Exploration Fund, 1890; reprinted Beirut: Khayats, 1965)

Lloyd, Simon, *English Society and the Crusade 1216–1307* (Oxford: Oxford University Press, 1988)

—— 'King Henry III, the Crusade and the Mediterranean', in Michael Jones and Malcolm Vale (ed.), *England and Her Neighbours, 1066–1453: Essays in Honour of Pierre Chaplais* (London and Ronceverte: Hambledon, 1989), pp. 97–119

—— 'William Longespee II: the making of an English crusading hero', *Nottingham Medieval Studies*, 35 (1991): 41–69, and 36 (1992): 79–125

Lower, Michael, *The Barons' Crusade: A Call to Arms and its Consequences* (Philadelphia, PA: University of Pennsylvania Press, 2005)

Macquarrie, Alan, *Scotland and the Crusades 1095–1560* (Edinburgh: Edinburgh University Press, 1985)

Maier, Christoph T., *Preaching the Crusades: Mendicant Friars and the Cross in the Thirteenth Century* (Cambridge: Cambridge University Press, 1994)

Marshall, Christopher J., 'The French regiment in the Latin East, 1254–1291', *JMH*, 15 (1989): 301–7

Mayer, Hans Eberhard, 'Ibelin *versus* Ibelin: the struggle for the regency of Jerusalem, 1253–1258', *Proceedings of the American Philosophical Society*, 122 (1978): 25–57; reprinted in Mayer, *Probleme des lateinischen Königreichs Jerusalem* (London: Variorum Reprints, 1983)

Menache, Sophia, 'Tartars, Jews, Saracens and the Jewish-Mongol "plot" of 1241', *History*, 81 (1996): 319–42

Ménard, Philippe, 'L'esprit de la croisade chez Joinville. Etude des mentalités médiévales', in Yvonne Bellenger and Danielle Quéruel (ed.), *Les Champenois et la croisade. Actes des quatrièmes journées rémoises 27–28 novembre 1987* (Paris: Aux amateurs de livres, 1989), pp. 131–47

Micheau, Françoise, 'Croisades et croisés vus par les historiens arabes chrétiens d'Égypte', in Curiel and Gyselen (ed.), *Itinéraires d'Orient*, pp. 169–85

Monfrin, Jacques, 'Joinville et la prise de Damiette (1249)', *Académie des Inscriptions et Belles-Lettres: Comptes rendus des séances* (1976), pp. 268–85

Morgan, David, *The Mongols* (Oxford: Blackwell, 1986)

Nicholson, Helen, 'Steamy Syrian scandals: Matthew Paris on the Templars and Hospitallers', *Medieval History*, 2/2 (1992): 68–85

O'Callaghan, Joseph, *Reconquest and Crusade in Medieval Spain* (Philadelphia, PA: University of Pennsylvania Press, 2003)

Pelliot, Paul, 'Les Mongols et la papauté: chapitre 2 (suite)', *Revue de l'Orient Chrétien*, 28 (1931–2): 3–84

Pouzet, Louis, *Damas au VIIe/XIIIe siècle. Vie et structures religieuses d'une métropole islamique*, Recherches, Nouvelle série, A: Langue arabe et pensée islamique, vol. 15 (Beirut: Dar el-Machreq SARL, 1988)

Powell, James M., *Anatomy of a Crusade 1213–1221* (Philadelphia, PA: University of Pennsylvania Press, 1986)

—— 'Frederick II and the Muslims: the making of an historiographical tradition', in Larry J. Simon (ed.), *Iberia and the Mediterranean World of the Middle Ages: Studies in Honor of Robert I. Burns, S.J.* (Leiden: Brill, 1995–96), vol. 1, pp. 261–9

Prawer, Joshua, *Histoire du royaume latin de Jérusalem* (2 vols, Paris: Centre national de la recherche scientifique, 1969–70)

—— 'Crusader security and the Red Sea', in Prawer, *Crusader Institutions* (Oxford: Oxford University Press, 1980), pp. 471–83

Pryor, John H., 'Transportation of horses by sea during the era of the crusades: eighth century to 1285 A.D. Part II: 1228–1285', *MM*, 68/2 (May 1982): 102–25

—— 'The naval architecture of crusader transport ships: A reconstruction of some archetypes for round-hulled sailing ships', *MM*, 70 (1984): 171–219, 275–92, 363–86

—— *Geography, Technology and War: Studies in the Maritime History of the Mediterranean, 649–1571* (Cambridge: Cambridge University Press, 1988)

—— 'The naval architecture of crusader transport ships and horse transports revisited', *MM*, 76 (1990): 255–73

—— 'The crusade of Emperor Frederick II, 1220–29: the implications of the maritime evidence', *The American Neptune*, 52/2 (Spring 1992): 113–32

Purcell, Maureen, *Papal Crusading Policy 1244–1291: The Chief Instruments of Papal Crusading Policy and Crusade to the Holy Land from the Final Loss of Jerusalem to the Fall of Acre* (Leiden: Brill, 1975)

Reeves, Marjorie E., 'History and prophecy in medieval thought', *Medievalia et Humanistica*, 5 (1974): 51–75

Riant, Paul, *Expéditions et pèlerinages des Scandinaves en Terre Sainte au temps des croisades* (Paris: A. D. Lainé and J. Havard, 1865)

Richard, Jean, *Orient et Occident au Moyen Age: contacts et relations (XIIe–XVe s.)* (London: Variorum Reprints, 1976)

—— 'Sur les pas de Plancarpin et de Rubrouck: la lettre de saint Louis à Sartaq', *Journal des Savants* (1977), pp. 49–61; reprinted in Richard, *Croisés, missionnaires et voyageurs. Les perspectives orientales du monde latin médiéval* (London, 1983)

—— *Saint Louis: Crusader King of France*, ed. and abridged by Simon Lloyd and trans. Jean Birrell (Cambridge: Cambridge University Press, 1992); original edition, *Saint Louis roi d'une France féodale, soutien de la Terre Sainte* (Paris: Fayard, 1983)

Riley-Smith, J. S. C., 'Government in Latin Syria and the commercial privileges of foreign merchants', in Derek Baker (ed.), *Relations between East and West in the Middle Ages* (Edinburgh: Edinburgh University Press, 1973), pp. 109–32

—— *What Were the Crusades?*, 3rd edn (Basingstoke: Macmillan, 2002)

Röhricht, Reinhold, 'Die Pastorellen (1251)', *Zeitschrift für Kirchengeschichte*, 6 (1884): 290–96

—— 'Der Kreuzzug Louis IX. gegen Damiette (in Regestenform)', in his *Kleine Studien zur Geschichte der Kreuzzüge*, Wissenschaftliche Beilage zum Programm des Humboldt-Gymnasiums zu Berlin, Ostern 1890 (Berlin: R. Gaertners Verlagsbuchhandlung, 1890), pp. 11–25 (no. IIIa).

Rüdt-Collenberg, Count W. H. , *The Rupenides, Hethumides and Lusignans: The Structure of the Armeno-Cilician Dynasties* (Paris: Librairie C. Klincksieck, [1963])

Sambin, Paolo, *Problemi politici attraverso lettere inedite di Innocenzo IV*, Memorie del Istituto Veneto di Scienze, Lettere ed Arti, Classe di Scienze Morali e Lettere, 31/3 (Venezia, 1955)

Schregle, Götz, *Die Sultanin von Ägypten* (Wiesbaden: Harrassowitz, 1961)

Sharon, M. (ed.), *Studies in Islamic History and Civilization in Honour of Professor David Ayalon* (Jerusalem: Cana, and Leiden: Brill, 1986)

Siberry, Elizabeth, *Criticism of Crusading 1095–1274* (Oxford: Oxford University Press, 1985)

Smith, Caroline, *Crusading in the Age of Joinville* (Aldershot: Ashgate, 2006)

Strayer, Joseph R., 'The crusades of Louis IX', in Wolff and Hazard, *The Later Crusades*, chapter 14

—— 'France: the Holy Land, the Chosen People, and the Most Christian King', in Theodore K. Rabb and Jerrold E. Seigel (ed.), *Action and Conviction in Early Modern Europe: Essays in Memory of E.H. Harbison* (Princeton, NJ: Princeton University Press, 1969), pp. 3–19; reprinted in Strayer, *Medieval Statecraft and the Perspectives of History* (Princeton, NJ: Princeton University Press, 1971), pp. 300–314

Wolff, Robert L. and Hazard, Harry W. (ed.), *The Later Crusades 1189–1311*, A History of the Crusades (general ed. K. M. Setton), vol. 2, 2nd edn (Madison, WI: University of Wisconsin Press, 1969)

Index

The definite article *al-* in Arabic personal and geographical names is ignored for the purposes of alphabetical order; thus 'al-Nāṣir' appears under N. The title *al-Malik* ('king', 'prince') found in the texts as part of the titulature of rulers is also omitted.

References to sources and documents are given in bold type under their authors.

Trinity, Order of the, 30n
Tripoli, 213
Troyes, bishop of, 30
Tunis, 154n, 170n, 205, 209n
Tūrān Shāh, al-Muʿaẓẓam Ghiyāth al-Dīn, sultan of Egypt, 4, 47, 72–3, 75n, 100n, 109–112, 125–8, 135–40, 142–3, 145, 148–9, 155–9, 214, 218, 223; his murder, 106, 111, 117, 127, 150–52, 161–2, 172, 205
Turcopoles, 212
al-Ṭūrī, Sayf al-Dīn Yūsuf, 148, 160n
Turkey, 20; see also Rūm, Seljük Sultan
Türkmen (Turcomans), 69, 76, 129n, 213
Tuscany, 48
Tyre, 102; see also Montfort, Philippe de

al-ʿUqayba, 224
Ushmūn Ṭannāḥ, River (Baḥr al-Ṣaghīr), 72, 91n, 116n, 131, 134n, 143–4; see also Tanais
Ushmūn Ṭannāḥ (town), 129–31
Utrecht, 56

Valéry, Jean de, 116
Vendôme, count of, 83, 120
Venetians, Venice, 24, 82, 197n
Verdun, 21, 29, 56
Villehardouin, see Guillaume II
Villeneuve, 181, 184
Vincent de Beauvais, 3–4; his *Speculum Historiale*, 3; **doc. 72**
Vitry, André de, 104; Jacques de, bishop of Acre, 70
vows, see crusade vows

Walter de Saint-Martin, Dominican, 208, 212
al-Wazīrī, Ṣārim al-Dīn Uzbak, 130
Wilbrand, Franciscan, 61–2
Willem van Eyk, Dominican, 59–60
William Longespee, 22, 24, 30, 100, 102, 104, 176
William, count of Holland and anti-king in Germany, 50–52, 56–60, 180
William of Rubruck, Franciscan and envoy to the Mongols, 68, 213n
William of Tyre, 1, 71
Worcester, bishop of, 28, 30, 37

Yemen, 153n, 216n

al-Ẓāhir Rukn al-Dīn Baybars al-Bunduqdārī, Mamluk officer (later sultan of Egypt), 134n, 150–52, 154n, 216
al-Ẓāhir Shādī, son of al-Nāṣir Dā'ūd, 133, 141, 219
al-Zarzārī, Nūr al-Dīn, 227
Zayn al-Dīn, *amīr jāndār*, 147, 150, 217
Zayn al-Dīn ʿAbd al-Raḥmān Ibn Marhūb, 142
Zayn al-Dīn al-ʿĀshiq, 139
Zealand, 56